Staging Desire

Staging Desire

Queer Readings of American Theater History

EDITED BY

Kim Marra and Robert A. Schanke

Ann Arbor

THE UNIVERSITY OF MICHIGAN PRESS

2005   2004   2003   2002   4   3   2   1

A CIP catalog record for this book is available from the British Library.

Library of Congress Cataloging-in-Publication Data

Staging desire : queer readings of American theater history /
edited by Kim Marra and Robert A. Schanke.
    p. cm. — (Triangulations)
Includes index.
    ISBN 0-472-09749-0 (cloth : alk. paper) — ISBN 0-472-06749-4
(pbk. : alk. paper)
    1. American drama—History and criticism. 2. Homosexuality
and literature—United States—History. 3. Theater—United
States—History. 4. Desire in literature. 5. Gays in literature. I.
Marra, Kim, 1957–   II. Schanke, Robert A., 1940–   III. Series.
PS338.H66 S73   2001
812.009'353   2001006446

For our partners,
Meredith and Jack,
sweet seventeen and counting . . .

Acknowledgments

We began work on this volume at the same time we started its prequel, *Passing Performances* (published in 1998), now nine years ago. Many individuals have supported us through a long, challenging process.

First we must thank our contributors, who have remained loyal to the project even as the mounting pressures of career development; life changes; and, regrettably, in a couple of cases, life-threatening illnesses have intensified their desire to see their work in print. The authors of these essays deserve our gratitude not only for their patience, but also for their responsiveness to numerous calls for revision over the years.

Jill Dolan, who together with David Romàn coedits the Triangulations Series, has been unflagging in her support of our efforts, helping us respond to readers' reports and offering invaluable additional guidance. In her former capacity as executive director of the Center for Lesbian and Gay Studies in New York City, Jill, along with the members of her staff, organized the symposium "Passing Performances: Queering American Theater History," which involved contributors to both volumes. We appreciate the efforts of Jill and her staff in connection with that symposium. Jill's mentorship continues to inspire us.

We remain indebted to our valiant editor at the University of Michigan Press, LeAnn Fields, who has steered this project through some especially trying times. We look forward to the next phase of our collaboration with her.

Numerous colleagues on our respective campuses have supported our efforts and offered helpful responses to various parts of this project. At the University of Iowa, we wish to thank Meredith Alexander, Art Borreca, Dare Clubb, Corey Creekmur, Jane Desmond, Kevin Kopelson, Teresa Mangum, and Judith Pascoe. At Central College, we thank Valerie Hedquist, Mary Jo Sodd, and the members of the Research and Development Committee.

Finally, we thank the many members of our extended families who so enthusiastically welcomed and intrepidly ventured into the prequel and have shared in our anticipation of this volume's publication.

Contents

CRITICS AND AUDIENCES

DESIGNERS AND DANCERS

Introduction

Kim Marra and Robert A. Schanke

"Teen's Play a Winner, But Its Performance Is Banned"—so read the headlines for a story in the *Charlotte Observer* on February 19, 1999.[1] Seventeen-year-old Samantha Gellar's play, *Life versus the Paperback Romance,* was selected as one of the winners of the local Young Playwright's Festival. Although the other winning plays were promised a production, the Children's Theatre of Charlotte and the Charlotte-Mecklenburg Schools refused to produce Gellar's. There was no nudity and no sex acts, but because the two main characters were lesbians who fall in love and kiss, officials declared that it was inappropriate for middle and high school audiences. As one school board member argued, "[T]houghtful citizens are not voyeurs that promote the display of such things."[2] Jill Dolan, then president of the Association for Theatre in Higher Education (ATHE), protested this decision:

> We at ATHE believe that theatre can be a strong voice in teaching cultural pluralism, and in helping people who are different from each other understand and respect the richness of their various lives. If the play was good enough to receive one of the festival's awards, preventing its presentation sends a censorious message.[3]

Censorship of gay and lesbian themes occurs in the professional theater as well. When word leaked out in the spring of 1998 that the Manhattan Theatre Club planned to stage Terrence McNally's *Corpus Christi,* a new play that depicted Jesus and his apostles as gay, the management reported anonymous death threats against the actors, audiences, and the playwright. Outraged callers threatened to burn the theater and exterminate everyone inside it. The Catholic League for Religious and Civil Rights vowed to "wage a war that no one will forget" unless the production was canceled. The theater initially succumbed to the pressure, but after advocates protested, they resumed their plans and hired a private security firm to guard the theater. On opening night, theatergoers were confronted by two thousand chanting protesters, funneled through metal detectors, and forced to have their bags X-rayed.[4]

Hundreds of organizations and individuals hailed the theater's decision in a statement prepared by the National Coalition Against Censorship.

> [T]he right of free expression includes the right to express unconventional and nonconformist ideas, even if offensive to some, or many. To safeguard this freedom, we must support arts organizations, even when they present works that may challenge our most heartfelt beliefs.[5]

Nevertheless, challenges to productions of the play continued. In Fort Wayne, Indiana, twenty-one state lawmakers sued in federal court to block performances of the play in August 2001 at Indiana University–Purdue University in Fort Wayne, charging that taxpayer money should not be used to subsidize its production. "This is not just an innocuous little play," the plaintiffs' attorney argued. "It's a full-blown, unmitigated attack on Christianity and its founders." Fortunately, the school disagreed, claiming that to suspend the performances would be an infringement of First Amendment rights to free speech and academic freedom.[6]

Even commercial, Broadway successes come under attack. Tony Kushner's *Angels in America,* part 1, *Millennium Approaches* won the Pulitzer Prize for Drama, Tony Award for Best Play, Drama Desk Award for Best Play, played on Broadway for eighty-five weeks, toured to thirty-four cities in the United States, and saw productions in over thirty countries. Yet when the Department of Drama at Catholic University of America scheduled a graduate student production in 1996, the university provost and its dean of arts and sciences banned the production. "Because of the content, it was deemed contrary to the mission of Catholic University," explained the university's director of media relations. "I think you must realize that the Catholic Church does not exactly endorse a homosexual lifestyle."[7] The department was offered an ultimatum: cancel the production, move it off campus, or limit attendance to graduate students, faculty, and people in the professional theater. Outraged by the conditions, the department moved the production to the Arena Stage, where every performance was sold out. Tony Kushner has denounced such attempts to suppress and stifle his writing.

> As a dramatist it's my job to find images which move an audience emotionally, and tell them a great deal of information economically and powerfully. . . . [T]he campaign against the play . . . is motivated by political disagreements with the play's author and the play itself. Those opposed to the production, those seeking to close it, have openly declared their objection to lesbian and gay rights, and wish to censor "Angels" for entirely political reasons.[8]

Kushner, McNally, and Gellar are part of a now thirty-year-old tradition of out lesbian and gay theater artists. Many in previous generations self-consciously appeared and acted straight in their public lives in order to be accepted by straight audiences and critics, thus appearing straight to straights. Unable to be honest about their sexualities, they used coded language, substituted straight for queer characters, and framed their plots in heterosexual contexts in order to gain acceptance and production of their plays. Since the infamous 1969 police raid and ensuing riots at the Stonewall Inn, a gay bar in Greenwich Village, that kicked off the lesbian and gay rights movement, playwrights have been more forthright in portraying characters and situations more overtly expressive of subaltern sexual identities. However, as Kushner's, McNally's, and Gellar's recent experiences show, it is still a traumatic decision and an enormous risk for artists to make open declarations of their sexual orientation and to reveal their same-sex sexual desires in their work. As Steven Drukman pointed out in *American Theatre,* such pressures and tensions are reminders "of how thorny questions about politics, morality and sexuality overlap and are ultimately borne by the artist in negotiation with his community and his own conscience."[9]

Like our previously published volume, *Passing Performances: Queer Readings of Leading Players in American Theater History* (University of Michigan Press, 1998), this book deals with a number of artists in the 125 years before Stonewall who worked primarily in the theater. Unlike Kushner, McNally, and Gellar, these figures were unable to "come out" because the risks were even greater than they are now and/or because the categories of what is "out" and what is "in," what is "gay," what is "straight," did not pertain or were differently drawn. Still, same-sex sexual desires significantly shaped their personal and professional affiliations and artistic sensibilities. Whereas the essays in *Passing Performances* dealt with actors, directors, producers, and agents, the fourteen in this volume, also by American theater historians, analyze the workings of subaltern desires in the careers of noted playwrights, lyricists, critics, and designers. While many of the same issues apply and thus will be similarly laid out in this introduction, this volume also emphasizes the different implications for theater artists who were not on stage themselves as actors but whose visions shaped the theatrical representation.

Even though concepts of sexuality and "outness" apply differently to many of our subjects than to our contemporaries, our project in both volumes has been, and will no doubt continue to be, seen in the current, highly controversial terms of "outing." This became clear in October 1998 when the Center for Lesbian and Gay Studies (CLAGS) at the City

University of New York sponsored a half-day symposium on *Passing Performances*. Nine contributors to that volume served on panels and engaged in lively discussion with over one hundred people in the audience, which included pioneering gay authors Larry Kramer and Kaier Curtin.[10] When Robert Vorlicky moderated one of the panels, he cited the response of a straight, female friend who had asked him the names of the subjects who would be discussed at the symposium. "Dear God, not Mary Martin?!" she exploded. "She was married! She had children! Not Mary! Isn't all this just academic snooping—speculation of the lowest kind? Why is it necessary?"[11]

Such objections reflect fear that reputations of cherished icons will be tarnished and the value of their art negated, attitudes rooted in homophobia that continues to permeate the theater world as well as the larger society. Although what we are doing is what historians do, that is, uncover information that enables new understandings of the past, when the subject is sexuality, especially transgressive sexuality, certain ethical questions are raised. Are we revealing information that will hurt people? Are we violating our subjects by taking it upon ourselves to reveal what they had fought hard to conceal? Are we breaking the time-honored code that queers cover for each other? We have always agreed with the point made at the symposium by Larry Kramer, a staunch defender of outing, that it is not enough simply to identify people as queer; the meaning of their sexuality and the value of that knowledge must be established. We argue that knowledge of the role of same-sex sexual desire in historical figures' theatrical careers is central to understanding their contributions and essential both to writing a fuller and more accurate account of history and to changing current attitudes. Indeed, not to write this history is to be complicit in what has been called "inning," the perpetuation of systematic denials that foster the climate of shame and risk surrounding same-sex eroticism within and without the theater.[12]

The rationales for our argument and the reasons why this knowledge matters are manifold. As Martin Duberman, George Chauncey, Martha Vicinus, and other historians of sexuality have powerfully demonstrated, this facet of humanity cannot be relegated to a discreet realm of the private and ignored in assessments of people's public activities.[13] Duberman noted in his closing remarks at the symposium that knowledge of sexual desire "explodes the tyrannical assumption that we should separate our private and our public presentations of the self—a separation that for many generations or centuries has kept us from understanding how the two, in fact, inescapably react upon and shape each other." Sexuality permeates people's beliefs, actions, and social relations; it is not only a question of whom they sexually desire but how they see and function in the world. We want to examine how larger societal and cultural attitudes shaped our subjects' sense of sexual difference in their respective periods, and the interplay of their on- and offstage lives in this context; how their sexuality affected their choices of intimates, professional associates, the kind of work they did, and how they performed it; how shared understandings with people of like persuasion both enabled and inhibited their collaborations; how they and their associates exploited as well as suffered from modes of discrimination and oppression. Far from irrelevant, these questions, in acknowledging sexuality as a historical force, inquire into the very fabric of the past.

Moreover, the knowledge we seek to produce doesn't just add to but transforms the record. Pulitzer Prize–winning historian Barbara Tuchman calls biography "the prism of history."[14] When acknowledged, the facet of sexuality, considered along with other facets of identity, such as gender, race, ethnicity, and class, changes the shape of the whole and vastly complicates what we see looking through it. At the turn into the twentieth century, Clyde Fitch became the nation's most commercially successful playwright by propounding a reassuringly codified ideal of American womanhood when traditional white, Anglo-Saxon Protestant patriarchal hegemony seemed to be threatened by a host of Progressive Era ills. Taking into account that Fitch, along with his producer, Charles Frohman, and agent, Elisabeth Marbury, arguably the three most powerful people in the business, all led queer lives underscores the highly constructed nature of putatively heterosexual American national identity and the deep involvement of same-sex sexual desire in its production.[15] Understanding Rachel Crothers's highly developed personal skills in passing as straight and respectable lends new insight into her abilities as a playwright and director to make a wider range of female types passable to a commercial audience. The hypermasculine images associated with the theater of the United States' most canonical playwright, Eugene O'Neill, take on a world of other meanings when read through the repressed homoerotic desire of his most famous designer, Robert Edmond Jones. That the well-muscled itinerant men, ostensibly proffered for female arousal, in William Inge's nostalgic visions of small-town American life in the 1950s sprang from the author's own forbidden desires and played to closeted spectators transforms and enlarges his place in the American dramatic canon. Information about these artists' sexualities prompts a reexamination of their careers and the social and cultural dynamics surrounding their work.

Ultimately what this knowledge affects is not just understanding of the past but understanding of human identity and historical processes in the present. As women and racial minorities throughout this century have shown, reclaiming one's history from systems of repression is an essential act of self-enunciation that inspires and sustains ongoing struggles for equality. For the last three decades, it has been vital to the lesbian and gay rights movement that such recovery work involves people whose contributions are well known but whose sexual proclivities have been kept "hidden from history."[16] Acknowledging and analyzing the sexualities of famous people both fills gaps and corrects distortions in their individual histories and debunks negative stereotypes oppressive to all members of the gay and lesbian community. In demonstrating the specificity and diversity of sexualities through time, historical recovery work counters constructions of a monolithic, unchanging "homosexuality" that stigmatizes and denies people their individual differences and individual rights.

The recovery work of this collection builds on the contributions of other scholars and addresses lacunae in the still small field of gay and lesbian theater studies. Research in the history of sexuality grounds the methodology and provides crucial material about the larger sociocultural context within which we read our respective moments of theater history.[17] The work of some of these historians—notably Martha Vicinus, George Chauncey, Lillian Faderman, Eric Garber, Esther Newton, and Martin Duberman—directly intersects the world of the theater.[18] Of the scholars centered in the theater who do gay and lesbian studies work, relatively few are theater historians, and fewer still are American theater historians. Kaier Curtin's pioneering *We Can Always Call Them Bulgarians* (1987) and Nicholas de Jongh's more recent *Not in Front of the Audience* (1992), which divides its focus between New York and London, usefully set the twentieth-century theatrical context. Rather than focusing on the relationships between individual subjects' lives and work, as this book does, they survey productions of plays featuring representations of homosexuality and lesbianism. Laurence Senelick's work is exemplary in its examination of the interplay of gender and sexuality in theater artists' careers.[19] Whereas he frequently deals with figures of the American popular theater, our project primarily concerns "legitimate" New York theater icons. Robert A. Schanke's biography of Eva Le Gallienne (1992), James V. Hatch's of Owen Dodson (1993), and Lisa Merrill's of Charlotte Cushman (1998) offer rigorous scholarly treatments of the issues of homosexuality and lesbianism in their subjects' lives and work.[20] Drawing on some of that research, this book gathers under one cover a variety of shorter case studies on a range of individuals covering 125 years of American theater history.

The majority of scholars currently working in lesbian and gay theater studies specialize more in the areas of theory and criticism than theater history. While many focus largely on contemporary theater, their perspectives have informed how we read theater history. In her engagements with postmodern theory, Sue-Ellen Case's insistence on the agency of a lesbian subject positioned both inside and outside ideology and able to change the conditions of her existence continues to be inspirational. Jill Dolan's paradigmatic theorizations of feminist spectatorship and the dynamics of lesbian desire in various kinds of performances have been especially important to this project. How Stacy Wolf has continued these and other queries in exploring the "use value" of Cold War–era American musicals in shaping lesbian subjectivity has also enriched our understandings of theatrical reception. John Clum, David Savran, and Robert Vorlicky provide leading readings of gay male sexuality in modern American drama and theater.[21]

Theoretical analyses of the intersections of sexuality and gender with race, ethnicity, and class by Kate Davy, David Romàn, and Jennifer Brody have pushed us to consider a variety of dynamics more fully.[22] For example, essays examine how Larry Hart's Jewishness and George Kelly's Irish Catholicism and the assimilationist ambitions of their respective families made their sexual deviance more threatening and shameful. By contrast, writers such as Fitch, Crothers, and Cole Porter were at least partially insulated by their native ties to upper-middle-class WASP respectability. Queer artists who were not themselves racially or ethnically othered took up the positions of those who were in gestures of empathy informed by their own experience of difference. This dynamic can be seen in Mercedes de Acosta's critique of anti-Semitism in *Jacob Slovak,* as well as the general affinity for outsiders she displayed in her work; in Robert Edmond Jones's direction of Ridgely Torrance's *Three Plays for the Negro,* which marked the first time that black actors performed on Broadway in dramatic roles; and in Eric Bentley's continued arguments against racism and anti-Semitism as well as homophobia throughout his long career. As James Wilson demonstrates, only an understanding of the interlocking oppressions of race, class, gender, and sexuality can unpack the complex of critical discourses surrounding the sensational production of *Lulu Belle,* a play that graphically depicted the purported pleasures and dangers of Harlem nightlife for largely white bourgeois audiences and spawned its own genre of nightclub drag performances.

Recent theoretical and historical work raises key questions about the ways knowledge of historical figures' same-sex sexual desires is produced, what constitutes that knowledge, and what its current ramifications are. A central question concerns how we as coeditors and contributors to this volume position ourselves in relation to our recovery projects. We are using a rubric of "queer readings" within which we can both retain the historical specificity and political agency of our respective identities and embrace the multiplicities, fluidities, and contradictions contained in contemporary notions of queerness. One can identify as lesbian, gay, bisexual, transgender, or straight, as the contributors to this volume variously do, and perform queer interventions. As Dolan stated in her keynote address at "Queer Theater, A Conference with Performances," "To be queer is not who you are, it's what you do, it's your relation to dominant power, and your relation to marginality, as a place of empowerment."[23] When we factor same-sex eroticism into the complex network of forces determining our subjects' careers, we and our contributors are doing queer theater history, working from various identity positions and rereading the past in ways that challenge the normalizing presumptions of heterosexuality.

If doing queer theater history involves affixing labels to our subjects' sexualities, the onus is on each of us to clarify the problematics of that recuperative gesture. Key questions to pose include: what were the salient conceptual frameworks of sexual normalcy and deviance within which our subjects functioned? How and to what extent did they identify their desires and behavior as transgressive? What were the terms for sexual deviance of their time, and how did they relate to those terms? Historians of sexuality have shown that the terms *homosexual* and *heterosexual* were not coined until the late 1860s and 1870s and were relatively obscure medical concepts that did not enter common circulation until the early decades of the twentieth century. The more popular terms *gay* and *lesbian* were in common subcultural usage in the decades prior to World War II, but even as many in the subculture embraced these terms as more affirming alternatives to the then pathologized *homosexual,* others vehemently eschewed them because of their connection to perversion and scandal. As terms used without as well as within subcultural circles, *gay* and *lesbian* gained widespread currency only in the last third of the twentieth century. Common usage of the term *gay* to refer to both men and women who sexually desire members of their own sex is problematic because it subsumes women into a male universal. Similarly, as lesbian theorists remind us, the term *homoerotic* primarily connotes male desire.[24] While many people of all sexes have reappropriated the term *queer* as a militant gesture of pride, its long history as an extreme pejorative still makes it difficult for some people to use, to describe either themselves or their predecessors. The essayists in this collection variously negotiate these terminological problems. How we do so is crucial to how we recover and relate ourselves to our subjects.

Even more vexed than the issue of what to call our subjects is the question of evidence. How do we know they desired members of the same sex? Most people's sexual desires—straight or queer—have not been conclusively documented with direct forms of proof, like eyewitness accounts, explicit photographs, or soiled bedclothes. Moreover, an individual's sexual behavior and desire may neither coincide nor remain consistent. The standard of "hard" evidence is elusive for different-sex desire as well, but biographers have not traditionally been faced with having to prove heterosexual subjects' sexuality; it is simply presumed, automatically buttressed less by facts than by hegemonic assumptions. Historically, many subjects never stated their subaltern desires publicly; often these subjects vehemently eschewed any imputations of sexual abnormality. Revelatory letters or photographs, if they ever existed, have likely been destroyed or kept hidden from researchers to protect reputations.

What, then, is the proof, if there is no self-identification, if there are no extant letters or diaries, if interviews with friends and colleagues are impossible or inconclusive? As Neil Miller points out, "to insist on evidence of genital sex or the unearthing of some lost 'coming out' manifesto to prove that someone was gay or lesbian sets up a standard of proof that cannot be met."[25] Absence of such evidence neither proves nor disproves the existence of the desire. In fact, in John D'Emilio's words, "absence" of or "inaccuracies" in evidence may be registering "ways misinformation is purposely used to deflect attention away from 'who one is' or 'who one is not.'"[26]

To recover our subjects' subaltern desires and their historical impact, we have had to build circumstantial cases in which all evidence is relative and most is ersatz. The process is one of reading multiple signs, including those of absence, relative to historically contingent sign systems. Dolan's argument that the "signs of sexuality are inherently performative"[27] enables us to read our subjects' erotically charged behaviors both within and without the theater as modes of staging their same-sex sexual desires. Most of our subjects appeared straight, which enabled them to circulate as acceptable in mainstream culture while registering signs of subaltern desire in strategies of self-concealment and subversion of dominant role expectations. In staging desire, the primary register of sexual identification is gender; that is, sexual deviance is often expressed through coded manipulation of gender stereotypes. Additionally, there are signs of concealment and erasure deployed by family and friends, the media, public opinion, and the scholarly community. Where possible, we have tried to find evidence of direct expressions of subaltern desire, in subjects' private papers if accessible, or in documented printed accounts by close associates. As noted, however, this kind of evidence is very rare because of the obvious risks involved in creating such documentation. Often what has remained is an ephemeral oral history handed down through generations within subcultural theatrical circles and recoverable through interviews.

In gathering this evidence and reading performances of sexuality, we cannot dismiss the value of gossip. As Edith Becker, Michelle Citron, Julia Lesage, and B. Ruby Rich have argued, gossip provides "official unrecorded history": "Long denigrated in our culture, gossip nevertheless serves a crucial purpose in the survival of subcultural identity within an oppressive society. If oral history is the history of those denied control of the printed record, gossip is the history of those who cannot even speak in their own first-person voice."[28] Of course, neither a piece of gossip nor any other single piece of evidence, such as cross-dressing, can be conclusive on its own. A circumstantial case about the workings of subaltern desire in a particular theatrical career must be built through an accretion of signs. Each sign must be read in relation to the others, and in relation to the subject's own level of consciousness about the meaning of her or his behavior within the larger framework of material and ideological circumstances that define prevailing standards of normalcy and deviance.

Vexed and elusive as it is, this evidence is vital to our project because of the highly influential and complex ways historical icons shape the self-conceptions of people across the social spectrum, both in their own time and now. The ramifications are both personal and political. While those of us who identify as gay and lesbian have always projected fantasies of desire and identification onto putatively heterosexual stars, it can be immensely validating, not to mention arousing, to know that these fantasies are not pure projection, that, in the face of our continuing degradation, widely worshiped icons were at least in some measure like us. For those who identify as straight, evidence of the role of same-sex sexual desire in leading practitioners' careers can be profoundly disorienting. Certainly it increases awareness of the constructed, contingent, and shifting nature of all sexualities, including their own. For queers and straights, it can change how we consume cultural products. Seeing Cole Porter's homoerotic play in the lyrics to the song "You're the Top" and Fitch's struggle with his own secret and, ultimately, lethal passions in the sexual scandals of his posthumous Broadway hit, *The City,* may irrevocably alter our reception of these old standards. As these and other examples throughout this volume indicate, desire for persons of the same as well as opposite sex has been deeply implicated in the production of icons that shape dominant cultural expectations of us all; who "we" are is part of who "they" are. Charting the diversity of sexual practices and sexual identities through time clarifies how "straight," "gay," "lesbian," "bisexual," "transgender," and "queer" are distinct but symbiotic formations, and none is monolithic or transcendently "natural."

This research has particular political ramifications for the institution of the theater, which has long borne the reputation of being a haven for homosexuality. The actual dynamics that constitute that "haven" and by which people with subaltern sexual desires have sought and operated in it until recently have been largely repressed in historical accounts and still warrant further study. Nicholas de Jongh relates the modern association between homosexuality and the theater to the Puritans who demonized the profoundly spectacular, sensual, and shifting presence of the actor's body in public performance, linking it to prostitution and the worst of all carnal sins, sodomy.[29] As modern theater capitalists cleaved to bourgeois morality and pushed the institution toward greater respectability, the dangers of revealing this allegedly sodomitical center became more acute while the possibilities of doing so became more tantalizing.

The primary means of negotiating this minefield—and the major source of theater's allure for those marginalized on the basis of sexual deviance—has been public performance, with its distinctive potentialities for both self-concealment and self-revelation. The theater grants its participants special license to imagine themselves and the world otherwise, affording them masks behind which they can express themselves in ways not possible in ordinary life. At the same time, the theater compels its artists to draw upon their innermost resources to bring those imaginings to life and demands that they subject their work to the immediate gaze and response of a collectively assembled live audience. Thus no matter how elaborate the pretense, theater artists' creations—and through them the artists themselves—are always extraordinarily vulnerable and exposed on stage. The essays in this volume explore how this has been at once the greatest promise and the greatest terror the stage holds for people who spend so much of their lives hiding who they are, and how those very skills—of dissembling, learning what passes, speaking and acting in codes—mastered from an early age have fitted them for a theatrical career.

If, historically, the theater has been a designated arena where people are given special license to perform a range of identities, it is also the place where the art of performance has been the most regulated by conventions. Among those conventions that queer practitioners have been the most expert at manipulating are those that allow the representation of otherwise socially transgressive behavior. In this sense, the highly conventional theater has been, to use Laurence Senelick's phrase, "a safe-house for unconventional behavior."[30] Even when direct representations of same-sex eroticism were strategically avoided and/or strictly forbidden, subaltern desires could be "smuggled in" through other kinds of transgression, such as extreme heterosexual passion, criminality, gender bending, and stylistic experimentation, which have traditionally been features of theatrical entertainment. Such smuggling helps explain, for example, de Acosta's Amazonian portrayal of Jehanne d'Arc for Eva Le Gallienne, the emasculating conduct of Kelly's *Craig's Wife,* the obtuse imagery of Djuna Barnes's "theater of restraint," and Loie Fuller's designs for hugely extending female form and movement. Also in coded fashion, others deployed what David Van Leer has called "queening," "the silent importing into heterosexual plots rhetorics and motifs more common to their own homosexual community."[31] This is evident not only in the ostensibly heterosexual "hunky" men of William Inge's plays but also in the ultrafashionable feminine worlds of Fitch and the multi-layered wit of Lorenz Hart and Cole Porter. We wish to explore the multiple ways our subjects exploited the "safe-house" where representations of certain social transgressions were permitted, and aesthetic distance allowed both performers and audiences to indulge in multiple readings without relinquishing claims to acceptability.

These explorations involve consideration of the peculiarly American exigencies placed upon both theater and sexuality that are tied to the persistent strains of Puritanism in white, middle-class U.S. culture. The formation of modern sexual identities coincided with the formation of American national identity on principles of supreme purity and progress.

The United States was to be the New Eden where humanity could begin again, unsullied by the sinful degeneracies that were thought to have corrupted the Old World, and attain unprecedented heights of civilization. Categories of hetero- and homosexuality arose in conjunction with other categories of gender, race, ethnicity, and class formed to further the project of nationhood. Because of dominant cultural anxieties about the relatively new status of American identity, these category boundaries were especially rigid and compulsively enforced in major social institutions and public discourse. In making the theater respectable, leading U.S. theater capitalists turned it into a showcase for exemplary American manhood and womanhood.

Given the sexism as well as heterosexism endemic to expectations and representations of American nationhood, the ramifications of on- and offstage role playing have been different for women than men. While injunctions of good character weighed heavily on both sexes, the construct of the New Eden hinged most pivotally on women's moral purity. Thus, the whole issue of female sexuality has been even more vexed in the United States than elsewhere in Anglo-European culture, a dynamic that has rendered female-female eroticism alternately more invisible and more insidious and demonic. For women in the theater, this has presented special challenges and opportunities that variously impacted our subjects. If they were uninsulated by ties to respectable bourgeois society, they could be branded as lesbian just for taking the "masculine" step of entering a public profession. The gender and sexual transgression was greater when women entered the theater not in the role of actress but in more authoritative roles such as those essayed by playwrights Crothers, de Acosta, and Barnes, or designer Jean Rosenthal.

If gender and sexual role expectations became less restrictive for women in twentieth-century U.S. theater and society, the reverse may be true for men. Lesbian therapist and author Betty Berzon explains that "men's roles are much more rigidly defined in this society than women's, so sometimes women can make changes that men can't." Michelangelo Signorile maintains that for most heterosexual men gay men having sex with each other is more threatening than lesbian women having sex with each other. "To many men," he insists, "the next step after the idea of having sex is those men coming after them. . . . On some level for them [straight men] there's something erotic about lesbians and something very scary about gay men." In an essay entitled "The Amazing Invisible Men of Show Business," author John Gallagher concludes:

> While coming out of the closet may pose a greater threat to men
> than to women, staying in offers advantages to men that it does not
> offer to women. If the decision makers are all straight men, a gay
> man who keeps his mouth shut will look like he belongs to the same
> club. . . . Forced to confront sexism, lesbians may decide to confront
> the closet as well.[32]

The different and changing stakes for men versus women involved in
being identified with same-sex desire are prominent among the specific
dynamics by which U.S. theater has functioned as a "haven for homosexuality." Taking such factors into account renders a fuller record and
helps dissipate oppressive and distorting generalizations about both the
institution and its practitioners.

The fourteen essays herein are grouped according to subjects' primary
positions within the theatrical profession—playwrights and lyricists, critics and audiences, and designers and dancers—to highlight particular
issues relevant to each specialization. Within these groupings, essays are
arranged chronologically to show developments related to changing concepts of sexual normalcy and deviance over time. For cross-referencing
among the volume's three sections and subjects' intersecting careers, we
have indexed the volume. Photographs accompany each essay to illustrate many of the queer aesthetics and dynamics discussed.

   In the opening section, historians consider the ramifications for playwrights and lyricists of the godlike power of creating whole worlds into
which both overt and covert fantasies can be projected and manipulated
to read differently to different audiences. Essays move through worlds
shaped by the Wildean desires of Fitch and the closeted maneuvers of
Crothers around the turn of the century; the tortured, barely repressed
passions of de Acosta and Barnes in the modernist teens and twenties; the
brilliantly coded wit of Porter and Hart through the Jazz Age and depression eras; and the darkly repressed and rechanneled homoeroticism of
Kelly and Inge amid Cold War paranoia.

   The critics examined in the second section are professional audience
members who make their livelihoods partaking of the spectatorial pleasures and reading the multiple meanings stage performance offers.
Because they are expected to publish their opinions in the mass media,
they must relate their private responses to the larger responsibilities of
influential public discourse. As Lisa Merrill puts it, their "texts become
part of the discursive frame through which the work of playwrights and
other artists are received." Her essay explores how the dynamics of per-

sonal, same-sex erotic passion find outward expression in the public writings of James Oakes and Adam Badeau about the performances of their respectively adored stars Edwin Forrest and Edwin Booth. Before the emergence of the category "heterosexual" and its pathological counterpart "homosexual," the same-sex desires of these critics could openly fuel moral, nationalistic arguments for the superiority of their stage favorites. By the time of the post-Freudian interwar years, as James Wilson demonstrates, both European American and African American critics, in their responses to the Broadway production of *Lulu Belle* and its Harlem drag cultural spin-offs, conflate same-sex erotics, female sexual lassitude, and miscegenation as forces of moral, social, and economic depravity. In the paranoically homophobic Cold War decades, Eric Bentley, operating as both critic and would-be playwright, kept himself closeted while defending homosexuality in other playwrights' works, and even took writers such as Tennessee Williams to task for not being more open about the same-sex desires inscribed in their plays.

Aaron Betsky's *Queer Space: Architecture and Same-Sex Desire* (1997) helps frame the final section on designers and dancers. Betsky shows how queers have manipulated the aesthetics of modern architecture and decor to create out of hostile environments living interiors that not only provided havens but served as "highly personal maps or mirrors of an unseen or unrepresentable self." Queer artists, he argues, are particularly enamored of artifice as being "against nature" and the purportedly "natural" laws their proclivities are alleged to violate.[33] Many have been drawn to work in the theater as the artificial space par excellence in which transgressive passions could be symbolized on a grand scale. Each of the three artists analyzed in this section was inspired to design stage space by the subaltern erotics of the dancing body. In Loie Fuller's case, that body was her own. She subsumed her "flawed" natural physique in enormous, swirling swaths of fabric and innovated lighting technology to magnify the effects. This self-styled "electric fairy" filled the stage with seemingly disembodied, yet flamboyantly sensual giant flowers, serpents, and flames. Bud Coleman relates her work to the lesbian erotics circulating in her private life and within her ardent following of female students and fans. Jane Peterson analyzes the ways Robert Edmond Jones queered the space in boldly modernist designs redolent with smoldering forbidden passions keyed to the highly choreographed movement sequences of his expressionist productions. As Jay Chipman demonstrates, Jean Rosenthal's same-sex desires were expressed in a lifetime of living and working with women and, most famously, in her long collaboration with Martha

Graham, whose fiercely passionate, moving body she loved to caress with beams of light.

While the careers of our subjects span the decades from the 1840s to the 1960s, the volume is not intended to be comprehensive but, like *Passing Performances,* is offered as a sampling of case studies. Many gaps remain. Again, some of the essays originally planned for the volume regrettably fell through because of authors' difficulties with evidence. Neither were we able, for some of the same reasons, to maintain a more equitable balance between male and female subjects. Some of these gaps and imbalances will be redressed in a biographical encyclopedia covering well over a hundred figures from the full range of theatrical occupations in the same period. We hope that many more scholars will further the project of analyzing same-sex sexual desire as a significant force in leading practitioners' lives and aesthetics and in the making of theater history.

Certain events have driven home how urgent the need remains for challenging received historical wisdom to change current attitudes. October 16, 1998, should have been an exciting day for us. We had been working on this three-volume project for five years, and on that day we received by special delivery our initial copy of the first book, *Passing Performances.* But our enthusiasm was dashed; it was the day of the funeral for Matthew Shepard, a young gay man who had been brutally beaten and hung on a fence post to die in the subfreezing cold of a Wyoming night. "We know that it could have been any one of us," warned Donna Red Wing, national field director of the Human Rights Campaign.

> And the message was clear: "Stay in the closet. Be silent." Well, we cannot allow ourselves to be silenced. We have to ask the questions: Why would two youngsters, the same age as Matthew, perpetrate such a crime? What information did they have about what it means to be gay? Who defined Matthew, and us, for them? What allowed them to reach so deeply into their personal fear and rage? Clearly, their perception of gay people did not allow them to see Matthew as an equal. Only if he were relegated to the place of someone who was "less than," or "different from" could they do what they did to him. Only if he became "the other" could they butcher him and hang his broken and bloody body to a fence post.[34]

Perhaps the ultimate goal of our project, then, is to focus our anguish and our rage toward making a difference. We are not remaining silent. Instead, we are challenging the misinformation and the stereotypes and seizing the opportunity through our own field of research to shape the national dialogue around queer issues.

NOTES

1. Tony Brown, "Teen's Play a Winner, but Its Performance Is Banned," *Charlotte Observer*, February 19, 1999.

2. Letter from Lindalyn Kakadelis to Ann Marie Costa, March 20, 1999.

3. Letter from Jill Dolan to friends in Charlotte, March 3, 1999.

4. Chris Michaud, "Controversial Gay Christ Play Opens," Reuters/Variety, October 15, 1998; Richard Zoglin, "Jesus Christ Superstar? Terrence McNally's Controversial Play about a Gay Messiah Finally Debuts. What's All the Fuss," *Time*, October 5, 1998, 86; John Leo, "Jesus and the Hustlers," *U.S. News and World Report*, June 15, 1998, 17.

5. "Arts and Free Speech Groups Support the Manhattan Theatre Club," National Coalition against Censorship.

6. "Indianans Sue to Block Play with Gay," *Des Moines Register*, July 6, 2001, p. 7A.

7. Stephen Nunns, "No 'Angels' on Catholic Campus," *American Theatre* 13 (December 1996): 46.

8. This statement appears in an affidavit signed by Tony Kushner, County of Mecklenburg (NC), 96-CVS-3662, and is his argument against censoring *Angels in America* at the Charlotte Repertory Theatre.

9. Steven Drukman, "A Standoff in Charlotte," *American Theatre* 13 (May–June 1996): 47.

10. Larry Kramer was a founding member of Gay Men's Health Crisis, helped to found AIDS Coalition to Unleash Power (ACT UP), and wrote *The Normal Heart* (New York: New American Library, 1985). Kaier Curtin wrote *"We Can Always Call Them Bulgarians": The Emergence of Lesbians and Gay Men on the American Stage* (Boston: Alyson, 1987).

11. Robert Vorlicky has edited *Tony Kushner in Conversation* (Ann Arbor: University of Michigan Press, 1997) and written *Act Like a Man: Challenging Masculinities in American Drama* (Ann Arbor: University of Michigan Press, 1995).

12. For a discussion of the concept of "inning," see Larry Gross, *Contested Closets: The Politics and Ethics of Outing* (Minneapolis: University of Minnesota Press, 1993). Choreographer and director Tommy Tune discusses being the victim of "inning" in his memoir, *Footnotes* (New York: Simon and Schuster, 1997).

13. Martin Duberman, Martha Vicinus, and George Chauncey Jr., eds., *Hidden from History: Reclaiming the Gay and Lesbian Past* (New York: Penguin, 1989).

14. Barbara W. Tuchman, *Practicing History: Selected Essays* (New York: Knopf, 1981), 73–74, 80.

15. We use the term *queer* in the way it was used, according to George Chauncey, prior to World War II to refer to people who led lives outside sexual norms. See *Gay New York: Gender, Urban Culture, and the Making of the Gay Male World, 1890–1940* (New York: Basic Books, 1994), 14–16.

16. See Duberman, Vicinus, and Chauncey, *Hidden from History*.

17. In addition to the *Hidden from History* collection, we are also especially indebted to the work gathered in Kathy Peiss and Christina Simmons, eds.,

Passion and Power: Sexuality in History (Philadelphia: Temple University Press, 1989).

18. See, for example, Martha Vicinus, "'They Wonder to Which Sex I Belong': The Historical Roots of the Modern Lesbian Identity," in *The Lesbian and Gay Studies Reader,* ed. Henry Abelove, Michele Ana Barale, and David M. Halperin (New York: Routledge, 1993), 432–52; Chauncey, *Gay New York;* Lillian Faderman, *Surpassing the Love of Men: Romantic Friendship and Love between Women from the Renaissance to the Present* (New York: Morrow, 1981) and *Odd Girls and Twilight Lovers: A History of Lesbian Life in Twentieth-Century America* (New York: Penguin, 1991); Eric Garber, "A Spectacle in Color: The Lesbian and Gay Subculture of Jazz Age Harlem," in Duberman, Vicinus, and Chauncey, *Hidden from History,* 318–31; Esther Newton, *Cherry Grove, Fire Island: Sixty Years in America's First Gay and Lesbian Town* (Boston: Beacon, 1993); Martin Duberman, ed., *Queer Representations: Reading Lives, Reading Cultures* (New York: New York University Press, 1997).

19. See, for example, Laurence Senelick's "Lady and the Tramp: Drag Differentials in the Progressive Era," in *Gender in Performance: The Presentation of Difference in the Performing Arts,* ed. Senelick (Hanover, N.H.: University Press of New England, 1992), 260–45, and "Boys and Girls Together: Subcultural Origins of Glamour Drag and Male Impersonation on the Nineteenth-Century Stage," in *Crossing the Stage: Controversies on Cross-Dressing,* ed. Lesley Ferris (New York: Routledge, 1993), 80–95. Senelick continues his recovery work with the more recently published *Lovesick: Modernist Plays of Same-Sex Love, 1894–1925* (New York: Routledge, 1999), and *The Changing Room: Sex, Drag, and Theatre* (New York: Routledge, 2000).

20. Robert A. Schanke, *Shattered Applause: The Lives of Eva Le Gallienne* (Carbondale: Southern Illinois University Press, 1992); James V. Hatch, *Sorrow Is the Only Faithful One: The Life of Owen Dodson* (Urbana: University of Illinois Press, 1993); Lisa Merrill, *When Romeo Was a Woman: Charlotte Cushman and Her Circle of Female Spectators* (Ann Arbor: University of Michigan Press, 1998).

21. See, for example, Sue-Ellen Case, "Toward a Butch-Femme Aesthetic," in Abelove, Barale, and Halperin, *Gay and Lesbian Studies Reader,* 294–306, "Performing Lesbian in the Space of Technology, Part I," *Theater Journal* 47 (March 1995): 1–18, and "Performing Lesbian in the Space of Technology, Part II," *Theater Journal* 47 (October 1995): 329–43; Jill Dolan, *The Feminist Spectator as Critic* (1988; reprint, Ann Arbor: University of Michigan Press, 1991), and *Presence and Desire: Essays on Gender, Sexuality, and Performance* (Ann Arbor: University of Michigan Press, 1993); Stacy Wolf, "The Queer Pleasures of Mary Martin and Broadway: *The Sound of Music* as a Lesbian Musical," *Modern Drama* 39 (spring 1996): 51–63, and "'Never Gonna Be a Man / Catch If You Can/ I Won't Grow Up': A Lesbian Account of Mary Martin as Peter Pan," *Theater Journal* 49 (1997): 493–509; John Clum, *Acting Gay: Male Homosexuality in Modern Drama* (New York: Columbia University Press, 1992); David Savran, *Communists, Cowboys, and Queers: The Politics of Masculinity in the Work of Arthur Miller and Tennessee Williams* (Minneapolis: University of Minnesota Press, 1992); Vorlicky, *Act Like a Man.*

22. See Kate Davy, "Outing Whiteness: A Feminist/Lesbian Project," *Theater Journal* 47 (May 1995): 189–205; David Romàn, "Teatro Viva! Latino Performance and the Politics of AIDS in Los Angeles," in *Etiendes? Queer Readings, Hispanic Writings,* ed. Emile L. Bergmann and Paul Julian Smith (Durham, N.C.: Duke University Press, 1995); and Jennifer Brody, "Hyphen-Nations," in *Cruising the Performative: Interventions into the Representation of Ethnicity, Nationality, and Sexuality,* ed. Sue-Ellen Case, Philip Brett, and Susan Leigh Foster (Bloomington: Indiana University Press, 1995).

23. "Queer Theatre: A Conference with Performances," Center for Gay and Lesbian Studies, New York, April 27–29, 1995.

24. The terms *homosexuality* and *heterosexuality* first appeared in print in the United States in the early 1890s as the theories of German sexologists, most influentially those of Richard von Krafft-Ebing, entered English-language medical discourse. See, for example, Jonathan Ned Katz, *The Invention of Heterosexuality* (New York: Penguin, 1996), 19–21. As Chauncey demonstrates, the medical profession did not "invent" homo- and heterosexuality; rather, doctors coined these terms in response to preexisting social phenomena. Well before the medical publications, people were self-identifying as "queer," "fairy," and "Sapphic" and did not just internalize but resisted the pathology the sexologists imposed upon them. See George Chauncey, "From Sexual Inversion to Homosexuality: The Changing Medical Conceptualization of Female Deviance," in Peiss and Simmons, *Passion and Power,* 109.

25. Neil Miller, *Out of the Past: Gay and Lesbian History from 1869 to the Present* (New York: Vintage, 1995), xx.

26. John D'Emilio, oral presentation at the Lesbian and Gay History Conference, City University of New York Graduate Center, October 6–7, 1995.

27. Dolan, "Breaking the Code: Musings on Lesbian Sexuality and the Performer," in *Presence and Desire,* 139.

28. Edith Becker, Michelle Citron, Julia Lesage, and B. Ruby Rich, "Lesbians and Film," in *Out in Culture: Gay, Lesbian, and Queer Essays on Popular Culture,* ed. Corey K. Creekmur and Alexander Doty (Durham, N.C.: Duke University Press, 1995), 31.

29. Nicholas de Jongh, *Not in Front of the Audience: Homosexuality on Stage* (New York: Routledge, 1992), 5–6.

30. Senelick, *Gender in Performance,* xi, 39.

31. David Van Leer, *The Queening of America* (New York: Routledge, 1995), 66–67.

32. All quotations in this paragraph are found in John Gallagher, "The Amazing Invisible Men of Show Business," *Advocate,* May 13, 1997, 26–32.

33. Aaron Betsky, *Queer Space: Architecture and Same Sex Desire* (New York: William Morrow, 1997), 5–6.

34. From an address given by Donna Red Wing before the First Friday Breakfast Club in Des Moines, Iowa, on April 2, 1999.

Playwrights and Lyricists

Clyde Fitch's Too Wilde Love

Kim Marra

Fashion . . . and Dandyism . . . had, of course, their fascination for him.
                              —Oscar Wilde, *Portrait of Dorian Gray*

. . . through Art, and through Art only, . . . we can shield
ourselves from the sordid perils of actual existence.
                              —Oscar Wilde, *The Critic as Artist*

By many estimations, Clyde Fitch (1865–1909) was the most successful
American playwright of his generation. Over a twenty-year professional
career beginning in 1890, he authored sixty-two plays: thirty-six original
works, twenty-one adaptations, and five dramatizations of novels.[1] More
than fifty of these received Broadway productions, and in a single year,
1901, he had four plays running simultaneously on Broadway. Fitch not
only wrote these plays, but, after proving his directorial talents to the
profession with *The Moth and the Flame* in 1898, he customarily staged
his own work. His longtime producer, Charles Frohman of the Theatrical Syndicate, proclaimed him "easily the leader in the line of play production in this country."[2] Cumulatively, Fitch's plays fed Syndicate cof-
fers more than those of any other author and made him one of the
nation's first dramatist millionaires.

While his work was immensely popular and profitable, Fitch endured
a troubled relationship with critics and commentators throughout his
career. His stock-in-trade was witty, urbane comedy of high society that
revolved around female characters and catered to the increasingly
female-dominated audience of the legitimate theater. With few excep-
tions, members of the male-dominated critical establishment disparaged
his emphasis on women's sphere as frivolous and commercially expedient
and made his preoccupation with fashion and manners into a metaphor
for his method. They claimed he did not plumb the depths of life to create "great art" but dealt only with outer appearances, tailoring characters and situations along with costumes, sets, and stage business to suit

23

FIG. 1. Clyde Fitch at the time of writing *Beau Brummell* (1889–90). Behind him on the wall of his apartment is the portrait of Salomé holding the severed head of John the Baptist on a silver platter.

From Montrose J. Moses and Virginia Gerson, eds., Clyde Fitch and His Letters *(Boston: Little, Brown, 1924).*

performers' personalities. Fitch's prodigious output—he staged as many as six new plays a season—fueled accusations of superficiality; critics contended no serious artist could possibly create work of substance at such a rate.[3]

These gender-based lines of criticism were tinged with innuendo regarding Fitch's own gender and sexual identity. Because of his public image as a dandy of legendary sartorial flamboyance, commentators attributed his preoccupation with fashionable femininity to his personal "effeminacy." Summing up such assessments, John Lowe titled a 1920 retrospective of Fitch's career "A 'Sissy Boy' Who Became a $250,000 a Year Dramatist."[4] While rumors circulated, Fitch was fastidiously discreet about his private life, and information confirming imputations that he was homosexual remained elusive.

Subsequently, scholars have redressed some of these criticisms of Fitch's work by positioning him as an important figure in the emerging genre of American social realism. These studies take their cue from Walter Prichard Eaton, who claimed that an illustrated edition of Fitch's works would give future generations a better idea of the upper echelons of American life from 1890 to 1910 than newspapers or historical records.[5] While imparting greater substance to the Fitch canon, such analyses marginalize gender issues—Fitch's expertise in female characterization is viewed as part of a general acumen as a social documentarian—and dismiss sexuality issues as spurious and irrelevant. I intervened in this discourse with a 1992 article placing gender at the center of the analysis. From written and pictorial documentation that the dandiacal Fitch also engaged in transvestism, I related his personal penchant for cross-dressing to his special talent for creating female characters.[6] Lacking any evidence about his sexuality beyond rumor and innuendo, I left that question open.

Since then, more concrete evidence has emerged in the form of letters from archives of two friends of Fitch, one of whom was Oscar Wilde. It has long been established that Fitch had met and admired Wilde, but letters unearthed and published by two Wilde scholars, Melissa Knox and Gary Schmidgall, in 1994 strongly suggest that they also had a passionate physical love affair in 1889 and 1890 during Fitch's trips to London.[7] The second correspondent was Fitch's friend DeWitt Miller, in whom he confided shortly after the affair about "certain temperaments of men for the not ordinary sexual enjoyment."[8] These letters provide the clearest indication to date that Fitch experienced same-sex sexual desire as well as transvestite impulses and that he was at once exhilarated and terrified by these proclivities.

Building on these findings, I wish to reexamine Fitch, who remains a minor figure in Knox's and Schmidgall's book-length studies of Wilde. Indeed, given their different aims, some of the evidence that prompts my analysis they relegate to endnotes. My project is to elaborate the evidence from Fitch's side, examining how the Wilde affair affected his career and how his conflicting responses to his sexuality shaped the artistic vision he expressed both on his own person and in his fictional representations. Though enormously commercially successful, Fitch was plagued by debilitating, ultimately fatal stress from overwork and constant deception. As he put it, "I live my life in the mist of shams."[9] The Wilde affair impassioned and inspired him, but also intensified his culturally imposed feelings of sinfulness and fear of exposure, especially in the wake of Wilde's sensational trials. Factoring such dynamics into the production of Fitch's art highlights the ways he used the theater both to express and contain his transgressive desires, especially through fetishistic stagings of femininity, baroque stylistic excess, ironic wit, and novel scenic effects. These methods align him aesthetically as well as sexually with his infamous lover and complicate traditional assessments of his work in terms of social realism.

When Fitch met and fell in love with Oscar Wilde, he was twenty-four years old. He had not yet had his breakthrough success as a commercial playwright, but he had developed sensibilities and manifested theatrical talents that help explain his affinity for Wilde and things Wildean. These need to be analyzed in the context of prevailing concepts of sexual and gender identity in the period. The decades following the Civil War were marked by increasing efforts within the dominant culture to solidify monolithic notions of Americanness based on the putatively triumphant values of the northeastern white, Anglo-Saxon, Protestant industrial capitalist bourgeoisie. These values mandated adherence to gender norms tied to the middle-class ideology of sexual control. For men, this meant conquest of chaotic passions and instincts inside the self, as well as external forces of purported "savagery" and "decadence";[10] and, for women, embodiment of the feminine ideals of passionlessness and domesticity.[11] Proper gender behavior culminated in a respectable marriage suffused in an ethos of conspicuous consumption to manifest socioeconomic success. Within these parameters of normalcy, the anomaly of same-sex sexual desire was understood chiefly in terms of sexual inversion, the concept of a being of the opposite sex trapped inside one's body. Thus, for a man, desire for another man was believed to be inherently feminine, the function of the woman contained within.[12] Both the being without and the oppositely sexed being within were constructed according to dominant gender ideology.

Raised in the northeastern, middle-class environment of Elmira, New York, and Hartford, Connecticut, Fitch, from an early age, displayed signs of inverted behavior. Both the markers of normalcy and patterns of deviance were inscribed in his nuclear family situation. His father, who served as a captain in the Union army, exemplified strict bourgeois utilitarian standards of Victorian masculinity, while his mother, a Southern belle, incarnated cultural ideals of feminine beauty and gentility. According to Elisabeth Marbury, his longtime friend and agent who knew his family firsthand, Fitch, an only child of frail health, favored his mother in temperament and acquired her love of art and continental culture.[13] Another family acquaintance and early biographer, Archie Bell, opined that Clyde's greater identification with his mother put him in conflict from an early age with his father's conventional expectations of developing manhood.[14]

By the time Fitch entered Hartford Public High School, his deviance from bourgeois patriarchal norms was strikingly apparent. Schoolmate William Lyon Phelps reported:

> He was even at the age of fourteen a complete individualist; he was unlike any other boy I have ever seen. He hated outdoor games and would have nothing to do with them; instead of speaking our dialect, he spoke English accurately, and even with eloquence, he was immaculately, even exquisitely clothed; he made no friendships among the boys and it was evident that he regarded us as barbarians, which we were; we showed it in many ways and particularly in our treatment of him. He seemed to be an impossible person. We treated him exactly as the graduates of Oxford ten years earlier had treated Oscar Wilde; they threw him in the Cherwell and wrecked the beautiful decorations of his room in Magdalen.[15]

Another of Phelps's accounts of Fitch during this period further foregrounds his deviant manner, declaring him "unlike the normal boy in clothes, appearance, gait, manners, tastes, language, and voice." Phelps writes of how "the radiance of [his] glossy garments almost hurt the unprotected eye. . . . His gait was strange, the motive-power seeming to dwell exclusively in the hips; if you can imagine a gay side-wheel excursion steamer, with the port and starboard wheels moving in turn instead of together, you will obtain a fair idea of [his] approach." Fitch's voice he characterizes as "very high, frequently breaking into falsetto, and even in ordinary conversation, it sounded like that of an hysterical woman who had just missed the train."[16]

Moving away from home for the first time, Fitch transferred to Holderness to prep for college. At age fourteen, he declared openly in a letter to his mother: "I am in love with one fellow here, *Livermore,* a great grandson of the old judge. He is rather small, very handsome, and a great athlete, is elegant on the ballground, and is very tony in knickerbockers there."[17] Significantly, this is the only such overt expression of desire for another man preserved in the volume, *Clyde Fitch and His Letters* (1924), edited by Montrose J. Moses and Virginia Gerson, which intermixes the text of selected letters with biographical narrative and still stands as the major published chronicle of Fitch's life. Moses writes in the preface to the volume, "If there is not much to draw on, written to his mother, and to Mrs. Homans of Boston, between whom and Clyde there sprang up the friendship of an old woman for a young man—it is that both destroyed their letters."[18] The preface also indicates that coeditor Virginia Gerson, another dear friend of Fitch, was also reticent about revealing his intimate side. It seems that those close to Fitch engaged in a concerted effort to protect him. The editors may have deemed this letter safe to include because it was addressed to his mother and might be dismissed as an innocent youthful effusion. However, in light of other evidence omitted from this official biographical record, the expression of love and attention to the boy's physique and fashion can be read as an early glimmer of homoerotic desire.

In the fall of 1882, the year Oscar Wilde was making his sensational lecture tour of the United States, Fitch entered Amherst College. Wilde's tour had begun in January of that year in New York to promote the American debut of Gilbert and Sullivan's *Patience.* In the ensuing months, it made its way to other eastern cities and headed westward. Courting and reveling in waves of publicity, "the high priest of aestheticism," dressed as a florid dandy addicted to gold-tipped cigarettes and exquisite objets d'art, impressed himself on American cultural discourse. His lectures expounded on matters of fashion and ornament and included "The English Renaissance of Art," "House Decoration," "Dress and Art in Home Decoration," "The House Beautiful," and "Art and the Handicraftsman."[19] While it is difficult to determine precisely how much exposure to Wilde Fitch would have gotten at this point, the Wildean persona and aesthetics were certainly available as a public image to inspire Fitch's budding tastes. Not only did Fitch "push the fashions hard" at Amherst and incur mounting tailor bills that his father had to cover, but, as Wilde had done at Oxford and advocated in his lectures, he lavishly beautified his rooms. A painted frieze of apple blossoms against a Pompeian background girded the walls, and shelves and tables overflowed with his extensive doll collection, china tea sets, and cut-glass bowls of potpourri.[20]

For his decorative and sartorial excesses, Fitch, as he had in high school and as Wilde had at Oxford,[21] initially suffered terrible taunts from his peers, but he soon made a place for himself as a font of amusement in the campus's small, isolated, and all-male community. Fitch's college years have been rightly termed his "apprenticeship," for it was at Amherst that he began exploiting the theater as a grander outlet for his aesthetic and performative impulses.[22] There his passions could find expression in stage decor, costuming, and, most infamously, female impersonation. While Amherst, like many other all-male colleges, had a venerable tradition of men playing women's roles in campus theatricals,[23] Fitch's activities in this area far exceeded traditional boundaries and long remained legend at his alma mater. Until his arrival, formal—that is, college-sponsored—dramatic endeavor was considered a privilege of the senior class, but Fitch began finding alternative venues for transvestite activity his freshman year. He enlivened cocktail parties and faculty teas with improvised female characterizations and delighted his fraternity brethren with original dramatic sketches featuring himself in female garb.[24] By his sophomore year, the senior class was tapping him to assist in their productions, making him the first underclassman ever to appear in this most prestigious college venue. In three successive annual Senior Dramatics Club presentations, Fitch selected the plays—all comedies dating from the famously dandiacal Georgian period—and assumed the leading ingenue roles.[25] His star turns as Constance Nevill in *She Stoops to Conquer* in 1884, Lydia Languish in *The Rivals* in 1885, and Peggy Thrift in *The Country Girl* in 1886 are well documented in the Memorabilia of College Productions in the Amherst archives. Photographs of his performance of Lydia, for example, illustrate how he affected girlish manners and poses that witnesses construed as remarkably "free from anything masculine."[26] Incarnating these coquettish ingenues in the relatively safe and insulated environment of all-male Amherst, Fitch could playfully express his transgressive desire in overt displays of gender inversion.

Moreover, Fitch extended his penchant for cross-dressing beyond his own body to occupy the entire representational apparatus. He costumed not only his own but all the other characters in the plays and fashioned the stage settings.[27] Fitch also brought to these productions a growing practical knowledge of the theater gleaned from marathon playgoing trips to New York on which he embarked several times a semester.[28] By taking control of the entire mise-en-scène in order to express his sexual and aesthetic passions, he single-handedly raised the level of production values at Amherst. In essence, Fitch was already practicing what Wilde, in the very same years, was advocating in his essay "Shakespeare and Stage Costume." A devotee of Wagnerian "total theater," Wilde praised the stage as "the meeting place of all the arts" and propounded the ideals of "the unity of artistic effect" and the necessity for "one single mind directing the whole production."[29] Although Wilde's affinity for these theatrical ideals was not tied like Fitch's to a personal need to cross-dress, he did, as trial testimony would later make graphically clear, like his younger lovers to play the woman's part.[30] This was a talent at which Fitch during his Amherst apprenticeship in theatrical autocracy became notoriously expert.

After graduation, Fitch and his mother had to convince his disapproving father to let him try to make his professional livelihood in the theater. Reluctantly, his father agreed to support him, but only for a three-year trial period by the end of which time, if he had not succeeded, he would have to switch to something useful, like architecture.[31] Achieving success in playwriting was slow, but several other significant things happened to Fitch during this trial period. The move to the city itself was momentous. He wrote to a childhood friend of his excitement about new opportunities and experiences as he plunged into the urban and urbane culture that became the characteristic world of his plays:

> You can't imagine what a different look the world puts on when you have to make your way *through* her, and by her. And *the City* . . . ! I wouldn't live anywhere else, now, I suppose, and I wouldn't *give up* for *anything* on God's Earth! But the life destroys pure enjoyment; you are surfeited like the little boy with the ice-cream. I have had a madly gay winter, after an equally gay summer at Newport. I've enjoyed myself hugely.[32]

Living in the city, Fitch could surfeit himself on fashion, high society, and theatergoing. The legitimate theater was thriving in New York in the 1880s, with Fitch's college favorite, Daly's, still the leading society house. Other managers were beginning to rival Daly in power and respectability, including the Frohman brothers, most notably Charles, who would become Fitch's major producer, and who made the foundation of his empire-building fortune with Bronson Howard's *Shenandoah* in 1888. That production among others indicated that while European imports, adaptations, and revivals still dominated the legitimate repertoire, there was a growing market for new American-authored plays.

Other stimulus for surfeiting abounded in the city. George Chauncey describes New York in this era as notoriously "wide-open" in terms of the availability of multiplicitous pleasures and dangers. Among these was an emergent subculture growing up around same-sex eroticism. According to Chauncey, the most visible figure of the subculture was the fairy. This was a flagrantly effeminate working-class type prominent in the Bowery, the waterfront, and parts of Harlem, who actively solicited sex with other men. If respectable society constructed proper womanhood as essentially passionless, it viewed the fairy's woman within as a trashy tart. Outwardly, the fairy displayed characteristics akin to those of a prostitute, most notably bleached hair, tweezed eyebrows, and painted face.[33] A man in Fitch's position could but did not have to "slum" in the fairy's haunts to encounter him. Beginning in the 1880s and 1890s, the genre of periodical press led by Pulitzer's *World* and Hearst's *Journal* burgeoned by capitalizing on the sensational appeal of stories of crime, scandal, and the urban underworld, many of which offered vivid glimpses into "degenerate resorts" and "fairy backroom salons."[34] A writer hungry for material and curious about the world around him, Fitch was an avid reader of multiple papers per day and undoubtedly had at least vicarious exposure to the working-class sexual subculture of the fairies.[35]

As part of Fitch's new city life, knowledge of the fairy is significant because of its potential impact on his emerging adult identity. By the 1880s and 1890s, when bourgeois male hegemony seemed to be threatened by corporate consolidation, mounting immigration, poverty, labor unrest, and women's rights, among other purported symptoms of "overcivilization," the fairy's high visibility and association with class and sexual degradation made it, in Chauncey's words, "the primary pejorative category against which male normativity was measured."[36] As such, the fairy "influenced the culture and self-understanding of all sexually active men."[37] To maintain respectability, middle- and upper-class men inclined to same-sex eroticism needed to keep a perceived distance from the fairy while signaling a certain difference from bourgeois masculine norms. Geographically, they were centered not in the Bowery but in the wealthier sections of the Village, Harlem, and Times Square. They also asserted their class differences from the fairy by adopting a highly mannered, refined style that could be passed off as a function of urbane sophistication rather than sexual deviance.[38] The protections higher class identification afforded, however, were by no means secure. Preoccupation with fashion and manners still risked being seen as effeminate and "overcivilized," and, therefore, degenerate. Fitch, with his high-pitched voice, swivel-hipped gait, and florid tastes, was at particularly high risk.

In part because of the tensions and risks of New York life, Fitch came to crave the added stimulation and relative freedom of European urban centers. In 1888, shortly after his move to the city, he began his annual pattern of spending summers—usually from April to October—abroad. Away from his professional base and the increasingly prurient and prying American press, he could indulge his exotic tastes, feasting on and procuring high-style antiques and adorning himself in the latest in Continental fashion. On his initial trip abroad, he went first to London and environs, where he attended at least one gathering hosted by André Raffalovich, a pioneer writer on same-sex erotic subjects in French, and a prominent figure in the high-class English and Continental sexual subculture.[39] Fitch wrote to his friend Grace Mosher: "A jolly visit I had with Raffalovich, Heath Lodge, lovely place on Thames, fourteen people in the house all clever and jolly."[40] Fitch then went to Paris, the putative capital of cultural decadence, where under the Napoleonic code there were no legal penalties for sodomy.[41] Subsequent summers would find him also frequently in Italy—Venice, Rome, Florence—and the more southern Mediterranean locales of Naples, Sicily, and Morocco, popular destinations for American and European men interested in same-sex sexual activity. On these annual trips, Fitch customarily traveled with a valet and often with a male companion with whom to savor the pleasures of these destinations. His friend and travel companion Robert Herrick wrote of how Italy, in particular, stimulated Fitch: "There was something colorful and expressive in his nature, quite un-American, that demanded the warmth and spontaneity of Italy for its satisfaction."[42]

Fitch may have met Wilde on that first trip, perhaps at Raffalovich's (Wilde and Raffalovich were quite close at the time),[43] but it was during his next two trips to Europe—in the summer and fall of 1889 and 1890—that their correspondence indicates the affair transpired. On June 22, 1889, Wilde telegraphed Fitch a brief line, "What a charming day it has been,"[44] which may mark the beginning of their friendship. All but one of the surviving letters are from Fitch to Wilde. The intimacy seems to have escalated rapidly, with the older Wilde seducing the less experienced Fitch through his writing, among other ways. Referring to Wilde's "The Portrait of Mr. W. H." about Shakespeare's love for the boy actor Willie

Hughes, Fitch called the story "*great*—and *fine*" and declared "*I* believe in Willie Hughes." He signed the letter, "Invent me a language of love. *You* could do it. Bewilderedly, All yours Clyde."[45] In the full flush of Eros, Fitch wrote again to the master after reading another of his works (the title is unspecified):

> Oh! You adorable creature! You *are* a great genius. And oh! such a sweet one. Never was a genius so sweet so adorable. . . . And I—wee I—I am allowed to loose the latchet of yr shoe. Am bidden tie it up—and I do, in a *lover's knot!* . . . You are my sight, and sound, and touch. Yr love is the fragrance of a rose—the sky of a summer— the wing of an angel—the cymbal of a cherubim.[46]

The affair inflamed Fitch's passion not only for Wilde himself but also for the artistic styles for which they shared a predilection. This manifested in Fitch's cultivation of the pose of the dandy, both on his own person and in the theater. Though Fitch had very little money at this point and lived in small humble quarters in a boardinghouse, he managed nevertheless to impress his acquaintances with his personal style.

> He would greet his callers in a blue velvet coat, with a rose-pink carnation in his buttonhole, while around was a pleasant consciousness of flowers, incense and brewing tea. Like a highlight in this dim picture of color, catching the full reflection of the fire, sat "Rosetta," a yellow kitten, wearing a wide yellow ruffle around her neck, immovable as a golden sphinx.[47]

According to Moses and Gerson, Fitch's dandiacal persona as well as his budding writing talent prompted the critic E. A. Dithmar to recommend him to actor Richard Mansfield to adapt the story of the legendary Georgian dandy, Beau Brummell, for the stage.[48] Fitch received the commission in November 1889, just as the three-year trial period imposed by his father was winding down. While Mansfield and his advocate, the critic William Winter, would later try to claim authorial credit, it is evident that Fitch, though he incorporated Mansfield's requests, had compelling personal interests in the subject matter, did his own historical research, and wrote the play on his own. The commission proved a most fortuitous opportunity for Fitch to draw upon his desires and offer a paean to his mentor, whom André Gide had described as "the most lord, the most Brummell, the most Byronian."[49] The result was Fitch's breakthrough professional theatrical success. *Beau Brummell* became a staple of Mansfield's repertoire and one of the most popular plays of the 1890s.

Compounding his already well-established dandiacal tastes, Fitch, as an intimate member of the Wilde circle, would have been infused with the Aesthetes' affinity for the Regency dandies, not only because of their love of fashion, manners, exoticism, and wit, but because those qualities constituted an expressly antibourgeois, aristocratic pose. As Stephen Calloway puts it, "The dandies had made art out of their lives, and this the Aesthetes found irresistible."[50] For Wildeans, the signal text of Brummell's life, Barbey d'Aurevilly's *Du Dandysme et de Georges Brummell* (1844), made his androgynous combination of masculine power and feminine elegance precisely the source of his artistic genius.[51] Though unmistakably effeminate, the dandy's aristocratic and artistic attributes clearly delineated him from the crass, low-class fairy. Moreover, the dandy's woman within historically had been construed as a priss devoid of carnal appetite. To the dandy, instinctual passions and bodily functions of any sort were supposed to be animal and undignified and thus anathema.[52]

Of course, many who adopted the pose knew their woman within to be something radically other than a bloodless priss. For Wilde and Fitch she took the form of an operatic femme fatale, the biblical Salomé, potentially even more dangerous than the fairy's trashy tart. In an endnote, Knox points out hints of the adolescent femme fatale in Fitch's imitation of the Song of Songs in a love letter to Wilde (cited above).[53] Wilde, of course, would soon immortalize her in his eponymous play. Significantly, Fitch's first major European purchase was an imposing baroque portrait of the seductress. She loomed large on the wall of his apartment for a decade (see fig. 1) until he could afford his own townhouse, where he had her permanently built in over the salon mantle there to greet him and his visitors fittingly from atop a fiery hearth.[54]

But in the early 1890s, it was still possible for queer men to take cover behind the dandy's lingering historical reputation for passionlessness. This reputation made dandies safe, even useful, exotics for display on the bourgeois stage. They provided an effeminate type against which bourgeois men could feel more manly. While these more manly men were busy at work, indolent dandies could amuse bored housewives with cultured conversation without threatening their chastity. And dandies' interest in fashion and decor fueled female consumerism to drive the economy.

Fitch's *Beau Brummell* was true to form, meticulously tending to his florid personal appearance and position at the top of the *haut ton,* deploying his supreme wit to stay ahead of creditors, and reluctantly pursuing a marriage of convenience. But other meanings are also imbedded in the Wildean scheme. Fitch wrote the play in the same months Wilde was writing *The Portrait of Dorian Gray.* One man was in New York, the other in London, but the love the two had exchanged during the previous summer was still very much aflame. That transgressive desire manifests in Fitch's play as it does in Wilde's novel. Where Mansfield and Winter's scheme made the Beau a romantic hero who sacrificed all for love of a virtuous woman,[55] Fitch's Beau pointedly eschews romance with his fiancée Mariana and instead directs his most ardent passions toward a handsome relatively uncultured young man named Reginald. Fitch makes Reginald the Beau's orphan nephew in order to create an acceptable framework for exchanges of intimacy and affection between men. Reginald enters midway through the first act, eager to please but comparatively naive in the ways of fashion. Fitch stages his visit to the older Beau's dressing room as an initiation similar to what Dorian Gray undergoes with Lord Henry Wotton and what Fitch himself likely underwent when he first worshipped at the feet of the master. Some of the same coded means of communication between same-sex-desiring men appear in both Fitch's play and Wilde's novel. Meaningful looks and adoring gazes are key purveyors of secret passion throughout *Dorian Gray*. The Beau instructs his protégé to eschew the common manly handshake and employ instead "the glance of the eye." As Henry does to Dorian in their first scene in the garden, the Beau "goes to Reginald, and puts his hand on his shoulder and speaks with real affection."[56] Lord Henry invites Dorian to visit him at home, after which the young man's dandyism blossoms. The Beau invites Reginald into his dressing room and then into the more private, offstage space of his bedroom, beckoning "come with me, and you shall see me having my coat put on."[57] When the characters emerge, Reginald, who had entered with the bounding energy of a bull in a china shop, proves his discipleship by flawlessly joining the Beau in an elaborately choreographed, highly suggestive exchange involving the taking of snuff, a ritual Fitch uses throughout the play as the proper dandy's mating dance.[58] The bond between this older and younger man becomes the central relationship of the play. When the Beau learns that Reginald wants to marry Mariana, he relinquishes his claim, not out of chivalry toward the young woman, as Winter and Mansfield postulated, but out of devotion to his nephew. Since Mariana is the Beau's only hope of financial salvation after his famous falling out with the prince regent, this constitutes a supreme self-sacrifice signifying the magnitude of his same-sex love.

As in *Dorian Gray*, transgressive passions are also inscribed in the lavish decor and clothes in which Fitch stages the play. The scenes involve not only the Beau's luxurious abode, "furnished more like a lady's boudoir than a man's dressing-room," but a sumptuous royal ball at Carlton House.[59] Critics have related the dandiacal excesses that extend throughout Wilde's mise-en-scènes to the author's preoccupation both with orgasmic satisfaction of forbidden desires and terror of the consequences. Whether or not one accepts the medical evidence that Wilde had syphilis, it is apparent that he, like other queer men of his generation, experienced his same-sex desire itself as contagion. A vast army of moralists cast the then incurable disease as the inescapable consequence of indulging evil passions and magnified its horrors to serve the middle-class ideology of sexual containment.[60] Fear that his sinful desire would erupt and, as Dorian tells Basil, "write itself across his face" in corrosive sores—indeed, his portrait assumes a markedly syphilitic decrepitude—prompted compensatory obsession with grooming, preservation of youth, florid attire, and acquisition of goods and objets d'art. Escape into a beautiful world of his own making was not only Aesthetic rejection of bourgeois philistinism but anodyne to the hideous ravages of syphilis his society took to be the visible manifestation of degenerate desire.[61] A Wilde lover, Fitch, too, was afflicted with syphilophobia, if not the spirochete itself. Deemed a "sickly" child, Fitch continued to suffer chronic bouts of illness as an adult. To his friend DeWitt Miller, in whom he confided about "certain temperaments of men for the not ordinary sexual enjoyment," he wrote that he took his illnesses to be "punishment" for his "sins."[62] Fitch's *Beau Brummell* is much lighter in tone than Wilde's *Dorian Gray*, but the underlying preoccupations are similar. Dandiacal excess remained a primary distinguishing feature of Fitch's stage productions, his personal style, and his homes that grew in lavishness as he earned more money.

Opening in May 1890, *Beau Brummell* ran through the summer and into the following season. *The Picture of Dorian Gray* was published in *Lippincott's* in July. When Fitch and Wilde reunited in London that summer, they had reason for mutual celebration. It may have been Wilde's novel Fitch had in mind when he exclaimed in one of his love letters: "Perfect. *Perfect . . Perfect*! . . It is the most delicate, the most exquisite, the most complete idyl I have ever read."[63]

As their time together ended, Fitch wrote to thank Wilde for inviting him to his Tite Street home on his last night in London:

> You have been the sun that has glorified my horizon, and if night come on, and the sun set in a sad splendor, the morning came with its own golden halo and shone sweetly into the thicket where the brown-eyed Fawn lay on his grass green bed, with a strangely

shaped wound—like this—♥—in his side. A hunter in snaring his shadow had wounded his heart.

But the Brown-eyed Fawn was happy. "He has my heart," he sang, "but the *wound*, the wound is mine—and no one can take it from me!" Clyde[64]

Fitch's poetic imagery evokes an amorous physical encounter between an older, more experienced man, the hunter and penetrator, and a younger, more innocent male lover, "he" the "brown-eyed fawn." If, as Schmidgall has noted, Wilde liked to refer to the youths he found sexually appealing as "fauns,"[65] Fitch's self-referential use of the homonym indicates his aspiration to a distinctive position among those ranks.

Parting was at least some sweet sorrow for Wilde, too; the only surviving letter from Wilde to Fitch is the one he wrote shortly after Fitch left:

Dear Clyde, Just a line to tell you how sorry I am that you have left town, and how I shall miss you.

When you return we must make merry over a flagon of purple wine and invent new tales with which to charm the world. O.W.[66]

Given that Wilde was known to be an incautious and effusive correspondent, this seems a rather perfunctory relic that on its own may register a certain fondness and friendship but not necessarily a love affair between the two men. However, it needs to be read in the context of at least two other considerations. First, the record indicates that the ardor was more intense on Fitch's part; young Clyde was one of a series of "fauns" for Wilde, whereas for Fitch, Wilde, in many senses, may have been the biggest love of his life. Second, the presence of this letter and the above-cited telegram in Wilde's papers and not Fitch's is itself suggestive. Someone—probably the protective Mrs. Fitch after her son's death—removed these items from Fitch's papers and sent them to be archived with Wilde's. These two items may have survived precisely because they were less revealing than others Wilde may have written to Fitch that she (or another interested party, or even Fitch himself) destroyed.

In another instance of significant absence, no letters from Fitch, a prolific correspondent, to his friends back home during either summer—1889 or 1890—of the affair with Wilde are included in the Moses and Gerson volume. The only inkling of anything special happening to him is contained in a letter to a close childhood friend, Grace Mosher, written on board the *S. S. Fulda* on October 1, 1890, when he was on his return voyage across the Atlantic. He tells her he is bringing her an inscribed copy of Wilde's book of fairy tales and takes pains to point out, "I got him to write in it as if it were my own, and now I send it to you. Oscar's inscription sounds as if he gave it to me, but he *didn't,—I bought* it."[67] He ends the letter thus: "To write you of ½ the beautiful things that have happened to me this year and to try to tell you ½ of my *new and wonderful friends* is impossible. I only say I shall miss not seeing you this winter, more than I can say, because you KNOW without my saying."[68] His gift to her of the fairy tales and the enigmatic ebullience of his closing suggest a desire to share his happiness with his sisterly confidant but an inability to be forthright. One wonders how much she knows without his saying.

If Fitch expressed exhilaration about the affair in his letters to Wilde and, indirectly, in his confidences to Mosher, and if he glorified his Wildean passions in *Beau Brummell,* elsewhere he exhibited considerable anxiety and reticence about his sexuality. In a letter he wrote to DeWitt Miller in January 1891, he argued that revelation of same-sex erotic proclivities

> would ruin the reputation of many men living and dead who had fought hard against their temptations and done all in their power to make up for their secret life . . . I believe this temperament belongs to them, and they are answerable for it to God (who perhaps is *also* answerable to them) and not to the world who would condemn and damn them. Their family, their *mothers,* should be remembered.[69]

This most explicit of Fitch's writings on the subject has survived for posterity because Miller apparently ignored Fitch's instructions—double and triple underscored—to answer but destroy the document.

Just a few weeks after he wrote this letter, Fitch's only novel, *A Wave of Life,* began serial publication in *Lippincott's* magazine.[70] He had started writing it in 1887 not long after moving to the city and had finished it during the period of the Wilde affair. Markedly different in tone than *Beau Brummell* and most of his subsequent plays, the novel depicts the destructive consequences of an illicit passion between two lovers, each betrothed to someone else. Alone on a sleigh ride, their lips meet for the first time, unleashing waves of forbidden desire and frightening the horses who bolt wildly out of control. The sleigh catches on a log that snaps the traces just before the runaway steeds plunge over a cliff to their deaths. Spared for the moment, the lovers are nonetheless doomed. Their irrepressible affair rends the social fabric, and the resulting guilt and shame eventually drive the lovers to suicide. On a sea voyage, one leaps overboard; the other watches him being engulfed by the waves and then dives in to join him in a spectacular love-death. Though these characters are ostensibly heterosexual, the young heroine can be read as Fitch in another ingenue role, and her older paramour, a tall man of artistic temperament with long, wavy hair and a moustache, as a conflation of Fitch and Wilde (Oscar was tall with long wavy hair, artistically inclined, and eleven years older than the considerably smaller, mustached Clyde). The fictional couple's experience reflects the fears about uncontrollable sexual desire and public revelation that Fitch expressed in his confidences to DeWitt Miller.

Fitch and Wilde's amorous relationship seems to have ended sometime in 1891, the year Wilde took up with his most infamous young paramour, Lord Alfred Douglas. However, the two playwrights remained friendly and attuned to each other's activities. After *Beau Brummell,* Fitch did not score another major commercial success with an original play for eight years. Wilde's theatrical fame, on the other hand, rose with stunning rapidity in London and New York with the series of celebrated social comedies that began with *Lady Windermere's Fan* in 1892. The older playwright continued to inspire Fitch with his brilliance even as his private life grew into an horrific cautionary tale that played into Fitch's deeply conflicted feelings about the sexuality they shared.

The impact of Wilde's example on Fitch in the early 1890s was a function not only of their former intimacy, but also of their shared aspirations and associations. They continued to move in many of the same social and professional circles. Both shared the same agent, Elisabeth Marbury, for the duration of their theatrical careers,[71] and the Frohman brothers, Charles and Daniel, became the major producers of both men's work in New York.[72] Shared lifestyle choices and affinities underpinned these long-lasting professional relations. Marbury and Charles Frohman eschewed conventional marriage, and each lived in same-sex domestic partnerships, Marbury with the actress and interior decorator Elsie de Wolfe,[73] and Frohman with his "sort of secretary" and later fellow producer, Charles Dillingham.[74] Their respective homes in town and in the country became favored social gathering places for close friends and associates, including Fitch and Wilde.[75] When Frohman built his Empire Theatre in 1893, Marbury moved her offices into the building, and the two shared numerous clients. In her memoir *My Crystal Ball,* she describes a special bond that developed between Frohman and Fitch based on what she called "shared personal tastes" that included private dessert orgies at Sherry's.[76] This bond sustained Fitch and Frohman through dozens of productions together over two decades.

Within this tightly knit circle of associates, it could not have been easy for Fitch to find himself displaced in Wilde's affections. To DeWitt Miller a year after the breakup, Fitch expressed feelings of sadness and betrayal in quoting verses by Sully-Prudhomme about his dreams of summers, kisses, and unions that "abide alway."[77] His continuing admiration of Wilde may thus have been tinged with jealous revenge when he agreed to adapt the Charles Brookfield–J. M. Glover travesty of *Lady Windermere's Fan, The Poet and the Puppets,* for a New York production. It was a remarkable confluence of Fitch/Wilde/Frohman/Marbury personal and professional interests, an insiders' piece shot through with queer desires and intrigue. The adaptation was produced without Fitch's name at the Garden Theater, one of the many into which Frohman booked productions, during the period of *Lady Windermere's Fan*'s Broadway run in the spring of 1893.[78] Not only was Wilde's play wickedly satirized, but also his decadent Aesthetic persona. Afraid of working too hard, the Poet, "O'Flaherty's child," for assistance conjures a fairy who greets him with a verse. The Poet enjoins him, "To employ your oratorical resources in private conversation is like going to bed in your evening clothes."[79] Now that he's invented Art, Flowers, and Fairies, the Poet wishes to invent plays and actors and actresses who must already be well known and successful. When the confused Fairy says, "But I don't understand," the Poet replies, "That's why you're so charming. That's why I delight to surround myself with the young and fairy-minded. It would be so dull to be understood. The greatest pleasure in life is to be misunderstood."[80] The Fairy summons a number of famous experts from eras past and present to help the Poet write the play. These include the Bard and his Hamlet and Ophelia who observes, "That picotee—and pink—and fair carnation / Have lately turned a mawkish, envious green! / They've all been dyed you know with anyline!"[81] In the ensuing spoof of selected scenes from *Lady Windermere's Fan,* Lord Pentonville, for whom "Nothing is so ennobling as crime," explains to Lady Winterstock why he has done time:

> A trifle, that's the pity.
> A Foolish little business in the city.
> And e'er my pals and I had time to off it,
> They copped us and the swag—I mean the profit.[82]

Such lines, followed by an exclusive cocktail party scene with the Poet and a cadre of witty, elegant young men, staged dynamics of the gay underworld à la *The Picture of Dorian Gray.*

The obligatory reference to the green carnation and the slip about the swag were delightfully naughty witticisms, but not nearly so naughty as the spritely fairy who flitted through a dizzying array of queer connotations. The immediate reference was to Wilde's notoriety as a writer of fairy tales based chiefly on his 1888 volume *The Happy Prince,* a copy of which he inscribed for Fitch with the line, "Faery-stories for one who lives in Faery-Land."[83] Inspired by the master, Fitch also wrote fairy tales and published his own collection in 1891.[84] Fairy tales were deployed by Wildeans to express same-sex desire in a thickly coded array of tropes. Writers could get away with the play upon "fairy" because fairy tales were presumed to be an allegorical genre tied to childhood fantasy far removed from the socioeconomic and sexual degeneracy associated with lower-class fairy prostitutes. The presumed distance from stigma was not only a convenient mask; the fairy-tale genre offered same-sex desiring men an escape into an idyllic preadolescent fantasy land, a vicarious refuge from the pain, suffering, and fear wrought by the real adult world where they were beset with traumatic injunctions to conform to bourgeois male standards and pursue conjugal relations with women. The genre also allowed free fetishizing of youth and beauty, a vital preoccupation for men whose sexual proclivities were aligned with moral depravity and syphilitic decay. Most appealingly, under the veil of innocent fantasy and allegory, fairy tales could be laden with sensual erotic content.[85] To cite just one germane example, Fitch culminated his volume with a story dedicated to Wilde entitled "The King's Throne," which ends with the image of the long, hard shaft of a crucifix falling to its final rest over a softly blossoming floral circle.[86]

Allusions to this fairy-tale tradition conjured by the fairy in Fitch's travesty would have been relished among Wildeans. Recalling Wilde's belief that "when a man is big enough to be burlesqued, he has attained much that the world holds valuable," the *New York Herald* postulated that he delighted in this piece, as he had in Gilbert's *Patience.*[87] *The Poet and the Puppets* was a way for Fitch to flatter Wilde in the coded manner of inverting the conventional order. That the adaptation was produced without Fitch's name compounded the inside joke by providing some professional cover for the still neophyte playwright and enabling pokes at contemporary American theatrical figures like the venerable manager, Augustin Daly, in which Frohman and Dillingham would have found particular amusement. If this closely knit circle of practitioners laughed up their sleeves, the review in the *New York Times* the next day lamented, "There is no particular fun in this for any large portion of the paying public. . . . Where it is ingenious caricature of Oscar Wilde, it seems to misfire with all but a very few."[88] The piece was quickly withdrawn, but even the *Times* acknowledged that it succeeded in awakening new interest in *Lady Windermere's Fan,* then nearing the end of its run at Palmer's Theatre. To have amused themselves while aiding business must indeed have been a delectable experience for the producers.

Whatever delight was shared among the members of this in-group over Wilde's success was short-lived. It has often been pointed out that had Wilde remained discreet about his proclivities, he would have avoided persecution.[89] But during his four pretrial years with Bosie, an evidently spoiled, impetuous young man who demanded all manner of extravagances and indulgences, Wilde grew increasingly reckless. To others in their circle and, eventually, to a much wider public on two continents, Wilde and Douglas's relationship became a spectacle of enslavement to destructive passions. Fitch saw his beloved mentor rocket to theatrical fame and then, as Wilde himself later put it, fall "prey to [the] absolute madness" of same-sex sexual desire.[90] Once the trials that began April 3, 1895, made Wilde's sexuality public, not even Marbury and the Frohmans, three of the most powerful people in the business, could protect Wilde or the reputation of his plays. Marbury writes that the Frohmans outlasted Wilde's London producer George Alexander in standing by him. Charles went ahead with the scheduled opening of *The Importance of Being Earnest* on April 22, and Daniel continued to run *An Ideal Husband* at the Lyceum until the play no longer attracted patronage.[91] Marbury corresponded with Wilde while he was in prison and tried to help him and his family financially by selling "The Ballad of Reading Gaol," a manuscript that, she reports, "moved her to tears." After his release, Wilde sought her out in Paris. Charles Frohman authorized her to advance Wilde five hundred dollars for a new comedy that was to be his "recall to honor and to fame," but Wilde died before he could fulfill the contract.[92] Neither did he live long enough to occupy the small house Marbury and de Wolfe purchased for him adjacent to their summer villa in Versailles, France.[93]

The public spectacle of Wilde's rise and fall greatly heightened the risk factor for those with same-sex affectional preferences and alternative lifestyles throughout Anglo-American culture.[94] Fitch, who had shared the master's bed as well as his theatrical aspirations, had particular reason to be afraid. Wilde had left him with a fully awakened sexuality and a mounting terror that it would run out of control and destroy him. The younger Fitch was still struggling for lasting success in a highly public profession where the stakes for his conduct were becoming much greater.

After Wilde, there is no evidence that he had any other such exhilarating romances. He traveled with a variety of male companions and kept valets and butlers around him at home, but he remained fastidiously discreet about his private life. At the most intimate level, as his correspondence with DeWitt Miller indicates, he remained profoundly lonely and drove himself to fill the void with his work. Years later, when a reporter asked him why he never married, he replied: "Well—even a dramatist may have a damaged heart, may he not? Hearts are hard to mend . . . I live alone in my house here among the things I love to gather and with my work."[95] His playwriting began to pay off steadily after 1898–99 when, after years of furnishing Frohman primarily with adaptations of foreign pieces, he established himself as a commercially successful author of original plays.

With increasing intensity, Fitch used the theater as his primary means of containing as well as expressing his transgressive desire. His strategy involved externalizing his Wildean inner Salomé and refashioning her through stage performance. Far from the pawn of her mother, Herodias, Wilde's Salomé, whom he repeatedly calls "Daughter of Sodom," is herself the instigator; it is for her own pleasure, she tells Herod, that she demands the head of Jokanaan on a silver platter.[96] Her inordinate lust and necrophilic kiss of the decapitated prophet's mouth signaled the catastrophic triumph of forbidden sexual desire over potentially saving artistic genius. Aubrey Beardsley, whom Wilde credited with knowing the secret of the Dance of the Seven Veils, revealed its hidden meanings in his illustration "The Stomach Dance" for the 1894 English edition of the play.[97] At Salomé's feet, strumming the lyre to which she dances, lurks a ghoulish, gleefully priapic minstrel whose misshapen and blemished features connote dread contagion.[98] Fitch's theater worked to transform this dangerously desirous, dancing syphilitic Salomé into a virtuous, statuesque, iconic beauty who defied physical and moral decay.

In this endeavor, his personal needs merged with those of the dominant culture and its commercial theater. Fitch became the leading theatrical fashioner of the emergent national feminine ideal, the American Girl, rendering in four dimensions the codified visual icon leading commercial illustrators such as Charles Dana Gibson and Howard Chandler Christy rendered in two. In an era when Theodore Roosevelt, fearing "overcivilization," inveighed his compatriots not to shrink from those manly contests that built the nation, the American Girl emerged as the ultimate trophy wife—reward for and signifier of heroic American manhood and its triumph over both Old World decadence and frontier savagery. Most jingoistically, Christy called her "a veritable Queen of the

Kingliest of races," "the culmination of mankind's long struggle upward from barbarism to civilization."[99] Unlike the sensuously dancing Salomé whose seduction catalyzed syphilitic decrepitude, the American Girl stood poised atop a pedestal with a tall, classical silhouette that, for both the nation and its most prolific playwright, expressly defied the feared degradations of time, gravity, pollution, and disease. If Fitch debuted in the commercial theater with a stage dandy who served dominant cultural needs by constructing manliness through negative example, he made his greatest fame and fortune with productions showcasing iconic femininity. He did manage a swan song, *The Last of the Dandies,* produced in London by Herbert Beerbohm-Tree the year after Wilde's death, that repeated many of the same tropes as *Beau Brummell.*[100] But American Girl plays premiering in New York overwhelmingly dominated the most successful phase of his career: *The Moth and the Flame* (1898), *Nathan Hale* (1899), *The Cowboy and the Lady* (1899), *The Climbers* (1901), *Captain Jinks of the Horse Marines* (1901), *Lover's Lane* (1901), *The Way of the World* (1901), *The Girl and the Judge* (1901), *The Stubbornness of Geraldine* (1902), *The Girl with the Green Eyes* (1902), *Her Own Way* (1903), *Glad of It* (1903), *The Coronet of the Duchess* (1904), *The Woman in the Case* (1905), *Her Great Match* (1905), *The Girl Who Has Everything* (1906), *The Straight Road* (1907), *The Truth* (1907), *Girls* (1908), *The Bachelor* (1909), *A Happy Marriage* (1909).

The two plays considered Fitch's best in this genre, *The Girl with the Green Eyes* and *The Truth,* illustrate how Fitch shaped his plots to express and contain transgressive passion. Each play features a heroine who appears to conform to the American Girl ideal except for one nearly fatal flaw: in the former play, it is pathological jealousy; in the latter, pathological lying. Both are highly significant transgressions for the playwright. The newly married Jinny Austin grows irrationally jealous over the attention that her husband seems to be paying another woman. In her carnation-green eyes, one can read Fitch's flashes of jealousy over Wilde's interest in Bosie Douglas, especially given Wilde's preference for his lovers to play the woman's part. Additionally, Fitch cleverly links Jinny's outbursts with homoerotically encoded scenography. Jinny flashes hotly when the newlyweds are on their honeymoon in Italy, one of Fitch's favorite summer travel destinations where he could express himself more freely. He sets their confrontation scene in Rome in the Tribune of the Apollo Belvedere. As in the entryway of Fitch's luxurious townhouse, which featured a life-size statue of Adonis,[101] the central visual element of the scene is the nude male form over which enraptured onlookers exclaim in ecstatic French, "C'est superb!" "Magnifique!" "Quelle grace!" "Quelle force!"[102] The scene caused a sensation in the theater and the press.[103]

In the second play, *The Truth*, Becky Warder's lying has more encompassing implications, since lying, the need to dissemble, the need to "pass," historically has been the queer modus operandi. Becky justifies her lying as artistic enhancement of life in the Wildean manner until her web of deceit shatters her husband's faith in her. Metaphorically, the lying is linked to shameful contagion because it is portrayed as a congenital illness, which makes Becky the perverse spawn of her profligate father. When her disgusted husband leaves her, she faces what moralists touted as the wages of sin—precipitous moral, physical, and economic decline. Echoing the rhetoric that condemned Wilde, one reviewer described her affliction as a "sickening perversity."[104] In both plays, Fitch pushes the pathological situation to a climax during which the shamed heroine bares her soul and repents, prompting her husband to forgive and save her from irretrievable ruin. Through this catharsis, she is restored more securely than ever to iconic, bourgeois wife status.

Fitch furthered his strategy of externalizing and containing his woman within by directing his own plays, which became his regular practice after 1898. Drawing on the transvestite expertise cultivated during his college days, he directed his plays by impersonating his female characters himself in rehearsal and instructing actresses to copy him. There are abundant testimonials to his skill, such as this one by an actress who worked with him on *The Climbers:* "Could the entire first act of the play—which you will remember is dominated by women characters—have been played by Mr. Fitch, it would have scored such a success as New York rarely knows."[105] Archie Bell, who wrote a personal memoir of Fitch, recalled of his work with actresses: "If they rose to unusual heights of dramatic expression, it was because they were able to grasp the manner and method from him. He knew the stage value of a drooping eyelash, a momentary pause, a whisper, and a step. He gave it all freely, that his pieces might approach as nearly as possible to ideal representation."[106] In addition to modeling their behavior, Fitch personally attended to his actresses' costumes, hair, wigs, and nails.[107] So assiduous were his ministrations that he repeatedly proved he could take a female performer of little or no stage training or experience and overnight turn her into a star. Indeed, that gesture of molding real, imperfect, desiring women into iconic stage beauties became central to his strategy and earned him the moniker "Maker of Actresses."[108] He was besieged by hundreds of requests from women wanting him to make them a star. While his methods served his own deeply personal need to keep his unruly Salomé a paragon of high-class virtue, they also helped these women fulfill dominant cultural injunctions of ideal femininity.

Along with his playwriting and directorial methods, the pace at which Fitch worked compellingly reveals his attempt to contain destructive desires. Montrose J. Moses and Virginia Gerson, his friends and the editors of his collected letters, write: "Plays began to dovetail faster and faster in the daily routine of [his] life. He was often rehearsing two plays at a time, writing on another, and planning ahead with managers for a fourth and fifth."[109] In 1901, he had four plays running simultaneously on Broadway. In the ensuing ten-month period, he wrote and directed six more full-length plays, prompting Frohman to make the extraordinary gesture of granting Fitch his own theater. Given how Fitch drove himself, it is not surprising that his chronic bouts of illness intensified to the point where he was spending several weeks of his summers abroad at spas like Karlsbad and Salsomaggiore. If not traceable to actual syphilis, his health problems were undoubtedly exacerbated by fears of the contagion that were intensely bound up with fears of exposure. He became gravely ill in the winter of 1902 from "stomach trouble aggravated by ragged nerves," symptoms attributed to extreme stress and overwork. While Fitch was in Europe that summer, there were reports he had appendicitis and that surgery might be in order, but, fearing the knife perhaps because it would not only disrupt his productivity but expose his insides, he found specialists who ruled surgery unnecessary.[110] In spite of the strictest orders to cease work, and having lost fifty pounds and "wasted to a skeleton," Fitch persisted. Even while taking the cure for what he described as "nervous prostration," he reportedly worked on four plays at a time (including *The Girl with the Green Eyes*) with a secretary stationed beside his steaming pool to take dictation. Against doctors' orders, he returned to New York that fall to stage the plays for which he was contracted. He told a reporter, "I am going to lead a strenuous life and see if mental activity won't knock out physical illness."[111] He wound up caught in a vicious, syphilophobic cycle where illness conjured sin, which he countered with obsessive stagings of iconic femininity, which caused more illness. However frivolous and superficial his work seemed to mainstream critics, his representations were animated by a deep-seated, even mortal urgency.

Fitch's workaholism continued unabated until it hounded him into an early grave. Unable to slow down, he took to writing plays on his purported vacations while motor touring with a driver as fast as possible around the European countryside. Writing and driving in this fashion through France in September 1909 with his health weakened from overwork, he suffered an attack of acute appendicitis near the small town of Chalon-sur-Marne. Rather than pressing on to Paris where specialists could operate, he ordered his driver to stop for the night at a hotel. He refused to summon a physician and instead had his traveling companion find him a room, ply him with brandy, and apply hot compresses to his abdomen, which turned out to be the worst possible remedy because it prompted the appendix to rupture. He was forced to submit to emergency surgery by the local doctor, and for a brief period it looked as if he might recover, but then he succumbed to blood poisoning.[112] He was forty-four years old, gone before his time, like Wilde, who died at forty-six.

Before Fitch had embarked on that fateful trip, sensing his days were numbered, he pushed fiercely to finish his play *The City*. "If I should die with 'The City' incomplete," he told actor Tully Marshall, "I should never be able to rest in my grave."[113] Rather than containing his woman within in a high-society comedy, the play reveals the character of the man without in a shocking melodrama. Fitch created a dramatic situation that allowed him to wrestle more openly with his worst fears and purge some of his shame and guilt. The hero, George Rand Jr., has moved his family from a small town to New York City to pursue his business and political ambitions. From his father he inherits some shady financial practices and the burden of providing a livelihood for a troubled youth named Hannock who is in the grip of a shameful affliction he cannot shake—in this case, drugs—and who, as only Rand knows, is his father's illegitimate son. The crisis develops when Hannock tries to blackmail Rand into naming him campaign manager and allowing him to marry Rand's sister Cicely. Rand is forced to tell Hannock she is also his sister. Repulsed, Hannock shoots Cicely to spare her the awful knowledge they are guilty of incest and tries to shoot himself, but Rand grabs the gun away from him. Rand considers letting Hannock kill himself to spare the family the shame and exposure of a trial, preserve the family secrets, and win the election. However, confronting his illegitimate brother writhing before him, the specter of his shadow self, whom one reviewer described as "a moral and physical degenerate, a nervous wreck, a mental ruin,"[114] he resolves to undergo total exposure and rebuild his life on an honest foundation. He hurls the gun out the window, exclaiming: "This is my *only chance to show I can be on the level! That I can be straight,* when it's plain what *is* the right thing to do!"[115]

When the play premiered in December, critics were thrilled finally to see something they thought was fully masculine from Fitch. The *Tribune* proclaimed it "strong as a raging bull, an elephant in passion or a hungry tiger." If Fitch feared the surgeon's knife, in this play, wrote Louis DeFoe, "He laid human nature bare and exposed its cankers in their most repellant forms. He cut through the quivering flesh to the very heart." DeFoe compared its riveting climax to that of Ibsen's *Ghosts,* the play Elaine Showalter has called "the *locus classicus* of syphilitic insanity."[116] Fitch's old schoolmate, William Lyon Phelps, was in the audience opening night and reported being overwhelmed because he felt Fitch crying out from the grave.[117] In Rand's famous speech in the last act we can hear the playwright's own reckoning with his New York–based career and the battles he fought with his Wildean desires:

> Don't blame the City. It's not her fault! It's our own! What the City does is to bring out what's strongest in us. If at heart we're good, the good in us will win! If the bad is strongest, God help us! Don't blame the City! *She* gives a man his opportunity; it is up to *him* what he makes of it! A man can live in a small town all his life, and deceive the whole place and *himself* into thinking he's got all the virtues, when at heart he's a hypocrite! But the village gives him no chance to find it out, to prove it to his fellows—the small town is too easy! *But the City!!* A man goes to the gates of the City and knocks!—New York or Chicago, Boston or San Francisco, no matter *what* city so long as it's big, and busy, and selfish, and self-centered. And she comes to her gates and takes him in, and she stands him in the middle of her market place—where Wall Street and Herald Square and Fifth Avenue and the Bowery and Harlem and Forty-Second Street all meet, and there she strips him naked of all his disguises—and all his hypocrisies—and she paints his ambition on her fences, and lights up her skyscrapers with it!—what *he wants to be and what he thinks he is!*—and then she says to him, 'Make good if you can, or to Hell with you!' And what is in him comes out to clothe his nakedness, and to the City he can't lie! I *know* because I tried!*[118]

NOTES

    1. See "List of Plays by Clyde Fitch," in *Clyde Fitch and His Letters,* ed. Montrose J. Moses and Virginia Gerson (Boston: Little, 1924), 389–93.
    2. "American Stage Authors in Favor: Charles Frohman Discusses Playwrights Now Making Fortunes," unnamed newspaper clipping, January 24, 1902,

in Clyde Fitch Scrapbook, Robinson-Locke Collection of Theatre Scrapbooks, New York Public Library, Lincoln Center, vol. 211, n.p.

3. For summations of these assessments, see H. T. Parker, "Clyde Fitch: The Man, His Traits, and the Sum of His Work," *Boston Transcript,* September 8, 1909, n.p.; Janet Ann Carnevale-Kanak, "Clyde Fitch and His Reception by the American Periodical Press," Ph.D. diss., Fordham University, 1978.

4. John A. Lowe, "Clyde Fitch, A 'Sissy' Boy Who Became a $250,000 a Year Dramatist," *Literary Digest,* November 13, 1920, 69, 74, 78–79.

5. See Walter Prichard Eaton, "The Dramatist as Man of Letters: The Case of Clyde Fitch," *Scribner's,* April 1910, 490–97; Robert William Masters, "Clyde Fitch: A Playwright of His Time," Ph.D. diss., Northwestern University, 1942; Walter Meserve, "Clyde Fitch and the Social World," in *An Outline History of the American Drama* (Totowa, N.J.: Littlefield, Adams, 1965), 155–59; Thomas Lowell Hellie, "Clyde Fitch: Playwright of New York's Leisure Class," Ph.D. diss., University of Missouri, Columbia, 1985.

6. Kim Marra, "Clyde Fitch: Transvestite *Metteur-en-Scène* of the Feminine," *New England Theatre Journal* 3, no. 1 (1992): 15–37.

7. Melissa Knox, *Oscar Wilde: A Long and Lovely Suicide* (New Haven: Yale University Press, 1994); Gary Schmidgall, *The Stranger Wilde: Interpreting Oscar* (New York: Dutton, 1994).

8. Letter to DeWitt Miller, February 9, 1891, in Clyde Fitch and DeWitt Miller Correspondence, Fitch Letters 1890–94, New York Public Library, quoted in Schmidgall, *The Stranger Wilde,* 442.

9. Quoted in Carnevale-Kanak, "Fitch and His Reception," 46.

10. George Chauncey, *Gay New York: Gender, Urban Culture, and the Making of the Gay Male World, 1890–1940* (New York: Basic Books, 1994), 35–36; David Pugh, *Sons of Liberty: The Masculine Mind in Nineteenth Century America* (Westport, Conn.: Greenwood, 1983), 59, 86.

11. George Chauncey, "From Sexual Inversion to Homosexuality: The Changing Medical Conceptualization of Female 'Deviance,'" in *Passion and Power: Sexuality in History,* ed. Kathy Peiss and Christina Simmons (Philadelphia: Temple University Press, 1989), 89.

12. Chauncey, *Gay New York,* 48–49.

13. Elisabeth Marbury, *My Crystal Ball* (New York: Boni, 1923), 86.

14. Archie Bell, *The Clyde Fitch I Knew* (New York: Broadway, 1909), 93–94.

15. William Lyon Phelps, *Autobiography with Letters* (New York: Oxford University Press, 1939), 122.

16. William Lyon Phelps, *Essays on Modern Dramatists* (New York: Macmillan, 1921), 142–44.

17. Letter dated October 1, 1879, in Moses and Gerson, *Fitch and His Letters,* 10.

18. Ibid., xiii.

19. See H. Montgomery Hyde, ed., *The Annotated Oscar Wilde: Poems, Fiction, Plays, Lectures, Essays, and Letters* (New York: Clarkson N. Potter, 1982), 370–71.

20. Moses and Gerson, *Fitch and His Letters,* 18. See also Andy Bohjalian,

"Salute to Clyde Fitch '86," in Memorabilia of College Productions. Amherst College Special Collections and Archives.

21. Stephen Calloway, "Wilde and the Dandyism of the Senses," in *The Cambridge Companion to Oscar Wilde*, ed. Peter Raby (New York: Cambridge, 1997), 44.

22. Chilton L. Powell, "Clyde Fitch's Apprenticeship," *Amherst Graduates' Quarterly*, May 1928, 157–66.

23. See Geraldine Maschio, "A Prescription for Femininity: Male Impersonation of the Feminine Ideal at the Turn of the Century," *Women and Performance*, 4.7 (1988/89): 43–50.

24. Albert S. Bard, "Some Recollections of Clyde Fitch in College," *Amherst Graduates' Quarterly*, October 1914, 39; Moses and Gerson, *Fitch and His Letters*, 18.

25. Powell, "Clyde Fitch's Apprenticeship," 164–65.

26. Review of *The Rivals*, *Amherst Student*, February 14, 1885, 116–17, Amherst College Special Collections and Archives.

27. Powell, "Clyde Fitch's Apprenticeship," 164–65.

28. John Lancaster, "Clyde Fitch," *Newsletter of the Friends of the Amherst College Library*, 1983, n.p.

29. Wilde's essay "Shakespeare and Stage Costume," the first incarnation of "The Truth of Masks," appeared in the *Nineteenth Century* in May 1885. See *The Artist as Critic: Critical Writings of Oscar Wilde*, ed. Richard Ellmann (New York: Random House, 1969), 341–71.

30. See, for example, the account of the testimony of Charles Parker, one of Wilde's young male prostitutes, in Michael S. Foldy, *The Trials of Oscar Wilde: Deviance, Morality, and Late-Victorian Society* (New Haven: Yale University Press, 1997), 32.

31. "Captain Fitch Did Not Understand Art," *Hartford Courant*, September 21, 1923, n.p.

32. Letter to Mollie Jackson, March 1888, in Moses and Gerson, *Fitch and His Letters*, 39.

33. Chauncey, *Gay New York*, 60–61.

34. Ibid., 39–44.

35. "Clyde Fitch Explains Why He Stopped Writing 'Smart Set' Plays and Says His Ambition Is to Depict the Melodrama of Real Life," *Sunday New York Herald*, February 5, 1905, sec. 3.

36. Chauncey, *Gay New York*, 112.

37. Ibid., 47.

38. Ibid., 106.

39. "Andre Raffalovich," in *The Gay and Lesbian Literary Heritage: A Reader's Companion to the Writers and Their Works, from Antiquity to the Present*, ed. Claude Summers (New York: Holt, 1995), 708.

40. Moses and Gerson, *Fitch and His Letters*, 45–46.

41. Neil Miller, *Out of Our Past: Gay and Lesbian History from 1869 to the Present* (New York: Vintage, 1995), 48.

42. Moses and Gerson, *Fitch and His Letters*, 184.

43. Richard Ellmann, *Oscar Wilde* (New York: Vintage, 1988), 282.

44. Telegram reprinted in *More Letters of Oscar Wilde,* ed. Rupert Hart-Davis (London: John Murray, 1985), 83.

45. "Fitch, Clyde, A.L.S. to Oscar Wilde" (Wilde F544L W6721 [1889?]), William Andrews Clark Memorial Library, University of California, Los Angeles, quoted in Schmidgall, *The Stranger Wilde,* 178; Knox, *Oscar Wilde,* 151 n. 1.

46. "Fitch, Clyde, A.L.S. to Oscar Wilde" (Wilde F544L W6721 [189–?]c), Clark Library, quoted in Knox, *Oscar Wilde,* 152 n. 1; Schmidgall, *The Stranger Wilde,* 178.

47. Moses and Gerson, *Fitch and His Letters,* 47.

48. Ibid, 48.

49. Quoted in Schmidgall, *The Stranger Wilde,* 181. In the course of a brief account of the Fitch/Wilde affair, Schmidgall asks in a footnote whether Fitch's *Beau Brummell* could have been inspired by Wilde.

50. Calloway, "Wilde and Dandyism," 36.

51. See Ellen Moers, *The Dandy: Brummell to Beerbohm* (New York: Viking Press, 1960), 256–64.

52. Moers, *The Dandy,* 18.

53. Knox, *Oscar Wilde,* 151 n. 1.

54. Moses and Gerson, *Fitch and His Letters,* 43, 204.

55. In a letter to the *Boston Evening Transcript,* September 13, 1906, William Winter elaborated the romantic plot he claimed to have given to Mansfield to pass on to Fitch.

56. Clyde Fitch, *Beau Brummell,* in *Plays,* Memorial Edition, ed. Montrose J. Moses and Virginia Gerson, vol. 1 (Boston: Little, Brown, 1920), 38–39.

57. Ibid., 51.

58. Ibid., 54–55.

59. Ibid., 11.

60. Elaine Showalter, "Syphilis, Sexuality, and the Fiction of the Fin-de-Siècle," in *Sex, Politics, and Science in the Nineteenth-Century Novel* (Baltimore: Johns Hopkins University Press, 1990), 92.

61. For more on the evidence and impact of syphilis on Wilde's career, see Knox, *Oscar Wilde,* 42–45, 61–62; Ellmann, *Oscar Wilde,* 92; Showalter, "Syphilis," 103–4.

62. Letter to DeWitt Miller, February 9, 1891, in Clyde Fitch and De Witt Miller Correspondence, Fitch Letters 1890–1904, New York Public Library.

63. "Fitch, Clyde, A.L.S. to Oscar Wilde" (Wilde F544L W6721 [189–?]c), Clark Library, quoted in Knox, *Oscar Wilde,* 152 n.1.

64. "Fitch, Clyde, A.L.S. to Oscar Wilde" (Wilde F544L W6721 [189–?]d), Clark Library, quoted in Knox, *Oscar Wilde,* 152–53 n. 1; Schmidgall, *The Stranger Wilde,* 180.

65. Schmidgall, *The Stranger Wilde,* 180.

66. Letter from Wilde to Fitch dated September 1890 (L275), Clark Library, quoted in Schmidgall, *The Stranger Wilde,* 154.

67. Moses and Gerson, *Fitch and His Letters,* 57.

68. Moses and Gerson, *Fitch and His Letters,* 58.

69. Letter to DeWitt Miller, January 2, 1891, in Clyde Fitch and De Witt Miller Correspondence, Fitch Letters 1890–1904, New York Public Library, quoted in Schmidgall, *The Stranger Wilde*, 442–43.

70. *A Wave of Life* was later published in full by Mitchell Kennerly in New York in 1909.

71. Elisabeth Marbury, *My Crystal Ball* (London: Hurst and Blackett, 1924), 80, 95.

72. Isaac F. Marcosson and Daniel Frohman, *Charles Frohman: Manager and Man* (New York: Harper, 1916), 150.

73. See Kim Marra, "A Lesbian Marriage of Cultural Consequence: Elisabeth Marbury and Elsie de Wolfe, 1886–1933," in *Passing Performances: Queer Readings of Leading Players in American Theatre History,* ed. Robert A. Schanke and Kim Marra (Ann Arbor: University of Michigan Press, 1998).

74. Marcosson and Frohman, *Charles Frohman,* 153–56.

75. See Jane S. Smith, *Elsie de Wolfe: A Life in the High Style* (New York: Atheneum, 1982), 70; and Marcosson and Frohman, *Charles Frohman,* 367–69.

76. Marbury, *My Crystal Ball* (1924), 82.

77. Letter to DeWitt Miller dated "Monday Night 1893," in Fitch Letters, 1890–1904, New York Public Library.

78. In their chronology of Fitch productions, Moses and Gerson give September 4, 1895, as the date of Fitch's adaptation of *The Poet and the Puppets.* However, I was able to find no corroborating record of this production date in the daily papers. Reviews in the *New York Times* and the *New York Herald* attest that the production opened on April 8, 1893.

79. Charles Brookfield and J. M. Glover, *The Poet and the Puppets* (originally printed in London by Mitchell, 1892), in *The Decadent Consciousness: A Hidden Archive of Late Victorian Literature,* ed. Ian Fletcher and John Stokes, vol. 35 (New York: Garland, 1978), 6.

80. Ibid., 7.

81. Ibid., 16.

82. Ibid., 16.

83. Quoted in Schmidgall, *The Stranger Wilde*, 154.

84. Clyde Fitch, *The Knighting of the Twins and Ten Other Tales,* with drawings by Virginia Gerson (Boston: Roberts Brothers, 1891).

85. See Kevin Kopelson, *Love's Litany: The Writing of Modern Homoerotics* (Stanford: Stanford University Press, 1994), 23–25 for a queer reading of Wilde's *The Happy Prince.*

86. Fitch, *Knighting of the Twins,* 251. Another story in the volume, "An Unchronicled Miracle," written in Chester, England, May 1889, is dedicated to Walter Pater, a mentor Fitch and Wilde shared.

87. Review of *The Poet and the Puppets, New York Herald,* April 9, 1893, 14.

88. "The Theatrical Week," review of *The Poet and the Puppets, New York Times,* April 9, 1893, 10.

89. See, for example, Schmidgall, *The Stranger Wilde*, 174–95.

90. Quoted in Schmidgall, *The Stranger Wilde*, 181.

91. Marbury, *My Crystal Ball* (1924), 95.

92. Ibid., 97–98. See also Ellmann, *Oscar Wilde,* 579. In spite of the major role Marbury played in Wilde's theatrical career as his agent and her loyalty to him until his death, she does not figure in Ellmann's account.

93. Smith, *Elsie de Wolfe,* 171.

94. Miller, *Out of Our Past,* 50.

95. "A Chat with Mr. Clyde Fitch in His Home about Things Theatrical," *New York Herald,* November 16, 1902, in Clyde Fitch Collection, Amherst College Special Collections.

96. See Joseph Donohue, "Distance, Death, and Desire in *Salome,*" in *The Cambridge Companion to Oscar Wilde,* 125, 135.

97. Quoted in ibid., 173.

98. William Tydeman and Steven Price, *Wilde: Salome* (New York: Cambridge, 1996), 118.

99. Howard Chandler Christy, *The American Girl as Seen and Portrayed by Howard Chandler Christy* (1906; rpt. New York: Da Capo, 1976), 69–70.

100. *The Last of the Dandies* premiered at Her Majesty's Theatre in London, October 24, 1901. Like *Beau Brummell,* the play features an older dandy based on an aristocratic English historical figure, Count d'Orsay, whose most ardent passions are directed toward a younger man in the acceptable framework of a filial relation.

101. See "Magnificent Home of Playwright Clyde Fitch," *Boston Herald,* August 10, 1902, n.p., Clyde Fitch Collection, Amherst College Special Collections.

102. Fitch, *The Girl with the Green Eyes: A Play in Four Acts* (New York: Macmillan, 1905), 75–76.

103. See Carnevale-Kanak, "Fitch and His Reception," 164–67.

104. Review of *The Truth, Theater,* February 1907, 30.

105. Clyde Fitch Scrapbook, Robinson-Locke Collection of Theatre Scrapbooks, New York Public Library, Lincoln Center, vol. 480, p. 65.

106. Archie Bell, *The Clyde Fitch I Knew* (New York: Broadway, 1909), 71.

107. Roi Cooper Megrue, "The Real Clyde Fitch," Ts., 1905, pp. 14–15, Clyde Fitch Collection, Amherst College Special Collections.

108. See E. Elderkin Fyles, "The Man behind the Stars: Clyde Fitch, Maker of Actresses," *American Illustrated Magazine,* November 1905, 72–78.

109. Moses and Gerson, *Fitch and His Letters,* 209.

110. Marbury, *My Crystal Ball* (1924), 83.

111. Reports of Fitch's 1902 illness are found in various clippings in the Clyde Fitch Scrapbook, Robinson-Locke Collection of Theatre Scrapbooks, New York Public Library, Lincoln Center, vol. 480, pp. 19–38.

112. Marbury, *My Crystal Ball* (1924), 84–85.

113. Quoted in "Clyde Fitch Foresaw His Death," advance program for *The City* at the Lyceum Theatre, January 1910, Clyde Fitch Clipping File, New York Public Library, Lincoln Center.

114. Channing Pollock, "The Thick of the Season," *The Green Book Album,* March 1910, 515.

115. *The City*, in Fitch, *Plays*, Memorial Edition, ed. Montrose J. Moses and Virginia Gerson, vol. 4 (Boston: Little, 1921), 605–6.

116. *Tribune* and DeFoe quotes appear in *Current Literature*, February 1910, 201–2; Showalter, "Syphils," 105.

117. Phelps, *Essays*, 150.

118. *The City*, 627–29.

Rachel Crothers

An Exceptional Woman in a Man's World

J. K. Curry

Rachel Crothers (1878?–1958) was a notable presence on Broadway from 1906 to 1937 with twenty-four plays produced, including *A Man's World* (1910), *He and She* (1920), *When Ladies Meet* (1932), and *Susan and God* (1937).[1] Distinguishing herself from her peers, Crothers directed all of her own plays, beginning with *Myself—Bettina* in 1908, and occasionally directed plays by other writers. Over the years, she also devoted extensive resources to charitable organizations, helping to form and lead the Stage Women's War Relief in response to World War I, the Stage Relief Fund to help members of the theatrical profession during the Great Depression, and the American Theatre Wing of the Allied War Relief during World War II. Frequently referred to in her day as "dean of the women playwrights," Crothers was included in a 1930 list of the "fifty foremost women in the United States."[2] She was a highly visible model of a modern career woman, even as she wrote many plays about women's domestic concerns and love lives. Always focused on mainstream, commercial success, Crothers wrote plays that raised timely issues of concern to women, without shocking her audiences or venturing too far from conventional values of the day. Many of Crothers's plays explore love, relationships, and changes in sexual morality, but always within a heterosexual framework.

Though a notable public figure, Crothers managed to keep her personal life private. Crothers was never married, and available documents do not record any romantic relationships with men. Her primary emotional attachment was apparently to a woman who shared her home for many years. The relationship was not discussed in any of the numerous articles about Crothers, with the exception of one fairly early profile. In this article, entitled "'What do Women Think of Other Women?' Men Are More Tolerant and Good Natured," Crothers answered several

55

FIG. 2. Rachel Crothers at her home, Roadside, in Redding, Connecticut.

(Courtesy Theatre Collection, Museum of the City of New York.)

interview questions about contemporary women. After denying that "there exists any new and widespread loyalty among women for women," Crothers commented on her own situation. She said, "Modern women are capable of splendid friendships for each other. That is a matter on which I feel very strongly. I myself have lived for ten years with a woman friend and the relation has been ideal. I have my work and she has hers. I write plays and she keeps my apartment." She also noted, "I have known of a number of similar instances, and I think many women are learning to make homes together. Two women, each earning a small salary, can turn a modest apartment into a home; something two men can't do, even if they can afford more luxuries."[3] The woman friend Crothers referred to was apparently Eula Seeley Garrison, who shared Crothers's home in Connecticut for decades. Garrison's daughter, Angeline G. Hoagland, who occasionally performed secretarial work for Crothers, was the sole beneficiary of Crothers's estate.[4]

Crothers never publicly identified as a lesbian. This may have been a business decision by a playwright whose commercial success was connected to her convincing depictions of the dilemmas faced by the "modern woman," always implicitly a heterosexual woman. Many of Crothers's theater colleagues were aware that she had a female companion, but there is almost no evidence of the details of the relationship and its impact on her personal identity.[5] As Leila J. Rupp cautions,

> Passionate love between women has existed, but it has not always been named. Since it *has* been named in the twentieth century, and since there *was* such a thing as a lesbian culture, we need to distinguish between women who identify as lesbians and/or who were a part of a lesbian culture, where one exists, and a broader category of women-committed women who would not identify as lesbians but whose primary commitment, in emotional and practical terms, was to other women.[6]

While it is clear that Crothers's closest intimate bonds were with women, we should be cautious about assigning her a label she did not embrace.

An emotional commitment to another woman was not part of Crothers's public persona. Instead, she was portrayed in the press as married to her work and too busy for a social or personal life. Alternatively, Crothers was presented as a schoolmarm type, in an era when female teachers were required to remain unmarried and childless. For example, in a profile of Crothers, Djuna Barnes wrote that "had she been born twenty years earlier she would, or one feels she would, have been the head of a young ladies seminary."[7] Another writer observed, "To call her a small-town, Middle West school teacher is to make more startling the fact that she has cracked the whip and made Broadway sit up for twenty-five years."[8] Indeed, it often seems the backstage glimpses into Crothers's life were provided primarily to explain the absence of a heterosexual relationship. If not the stern, celibate, schoolteacher disciplining unruly actors, Crothers was presented as a woman whose passion was directed entirely to the theater. A 1931 article noted,

> The fact that Miss Crothers writes knowingly and shrewdly about married life often raises the questions of her own private life. The answer is that Miss Crothers has never married. She says she has never had the time. She waves a hand toward the stage where her company is playing and says: "Those people are my husbands and my lovers, my sons and my daughters."[9]

Emphasizing the presumed sacrifice of a family life, the article continues, "Then she smiles a little. 'The road to the stars is over stony ground.'"

The idea that Crothers was too busy for a husband and children, had she wanted them, was certainly plausible. Writing and revising twenty-four full-length plays for production on Broadway was only one portion of Crothers's professional output. She considered her work as a director equally important. In fact, over the years Crothers often advanced her theory that the well-trained playwright was the best possible director of her own play. In a lecture on playwriting she explained,

> Great directors do much for plays, but no matter how fine the director and all the other minds which are brought together in the production, they can't see and know the play as deeply and vividly as the author does; and if the author is trained and equipped and has a gift for all that goes into the staging of a play, he gets a result which does more for the play than the outsider can do. Some subtle quality escapes when it goes through other minds.[10]

Although her reputation was made as a playwright, Crothers stressed the director's contribution to each production. As early as 1916 she insisted that the future of the American stage depended on the director, arguing, "What is needed is not genius among the actors so much as genius among the directors."[11] Crothers, herself, was the only woman included in a short list by playwright Owen Davis of playwrights who were "first rate directors of their own plays."[12] Given her awareness of the significance of the director's job, it is not surprising that Crothers took on so many of the production responsibilities. "Personally I care as passionately about the production of my plays as I do about the plays themselves," she wrote.

> It became a natural and apparently inevitable thing that I should stage and direct my own plays and I find it infinitely easier to make myself responsible for the slightest details of production and carry the whole burden than it is to delegate different things to different heads, not knowing whether the details are going to fit correctly into the main scheme or not.[13]

Crothers regularly put a great deal of effort into casting and coaching the actors. She reportedly drew her own sketches of the scenery and kept a close eye on the scene painters and property men. Concerned with every detail of costume and setting, Crothers spent her hours away from rehearsals scouting for necessary costume items and also for the precise props and furniture she required. She monitored the promotion of her productions, rehearsed road companies, and frequently reviewed her long-running productions and gave new notes to the actors. Even by theatrical standards, Crothers was a remarkably busy woman. A reference to her full schedule was a simple way to explain her lack of a husband to curious fans.

Crothers also promoted an image of herself as a woman too remarkable and talented to easily find an acceptable male partner. In 1923 she told an interviewer,

> I have never found a man who was big enough, strong enough, and intellectual enough who did not also have the vices of those great qualities. Such a man has been taught by millenniums of generous providing for his women folks that his woman should depend on him economically and mentally. The superior man will not have the superior woman—not on the superior woman's terms.[14]

Other women in theater sometimes opted for a convenient marriage to divert attention from their primary relationship. In another essay in this volume, Robert A. Schanke examines the choice of a convenient marriage made by another woman writer, Mercedes de Acosta. Crothers chose, instead, to emphasize the lack of a suitable male partner, along with the difficulties of combining career and marriage. Certainly, Crothers was often identified as a woman who had chosen a career instead of marriage and family. Through the years of Crothers's career, journalists readily accepted the idea that a woman's choice between career and family was an either/or decision.

Crothers, herself, made a clear distinction between the majority of women, who would assume traditional roles as wives and mothers, and career women, in comments she wrote after the Broadway production of her play *He and She* (1920). The play generated a fair amount of controversy, as it weighed in on the timely issue of a woman's proper role in and out of the home and because many admirers of Crothers's earlier work thought Crothers was reversing her own position on some key feminist issues. The title characters of *He and She,* Tom and Ann Herford, are a married couple, who are both sculptors. Tom is planning to enter an important competition for a big commission and believes he has a good chance of winning. Ann offers Tom her own design ideas, which he admires, but rejects as not big enough or in the same class with his work. Ann then asks permission to enter the drawings on her own. When Ann wins the contest, no one in the family, not even the previously supportive husband, is happy for her. Meanwhile, a crisis develops as the couple's teenaged daughter Millicent contemplates an ill-advised marriage to the chauffeur at her boarding school. Feeling guilty for neglecting her daughter, Ann decides she must devote her full attention to Millicent, and she turns the commission over to her husband. The play thus ends with a woman sacrificing her career for the sake of her marriage and family.

Many audience members were apparently surprised by the resolution of *He and She.* Describing the audience, Louis Reid of the *New York Dramatic Mirror* noted that "the feminine portion gave enthusiastic approval to the idea of woman carving out a career for herself at the same time that she lives a normal domestic life."[15] Some members of this enthusiastic crowd were undoubtedly familiar with Rhy MacChesney, Crothers's spunky heroine in *The Three of Us* (1906), Crothers's first Broadway hit. Rhy MacChesney struggles to raise her younger brothers and hold on to the family's mining claim. In the play's big scene Rhy is discovered at night in the rooms of a man, the play's villain. Rhy insists that outward appearances are not important while she knows she has not done anything wrong, and she will not be coerced into marrying the man to save her "honor." Though the play is resolved conventionally with Rhy's marriage to her sweetheart, the audience first must see Rhy as a strong woman of her word who will make her own decisions. Another memorable character that had been written by Crothers was Frank Ware, the woman who rejects her male suitor, rather than compromise her values, in *A Man's World* (1910). Ann Herford was presented in *He and She* as a talented, unconventional woman, like Rhy MacChesney or Frank

Ware, and this made her final decision to sacrifice her career all the more disturbing to a key segment of the audience.

Some critics happily accepted Crothers's apparent message that woman's place is in the home. Others used their reviews to argue against the idea. Heywood Broun, for example, wrote in the *New York Tribune*,

> We have always found that the soup tastes just the same whether it was opened with loving care or by the hired help. Nor are we convinced that young daughters tend to become entangled in unfortunate love affairs the instant a mother begins to paint a picture or deliver a series of lectures or write short stories for the magazines.[16]

The critical response indicated that *He and She* had struck a nerve. Burns Mantle wrote that the play "focuses attention on a present-day problem that will not find its solution until generations of men and women yet unborn have struggled with it."[17] Even secondary issues in the play prompted discussion. The *Evening Mail* sponsored a contest inspired by the play, offering cash prizes for the best "letter discussion" on the question "Which do you consider more dangerous for a young girl—the wiles and temptations of the city or the possible neglect of absentee motherhood?"[18]

Crothers felt compelled to explain that she was not arguing against married women in the workforce. She began defending her play in 1912 when an early version, titled *The Herfords,* was presented in Boston. "Some people who see the play will go away with the idea that I think it is wrong for married women to work and this is not at all the idea I mean to convey," wrote Crothers. "I certainly think that the home should come first in a woman's life, but I do not see why she should not also have some other occupation besides keeping house and taking care of her children, if she has any."[19] Crothers continued,

> I also think that a profession need not necessarily upset a woman's home life or her relationship to her husband. It is right, I suppose that the man should be the bread winner; in fact, to me the assertion of this belief is the finest characteristic of American men, but in many ways I do think men are hopelessly benighted in regard to women. As long as they are taken care of and the home is attractively kept they are perfectly amiable; but as soon as a woman has any other interests outside of the household they are at once disgruntled and cannot understand the existence of such a possibility. *Mrs. Herford, however, gave up her profession not because her husband wanted her to, but because her daughter absolutely needed her care.* (Emphasis added)

While Crothers always believed women to be capable of any profession, she argued that women should not put career goals ahead of their children.

It is not hard to speculate about a connection between Crothers's view on this issue and her relationship to her own working mother. Marie Louise Depew Crothers began her study of medicine only after her husband, Dr. Eli Kirk Crothers, ran into serious financial difficulty. Rachel, the youngest of the Crothers's nine children (four survived childhood), included her mother's preoccupation with her studies among her earliest memories. Recalling hours spent playing alone with her paper dolls, Crothers wrote,

> I knew that I must be very quiet about all this. The woman sitting before the fire was my mother who must *not* be disturbed. She held on her lap the biggest book bound in pale leather. Over this book she bent—never looking up. After several years I knew that the book was 'Gray's Anatomy' and that Mother was going to be a doctor.[20]

When she had completed her home study, Marie Crothers traveled east to attend the Women's Medical College in Philadelphia, leaving Rachel in the care of an aunt.[21] After graduating with honors, Marie Crothers returned home and became the first woman to practice medicine in central Illinois. An exceptional woman succeeding in a male-dominated field, Marie Crothers served as a unique role model for her daughter.

On the other hand, Rachel Crothers viewed herself to some extent as an abandoned child, noting in her attempted autobiography, "How much a child suffers only that child knows." Several of Crothers's plays, including *The Three of Us, A Man's World, Once upon a Time, A Little Journey, He and She, As Husbands Go,* and *Bill Comes Back,* have the plot element of a child or children requiring adult guidance and care. Still, as an adult, Crothers demonstrated an understanding of the challenges her mother faced, writing,

> What it cost her to give up her home and put her children here and there—the courage it took to tackle the long difficult course in medicine—when she had never studied anything since she left a small private school and was married at seventeen to the handsome doctor who was ten years older than she—all this I didn't know until I was at least seventeen myself.

Crothers also noted that her mother had to "struggle against the strong prejudice and skepticism which prevailed against women in that profession. . . . This shy sensitive woman gave up her personal life and her fastidious housekeeping and became the leading woman physician in that part of the country."[22]

The personal mythology of a lonely childhood is repeated in many statements about Crothers's early days, though the positive aspect is stressed since Crothers traced her vocation back to her interaction with her paper dolls: "My theatre came into being on the floor with my paper dolls when I was four years old—building houses for them out of books—speaking their dialogue—living their lives—finishing one set of lives before I began another."[23] By age twelve Crothers had moved from creating a fantasy world with her dolls to writing and staging a play, with Crothers and her girlfriend playing all five roles. Years later Crothers recalled her young collaborator, saying, "I remember her so vividly. She was so pretty and I loved her so very much—but oh how I made her work and how tired she became of the whole thing! But I drove her on till it was brought to production in the back parlor."[24] On another occasion after again recounting how she "loved and admired" her "adorably pretty" friend, Crothers noted that the two worked in secrecy, even shutting out their other friends.[25] When Crothers's parents finally learned what she was up to, they were not thrilled since they considered the theater a disreputable institution. However, they did not restrict her activities, for soon their daughter was writing and staging "sketches" for a Sunday school class and performing with an amateur dramatic club.

Crothers's eagerness to continue exploring the imaginary world discovered in her childhood led her to look beyond the limited opportunities available in her hometown. Soon the teenaged Crothers was off for a year of study at the New England School of Dramatic Instruction, which she followed with additional training at the Stanhope-Wheatcroft School of Acting in New York City. Making this move, she demonstrated remarkable independence for a small-town Midwestern girl in the 1890s. Perhaps she already knew she would never comfortably settle into a conventional adult life in her hometown. She was determined to "be the greatest actress the world had ever known," but soon realized her real talents were in playwriting and directing.[26]

As an adult working in professional theater, Crothers chose not to divide her attention between work and family. Crothers had survived her own lonely childhood and prospered, perhaps even owing her successful career to the strength of the imagination she developed as compensation for her perceived isolation. However, she clearly did not approve of absentee motherhood. Her comments following the production of *He and She* emphasize the importance to women of choosing one of two possible paths, career or family. Crothers wrote that "it is absolute folly for any woman to try and convince herself that happiness will be hers if she will try to divide her interest between her work and her home."[27] Crothers insisted that she had not changed her views and still believed women were capable of competing with men in any field. However, only one group of women was free to enter the competition. If a woman decided to pursue a career, Crothers insisted,

> she must understand that she is automatically giving up the other great privilege—the privilege of being a wife and a mother in the truest sense of the term. She must understand that she is treading on ground that has proven treacherous to others and on which many have come to grief, that is, if they endeavored to play both games at once.

Crothers went on to stress the importance of the domestic sphere. Perhaps Crothers saw some commercial value in praising motherhood or hoped to avoid alienating her audience, while taking the other path herself.

> [A point] I cannot make forcibly enough is that woman should always remember that her duties as a wife and mother come first, that the building of a home and the caring for a family should be, by far, the foremost aims in her life. But, and here is my qualification, if she believes that she is totally unsuited for this plan of life and that she is better suited for the active world, then by all means it is her business to steer clear of matrimony.[28]

In that statement, Crothers also defined herself as a woman who could not tolerate marriage.

Women were thus divided into two distinct camps, those who would attempt to accomplish things in the world and those who would have families. Crothers often made comments that indicated she was pleased to belong to the former group. The public debate over *He and She* had prompted Crothers to praise motherhood, while exempting a select group of women, but during the same period she also had championed the other side. Crothers claimed that

> there are two classes of women in the world, and the dividing line between them is sharp. There are the women who are economically independent of men, and the women who are not. . . . The dependent wife and mother and the dependent woman generally is not going to benefit by changes that are occurring. . . . But—the independent woman is going to have glorious opportunities.[29]

Further, she noted that "the dependent women were always poor things, deserving of pity." Having found glorious opportunities in her own career, Crothers never asked for pity for herself. Yet journalists sometimes presented Crothers, a woman with a great career and no husband, as an object of pity. One article noted,

> The impression that Rachel Crothers gives is of a mighty executive mind that controls her destiny. But this great mind of hers . . . has been fed, nurtured on her personal life. In entering a man's world, the world where careers are made, it would seem that a woman must sacrifice certain human experiences. The same sacrifices are not exacted of man.[30]

Certainly the rejection of heterosexual relationships is implicit in the distinction Crothers makes between the potentially high-achieving career women and ordinary, domestic women. In Crothers's day, more than in our own, heterosexual relationships normally carried the possibility of reproduction. In her view, a woman who created a child had an obligation to put the child's needs ahead of her own professional development or artistic fulfillment. One sure way to avoid the burden of motherhood was to opt to avoid sexual relations with men.

In *He and She* Crothers presents a character, Ruth, who belongs in the group of exceptional women choosing career instead of marriage. Crothers calls Ruth "one of the world's 'doers.'"[31] Other female "doers" in Crothers's plays include Frank in *A Man's World* and Mary in *When Ladies Meet*. All three of these characters, among the most appealing to later feminist readers of Crothers's plays, desire love relationships with men, but ultimately reject the men who do not meet their expectations. Crothers presents an admirable picture of the woman who chooses to live without a man. In her plays, Crothers does not go so far as to propose that women form romantic or sexual relations with women instead of men, though, perhaps, this was the solution in her own life. It is interesting to note that Frank, not only rejects a heterosexual pairing, but also forms her own unconventional family unit and forms a community of women. As Serena Anderlini-D'Onofrio has pointed out, Frank was a member of a "homosocial community" even during her involvement with Malcolm Gaskell.[32] Frank has decided to open a club for disadvantaged young women and invites her friend Clara, a woman disappointed in both love and career prospects, to help run it. Frank acknowledges that Clara might have been best suited to married life had she had the opportunity. She says, "I believe in women doing the thing they're most fitted for."[33] The implication, of course, is that Frank, despite her immediate unhappiness, is not "most fitted for" marriage.

Crothers's own early partnership does not appear to have offered a radical critique of heterosexual pairings. It was clearly not a case of two equally ambitious and successful career women making a life together. Crothers herself avoided subordination to a man in her personal life and, perhaps, actually usurped a male privilege by, in effect, taking a wife. While making her way in a competitive field, Crothers apparently had someone to keep her house and provide domestic comfort and companionship.

Of course, the details of Crothers's domestic situation were largely hidden from view. Occasionally, the press reported that Crothers was able to escape the demands of her hectic professional life in the city and to retreat to her beautiful country home, Roadside, in Connecticut (see fig. 2). In mentioning Crothers's part-time residence, writers were able to emphasize domesticity and the more traditionally feminine aspects of Crothers's personality. For example, Charlotte Hughes noted, "Rachel Crothers's large, hospitable farmhouse in Connecticut is meticulously neat and exudes charm and comfort."[34] A domestic partner is not included in the picture. In fact, some glimpses into Crothers's home life stress the absence of companions. One writer insisted that Crothers "lives alone and no more has a guest chamber than a business man would keep a guest chamber in his office."[35] Crothers attempted to limit what aspects of her private life were revealed to the public: "Finally, I want just to touch on the way that many people have of puzzling over my very normal life. Simple domesticity—as you see for yourself here."[36] This statement sounds a bit like the disingenuous assertion of a child performer that she is just a normal kid.

Whatever the particulars of her household, Crothers's active professional life as a director and extensive volunteer work with organizations such as the Stage Women's War Relief would have interfered with a regular domestic routine. Yet Crothers liked to point out parallels between traditional women's work and her work as a director. In promoting her pet theory that writers should direct their own plays, Crothers noted, "Women writers should find matters of production and direction somewhat easy because they know by nature so much about dress, color, decoration and executive housekeeping. And these are the things that are inseparable from the play—the house, the background."[37] When it came to remodeling and furnishing her newly acquired country home, Crothers wrote, "So I furnished my whole house, drawing plans for it myself, as I went along, on the back sheets of plays I was writing at different times. . . . It was just like a play!"[38] Crothers assumed she was using skills possessed by many women, but she applied them primarily in the theater and almost as an afterthought in her own home.

Taking on the double role of playwright and director, along with many additional responsibilities, Crothers often appeared as a lone figure, reluctant to share the burden of production. However, she was willing to acknowledge valuable assistance from other women in establishing her career. She said, "I realize it is to three women that I owe my freedom—Carlotta Nielson, who liked my play; Mrs. Wheatcroft, who asked me to be coach; and Maxine Elliott, who let me in on the professional work."[39] The play that Nielson liked and chose to perform was *The Three of Us,* and her interest helped Crothers achieve her first major professional production. An equally significant break was provided by Maxine Elliott. When she appeared in Crothers's play *Myself—Bettina* (1908), she asked Crothers to stage the production. Crothers wrote, "Miss Elliott has such tremendous executive ability herself, such business capacity, and such an admiration for and faith in the work of women, that she was delighted to find a woman who could shoulder the entire responsibility."[40] Crothers, who had significant experience staging student productions of her one-act plays with the Stanhope-Wheatcroft School, had been frustrated by the experience of surrendering her work to other directors and was eager to take up Elliott's offer. Although *Myself—Bettina* was not a hit, Crothers was able to prove her competence as a director.

The third woman that Crothers acknowledged, Adelaide Wheatcroft, had offered Crothers a teaching position at her dramatic school after a short period as a student. In an early article, Crothers noted, "Mrs. Wheatcroft is a strong woman, and has come in contact practically, with all the vicissitudes of life, enough to discourage the ordinary woman. She manages her business, the school, superintends her own productions and does quite a little teaching herself. Such a woman is especially helpful to the earnest student."[41] Late in her career, Crothers would recall that the opportunity to take charge of the student plays had provided an important apprenticeship. She said, "This was an experience of inestimable value because the doors of the theatre are very tightly closed to women in the work of directing and staging plays. Here in this school of acting I had the theatre in miniature—a great chance to learn something about what I've been doing ever since."[42]

Once the door was open, Crothers did seem to think a woman could do just as well in the theater as a man. Certainly her own success as a playwright lent support to that idea. Crothers's early hit, *The Three of Us,* which might seem a bit old-fashioned to theatergoers today, won wide praise from contemporary critics and playwrights for its realism and originality. Praise of the work from the early master of American realistic playwriting, Bronson Howard, was especially meaningful to Crothers.[43] Despite the early promise, Crothers's plays were never judged to have the depth and merit of the great American playwright of her era, Eugene O'Neill, who won the Pulitzer Prize for his Broadway debut, *Beyond the Horizon* (1918). However, Crothers was a consistent presence on Broadway for thirty years. Though Crothers never won a Pulitzer, she achieved more commercial success than the three women who did win the prize for drama in the 1920s and 1930s, Zona Gale, Susan Glaspell, and Zoë Akins. Six of Crothers's plays, *Nice People, Mary the Third, Let Us Be Gay, As Husbands Go, When Ladies Meet,* and *Susan and God,* were selected by Burns Mantle for inclusion in his annual publication of the year's best plays. Reviews of Crothers's later plays regularly praised the production values and Crothers's skill as a director, even when criticizing the writing.

As for directing and other behind-the-scenes duties, Crothers noted that "once she had proved herself men were very willing to let her do the work."[44] Crothers thrived in a situation where she carried most of the responsibility. For years Crothers worked with producer and theater owner Lee Shubert, one of the most powerful businessmen associated with the American theater. About Shubert, she once said, "We have never had any trouble, and he has always left the decision on any of the little vexing details of a production to me, never questioning my decision." In the same article she insisted that she had always been well treated in the theatrical world and praised Shubert, calling him "one of America's business geniuses" and a "chivalrous co-worker."[45] Crothers would continue to have a good working relationship with the Shuberts for another ten years.

Complicating Crothers's business relationship with the Shuberts was an association Crothers formed with Mary Kirkpatrick around this time. Crothers's play *Everyday* was produced by Kirkpatrick at the Shuberts' Bijou Theatre in 1921. A contemporary newspaper account reported that "the fact that [Crothers's] play "Everyday" is produced by a woman theatrical manager—the first and only feminine member of the Theatrical Producing Managers Association—gives this forthcoming presentation added interest."[46] Although the production of *Everyday* was the most public indication of a business association between Crothers and Kirk-patrick, the two had been working together for at least two or three years. Correspondence in the Shubert Archive indicates that by 1918 Kirkpatrick was representing Crothers in some communication with the Shuberts and had a financial stake in the productions, beginning with *A Little Journey* (1918). Kirkpatrick received billing for Crothers's *Mary the Third* (1923), produced by Lee Shubert in association with Mary Kirk-patrick, but was also involved in the production of *39 East* (1919), *He and She, Nice People* (1921), *Expressing Willie* (1924), and *A Lady's Virtue* (1925). In 1923 Kirkpatrick wrote to Shubert, telling him she would not take part in a repertory company project he had proposed for Crothers, as she saw no role for herself.[47] However, the repertory experiment did not materialize, and Kirkpatrick continued to work with both Crothers and Shubert at least through the close of *A Lady's Virtue* in early 1926.

It is not known how Crothers and Kirkpatrick began their associa-tion. Earlier in her career, Crothers had been represented by Elisabeth Marbury's play agency, working primarily with Marbury's associate Roi Cooper Megrue.[48] While later accounts of Crothers's career indicate Crothers did not need an agent to place her works after her first couple of productions, Marbury and Megrue continued to represent Crothers's work in some capacity through 1913.[49] It is possible that Crothers decided to use Kirkpatrick's services in business management and production because of a personal relationship between the two women. Actor Wal-ter Abel, interviewed by a dissertation writer in 1977, said that Crothers lived with Mary Kirkpatrick for many years.[50] Unfortunately, there is no other information available on the nature of the relationship or to confirm Abel's assertion.[51] The professional association between the women appears to have ended with the spectacular failure of *Thou Des-perate Pilot* in 1927. Crothers, who directed the play by Zoë Akins and shared the producer credits with Kirkpatrick, ended up fifty-five thou-sand dollars in debt.[52] A later newspaper profile of Crothers mentioned *Thou Desperate Pilot*, remarking that "guests as well as servants at her country place at Redding, Conn., are cautioned never to mention the name of this piece save in whispers."[53] Accepting an award in 1939, Crothers referred to this failure, claiming she was duped into signing var-ious vouchers and contracts with assurances there was money in the bank to pay for everything.[54] Perhaps the financial strain, public embarrass-ment, and sense of betrayal connected with this incident led to the termi-nation of any relationship between Crothers and Kirkpatrick.

Crothers's business relationship with Lee Shubert was also indirectly affected by this failure, followed late in 1927 by the ill-fated *Venus,* the biggest failure of a play written by Crothers. In 1928 she signed a contract with the Shubert Theatre Corporation agreeing to serve as a play reader, direct various plays (for an additional fee), and submit her own plays in return for a weekly salary, which would be deducted from future royalties.[55] Clearly, Crothers needed a steady income as she worked her way out of debt and tried to write another hit play. Crothers was able to reverse her fortunes with *Let Us Be Gay* (1929), but she took that play to rival manager John Golden. The title of the play was not a public endorsement of homosexuality by Crothers. Rather, it referred to the falsely cheerful attitude the character Kitty Brown was determined to maintain when she was forced to spend a weekend with the man she had divorced because of his infidelity. Crothers later reported, "A manager was about to produce [*Let Us Be Gay*]—but I suddenly and precariously took it away from him because of the unfair terms which he was offering—knowing the desperateness of my situation."[56] Crothers was removed from the Shubert payroll in January 1929, and her subsequent plays were produced on Broadway by John Golden. These included *As Husbands Go* (1931), *When Ladies Meet* (1932—another play with a provocative title that does not actually refer to lesbian encounters), and the popular *Susan and God* (1937).

Crothers's great achievement in the theater was to gain commercial success and longevity, with an active Broadway presence from 1906 to 1938. While her works, to the disappointment of later critics, did not all offer feminist social criticism, they did often raise timely issues related to women's evolving place in society and put these issues before a large, mainstream audience. Crothers's primary goal was to succeed in the professional theater, rather than to find a creative outlet before a small audience in a little or art theater environment. She regularly criticized the "so-called small art theatre," especially when it was divorced from the practical concerns of pleasing a paying audience. She noted, "It is always made up of little rebellious groups who are determined to elevate the stage . . . and produce the play they think too good for the commercial manager to produce. It's usually something with some literary value in it, not good enough for the commercial theatre."[57] Crothers was not opposed to reform in playwriting and stagecraft, but she saw little point in experiments not connected to the professional stage. Perhaps in an effort to encourage an art theater with professional standards, Crothers did allow the Actors Theatre to premiere her play, *Expressing Willie,* at the 48th Street Theatre, in 1924. This proved to be a financial success for the company. Undoubtedly, Crothers's concern with competing in the commercial arena had an effect on her choice and treatment of subject matter.

According to Crothers, many of her plays could be considered "a sort of 'Comedie Humaine de la Femme,' or a 'Dramatic history of Woman.' "[58] However, she insisted that this was a subconscious process, rather than a deliberate chronicle of women's social progress. She often wrote about what was timely or "in the air," examining, for example, the new morality of the flapper set in *Nice People*. Though some of Crothers's characters were in the vanguard of independent women, others reflected the wide range of female experience during the early decades of this century. Colette and James Lindroth have noted that "the chorus of voices in a typical Crothers play reveals an honest picture of middle-class female life in years of drastic change for women."[59] The voices included those of women who lacked the resources or will power to resist the status quo. For example, *Everyday* included not only Fannie, a young idealist who is willing to oppose her domineering father, but also the timid Mrs. Nolan, who has nearly lost herself completely in her efforts to appease her husband.

The plays that focus on independent women show characters rejecting the double standard of sexual morality, insisting on their right to pursue careers, and seeking greater sexual equality. Crothers's first hit play, *The Three of Us*, was a play of this type. Crothers confirmed her reputation as a chronicler of the new woman with her 1910 production of *A Man's World*. Critic and historian Arthur Hobson Quinn called the play "one of the most significant dramas of the decade."[60] Crothers's heroine is a novelist with a man's name, Frank Ware. Besides being a writer, Frank is a social reformer, with her work among poor and troubled women providing subject matter for her books, and she is the adoptive mother of an illegitimate child. Frank lives among a bohemian set in an apartment house, but even in this atmosphere her reputation is in jeopardy. Some of her friends think Frank must have a man's assistance in writing her books and most of the inhabitants of the house suspect Frank actually might be the biological mother of the child in her care. Frank is romantically linked to successful newspaperman Malcolm Gaskell, but even he is troubled by the possibility of an illicit affair in Frank's past. Frank has not felt the need to justify her present circumstances by explaining that young "Kiddie" is the child of an American woman she befriended while living in Paris. The shame and misfortune of the young woman, who died in childbirth, has filled Frank with a hatred for the unknown father of the child and has fueled her social activism and writing about the plight of women. In a rather improbable turn of events, it is ultimately revealed that Gaskell, though previously ignorant of the fact, is the child's father. When Gaskell refuses to admit any wrongdoing on his part, Frank rejects him. Having earlier in the play argued that men won't change until women hold them accountable for their actions, Frank lodges her protest, refusing to accept that the world must inevitably remain a man's world.

Crothers continued to demonstrate the damage done to women under the double standard in her 1913 play, *Ourselves*. In the play, Beatrice, a concerned philanthropist, visits a reform school for girls from the streets. Beatrice decides to give Molly, one of these victims of male predators, a chance to turn her life around by inviting her to live in her own home. Molly does begin to change and is willing to break off relations with the man who got her into trouble. However, Molly is still at risk and is seduced by Beatrice's brother Bob. The affair is discovered just before Bob's wife, Irene, reveals that she is expecting their first child. Molly truly repents when she understands the misery she has caused Irene and Beatrice, but Bob tries to justify his actions. Irene refuses to see things his way and may carry out her threats to end the marriage.[61]

In *Ourselves,* all the women, despite their different circumstances, are hurt by a man's assumption that he can hold himself to a lower standard of morality. Many of Crothers's plays offer a complex assessment of the progress of women, by contrasting female characters with different goals and obstacles. A good example of this is seen in *He and She.* The central character, Ann Herford, has attempted to combine work and family, but ultimately decides to focus on her child, though she has to sacrifice a major development in her career. Ann's sister-in-law Daisy competently earns her keep as a secretarial assistant to her brother, but she longs for the opportunity to marry and devote all her efforts to her home and family. Ann's friend Ruth loves her career as a magazine writer and editor. Although Ruth would like to marry Keith, he will only accept her as a wife if she will abandon her career. She breaks off their relationship rather than give up everything she has worked to achieve. Like Frank Ware, Ruth, finding her potential mate is not sufficiently advanced in his thinking, chooses to live without a man.

Many of Crothers's works focused on women who asserted their independence by testing the boundaries of acceptable behavior in a time of evolving sexual morality. In *Young Wisdom* (1914), for example, sisters Gail and Victoria decide they should attempt "trial marriages" with their boyfriends before committing to any permanent arrangement. In *Mary the Third* (1923), Mary and her brother are horrified to discover the hypocrisy of their parents' marriage and suggest they should divorce rather than continue to live a lie. *As Husbands Go* (1931) concerns an Iowa housewife, Lucile, who meets a man while vacationing in Europe and contemplates leaving her husband. Mary Howard has nearly talked herself into having an affair with a married man at the beginning of *When Ladies Meet* (1932).

Of course, in most cases, the contemplated action is not taken and danger is averted. Not only in *Young Wisdom,* but also in *Nice People* (1921) and *Mary the Third,* young, single women arrange or find themselves in the situation of spending a night with a man. Yet, in each case, it is made clear that they do not actually go through with having sex. In this way, Crothers got the most mileage out of her provocative plots while offering little offense to her audience. Crothers chose timely subjects but was careful to treat them in a manner that was commercially viable. As early as 1916, Crothers defended her practice, saying that "commercialism really only means professionalism."[62] She added that "it's only by money and business methods that the big machinery of the theatre can be moved. . . . No commercial manager—no audience—no theatre."

Crothers crafted her plays with the intention of appealing to a wide audience. Perhaps, just as she guarded the details of her personal life, she was careful not to reveal too many of her own beliefs that would depart from those of her middle-class target audience. An examination of early versions of *A Man's World* and *He and She* is revealing. In both cases the plays were first written with conventional happy endings. In the earlier version of *A Man's World* called *Kiddie,* Frank Ware forgives Gaskell, and presumably the couple and their "kiddie" live happily ever after.[63] A straightforward happy ending is also found in *The Herfords,* an early version of *He and She,* where Ann appears delighted to tend to her daughter, rather than completing the frieze she had been commissioned to create.[64] The Broadway version of *He and She* still ended with Ann giving up the commission. However, it was a troubled resolution with Ann recognizing the depth of her sacrifice and admitting she might almost hate her daughter because of it. Contemporary critics were divided in their assessment of whether the ending was happy or not. In the case of *A Man's World,* the unhappy, and more artistically satisfying, ending was played on Broadway. Of course, Crothers tested both endings in out-of-town tryouts before deciding an audience would accept the more sober version.[65] In almost all of her other plays Crothers opted for crowd-pleasing, happy endings. Indeed, several of Crothers's plays, not part of her examination of modern women, were sentimental comedies. These pieces, including *Old Lady 31* (1916) and *The Heart of Paddy Whack* (1914) were calculated to soothe, rather than challenge audiences.

In several of Crothers's plays about women's concerns, the focus is not the rejection of the double standard, the right to pursue a career, or the right to greater sexual equality. Instead, the issue becomes the search for true love. In many ways, the plays suggest that independence, though an admirable goal for a woman, is not everything. Though Crothers's departure from her more overtly feminist concerns has troubled some critics, her change in focus makes a certain amount of sense. After all, Crothers, herself, was a woman who had achieved a remarkable career, but whose love life was either nonexistent or closeted. Worry about missing out on love is a motivating factor in the character Mary Howard in *When Ladies Meet*. Though she is a successful writer, Mary also longs for love and decides to pursue a relationship with her publisher, even though he is married. The interesting twist in this play is that the wife and the would-be mistress happen to meet and, largely due to their respect for one another, both decide to leave the man.

The happy ending of *Let Us Be Gay* is achieved when Kitty agrees to remarry her ex-husband, Bob. Kitty had divorced Bob after learning of his infidelity. By pursuing her own sexual experimentation, Kitty eventually recognizes the emptiness of such encounters and is ready to try again with the man she loves. Also in *As Husbands Go* sexual freedom is presented not as an end in itself, but as a means to confirming romantic love. Lucile, an Iowa housewife, enjoys the novelty and excitement of an extended flirtation while vacationing in Europe. However, when her new beau follows her back to Iowa, she is given a chance to reassess her relationship with her husband and reaffirm her marriage vows.

Although not all of Crothers's plays were moneymakers, she only experienced one dismal failure. That play, *Venus*, is worth reexamining because of its fascinating theme. The play is set in the future, at a time when humans have just completed their first space flight to the planet Venus. It is not surprising that the play failed. The fantasy setting was not Crothers's milieu as writer or director, and as a result the production could not draw on Crothers's sure touch at creating a realistic, contemporary living environment on stage. In addition, the script featured weak jokes repeated too many times and a fantasy plot twist that at some moments seemed illogical.[66] However, the play does promote the interesting idea that the ideal human intelligence combines both masculine and feminine attributes. Ross and Diana, young lovers and space travelers just returned from Venus, are guests of honor at a party. Dr. Richard Wakefield, inventor of an experimental potion designed to minimize gender differences, has brought the concoction along to the party. Also in attendance are Herbert, a macho thrill-seeker, and Agnes, his ultrafeminine, devoted wife. The guests all agree to try the drug, which does not work exactly as predicted. Instead, all the characters experience a gender reversal, except that Ross and Diana, already nearly androgynous, experience only slight changes. The most notable effect on the featured duo is that they each are able to see the other's point of view on a recent quarrel. Changes in Herbert and Agnes, on the other hand, call attention to the ridiculous extremes of their gendered behavior. The audience learns that the higher life form on Venus has not wanted any additional contact with the people of Earth. By the end of the play, however, Ross and Diana, shown to be more highly evolved than their contemporaries, are invited to return to Venus.

Why did Crothers turn to science fiction, a genre so different from anything she had attempted previously in her career? It gave her a way to provide a pointed critique of typical heterosexual pairings in contemporary society. Encouraging an audience to laugh at the extremes of feminine and masculine social behavior was one way to demonstrate the artificiality of gender role divisions. Writing *Venus* also gave Crothers an opportunity to promote a utopian vision of alternative sexuality. The androgyny of the central figures can be read as a stand-in for more controversial lesbianism. This is supported by the fact that the central characters' destination and the source of higher intelligence is the planet whose mythological name is associated with female sexuality. Crothers most likely thought the play's imaginative distance from contemporary society would allow her more freedom to explore a topic of personal interest. However, *Venus* was a resounding critical and financial failure. It ran just eight performances and was ridiculed by the press. In one of the least harsh reviews, Brooks Atkinson wrote,

> Miss Crothers posits her question of sex equality and pure intelligence in the light of the distant future. Even with that additional perspective, she does not illuminate them nor develop them. They remain questions rather than answers. And before the play is concluded they begin to seem tedious.[67]

It is easy to see why this experience would push Crothers back to safer territory. Unlike Djuna Barnes or Mercedes de Acosta, who regularly experimented with nonrealistic styles of playwriting that fit their bohemian personas, Crothers usually offered fairly conventional dramaturgy along with a public persona of carefully crafted respectability. With her next plays Crothers returned to more familiar subject matter of contemporary women contemplating divorce or an affair, or struggling to make their marriages work.

Although Crothers is not nearly as well known today as she was seventy years ago, she is a significant figure whose contribution to the American theater should not be forgotten. It is worth considering the ways her sexuality and lifestyle may have both facilitated and limited her career. Though it is quite likely that Crothers had at least one long-term, intimate relationship with another woman, she also made an effort to keep her personal life hidden from public scrutiny. As a result, there is not a great deal of evidence available. Of course, this very secrecy supports the idea that she was concealing the intimate nature of her relationships with other women. Certainly, she would have had strong commercial motivation to avoid announcing herself as a lesbian. Crothers's plays spoke to a mainstream audience of contemporary, heterosexual women, even as she publicly positioned herself as an exception, a woman without the time or interest in pursuing the heterosexual relationships that are frequently the concerns of her characters. In defining a conflict between a woman's career, on the one hand, and heterosexual relationships, home, and family, on the other, Crothers connected to a major social issue of her day. Under this system, qualification for membership in the more select category of successful career women involved the absence of heterosexual relationships. While the women in the special category might be understood by the public at large to be abstaining from sexual relations, they might just as well have been involved in homosexual relationships. Crothers may have feared social or professional rejection if she was perceived as a lesbian. Instead, she scripted a public identity of herself, through her plays, interviews, press releases, and the like, that not only explained away the lack of husband and children, but to some degree even celebrated her lack of conformity to a traditionally feminine, domestic role.

Embracing an alternative lifestyle with no husband or children gave Crothers the flexibility to pursue her career. She apparently found plenty of companionship and personal support, not only from the women who shared her home, but also through the service organizations, such as the

Stage Women's War Relief, which she founded and to which she devoted many hours of her time. Unfortunately, Crothers apparently felt compelled to limit the subject matter of her plays in order to maintain public approval and commercial appeal. *Venus* gives an indication of other directions Crothers might have pursued in her writing if she had experienced more tolerant social conditions. Perhaps Crothers's work would seem more timely and relevant today if she allowed any of her characters to fully embrace the lifestyle choices that she herself did. However, though Crothers kept her sexuality hidden from view, her personal experience still informed her themes on some level. This is seen most readily in the feminist issues that are raised in her plays and also in the recurring theme of pursuing love despite social prohibitions. One of Crothers's greatest strengths as a playwright was her ability to present a great variety of contemporary female experiences in her plays. Perhaps the most interesting and inspiring of her female characters were the ones, like Frank Ware, who in their independence most resemble Rachel Crothers herself.

NOTES

1. An award from the National Endowment for the Humanities to participate in a Summer Seminar "American Drama 1920–1950" allowed me to begin research on Rachel Crothers.

2. Charlotte Hughes, "Women Playmakers," *New York Times Magazine,* May 4, 1941, 11; Ida M. Tarbell, "Fifty Foremost Women of the United States Listed by Ida Tarbell," *Los Angeles Times,* September 14, 1930.

3. Marguerite Mooers Marshall, "'What Do Women Think of Other Women?' Men Are More Tolerant and Good Natured," clipping in local history clipping file in the Bloomington Public Library (Illinois), publication not identified. No date, but internal evidence suggests 1915.

4. Danbury, Conn., Probate Court, District of Danbury, copy of will of Rachel Crothers. Also, telephone conversations with Anne Sheffield, Crothers's literary executor, on December 15 and 21, 1998. Anne Sheffield spent many summers with her grandmother and Rachel Crothers at Crothers's home in Connecticut in the 1930s and 1940s. Eula Seeley Garrison died c. 1951. As a child, Sheffield knew the women were best friends, and as an adult she has reached the conclusion that both women were lesbians. In a letter of January 1, 1999, to the author, Sheffield mentioned numerous postcards in her possession (later viewed by the author) that document trips Crothers and Garrison made together to Europe in 1907 and 1910. It appears that Crothers and Garrison were travel companions and housemates for about forty-five years.

5. Zoe Coralnik Kaplan, "Rachel Crothers," in *Notable Gays and Lesbians in American Theater History: A Biographical Encyclopedia,* ed. Robert A. Schanke, Kim Marra, and Billy J. Harbin (Ann Arbor: University of Michigan Press, forthcoming). Kaplan interviewed some of Crothers's surviving colleagues for her dissertation, "Woman in Focus in Major Plays of Rachel Crothers," City University of New York, 1979.

6. Leila J. Rupp, "'Imagine My Surprise': Women's Relationships in Mid–Twentieth Century America," in *Hidden from History: Reclaiming the Gay and Lesbian Past,* ed. Martin Duberman, Martha Vicinus, and George Chauncey Jr. (New York: Penguin, 1989), 408.

7. Djuna Barnes, "The Tireless Rachel Crothers," *Theatre Guild,* May 1931, 18. Barnes's own playwriting career is discussed in a another essay in this collection by Susan F. Clark. Even if Barnes was aware of Crothers's sexual identity, it is not surprising that she would not reveal more in her mainstream journalism.

8. Mildred Adams, "Rachel Crothers, Playmaker," *Women's Journal,* May 1931, 11.

9. "Tenacious Miss Crothers!" *N.Y. American,* March 8, 1931, in the Shubert Archive, New York.

10. Rachel Crothers, "The Construction of a Play," in *The Art of Playwriting,* lectures by Jesse Lynch Williams, Langdon Mitchell, Lord Dunsany, Gilbert Emery, and Rachel Crothers (Philadelphia: University of Pennsylvania, 1928; rpt. 1967), 130.

11. "Future of American Stage Depends on Directors," *New York Times Magazine,* December 3, 1916, 136.

12. Owen Davis, *I'd Like to Do It Again* (New York: Farrar and Rinehart, 1931), 57. Other playwright-directors noted by Davis included Elmer Rice, James Forbes, and George Kelly.

13. Rachel Crothers, "Our Own Daisy Ashford Urges Dramatists as Directors," unmarked clipping, Shubert Archive.

14. "They Stage the Modern Woman," clipping in Illinois State University archives, marked *Pictorial Review,* April 1923.

15. Louis R. Reid, *New York Dramatic Mirror,* February 21, 1920, 310.

16. Heywood Broun, "'He and She' Puts Woman in Her Place," *New York Tribune,* February 13, 1920.

17. Burns Mantle, *New York Evening Mail,* February 13, 1920.

18. *Evening Mail* clipping, n.d., in Rachel Crothers File, Theatre Collection, Museum of the City of New York (hereafter MCNY).

19. "Miss Rachel Crothers, Author of 'The Herfords,' Discusses the Motive of her play," clipping marked *Boston Herald,* January 31, 1912, Robinson Locke collection, Billy Rose Theatre Collection, New York Public Library for the Performing Arts.

20. Rachel Crothers, "The Box in the Attic," autobiographical fragment, Crothers File, MCNY, 13.

21. Berenice Skidelsky, "Dr. Marie Louis Crothers," *Today's Housewife,* June 1923, clipping in Crothers File, MCNY.

22. Crothers, "Box in the Attic," 16, 17, 18.

23. Crothers, "Box in the Attic," 10.

24. *The Eleusis of Chi Omega*, September 1939, 427, copy in Crothers File, MCNY.

25. Crothers, "Box in the Attic," 18.

26. *Eleusis of Chi Omega*, 428.

27. "The Story of Rachel Crothers; America's Leading Woman Playwright," typescript in Crothers File, MCNY.

28. Rachel Crothers, "Woman's Place in the World," typescript (press release) in Crothers File, Shubert Archive.

29. "The Feminist Urge," unmarked clipping, Crothers File, Shubert Archive.

30. "They Stage the Modern Woman," clipping in Illinois State University archives.

31. "Woman's Place in the World," 2. The press release refers to the character as Ethel, but no there is no character named Ethel in the play, and the description fits Ruth.

32. Serena Anderlini-D'Onofrio, *The "Weak" Subject: On Modernity, Eros, and Women's Playwriting* (Madison, Wis.: Associated University Presses, 1998), 132, 149.

33. *A Man's World,* in *Plays by American Women: 1900–1930,* ed. Judith E. Barlow (New York: Applause, 1985), 52.

34. Hughes, "Women Playmakers," 10.

35. "They Stage the Modern Woman."

36. Henry Albert Phillips, "Miss Crothers Talks of Her Plays," *New York Herald Tribune,* March 15, 1931.

37. "Rachel Crothers Points Way for Women Who Seek Expression," *New York Tribune,* April 15, 1923, clipping in MCNY.

38. Phillips, "Miss Crothers Talks."

39. Barnes, "The Tireless Rachel Crothers," 18.

40. Rachel Crothers, "Troubles of a Playwright," *Harper's Bazaar,* January 1911, 14.

41. "Behind the Scenes: Rachel Crothers Tells Annette of Stage Realities," *Bloomington Pantagraph,* August 5, 1899, MCNY.

42. *Eleusis of Chi Omega.*

43. Kaplan, "Woman in Focus," 16.

44. Barnes, "The Tireless Rachel Crothers," 18.

45. Colgate Baker, "Rachel Crothers and the Little Journey," *New York Reviews,* January 4, 1919, clipping in Shubert Archive.

46. "Rachel Crothers' New Play 'Everybody,'" clipping in Tallulah Bankhead scrapbook, NYPL.

47. Kirkpatrick letter to Shubert, May 4, 1923, Mary Kirkpatrick general correspondence, file 2900, Shubert Archive.

48. For more on Marbury, see Kim Marra, "A Lesbian Marriage of Cultural Consequence: Elisabeth Marbury and Elsie de Wolfe, 1886–1933," in *Passing Performances: Queer Readings of Leading Players in American Theater History,* ed. Robert A. Schanke and Kim Marra (Ann Arbor: University of Michigan Press, 1998), 104–28.

49. Elisabeth Marbury/Roi Cooper Megrue, general correspondence, File 51, Shubert Archive.

50. Kaplan, "Woman in Focus," 243.

51. The lack of information about Crothers's personal life is frustrating, but hardly surprising given her efforts to guard her privacy. It is certainly possible that Abel, learning from other actors that Crothers was a lesbian, mistakenly assumed that her business partner was her lover. Crothers had to spend a great deal of time in New York City while directing and had a number of New York addresses over the years. However, Eula Seeley Garrison apparently was kept more or less out of sight in Connecticut. Sheffield reported that Garrison lived in the Connecticut home, but was not aware of her sharing apartments with Crothers in New York City.

52. Irving Abrahamson, "The Career of Rachel Crothers in the American Drama," Ph.D. diss., University of Chicago, 1956, 13–14.

53. Ward Morehouse, "Broadway after Dark," *New York Evening Sun,* May 18, 1931.

54. *Eleusis of Chi Omega.*

55. Contract dated June 26, 1928, Shubert Archive.

56. *Eleusis of Chi Omega.*

57. Crothers, "Construction of a Play," 133.

58. Phillips, "Miss Crothers Talks."

59. Colette Lindroth and James Lindroth, *Rachel Crothers: A Research and Production Sourcebook* (Westport, Conn.: Greenwood Press, 1995), 10.

60. *A History of the American Drama from the Civil War to the Present Day,* vol. 2 (New York: Harper and Brothers, 1927), 52. Crothers is the only female dramatist to receive her own chapter in Quinn's history.

61. *Ourselves* was not published. Plot synopses were included in several reviews. Some of the reviews are reprinted in the Abrahamson dissertation. The Lindroths also provide a summary. An typescript of *Ourselves* is in the Shubert Archive.

62. Crothers's talk to the Cosmopolitan Club in 1916, quoted in Kaplan, "Woman in Focus," 260.

63. A typescript of *Kiddie* is located in the Shubert Archive.

64. A typescript of *The Herfords* is in the Billy Rose Theatre Collection, New York Public Library for the Performing Arts.

65. A review marked *Cincinnati Commercial,* November 23, 1909, in a scrapbook in the Billy Rose Theatre Collection, New York Public Library for the Performing Arts, notes the happy ending. A letter, dated May 23, 1911, to Lee Shubert from Roi Cooper Megrue, in the Shubert Archive, says that Crothers was willing to let stock companies perform the happy-ending version.

66. *Venus* was never published. A typescript is located in the Rachel Crothers Files, Theatre Collection, MCNY.

67. *New York Times,* December 26, 1927.

Say What You Will about Mercedes de Acosta

Robert A. Schanke

Truman Capote was so fascinated by the amorous lifestyle of Mercedes de Acosta (1893–1968) he devised a card game called International Daisy Chain. The challenge was to link people sexually, using as few beds as possible. "Mercedes is the best card to hold," he quipped. "You could get to anyone from Cardinal Spellman to the Duchess of Windsor."[1]

She was notorious for walking the streets of New York in mannish pants, pointed shoes trimmed with buckles, tricorn hat, and cape. Her chalk white face, deep-set eyes, thin red lips, and jet black hair slicked back with brilliantine prompted Tallulah Bankhead to call her Countess Dracula (see fig. 3). She often boasted of her sexual prowess: "I can get any woman from any man."[2] Among her supposed conquests were such international beauties as Greta Garbo, Marlene Dietrich, and Isadora Duncan, as well as Alla Nazimova, Eva Le Gallienne, Tamara Karsavina, and Ona Munson. Additional, unsubstantiated chatter included Eleonora Duse, Katharine Cornell, Gertrude Stein, and Eleanor Roosevelt. There was perhaps justification for Alice B. Toklas's observation: "Say what you will about Mercedes, she's had the most important women of the twentieth century."[3]

Until she was seven, Mercedes was convinced she was a boy. Her mother called her Rafael, dressed her in Eton suits, and encouraged her to play boys' games. But one day, a boy challenged her:

"Have you got this?" he demanded.

I was horrified. I had heard about grown people and children being deformed. . . .

"You're deformed!" I shouted.

"If you are a boy and you haven't got this, you are the one who is deformed," he shouted back.

By this time the other boys had joined us, each boy speedily show-

Fig. 3. Portrait of Mercedes de Acosta painted by her husband, Abram Poole

(Courtesy Santa Barbara Museum of Art, Gift of Mercedes de Acosta in honor of Ala Story.)

ing me the same strange phenomenon the first boy had exhibited. . . . They demanded that I produce the same "phenomenon."

"Prove that you're not a girl," they screamed.

Mercedes was sent to a convent school to learn "feminine ways." While there, she befriended two lesbian nuns, delivered notes between them, and even stood guard in the corridors while they stole some privacy. Mercedes witnessed in grief and horror their forced separation: "For a second they stood mutely." Then came "a cry like the cry of death."[4] Mercedes ran down the hallway screaming hysterically, "I am not a boy and I am not a girl, or maybe I am both—I don't know. . . . I will never fit in anywhere and I will be lonely all my life."[5]

In the first draft of her autobiography, she recalls her bewilderment at the convent:

> I cannot understand these so-called "normal" people who believe that a man should love only a woman, and a woman love only a man. If this were so, then it disregards completely the spirit, the personality, and the mind, and stresses the importance of the physical body.[6]

In another place, she picks up the theme again. "How am I to convey to the reader the diverse people I feel within me," she pleads? "Who of us is only one sex? I, myself, am sometimes androgynous."[7]

Following her trauma at the convent, her affliction with what she called "moaning sickness" began. She would hide in a corner of a room, put her face to the wall, and moan. The attacks would start about five o'clock in the morning when she would awaken with a sense of fear and fatigue. Sometimes she would lie listless for hours and become obsessed with thoughts of ending her life. Adding to the torment of her teenage years were the suicides of both her father and older brother.

When Mercedes was about twenty years old, Elisabeth "Bessie" Marbury, a theater producer and "doyenne of Sapphic Broadway,"[8] assumed the role of matchmaker and introduced Mercedes to several available women; one was dancer Isadora Duncan, who penned a poem to Mercedes:

Beneath a forehead
Broad and Bright
Shine eyes
Clear wells
of sight—

A slender body, hands, soft and white
To be the service of my delight . . .
Two sprouting breasts
Grand and sweet
Invite my hungry
Mouth to eat—
From whence two nipples firm and pink
persuade my thirsty soul to drink
And lower still a secret place
Where I'd fain hide my loving face.
Arch Angel from another sphere
God-send to light my pathway
Here.
I kneel in Adoration.
Dear,
My kisses like a swarm
of bees
Would find their way
Between thy knees—
And suck the honey of thy lips
Embracing thy too slender hips.[9]

In an early draft of her autobiography, Mercedes remembered that "Many days and nights we spent together. . . . Often she would dance for me at night, three or four hours at a time."[10] One occasion was particularly unforgettable, even though she did not include the account in her completed manuscript.

> I don't know how long she danced, but she ended with a great gesture of Resurrection, with her arms extended high and her head thrown back. She seemed possessed by the dance and utterly carried away. When she finished she dropped her arms to her sides and stood silently. I dropped my eyes and did not look at Isadora. . . . In that pause I think we both lived many lives. Then Isadora seemed to return from a far land and again she became conscious of me. I moved toward her and in a mutual gesture we flung our arms around one another, and stood there clinging to each other in silence and tears.[11]

The two women continued their casual but romantic relationship for many years. Shortly before Duncan's tragic death in 1927, Mercedes peddled the manuscript of the dancer's 1927 autobiography to several publishers. Perhaps Duncan was remembering their liaison when she wrote, "I believe the highest love is purely spiritual flame which is not necessarily dependent on sex."[12]

Another liaison was with the exotic and sensual Russian actress Alla Nazimova.[13] Inspired by both Nazimova's thrilling performance in *War Brides* (1915) and their romance, Mercedes wrote a short one-act that appeared in the *Outlook* magazine. In *For France* (1917), Mercedes depicts a woman who has lost her husband and two sons in the war effort and now learns her third son has been drafted. "I cannot give you up!" she cries. "This devouring to the last shred all that we love! Devouring! Devouring! And never satisfied!"[14] Although there is no record of the play's being produced, the script suggests Mercedes' writing talent as well as her interest in women's issues.

This is not the first evidence of her interest in contesting the expected role of women in society. A few years earlier, while studying to be a nurse's aide, she would start writing at midnight and continue until the "early hours of the morning."

> My mother sometimes saw my light and was angry with me for staying up so late. . . . Like most mothers then she thought a woman's career was in the home and marriage—a view I did not share. I believed, without a shred of humor, in every form of independence for women and I was already an enrolled worker for Women's Suffrage.[15]

She went on to become a captain for the women's suffrage movement and "canvassed every house and verbally armed with every reason why women should have the vote, rang each doorbell."[16] Because of her mother's attitude, however, she kept her writing and her poems "a dead secret" for several years. She did not show them to her good friend, Bessie Marbury, or even to her sister.

In *Moods,* which appeared in 1919, her first book of poems bearing her name as author, she explores further her mysterious desire for sexual intimacy.

> A vast and deep silence has come over everything;
> and I, with all else, find myself holding my
> breath as I steal back into the room and sink
>   into a chair.
> Leaning languidly I half close my eyes,
>   while

far off I smell the salt and sadness of the sea . . .
    Weirdly and ghostlike you creep in and, in my
twilight dreams, you come to me![17]

The haunting quality of her mood poems prompted Charles Hanson
Towne to declare that her poetry "bears promise of even finer achievement. . . . She may go far."[18]

The following year, she shifted from serious writing when she
teamed with Deems Taylor and wrote lyrics for the musical *What Next!*
A Musical Indiscretion in Three Unwarranted Acts, a comic tale of a
fraudulent duke who steals a pearl necklace and is apprehended by
rookie detectives. The completely amateur cast played to capacity audiences for a limited, two-week engagement at the Princess Theatre—all
proceeds donated to the Girls' Protective League and the New York Pro-
bation and Protective Association. The catchy songs, clever dancing, and
twenty specialty acts prompted a *New York Herald* reviewer to call it
"one of the snappiest and most unusual diversions in the record of new
musical comedy." Another critic claimed that the daring costumes "out-
Ziegfelded 'Flo' Ziegfeld. . . . Who bothers about a plot when one can
look at such pretty chorus girls?"[19] At first glance, this diversion of Mercedes' with such lightweight material might seem bizarre, but it undoubtedly afforded her the opportunity to see and work backstage with scant-
ily clothed, beautiful young women who displayed their bodies.

In spite of the confusion she was feeling over her female romances, in
1920, to please her mother and maintain at least a semblance of propriety, Mercedes married Abram Poole, a handsome and wealthy portrait
painter who had studied in France and Germany. Even from the beginning, it was hardly a conventional marriage. Rather than traditional
white, she wore a gray chiffon wedding dress, objected to having music
during the ceremony, and refused to renounce her surname for his. A few
years later, in fact, it was reported in the *New York Sun* that Mercedes
was elected into membership in the Lucy Stone League, an organization
espousing a woman's right to keep her name when she married.[20]
Although they planned to spend the wedding night at the Hotel Vander-
bilt, Mercedes spent the night at home with her mother. It was even
rumored that she took a young girlfriend with her on their honeymoon.[21]

In another essay in this volume, J. K. Curry notes that Rachel
Crothers "identified as a woman who had chosen a career instead of marriage and family. Through the years of Crothers's career, journalists
readily accepted the idea that a woman's choice between career and fam-

ily was an either/or decision."[22] But Mercedes chose a different path. Even though it may only have been to please her family and to serve as a convenient cover, she consented to a marriage but, at the same time, continued to write.

The same year as her marriage, in fact, she published her first novel, *Wind Chaff,* which is the story of a young girl, Paula, whom she describes as "oddly quiet and reserved . . . unlike other children." While attending a boarding school, she receives love letters from other girls. Paula, like Mercedes, struggles with her sexuality. Sitting before a mirror, she "peered into her own eyes, 'What is the matter with me?' she said aloud. Hot tears came to her eyes" as she envisioned seeing a man and a woman embracing. "'Am I jealous, and if so, of which one?'" As her girlfriend Faith was dying, Paula "cried despairingly. 'Speak to me, *speak* to me! It's Paula, Paula, who loves you, Paula who . . .' her voice was muffled as she leaned over and kissed Faith frantically, then dropped to the floor unconscious."[23]

Undoubtedly adding to Mercedes' personal torment at the time was meeting Eva Le Gallienne, a young, attractive, and ambitious actress who was stunning all the Broadway critics.[24] Actually, just three days before Mercedes' marriage, they arranged to have lunch at the Ritz Hotel. By the time lunch was over they had worked themselves into "a pitch of excitement." When they were asked finally to leave the table, they left for Mercedes' apartment. Mercedes recalled in an early typescript of her autobiography that Eva "was surprised when I told her that I was being married within a week and would be going to Europe with Abram for the summer."[25]

Two months after they met, Mercedes designed a costume for Eva's character in a special matinee production of Maeterlinck's lyrical *Aglavaine and Selysette.* The production was unsuccessful, but it began a relationship that lasted for five years. When Eva left New York on a national tour of *Liliom,* she sent Mercedes flowers and wrote two or three love letters daily. On stage every night, though she vowed love to Liliom, her thoughts were of Mercedes. Since Mercedes was married, their relationship had to be hidden and very discreet. When Eva stole back to New York during breaks in the tour or on weekends, they met secretly in Eva's apartment. Although they exchanged rings as tokens of their love and swore everlasting fidelity, their correspondence reveals doubts, fears, jealousies, and even talk of suicide.[26]

In two more books of poetry, *Archways of Life* (1921) and *Streets and Shadows* (1922), Mercedes reveals the personal thoughts and anxieties she was having during her relationship with Eva. In "Soiled Hands" she recalls the thrill of sitting in a darkened theater with one of her lovers.

> Do you remember how we always sat silently?
> I would shut my eyes to feel your closeness nearer.

Even in a public place, the darkness seemed to provide her the necessary shield from prying eyes. Her overwhelming yearning to commit to a woman was consummate.

> I will offer all my love
>   Recklessly, without rest,
> And give myself completely
>   Upon my darling's breast—
> Our pulses shall beat as one pulse,
>   And in that sacred breath
> I shall feel the touch of Life
>   Yet know the truth of Death!

A closeted woman living in shadows, Mercedes was tormented by her need to hide her feelings.

> Today is your birthday.
> Many people will come to you with offerings,
> While I,
> Who seemingly know you so slightly,
> Yet who truly know you so well,
> Must stand aside with empty hands.
> If love could make this day perfect,
> My love would weave for you
> A web enmeshed with all your desires.
> On your pathway
> I would fling stars for pebbles
> And tear down the moon
> So that you might wear
> The radiance of its silver
> In your hair.
> But instead—
> I stand outside like a wall
> And quite powerless
> I send no gift at all.[27]

On June 4, 1922, Mercedes sailed for Europe with her husband, along with a packet of love letters from Eva to be opened on each day of the journey. Two days later, Eva sailed for England, reassuring Mercedes that she would lock away in a box any letters she received so that her mother would not see them. When they parted at the wharf before their separation, Mercedes was overcome by the agony of hiding their love and trying to appear "indifferent before the others."

> Going off the pier
> My throat closed with pain—
> Eyes dim—staggering just a little. . . .
> The desperate regret
> For all the trivial things I said,
> And because I did not kiss you
> The way I wanted.[28]

The lovers eventually reunited in Paris, where they stayed for several nights in adjoining rooms at the Hôtel Foyot. Every evening Mercedes rushed to her window after her husband left and whistled for Eva, who then stole to her room and crept to her bed. Toward the end of the summer, Eva wrote Mercedes from London that her mother and three old friends had been held spellbound as she read to them Mercedes' new play, *Jehanne d'Arc*. When Eva showed them a picture of Mercedes, they admitted they thought it was a man. Eva was tempted to confess it was her husband.

By the time they were both back in New York, Mercedes learned that Eva had broken their mutual vow of fidelity.

> To have returned and found you changed.
> To have left you trembling from my touch—
> With smouldering fires in your eyes—
> Now to find your flame
> Burning at another's altar.[29]

In spite of the rift in their relationship, the next year they embarked on a major theater venture—to produce *Jehanne d'Arc*. Director Arthur Hopkins had already rejected the script, complaining that Eva's restrained acting style would spoil the play. The Shuberts had expressed some interest but ultimately declined since they felt the cost of production would be staggering. Producer Sam Harris also turned it down, but when he asked if Mercedes had any other vehicles for Eva, she quickly finished another play, *Sandro Botticelli*. It focuses on a maiden who is beloved by all Florence but who has remained chaste and aloof to all men until she meets the handsome Botticelli. Hoping to spark a romance, she offers to pose nude for the artist's painting of *The Birth of Venus*. Although Botticelli is in love with her, the artist in him prevails, and as she strips in his studio, he forgets his passion and starts to work feverishly on his canvas. Feeling rejected and exploited, the enraged maiden runs from the studio into the pouring rain, becomes ill, and dies.

Theatergoers chattered curiously during intermission—how would Eva appear nude in act two? She simply dropped her cape while concealing her bare body with her long hair and a high-backed chair. Ironically, the painting of *The Birth of Venus* used in the final scene of the play was painted by Abram Poole, Mercedes' husband and Eva's nemesis.

In the play, Mercedes had again created a drama that depicted feminine issues, but the critics were not kind. The dialogue was called artificial, stilted, and "so flowery . . . that it resembles a seed catalogue." Eva was criticized for her inability to portray feminine passion.[30] Though it ran only briefly, it was published by Moffat, Yard Books.

Mercedes next wrote *The Mother of Christ*. One of Mary's prayers sounded very much like Mercedes:

> With your death has died the warrant of prejudice—cruelty—intolerance—greed. . . . With your resurrection has come everlasting life, the eternal promise of compassion—tolerance—forgiveness. . . . for which you gave your life.[31]

As a woman who was living a complicated life with both a husband and a female lover, Mercedes was undoubtedly expressing her own need for compassion, tolerance, and forgiveness. Although Eleonora Duse had promised to tour the play, it never materialized; the actress died quite suddenly during an engagement in Pittsburgh.

For the next many months, Mercedes struggled to find backers for productions that would see Eva starring in Mercedes' *Jehanne d'Arc* and *The Mother of Christ*. Mercedes' personal life informed her writing of Joan's character. In the first scene, Joan begs for help to escape from an arranged marriage. She is praised for "remaining unburdened by the low domestic things of life; free from slavery and the breeding of children." Throughout the script, Joan is jeered and spat upon for dressing in men's clothes and cutting her hair like a man's. She is told that her unnatural behavior defames herself before Heaven. Voices in the crowd call her "a woman trying to be like a man" and "a sexless woman." At one point, Joan explains, "We are each one of us chained to something. Each one of us in a different way. I have my battles too."[32]

Eventually, Fermin Gémier, director of the Théâtre de l'Odéon in Paris, was interested in producing both *Jehanne d'Arc* and *The Mother of Christ* under the auspices of the Ministry of Beaux-Arts, but only if Mercedes could find some American backers. The very wealthy Mrs. Harold McCormick of Chicago initially showed interest. But in November 1924, when she met Mercedes and Eva and learned that the two women were lovers and that Mercedes was married, she quickly withdrew her support. There was no way that she would link her name with such disreputable people. Understandably, they were outraged over the provincial and narrow thinking that was preventing their dream. At virtually the last hour, a new benefactor saved them, Alice DeLamar. A reclusive lesbian with homes in Paris, Palm Beach, and Connecticut, she had inherited $10 million from her father and was seeking ways to support the arts and please Eva.

As they left for Paris in late March 1925, Mercedes was bubbling with anticipation, for they had solid financial backing, a theater, and, as designer, Norman Bel-Geddes, who had achieved great notoriety a year earlier when he converted New York's Century Theatre into a cavernous Gothic cathedral for Max Reinhardt's production of *The Miracle.*

Complications pursued them endlessly. Since the Théâtre de l'Odéon theater that they had been promised rent-free was too small for Bel-Geddes' sets, they had to go elsewhere, reluctantly settling on the Théâtre de La Porte-Saint-Martin, which cost them seven thousand dollars for thirty days. Mercedes and Eva had raised a total of twelve thousand dollars before leaving New York, thinking that would be sufficient. Suddenly, more than half their funds were depleted, and they had to ask Alice DeLamar for another twenty-eight thousand dollars. Also, with their agreement to rent the Porte-Saint-Martin, they were obliged to use that theater's permanent company of actors. When it came to extras, Bel-Geddes insisted on hiring a minimum of 150, a third of whom were Russian immigrants who spoke neither French nor English. Mercedes wrote about still another problem they experienced: "To add to our many troubles we had to 'police' him [Bel-Geddes] . . . and spend much of our time and devitalized nerves in sobering him up. . . . Our young American genius discovers sex, night life, vie de Bohème and Paris!"[33]

When they finally opened on June 12, 1925, the theater world was bustling with excitement. American newspapers in such far-flung corners as Walla Walla, Washington; Grand Forks, North Dakota; and Duluth, Minnesota, proclaimed the opening. *Theatre* magazine ran photos of the sets along with detailed descriptions.[34] The French press had capitalized on the novelty of an American author and actress presenting, in French, a play about one of the French heroes. Front-page headlines of the Paris edition of the *Chicago Tribune* read, "Eva Le Gallienne to Play *Jehanne d'Arc*."[35] Opening night dignitaries included Elsie de Wolfe, Elsa Maxwell, Arthur Rubenstein, Mrs. Vincent Astor, Condé Nast, the Cole Porters, Ivor Novello, Dorothy Parker, Zoë Atkins, and Constance Collier.

The excitement was short-lived. Even prior to rehearsals, Bel-Geddes had complained to Mercedes about the script:

> your play is episodic and undramatic. We all know the story, so there has to be a special reason for writing a play. Why did you write yours? What contribution have you made? . . . I have the utmost confidence that the spirit of Jeanne will radiate through Eva, but I do not feel the same spirit radiating from your play. . . . Unless your play is right, Eva's effort and mine won't help it.[36]

Hoping to compensate for the uninspired writing, he conceived the production as a spectacle, emphasizing lighting, sound, and movement of the actors. He designed a single, architectural setting with multilevel platforms. By means of banners, costumes, and properties, he transformed the stage into the Dauphin's throne room, Rheims Cathedral, the battle of Compeigne, and a Rouen marketplace. As Joan's moods shifted, the lighting and the mood changed around her. The French critics were impressed with the spectacle and pageantry, but they were unanimous that Bel-Geddes had exaggerated his role as designer. A critic for *Le Matin* concluded, "It is a 'great show' for the eyes, and nothing at all for the brain and spirit."[37] The contribution of Mercedes suffered from all the dazzle. Sometimes ten minutes would pass before a word of dialogue was spoken. One French critic was so overwhelmed by the visual display that his only comment on the script and Eva's acting was that Eva spoke "French without the slightest accent."[38] Although plans to add *The Mother of Christ* to their repertory were quickly dropped, the press reported that *Jehanne d'Arc* would move to London in August and to Broadway in the fall of the year. Neither plan materialized.

Motives for dropping the project were complex—lackluster reviews, the exorbitant cost of production, and Bel-Geddes' focus on other, more promising productions. Certainly another reason was the growing conflict between Mercedes and Eva. Actually, their relationship had been declining for many months. Although Eva argued that she had never loved anyone other than Mercedes, she did not deny having sexual affairs with other women. She even encouraged Mercedes to seek an alternative, physical outlet. As they sailed back to New York on board the *Majestic* after the closing of *Jehanne d'Arc*, fellow passenger Noel Coward complained that during the entire trip the two women "alternated between intellectual gloom and feverish gaiety—and wore black indiscriminately, for both moods."[39]

By the time the ship docked in New York, their relationship had ended. Many of Mercedes' friends were concerned for her welfare. Dancer Tamara Karsavina wrote that news of the split upset her dreadfully: "I cannot bear to think of you lonely *and* unhappy. . . . I can hardly believe Eva left you. . . . It seems so cruel. . . . It haunts me."[40] Mercedes found herself totally abandoned. To survive, she threw herself into her writing. She finished *The Dark Light* and auditioned actresses. Nothing came of her efforts.

She then turned to a play she had been writing for several years, *Jacob Slovak*. "Perfectly cast, perfectly acted and perfectly directed," wrote one critic when it opened on October 5, 1927. The *New York Times* called it "an honest and interesting play . . . with fine emotional and touching scenes," and a critic for the *New York World* praised Mercedes' originality and conviction and described the play as an "interesting study of prejudice and desire under the eternal elms." *Billboard* thought it was "strong meat. . . . an excellently written play presented with real skill and understanding."[41] Just ten days after the off-Broadway tryout, the Shubert brothers moved *Jacob Slovak* to a Broadway house.

Mercedes' personal experiences as a woman marginalized because of her same-sex desires fueled her writing with the conviction and understanding that was noted by the critics. The title character, young Jewish Jacob Slovak, experiences prejudice in a little New England town. He has been hired as a shop clerk because "the sharpness of Jews" will help his employer compete with the other stores. But when he falls in love with Myra, the boss's daughter, the conservative Protestants of the town turn on him. They argue that all "foreigners are dangerous" and fear a Jew "ruinin' our gals." A friend warns him to move away: "I jest know yer don't fit. Yer never will. Yer are not like these people." He finally leaves after Myra refuses to renounce her family and town to marry him.

The final act takes place three months later. Jacob, who now has a respectable position playing in a symphony orchestra, has returned for Myra. She is pregnant with his child but tells him that she gave herself to another man who wanted to marry her in order to make him think it was his child. Myra still cannot run away with Jacob: "I can't go against everythin'. . . . I've been taught all my life ter hate your race. . . . It's no use, Jacob. I can't go against the way I've been brought up." Jacob replies:

> And are you going to bring my child up the way you've been brought up? Taught lies and hypocrisy. Taught to judge a man by color, race and creed rather than by the fitness of him! I won't allow those prejudices to ruin your life and mine.

Though tempted, Jacob cannot reveal Myra's lie: "Another man may bring up that child, but it will be my child and my race. My race that will come in here and go on."[42]

Although the production drew more critical praise when it moved uptown, it closed after only a handful of performances. The public was confused when Lee Shubert, without ever consulting Mercedes, changed the title to *Conflict* and then refused to advertise the change. When the Shuberts were sued by another author who claimed the new title was his, the production was withdrawn. Mercedes was overwhelmed since all signs suggested that the play was going to settle into a successful run that would have meant boosting her credibility as a playwright as well as rescuing her financially.

Her hopes for the play were renewed when a London production was announced for the Arts Theatre Club. John Gielgud and Ralph Richardson would star in their first production together. Using the new title of *Prejudice*, Arthur K. Phillips directed, and Gladys E. Calthrop, the woman who had come between Mercedes and Eva after *Jehanne d'Arc*, designed the production. The critics were certainly enthusiastic when the play opened on June 17, 1928. The *Daily Sketch* called it "a remarkable and powerful religious play," and the *Evening Standard* stressed that Mercedes had "a sense of character and of writing for the stage, and she avoids mincing matters, sometimes to the verge of brutal frankness." Other critics said it was "a moving play . . . finely acted," and that it went "far to restore one's faith in the London theatre."[43]

There were questions, however, about the play's relevance. Mercedes' script was compared with another American drama about prejudice that was running in London, *Show Boat,* starring Paul Robeson. Reviewers questioned why she had portrayed Americans "as hostile to the Jew as to the negro." They recognized that racial prejudice was present in America and England, but they denied the existence of anti-Semitism: "Jew-baiting in this country belongs . . . to the past."[44] In 1928, just a few years before the Holocaust, English audiences would not acknowledge that persecution of Jews existed. John Gielgud gave one of the best performances of his early career, though he remembered little about the production or audience reaction years later, only that Mercedes was "always very strikingly dressed in tricorn hats and becoming cloaks."[45]

When she returned to New York, she continued writing. At first, she completed a series of essays.[46] "On Great Men Recognizing Greatness" describes poets Byron and Shelley as "singers and passionate slaves of beauty. They had the good fortune to find in each other, not only a mental beauty, but also a rare physical beauty."

Her most explicit affirmation of same-sex desire appears in an essay simply called "Walt Whitman."

> He proclaims sex in all things; the man to the woman, the man to the man, the woman to the woman. . . . He proclaims sex not disgustingly or lewdly, but frankly, openly, truthfully. He proclaims all parts of the human body beautiful, to him the body is in the soul and the soul in the body.

Because the essays contained such radical thinking for the time, especially from a female author, she was never able to find a publisher.

She did find a publisher, however, for her novel *Until the Day Break*. A young, married woman, Victoria, admits that she hates herself and is confused about her sexual longings: "It's something in me, something struggling for expression that I don't understand."[47] Like Mercedes, the character rejects a life of domesticity, moves away from her husband, and embarks on a career in the theater. She moves to Paris, where she meets a woman who confesses her desire for other women.

> I have had more emotion through women; they give me that sense of beauty. . . . As for worrying about the sex end of it, that seems to me unimportant. In America I suffered much. They are not old enough to comprehend these things. It is perhaps their youth, which does not recognize that real love is real love, no matter whom it is for. . . . It is curious, the world does not blame people for having black or blond hair. They are just born that way and it is accepted. But for something deeper; something *more* "you" than colour of hair or eyes, one is condemned. They do not realize that God made each one for some ultimate reason; with his own salvation to work out, a pattern to follow and unfold, as his own spirit sees it.[48]

The year she published *Until the Day Break*—1928—saw another novel portraying same-sex desire, but one that became much more controversial. In *The Well of Loneliness,* when author Radclyffe Hall depicted lesbians as "more or less healthy people leading more or less normal lives," she brought "female homosexuality out of the closet."[49] Because the public had considered lesbians as perverts and degenerates, they were outraged at this new, sympathetic portrayal and condemned and censored the book. Just two years earlier, Broadway had been introduced to lesbianism in *The Captive.* Though hailed as a masterpiece when it was produced in Europe, New York reaction was quite the opposite and echoed the country's homophobia. Brooks Atkinson of the *New York Times* despised the "revolting theme," the "loathsome possibility" of a "twisted relationship with another woman." Other reviewers were equally damning: "a cancerous growth," "gangrenous horrors of sexual perversion," "a decadent woman." George Jean Nathan fumed that the play was corrupt and evil and "a documentary in favor of sexual degeneracy."[50] When the production was finally closed by a police raid after four months, stars Helen Menken and Basil Rathbone were arrested. Prompted by this production, a bill to amend the penal law in relation to immoral plays soon became a New York state law.

The temper of the times had changed from when Mercedes had begun her writing career. Although she had shown great promise in the early 1920s with her novels and poetry, the last years of the decade had been extremely frustrating. Three of her plays, *Sandro Botticelli, Jehanne d'Arc,* and *Jacob Slovak,* had failed to spark either critics or audiences. Several of her scripts, including *The Mother of Christ* and *The Dark Light,* were never produced. The public outrage against lesbian themes convinced Mercedes that she could never again write as openly as she had been accustomed.

To add to the strain, she was married to a man she did not love, and she had lost a lover of five years. It must have been painful to receive this note from Edward Gordon Craig: "I recall your visit to my house with that young warrior Miss Le Gallienne, who has . . . since then captured fortress after fortress in New York."[51] Eva's new Civic Repertory Theatre had captured front-page headlines across the country and had earned her a place on the *Nation*'s Roll of Honor for 1927 along with Eugene O'Neill, Ernest Hemingway, and Max Reinhardt. Mercedes' career, by contrast, was in a major slump.

Though a New Yorker by birth, Mercedes decided on moving to Hollywood, where she knew she would find a community more accepting of her sexuality. Soon after her first film script, *East River,* was rejected as a vehicle for Pola Negri, she began a lifelong infatuation with Greta Garbo. From 1931 when they met until she died thirty-seven years later, Mercedes' life was linked with Garbo's. They vacationed, sunbathed in the nude, and even lived together for a short time in 1932. But it was a very unpredictable and stormy relationship. Sometimes Garbo would scatter blossoms on the threshold when Mercedes entered her home and then usher her to the bedroom; other times she would parrot her famous screen line and beg to be left alone.[52] She would sometimes refuse to acknowledge Mercedes' presence. "It is really so idiotic," Mercedes explained. "One has to . . . go on handling her with absurd 'kid gloves,' or else suffer a falling out of some kind."[53] But perhaps there was another side to the story and Garbo had ample reason for her behavior. As their mutual friend, Cecil Beaton, observed, Mercedes became "rather idiotic, petty & petulant. Looking for grievances, she found them. . . . She managed to make it difficult for friends, impossible for her lovers."[54]

Her first film script for Garbo was *Desperate.* To avoid being recognized by the police, Garbo's character was to disguise herself as a boy, a "beautiful, pale, Shelley-like boy." "I made myself into a boy," she explains, "to avoid the things my life as a woman would have made for me."[55] The speech sounds like something Mercedes might have said to defend the masculine fashions she herself wore. Irving Thalberg, head of production at MGM, stopped the project when he learned that Garbo would be dressed as a boy for over half the film: "We have been building Garbo up for years as a great glamorous actress, and now you come along and try to put her into pants and make a monkey out of her."[56] It brought an abrupt end to her dreams of film writing.

For the next thirty-some years, Mercedes' life and career were a series of disappointments and rejections. Although she received no official credit for her work, she assisted on Garbo's *Queen Christina* (1933) and *Camille* (1937), primarily because she believed in Garbo's promise to star in her revision of *Jehanne d'Arc.* In 1932, when Garbo was being particularly aloof and quarrelsome, she engaged in a torrid love affair with still another screen goddess—Marlene Dietrich. Though Dietrich was married, it did not prevent her from showering Mercedes daily with bouquets of roses or carnations or orchids. When Dietrich was setting off for Europe, she wrote, "It will be hard to leave Hollywood now that I know you." She mailed Mercedes dozens of letters and telegrams, always signing off with love and kisses and saying, "I kiss your beautiful hands and your heart."[57]

Mercedes called Dietrich her "Golden One" and composed a small love poem for her:

For Marlene,
Your face is lit by moonlight
breaking through your skin
soft, pale, radiant.
No suntan for you glow
For you are the essence of
the stars and the moon and
the mystery of the night.[58]

Still another time, she promised, "I will bring anyone you want to your bed! And that is not because I love you little but because I love you so much! My Beautiful One!"[59] The passionate affair lasted little more than a year. Mercedes, heartbroken when Dietrich fell in love with actor Brian Aherne, fell into a deep depression that was further complicated by a serious injury when she was thrown from her car. Although she escaped permanent disfigurement, she needed extensive plastic surgery on her face.

In 1935, Mercedes' husband of fifteen years sued for divorce. "That we could no longer make a success of our sexual life seemed to me no reason to separate," she argued. "I was too European to feel, as Americans do, that the moment the sex relation is over one must fly to the divorce courts."[60] Once again she felt rejected: "It was as though my father or some close friend had written to me that he wanted me out of his life."[61]

In an effort to alleviate her depression, Mercedes took off for Italy, where she spent time meditating with twelve nuns.[62] She had grown up as a devout Roman Catholic, often kneeling in prayer for hours at a time. Once, she even put nails and stones in her shoes as a kind of penance. But now she rejected Catholicism to embrace the teachings of Kahlil Gibran and Jiddu Krishnamurti. In 1938 she flew to India and met with gurus Sri Meher Baba and Ramana Maharshi.

Their mutual interest in spiritualism drew Mercedes and Ona Munson together. By 1940, Munson had become the talk of the town for her portrayal of the voluptuous Belle Watling in *Gone with the Wind*. She had a long history in the theater, having performed in vaudeville, on Broadway, and on tour with Alla Nazimova in *Ghosts*. Munson reveals the depth of her love for Mercedes in her letters: "Your absence is a terrific void in my life and I long to hold you in my arms and pour my love into you." "I kiss your dear face all over, every little crevice." In a Christmas letter she acknowledged having "shared the deepest spiritual moment that life brings to human beings" and having "created an entity as surely as though [we] had conceived and borne a child." She even rented a new duplex that provided separate entrances and living quarters for her and her mother so that Mercedes "can visit me any time of day or night without even being seen."[63]

The relationship, however, was fraught with problems. Mercedes doubted Munson's sincerity and faithfulness. She became insanely jealous, for instance, when Munson told her that Marlene Dietrich had made an overture to date her. Still another thorn was the status of Mercedes' career; it was practically nonexistent. Garbo and Dietrich were at the height of their careers and Munson was turning heads, but Mercedes had nothing. Munson kept comforting her and telling her to "please get that thought out of your head that you're a failure."[64] Within a year, their relationship was over.

Mercedes' affair with Poppy Kirk began in the autumn of 1948. Poppy, the daughter of a Philadelphia diplomat, was married to a man working in the British Foreign Office when Mercedes met her. Poppy wrote that she longed to "kiss the tips of your ten fingers" and that she hated "to turn around in my bed . . . and not see my lovely one near me. . . . I need you my boy. Never forget it day or night. . . . Your girl needs you and loves you with all her heart." She admitted that when she received Mercedes' letters she would sneak away to the bathroom to read them in private.[65] During their six-year relationship, Poppy periodically left her husband for Mercedes, only to return to him after a few months. Then Poppy began to refuse Mercedes' telephone calls. "The time has come," wrote Poppy, "when I must have time to myself." In truth, Poppy had decided to live permanently with her husband.[66]

Through the 1940s, 1950s, and 1960s Mercedes' health deteriorated dramatically. A few years before she had met Poppy, she accidentally poured cleaning fluid into her eyes instead of eyewash. It almost blinded her. She continued to have so many infections in her right eye that she took to wearing an eye patch. Added to her already eccentric costumes, it gave her the look of a pirate. Then she contracted a bad case of shingles. In the early 1960s she underwent a painful leg operation as well as brain surgery. After the third of her close acquaintances committed suicide— Eleanora von Mendelssohn in 1949, Ona Munson in 1955, and William McCarthy in 1965—she suffered a nervous breakdown, fell into a severe state of depression, and contemplated suicide herself. Her old friend, Tamara Karsavina, advised, "What you need is someone who might help you to pull through, to some objective." She invited Mercedes to visit her in London: "With your fear of being alone it might help you to have someone to talk to."[67]

Through these bleak years, she continued to write. When she learned that the Office of War Information was publishing a propaganda magazine called *Victory*, she moved back to New York and joined the editorial staff in 1942. Two years later she embarked on a tour for the National Concert and Artists Corporation, lecturing on "The Challenge of a Changing World," "New Trends in Art and Literature," and "Friends and Celebrities." Other lecturers on the circuit included Lee Simonson, Lillian Gish, and Guthrie McClintic. For over a decade, she and Natacha Rambova worked together on a play called *The Leader*, which was an adaptation of Mercedes' earlier *The Mother of Christ*.

Her major undertaking, however, was her autobiography. When *Here Lies the Heart* finally appeared in 1960, reaction was mixed. Her close friends praised the book. Cecil Beaton wrote her that "there is so much good stuff in it & I have enjoyed it a lot."[68] Alice B. Toklas was another fan: "Your book has left me breathless—excited and very happy. I curtsy before your tremendous accomplishment."[69]

Her early, unpublished manuscripts and writings contain coded accounts of Mercedes' lesbian relationships. Although the finished book discusses all of her female friends with no reference to their sexual orientation, many readers were outraged by the implications. In 1960, the subject of lesbianism was still unpopular.

For many years, Garbo had carefully avoided seeing Mercedes. "She's always trying to scheme and find out things and you can't shut her up," Garbo complained.[70] The publication of the book made her so furious that even when Mercedes lay on her deathbed, Garbo refused to visit or send flowers. Eva Le Gallienne's reaction was just as unkind. If someone mentioned Mercedes' name, she would storm from the room in disgust. She and Mercedes had worshiped Duse. They had met Duse together, and later had stood vigil with their arms linked at her coffin. Yet when Le Gallienne wrote her memories of Duse in *The Mystic in the Theatre* in 1966, she did not give Mercedes even a footnote reference. She told her friends that Mercedes' book should have been called "Here the Heart Lies." In spite of their sharp rebuke, Mercedes kept snapshots of them in her family Bible until the day she died.[71]

The book's publication should have excited Mercedes, but instead it threw her into a deeper depression. By now, she was living a threadbare existence. She had been receiving alimony from Abram Poole since their divorce in 1935, but when he died in 1961, her allowance was frozen. Because royalties from her book were very slim, she was forced to sell her jewels and move into a tiny, two-room apartment on East Sixty-eighth Street. Although she was offered ten thousand dollars for her Garbo correspondence, she refused to sell. Fortunately, old lovers such as Marlene Dietrich and Poppy Kirk lent her money to cover her bills.

Her only visitors in the end were "Les Girls," young women hoping they would be introduced to Garbo. Although she had been labeled a social butterfly and tagged "the dyke at the top of the stairs," she whispered to one of the few friends who still visited her, "I'm sitting here all alone."[72] She pointed to the autographed photographs in her room signed "To Dearest Mercedes," "To the One and Only Mercedes," and others, and admitted that she had been forgotten by all the famous personalities in her past now that she was penniless. "I don't think it's made me bitter—just damned bewildered. And I'm not ashamed to say I'm lonely."[73] She died on May 9, 1968.

The nine years between 1919 and 1928 had been extremely productive for Mercedes: three books of poetry, two novels, and three produced plays—one off-Broadway, another in Paris, and a third both on Broadway and in London. However, with the exception of her 1960 autobiography, her last forty years were fruitless. The early promise she had shown as a poet, novelist, and playwright never materialized. In the pantheon of theater history, she is now virtually unknown, except perhaps as a starstruck social butterfly and confidante of the stars.

Although Mercedes' literary work has been forgotten, her story provides an important case study on how a writer's same-sex desire can affect a career. Her love for other women and her struggle for acceptance were certainly sources of her originality and fueled her writing. But the need for fame and celebrity, along with the cloying emotionalism with which she suffocated her lovers, turned to fanaticism, clouding her vision, taste, and artistic decisions. She was blinded by sexual passion. When he learned of her death, Cecil Beaton wrote an epitaph in his diary:

> I cannot be sorry at her death. I am only sorry that she should have been so unfulfilled as a character. In her youth she showed zest and originality. She was one of the most rebellious & brazen of Lesbians. . . . I am relieved that her long drawn out unhappiness has at last come to an end.[74]

NOTES

1. Hugo Vickers, *Loving Garbo: The Story of Greta Garbo, Cecil Beaton, and Mercedes de Acosta* (New York: Random House, 1994), 12.

2. Ibid., 12.

3. Quoted in Steven Bach, *Marlene Dietrich: Life and Legend* (New York: William Morrow, 1992), 172.

4. Mercedes de Acosta, *Here Lies the Heart* (New York: Reynal, 1975), 36.

5. Mercedes de Acosta, "First Writing," a typed manuscript of her autobiography, 30–32, in folder 01:05, Rosenbach Museum, Philadelphia. Both Hugo Vickers, *Loving Garbo,* and Karen Swenson, *Greta Garbo: A Life Apart* (New York: Scribner, 1997), cite as sources the "First Draft" and the "Second Draft" of *Here Lies the Heart.* The librarian at the Rosenbach Museum, Elizabeth Fuller, has confirmed that those citations are not accurate. The Rosenbach has no manuscripts labeled "First Draft" or "Second Draft." The citations I am providing are the correct ones.

6. Acosta, "First Writing," 33–34.

7. Mercedes de Acosta, typescript with corrections, in folder 02:02, 338, Rosenbach Museum, Philadelphia.

8. Axel Madsen, *The Sewing Circle: Hollywood's Greatest Secret, Female Stars Who Loved Other Women* (New York: Birch Lane Press, 1995), 41.

9. Isadora Duncan to Mercedes de Acosta, 1927, in Rosenbach Museum, quoted in Vickers, *Loving Garbo.*

10. Acosta, "First Writing," 64.

11. Ibid., 75.

12. Isadora Duncan, *My Life* (New York: Boni and Liveright, 1927), 285.

13. See Robert A. Schanke, *Shattered Applause: The Lives of Eva Le Gallienne* (Carbondale: Southern Illinois University Press, 1992) as well as his essay on Nazimova in *Passing Performances: Queer Readings of Leading Players in American Theater History,* ed. Robert A. Schanke and Kim Marra (Ann Arbor: University of Michigan Press, 1998).

14. Mercedes de Acosta and Stuart Benson, "For France," *Outlook,* July 25, 1917, 483. In January 1921, Stuart Benson married Mary ("Mimsey") Duggett, an actress who had been the emotional center of Eva Le Gallienne's life for three years. By the end of the year, Mercedes had initiated her own relationship with Le Gallienne.

15. Acosta, *Here Lies the Heart,* 76.

16. Ibid., 85.

17. Mercedes de Acosta, *Moods* (New York: Moffat, Yard, 1919), 45.

18. Ibid., 2.

19. *New York Herald,* January 27, 1920; *New York American,* January 27, 1920.

20. *New York Sun,* February 27, 1922.

21. Vickers, *Loving Garbo,* 12.

22. See J. K. Curry, "Rachel Crothers: An Exceptional Woman in a Man's World," in this volume.

23. Mercedes de Acosta, *Wind Chaff* (New York: Moffat, Yard, 1920), 11–12, 188–89, 225, 232.

24. See Schanke, *Shattered Applause.* There are discrepancies between what I have written in this essay about the relationship between Mercedes and Eva Le Gallienne and what I wrote in *Shattered Applause.* When I was writing the

earlier biography, Le Gallienne was still alive, and her letters to Mercedes were sealed at the Rosenbach Museum. Those letters, which were made available to readers after she died in 1991, provide more accurate information than was earlier available.

25. Acosta, typescript with corrections, 200.

26. The letters from Eva Le Gallienne to Mercedes de Acosta are in the Rosenbach Museum.

27. Mercedes de Acosta, *Archways of Life* (New York: Moffat, Yard, 1921), 13, 14, 33, 24.

28. Mercedes de Acosta, *Streets and Shadows* (New York: Moffat, Yard, 1922), 33.

29. Ibid., 26, 36.

30. Percy Hammond, "The Theaters," *New York Tribune*, March 27, 1923; Heywood Brown, *Democrat Chronicle*, April 1, 1923; Gordon Whyte, *Billboard*, April 7, 1923.

31. Typed manuscript of "The Mother of Christ," Rosenbach Museum.

32. Typed manuscript of "Jehanne d'Arc," Rosenbach Museum.

33. "First Writing," 175–76.

34. *Theatre*, May 1925.

35. *Chicago Tribune* (Paris edition), June 11, 1925.

36. William Kelly, ed., *Miracle in the Evening: An Autobiography by Norman Bel Geddes* (Garden City, N.J.: Doubleday, 1960), 329–30.

37. *L'Action Francaise* (Paris), June 18, 1925.

38. *New York Review*, July 11, 1925.

39. Noel Coward, *Present Indicative* (New York: Doubleday, 1937), 216.

40. Letter from Tamara Karsavina to Mercedes de Acosta, July 23, 1926, Rosenbach Museum.

41. *New York Times*, October 6, 1927; *New York World*, October 6, 1927; *Billboard*, n.d.

42. Typed manuscript of "Jacob Slovak," Rosenbach Museum.

43. *Daily Sketch*, June 18, 1928; *Evening Standard*, June 18, 1928; *Morning Post*, June 18, 1928; *Western Morning News and Mercury* (Plymouth), June 19, 1928.

44. *Outlook*, June 23, 1928; *Times* (London), June 18, 1928.

45. Letter from John Gielgud to the author, August 7, 1995.

46. The essays are all located at the Rosenbach Museum.

47. Mercedes de Acosta, *Until the Day Break* (New York: Longmans Green, 1928), 24.

48. Ibid., 170–86.

49. Vern L. Bullough, *Homosexuality: A History* (New York: New American Library, 1979), 124–25.

50. *New York Times*, September 30, 1926; *New York Morning Telegraph*, October 10, 1926; Arthur Hornblow, "Mr. Hornblow Goes to the Play," *Theatre*, December 1926, 16; George Jean Nathan, "The Theatre," *American Mercury*, March 1927, 373.

51. Letter from E. G. Craig to Mercedes de Acosta, January 23, 1928, Rosenbach Museum.

52. The letters of Garbo to Mercedes are located at the Rosenbach Museum. They were closed to the public until ten years after Garbo's death, but were finally unsealed on April 17, 2000. Although the letters provide no concrete evidence of a sexual relationship between the two women, the headline for Dinitia Smith's article in the *New York Times,* April 18, 2000, is accurate: "Letters Push Garbo Slightly into View." As of this writing, the Garbo estate was not granting permission to quote from these letters. I will deal with these letters more substantively in my forthcoming biography of de Acosta.

53. Quoted in Vickers, *Loving Garbo,* 210.

54. Ibid., 532.

55. Typed manuscript of "Desperate" at Rosenbach Museum.

56. *Here Lies the Heart,* 233.

57. From Marlene Dietrich to Mercedes de Acosta, September 15, 1932; July 28, 1933; Rosenbach Museum.

58. Mercedes de Acosta, note in her address book, Georgetown University, Washington, D.C.

59. Mercedes to Marlene Dietrich, ca. 1932, quoted in Maria Riva, *Marlene Dietrich* (New York: Knopf, 1992), 168.

60. Acosta, *Here Lies the Heart,* 261.

61. Acosta, typescript with corrections, 419.

62. Mercedes de Acosta, "Study in Sainthood," *Tomorrow,* May 1942, 37–40.

63. Ona Munson to Mercedes de Acosta, February 26, 1940; March 6, 1940; Christmas, 1940; February 20, 1940; Rosenbach Museum.

64. Ona Munson to Mercedes de Acosta, February 26, 1940; March 11, 1940; March 20, 1940; March 1, 1940; March 6, 1940.

65. Poppy Kirk to Mercedes de Acosta, 1949; January 25, 1950; Rosenbach Museum.

66. Poppy Kirk to Mercedes de Acosta, August 23, 1954, Rosenbach Museum.

67. Tamara Karsavina to Mercedes de Acosta, August 12, 1956, Rosenbach Museum.

68. Cecil Beaton to Mercedes de Acosta, March 26, 1960, Rosenbach Museum.

69. Quoted in *Staying On Alone—the Letters of Alice B. Toklas,* ed. Edward Burns (New York: Random House, 1974), 380.

70. Quoted in Madsen, *The Sewing Circle,* 200.

71. The Bible, dated 1922, was on exhibit in the parlor of the Rosenbach Museum on May 17, 2000. There were also photos of Eleonora Duse, Isadora Duncan, Rita Lydig, and Mercedes' mother.

72. Kieran Tunney, *Interrupted Autobiography and Aurora* (London: Quartet Books, 1989), 37; Wilder Luke Burnap to Hugo Vickers, September 30, 1992, quoted in Vickers, *Loving Garbo.*

73. Quoted in Tunney, *Interrupted Autobiography and Aurora,* 37.

74. Cecil Beaton, unpublished diary, May 1968, quoted in Vickers, *Loving Garbo.*

Djuna Barnes
The Most Famous Unknown
Susan F. Clark

Djuna Barnes (1892–1982) is rarely associated with the theater in America, despite her prolific accomplishments as a playwright, critic, and interviewer. Before the age of thirty, she had three plays produced by the Provincetown Players and had gained the attention of New York's top drama critics; by 1926, over eighteen Barnes plays had been published in various newspapers, periodicals, and in a book of her collected works; between 1916 and 1931, she wrote over seventy-five articles, interviews, and reviews of the plays, people, and ideas current on the Broadway stage; and, in 1961, Stockholm's Royal Dramatic Theatre gave the premiere production of her only published full-length play, *The Antiphon* (1958).[1] Barnes's short play *The Dove* (1923) was one of the first lesbian plays by a lesbian-identified playwright produced on the American stage.

Since her death in 1982, Barnes has been the subject of significant scholarly attention, much of it focused on her short stories and novels, in particular the lesbian classic *Nightwood* (1930), and her colorful, if unusual, life. Yet, despite the thirteen books she authored, including *A Book of Repulsive Women* (1915), *Vagaries Malicieux* (1922), *A Book* (1923), *Ryder* (1928), *Ladies Almanack* (1928), *A Night among the Horses* (1929), *Spillway* (1962), and *Creatures in an Alphabet* (1982), the recognition Barnes longed for eluded her during her lifetime. Barnes lamented this fact when she wrote in a letter to Natalie Barney, "I am the most famous unknown of the century! I can't account for it, unless it is that my talent is my character, my character my talent, and both an estrangement."[2]

Barnes's perception of the causes of her estrangement is remarkably self-aware. The "most famous unknown" was, indeed, a walking paradox. Raised in rural New York state, she felt most at home in the cafés and nightlife of Europe. Though she refused to compromise her artistic principles for money, poverty was a constant fear and threat that caused her to rely on the financial assistance of several benefactors. Despising most things American as petty and bourgeois, for twenty years she made her living reporting on American culture and events. Highly attractive to men, she vowed early in her life never to marry and formed her most serious relationships with women. Though she wrote several lesbian works, she never publicly embraced her own lesbianism. A bold, witty, arrogant woman, Barnes spent the first forty-five years of her life searching for a relationship that would provide protection and comfort. Within her own circle of chosen friends, many of whom were the leading literary figures of the day, she was famous and an equal; yet the public recognition achieved by her friends James Joyce and T. S. Eliot would never be hers.

Part of her lack of recognition was due to her talent, which led her to write in language that was poetic, challenging, and, to many, inscrutable. The larger part of her failure to achieve success, particularly in the theater, was her character, which dictated the subjects and themes she chose to write about. This essay will examine some of the events that influenced the Barnesian character, the enmeshment of her talent and character, and their reflection in the theater.

In a review of Marlene Dietrich's 1931 film, *Morocco,* Barnes expressed what might be viewed as her artistic credo: "I like my human experience served up with a little Silence and Restraint. Silence makes experience go further and, when it does die, gives it that dignity common to a Thing that has been touched but not ravished."[3] The complex nature of theatrical representation in many ways matches the complexity of Barnes herself. In contrast to the explicit representations common to the commercial stage, Barnes wrote her plays for a theater of "restraint" that could explore intimate realities and inner worlds through the subtleties of language, silence, gesture, and visual art.

Though a highly public figure, Barnes was an intensely private person, and many of her works explore the most hidden aspect of her life, her sexuality. In this sense, Barnes used the theater to "touch" her life truths without subjecting them to "ravishment." Just as the tools of theatrical expression, language, music and art, were essential elements of Djuna's education, the bohemian "free love" environment of her childhood permeated every aspect of her character and adult life. The "taboo" nature of many of her early sexual experiences (which included incest, rape, and homosexuality) required "silence," while Barnes's artistic temperament demanded expression. The theater's ability to assimilate these public and private elements into an organic whole appealed to Djuna's aesthetic sensibilities and helped to assuage her personal demons. Existing on levels of text and subtext, realism and symbolism, the theater embodied a duality that appealed to a woman who was both gregarious and intentionally mysterious.

Excluding her journalism and contracted writing assignments, all of the Barnes literary heritage is a complicated and consuming exploration of sexuality. Throughout her life, Barnes struggled to find her sexual identity. A childhood victim of incest and rape, Barnes actively sought and experienced a variety of human sexual interactions, including multiple partnerships, infidelity, and homosexuality. The translation of these experiences into artistic form, particularly for the highly public and visual venue of the stage, required that Barnes negotiate between the boundaries of censorship laws and her innate sense of artistic integrity. The resulting literature is coded by layers of archaic language, mystifying actions, and symbolic atmosphere. Largely inscrutable to the general public, the major portion of Barnes's plays remains unread and unperformed.

Barnes's unconventional upbringing and rather extraordinary childhood have been the subject of several studies, including Phillip Herring's recent book, *Djuna: The Life and Times of Djuna Barnes* (1995). Born in Cornwall-on-Hudson, Djuna, along with all of the Barnes progeny, was educated at home by a highly literate and liberal group of adults who mistrusted public schools. Though they were constantly on the verge of poverty, intellectual life in the household was rich, and Chaucer, Montaigne, and Proust were but a few of the early childhood readings. Each child also learned to draw, to play one or more musical instruments, and to do most of the work on the small farm, leaving the adults free to pursue their various interests.

From her earliest days on Storm King Mountain, Djuna had ample opportunity to observe the "free love" movement firsthand. Her paternal grandmother, Zadel, was an outspoken supporter of women's rights (including the right to sexual freedom) and helped to support the growing family by her writing and journalism. Wald, Djuna's father, fancied himself an artistic "gentleman farmer" and practiced bigamous free love, sharing his home with Elizabeth, his legal wife and Djuna's mother, as well as with his mistress, Fanny. Altogether, eight children (five belonging to Elizabeth and three to Fanny) and four adults shared the tiny cabin on property owned by Wald's brother; privacy was a rare luxury.

Letters between Barnes and her grandmother indicate that they shared a bed for many years. Though there is controversy among Barnes scholars regarding the nature of their relationship, the letters are highly suggestive of a homoerotic involvement between grandmother and granddaughter. Private pet names for intimate body parts, bawdy sketches, and fantasies of joyful times shared in bed are contained in the correspondence. In her article, "My Art Belongs to Daddy," Mary Lynn Broe describes the drawings that accompany one correspondence from Zadel to Djuna:

> "Oh, Misriss! When I sees your sweet hands a huggin your own P.T.'s [the drawing is a set of breasts]—I is just crazy and I jumps on oo. Like dis. Wiv dis wesult." [The drawing is of two women in bed, breasts together, one overpowered by the other. Another drawing is of two breasts reaching to meet, nipple to nipple.]⁴

Barnes's introduction to sexuality was not limited to her experiences with her grandmother. In her adult life, Djuna spoke with close friends regarding the nature of her father's sexual activities, including an anecdote she told of his riding the countryside with a sponge attached to the saddle of his horse so he could clean up if an unexpected sexual encounter with one of several women neighbors should occur. Just as she later fictionalized this family tale in *Ryder,* some of Barnes's mature work, most notably *The Antiphon,* includes the rape of a young girl by a father figure. Whether Wald Barnes sexually violated his daughter, or, as Barnes sometimes implied, persuaded another adult male to do so, it is clear that by the time Barnes was sixteen, her life had already been steeped in the rhythms of sexuality, both heterosexual and homosexual.

Personally and artistically, Djuna bore the mark of these early sexual experiences. Attracted to women, Djuna's longest and most enduring female friendships might be seen as her attempt to regain the comfort and security she had experienced with her grandmother. Indeed, she often remarked that she fell in love with Thelma Wood (her only acknowledged lesbian partner) because Thelma reminded her of Zadel (see fig. 4).⁵ Though she also had many relationships with men, including one that resulted in an abortion, rarely did they last more than a few months. A great deal of her fictional writing may be read as an attempt on Barnes's part to reconcile conflicting feelings of love and hate, incest and sensuality, heterosexuality and homosexuality. This can be seen most clearly in Barnes's famous work, *Nightwood,* a fictionalized purging of her eight-year relationship with Thelma. In Shari Benstock's analysis:

> *Nightwood* constructs a society doomed to misread itself and to misinterpret the signs of its own operations. Nora Flood [Djuna] cannot "read" Robin Vote [Thelma] because Robin's behavior, appearance, and efforts to communicate are not inscribed in the

FIG. 4. Thelma Wood and Djuna Barnes on a beach
in Provincetown, Massacusetts

*(Courtesy, Special Collections, University of Maryland at
College Park Libraries.)*

societal code to which she is asked to conform. A product of a culture that has suppressed female *difference,* Nora Flood sees Robin
as a man would see her: as an object of desire. Like a man, Nora
constructs Robin in her own image. Thus Robin simultaneously
serves as a "sign" of female difference repressed by Western culture and is misread by Nora into conformity with the cultural
code. . . . Nora both loves and fears Robin, but she loves her own
"re-made" image of Robin and fears the Robin who signals
woman's difference, the Robin who stands outside the sexual
economy of this culture.[6]

Bohemian Greenwich Village was a perfect setting for Djuna, who moved to New York with her mother, Elizabeth, following her divorce from Wald in 1912. Djuna was attractive, witty, sexually adventurous, talented, and imbued with a cynically pessimistic attitude that found soul mates in the heavy-drinking, free-loving, radical atmosphere. After a brief period studying at the Pratt Institute, Djuna began her career as a journalist writing feature stories. Her participatory style of journalism, which included allowing herself to be force-fed in imitation of the English suffragettes, gained her prominence as a writer. A "woman about town," her subjects included the IWW, preacher Billy Sunday, war veterans, and Diamond Jim Brady, as well as some of the most prominent figures in the performing arts.

Although Barnes is not listed as a member of Heterodoxy, the Greenwich Village organization of radical feminists, many of her associates and affiliates at the Provincetown Players were, including Susan Glaspell, Ida Rauh, Mary Heaton Vorse, Mabel Dodge Luhan, Zona Gale, Crystal Eastman, and Helen Westley. In addition, several of the male members of the Provincetown, including leader Jig Cook, lent their support to the group. Judith Schwartz describes the climate:

> In Greenwich Village in particular, the options for sexual expression seemed suddenly limitless. Now, a woman could at least consider the choices presented around her before deciding whether or not to obey the old morality she may have grown up hearing. Those choices included whether to enjoy sex with men, women, or both sexes separately or together. A woman could wait until she felt romantic attachment to the other person, or accept the new view that sexual attraction was a perfectly good reason to go to bed with someone, whether you felt you loved them or not.[7]

By 1917, at the age of twenty-five, Barnes was living in a common-law marriage with Courtenay Lemon and several other artists in a house leased by Susan Light, the editor of *All-Story Weekly*, and her husband, Jimmy Light, who acted and directed for the Provincetown Players. Barnes's first play, *The Death of Life: Death Is the Poor Man's Purse—Baudelaire*, had been published in the *New York Morning Telegraph Sunday Magazine* on December 17, 1916. Barnes's circle of friends and acquaintances at the time included many of the luminaries of the contemporary art and political scenes, including the left-wing radical Jack Reed, playwrights Floyd Dell, Eugene O'Neill, and Edna St. Vincent Millay, photographer Alfred Stieglitz, and Marcel Duchamp, the artist.

It was here, in Greenwich Village, that Barnes established what

Phillip Herring refers to as Barnes's "philosophy of the artistic life": "For Barnes and her circle, sex was essentially recreational, part of a lifestyle that they believed left them free for more important matters, such as art. Provincetown's high artistic standards, which implied a contempt for financial success, combined with sexual freedom, remained at the core."[8]

In addition to her personal friendships with members of the group, Barnes was attracted to the vitality and idealism of the Provincetown Players. The Provincetown was one of several growing little theaters across the United States, dedicated to rescuing the theater from the commercial pablum of the contemporary stage. It was a place where talented amateurs toiled alongside those with some professional knowledge, a theater where actors, playwrights, designers, and directors mingled and shared ideas, concepts, and work. Barnes, in her work as a journalist and reporter, was acutely aware of the New Drama movement taking place in Europe. Jan McDonald discusses the new movement in Great Britain in her introduction to *The "New Drama," 1900–1914*:

> The philosophy common to all those involved included first, a belief in the importance of the theater as a social force rather than as a social event; secondly, a desire to experiment with new dramatic forms and to break away from the rigid structure of the conventional "well-made" play that dominated the commercial stage; thirdly, to make the theatre a reflection of everyday life rather than a closed, unreal, "limelit" world; and finally, to create a more intellectually demanding literary drama than was currently available.[9]

One of the goals of the Provincetown Players, also known as the "Playwright's Theater," was to foster playwrights in the development of their own distinct voices and styles. Barnes's plays reflect this attempt to create a "new drama," informed by her familiarity with the works of Synge, Ibsen, and others, to form a body of work that stands out as iconoclastic and unsuited for the commercial stage. It was during her time with the Provincetown Players (1919–21), a period marked by its experimentation and movement toward more professional production standards, that Barnes formulated her principles for theater and concentrated on developing her mastery of the craft. Jig Cook, the founder of the Provincetown Players, took a sabbatical from the theater in 1919 out of his frustration with the failure of the group to succeed in his idealistic vision of devoted amateurs. Robert Sarlos, in his book about the Provincetown Players, describes the conflict between Cook and the younger members of the group:

The crucial factor . . . was an alienation between the spiritual mentor and his disciples. . . . Expending all his faith and energy on others—without consistently hitting paydirt—turned Jig increasingly
bitter. Not just one of the older generation, he was *the* founder and
sustainer, who seemed to have given up all other ambition . . .
besides the Provincetown Players. . . . He developed a phobia about
conflict with Youth: he felt challenged to compete and feared defeat.
. . . Jig Cook expressed irritation with the independent views, the
openly professional interest of the most ambitious and most aggressive young and talented Players.[10]

For Barnes, and the rest of the members of the Provincetown "Youth,"
the vision of a theater that was both artistically satisfying and professionally acclaimed was not contradictory. Unlike Cook's gathering of
dedicated "amateurs," most of the members from this period of the
Provincetown went on to successful professional theater careers. The
three Barnes plays produced by the Provincetown during the "Season of
Youth," *Three from the Earth* (1919), *An Irish Triangle* (1920), and
Kurzy of the Sea (1920), reflect her growing skill with the medium, as well
as her maturing aesthetic sensibility. At least two of these plays exhibit
the strong influence of John Synge, of whom Barnes wrote:

I find myself in the strange position of one who must write an
atmospheric article on an atmosphere. The task, did I love the cause
less, would be almost insurmountable. I am not a critic; to me criticism is so often nothing more than the eye garrulously denouncing
the shape of the peephole that gives hidden access to treasure.[11]

Barnes's plays, as well as most of her prose writing, are similarly laden
with "hidden treasure." Like Synge, Barnes valued atmosphere in her
plays, sometimes to the detriment of clear communication but oftentimes
to express what she dare not say plainly.

Understatement, both artistically and personally, is the key to the
Barnesian style. Those who failed to live up to her artistic standards
received her scorn, or, at the very least, her disappointment, including
some of her fellow Provincetown playwrights. Of Susan Glaspell's play,
Alison's House, Barnes wrote, "It is . . . Emotionally infirm. The characters do not enhance, but detract from the Spirit of the Poet by their ghoulish approval. They are like People about a Corpse who make themselves
presentable in Raiment that cries Aloud of the Departed."[12]

Those who fell prey to the temptation of easy success on Broadway similarly met with Barnes's disdain. Even Alla Nazimova, who clearly had Barnes's admiration and respect, met her harsh judgment:

> To Nazimova the memory . . . is a neurosis, the radix of which is pain and calamity, because they obliged her to feed her great talents to a public which had appetite for nothing more than the conventional stage vampire . . . she began playing that series of lust-and-vengeance drama which brought her nationwide fame—and grief. . . . She made huge sums of money, she was the darling of every tea, she was feted and cried over, complimented and kissed! One can see her longing in every fiber to play parts that call for overtones and underacting. . . . One can see her valuing that sort of thing, the kind of thing she once portrayed in Ibsen.[13]

For Barnes, every aspect of theater, including acting, should be "a Quiet, wise thing, in which the world is told off without a gesture, in a silence white and dumbfounding."[14] These qualities were as much a part of Barnes's personal beliefs as they were integral to her artistic standards. Even in her later years, when it could hardly matter, Barnes refused to discuss the nature of her partnerships with other people, most specifically those which involved women. Though she admitted to her relationship with Thelma Wood, Barnes disclaimed any suggestion that she was a lesbian herself, despite the fact that she had had many relationships with women. Questioned about her lesbianism, Barnes responded: "I might be anything. If a horse loved me, I might be that."[15]

Shari Benstock attributes Barnes's ability to negotiate the expatriate literary experience, divided between the male literary giants (such as James Joyce and Ernest Hemingway) and the "Amazons" (i.e., Gertrude Stein, Natalie Barney) to her efforts to keep her personal life private. According to Benstock, "Her writings . . . divided themselves along lines of sexual orientation: her journalism, short essays, and certain fictions (*Ryder,* for example) were directed toward the larger heterosexual community, while other writings, including much of her poetry and the *Ladies Almanack,* were intended primarily for a lesbian readership."[16] One might extend this analogy further and state that Barnes's writings also divide themselves along lines of intellectual orientation: her journalism and short stories were aimed primarily at a middle-class audience, while her poetry, drama, and novels were intended for her artistic peers and equals. The former she wrote to make money; the latter, to assuage her muse.

Despite the lack of critical acceptance by theater professionals,

Barnes persisted in writing plays. Long after her association with the Provincetown Players, Barnes continued to work on several full-length plays, though only *The Antiphon* was ever published. This suggests an affinity for the theater and the dramatic form that extended beyond her desire for recognition and success.

Barnes's devotion to the dramatic form may be read in the idealism of the Provincetown Players, which was "in part, a social effort to live again spiritually, to recover from discouragement and disappointment, to be free of the poison of self and the poison of the world."[17] In a letter to Natalie Barney dated October 16, 1963, Barnes looked back on these early days with longing:

> How do *you* think of that time of ours, which people seem to regard as the "disastrous twenties?" (thirties, forties, fifties, sixties?) now that we are well out of it? It seems like a time of complete (tho corrupt) innocence to the fearful time it has climbed into. I presume myself not to be exactly prudish, but quite simply I am shocked with what is written now, at plays now on the boards, at magazine covers on the stalls, at speech and action on the streets, and as for the recordings of horrors abroad and "things to be" . . . who can contain or understand it?[18]

Barnes embraced the theater as a source of relief from the sexual confusion that clearly tormented and confused her throughout her life. By using formal (and sometimes archaic) language, sets redolent with symbolism and muted physical action, Barnes was able to express her deepest conflicts and fears while remaining safely within the boundaries of acceptability.

Yet Barnes's plays (and many of her other works) were ignored or dismissed either because of the content or because of the heavily coded action (or nonaction) and language that Barnes was compelled to use. Nevertheless, the first Barnes play produced by the Provincetown Players in 1919 earned the following laudatory praise from S. J. Kaufmann in the *New York Globe and Commercial Advertiser*:

> The Provincetown Players prove one thing. They prove of what little value A theatre is. And of how great value THE theatre is. Last night we saw a new bill there. The moment the curtain parted we knew we were in THE theatre. The play's really the thing there. And Eugene O'Neill's *The Dreamy Kid* and Djuna Barnes' *Three From the Earth*—half the bill—are justification for THE theatre in America. Miss Barnes' play is so near to being great that we hope we shall be able to see it again. And we hope it's printed. Does Arthur Hop-

kins know there is a Djuna Barnes? She has been doing odd jobs. Now she has arrived. He should see her playlet and insist upon her writing for him. We anticipated all sorts of disagreement as to the strength of *Three From the Earth*. That is one of its strengths. Even now as we write the power, simplicity and withal the incalculable depth has us enthralled.[19]

Yet Kaufmann's enthusiasm stands practically alone among those critics who had the opportunity to view Barnes's work. Others referred to her plays as "obscure," "esoteric," and occasionally, "obscene." Most critics failed to see the value or meaning in a play such as *Three from the Earth*, in which three grown men approach their prostitute mother for proof of their birth, and leave, taking an uninvited, but clearly sexual (and incestuous), kiss in parting. In contrast to Kaufmann's enthusiastic reception of the play, Alexander Woollcott renamed the piece "Three From the Birth: A Malthusian Sardonicism in One Act," in his review:

the greatest indoor sport this week is guessing what it means. . . . It is really interesting to see how absorbing and essentially dramatic a play can be without the audience ever knowing what, if anything, the author is driving at. . . . The spectators sit with bated breath listening to each word of a playlet of which the darkly suggested clues leave the mystery unsolved. The trick of hinting at things which are never revealed, of charging an act with expectancy never satisfies, of lighting fuses that lead to no explosion at all is a trick used occasionally to intensify a scene. It is a trick which, played often, would enrage an audience.[20]

The review from the *New York Tribune* reflects a similar refusal to make sense of what is clearly apparent:

Djuna Barnes' play, *Three From the Earth*, evades classification. It is the extreme of impressionism. It floats in a nebula of its own connotations into which the audience tries to force a baffled entrance. Now and then something familiar in the dialogue swims past— "you have come for the letter?" But it is useless to catch at this spar. You are floated despairingly out to sea, far past the hope of negotiating a landing on any simple basis of understanding.

Now and then Ida Rauh seemed to make the play say something—but out of much fascinated juggling with the jig-saw of its references one comes to the conclusion that *Three From the Earth* is proof that movement and light and color and semi-intelligible sounds may be fascinating in the same way dreams are fascinating. Its purpose may be only to convey a dream—and, if so, one emerges from it in the same state of mild exasperation as out of a dream to which one has lost the clue.²¹

This bemused, if sometimes fascinated, attitude on the part of the critics dogged Barnes throughout her playwriting career. None of her plays, including *The Antiphon,* which was the one play to receive a full-scale professional production and which Barnes considered to be her finest piece of professional work, had any greater success in communicating with those powerful "makers-or-breakers" of plays and playwrights. To be certain, the language of a Barnes play is rarely commonplace, nor do the plays rely on rapidly changing plot events, witty cocktail repartee, exciting visual effects, or any of the accustomed devices of the commercial theater.

At the time of Provincetown Players' birth, however, critics had begun, somewhat consistently, to speak out against vacuous dramas, fastidiously sterile scenery, contrived melodramas, and the extravagant leg shows that currently inhabited the Broadway stage. George Jean Nathan's voice repeatedly spoke out against what he considered to be the "dry rot" in the American theater. Several critics (including Acton Davies, Alan Dale, and William Winter) were fired from their jobs for failing to praise inferior Syndicate productions.

Yet what separated Barnes's plays from even the "art theater" pieces was their subject matter and style. The fact that Barnes, because of both practical and psychological necessity, couched the messages of her plays in terms that were vague, obscure, and distinctly subtextual, may account for her failure to achieve any modicum of theatrical success. In addition, incest, homosexuality, and infidelity were hardly the stuff and substance of the commercial theater world, though they were the subjects Barnes felt most compelled to explore.

Even the most benign of Barnes's plays address the impossibility of achieving a harmonious, or even pleasant, relationship between members of the opposite sex. Furthermore, women characters dictate the action of the plays and generally exist as independent and superior to the male characters. Because the subjects of open marriages *(An Irish Triangle),* Christ-like crucifixions that revolve around lustful passions *(Passion Play),* and a woman who collects the body parts of her former lovers *(Madame Collects Herself),* to list a few of the Barnesian themes, are unconventional and more than slightly risqué, the plays remained (and remain) largely unproduced and unexamined.

The Dove represents Barnes's most accomplished synthesis of her "character" and "talent" and is, predictably, the play most "estranged" from the commercial theater. It is the only lesbian-identified play that Barnes wrote, containing an all-female cast and a sexually explicit scene. *The Dove* was published soon after Barnes had begun her live-in relationship with Thelma Wood at 9, rue St. Romain in Paris. Though not Barnes's first lesbian experience, the love affair with Thelma was to prove the most significant and the only highly public demonstration of Barnes's attachment to a woman. Considered to be the one "great love" of her life, Barnes's existence with Thelma was marked by Thelma's bouts of drunkenness, fighting, and infidelity, with brief periods of domesticity. Even after Thelma left Djuna for another woman, Barnes remained obsessed with the relationship for many years.

Though it did not receive a professional run, *The Dove* was featured in the Fourth Annual National Little Theater Tournament in New York and produced by the Studio Theater of Manhattan. That *The Dove* was ever seen on stage at all can be credited to Samuel A. Eliot Jr., professor of English and drama advisor at Smith College and an enthusiastic champion of "experimental" drama. The premiere production of *The Dove* took place at Smith College in Northampton, Massachusetts, on November 18, 1925, as part of the annual student workshop productions. Directed by third-year student Margaret Wall, the production was reviewed in the *Smith College Weekly:*

> Modernism, as expressed by Djuna Barnes, seems to have reached a peak in *The Dove*. The work of the authoress is infused with Greenwich Village spirit, with the result that it is rather obtuse. In fact, the inclusion of *The Dove* in the program is in the nature of an experiment, since we are assured that we "will probably not understand it." The play itself is fairly simple. Of the three characters, all of whom [are] women, two, Vera and her sister Amelia, are trying to reconstruct for themselves a fictitious world in which all their starved and frustrated desires will be satisfied. *The Dove,* the third character, is a woman of strong personality who, having actually lived the dream fantasies of the other two, is the embodiment of what they would like to be. It is with their life, more particularly their desires to be "wicked," that the action is concerned.[22]

The "fantasies" to which the writer refers are largely expressed through Barnes's description of the setting and its inhabitants: there are a few animals kept about in the hope that the sisters will "see something first hand"; French novels and flies abound; Amelia keeps, in her bed, a picture of a Parisienne bathing girl which is "stuck full of pin-holes"; Vera dreams that she is a Dresden doll broken all to pieces, except for her china skirt, which has become "flexible," made of "chiffon and lace"; the title character is precariously misnomered "The Dove," ordinarily a symbol of peace and purity. During the course of the play, additional information is revealed by suggestive action. As the scene first opens, the Dove, a confident young woman, is clearly in command of the situation, as she sits and polishes the blade of an immense sword. Her self-assurance is apparent when she responds to the question "why don't you do something?" with "A person capable of anything needs no practice."

Slowly, the mystery of why the Dove is living in the Burgson sister's apartment is revealed. The Dove is, by her own admission, always waiting for the climactic moment.

> *The Dove.* I suppose I'm waiting for the person who will know
>   that anything is a reason for using a pistol, and the obvious has
>   never been sufficient reason.[23]

The Dove, a person of "superior sensibilities," is beyond ordinary needs and ordinary means of expression. Early in the script, Barnes establishes that any action taken by the Dove will be a significant one; indeed, it is only the Dove who has the ability to act. By contrast, the Burgson sisters are trapped by their fear of sexual expression in any form: they live vicariously through immoral pictures, dangerous weapons hanging on the walls, decadent red plush draperies, and copulating animals kept just for that purpose. Each of the sisters longs for the sexual freedom of the Dove, yet lacks the courage to commit to life by fully living. In response to the question of why she is so restless, Vera responds:

> Because I am a woman. I leave my life entirely to my imagination
> and my imagination is terrific. . . . Some people would say [I want]
> a lover, but I don't say a lover; some people would say a home, but
> I don't say a home. You see I have imagined myself beyond the need
> of the usual home and beyond the reach of the usual lover. . . . Per-
> haps what I really want is a reason for using one of these pistols![24]

Passion, intensity, and danger, bound up in the symbolic use of pistols, are the forte of the Dove, not the Burgsons. The second sister, Amelia, foresees a similarly bleak future for herself.

> *Amelia.* . . . Aren't there a great many flies in here?
> *The Dove.* Yes, the screens should be put up.
> *Amelia.* No, no, no. I don't want anything to be shut out. Flies
>   have a right to more than life, they have a right to be curious.
> *The Dove.* A bat flew into the room last night.

Amelia. Some day I shall look like a bat, having beaten my wings
   about every corner of the world, and never having hung over
   anything but myself.[25]

Amelia's virginity, "never having hung over anything" but herself,
and likely continued celibacy, stands in stark contrast to the Dove's
refusal to live incompletely. The play's conflict arises from Vera and
Amelia's denial of their lesbian natures in the presence of the Dove, who
accepts everything and wants the most out of every experience. Barnes
thus links Vera and Amelia's rejection of their sexuality, and their subsequent unhappiness, to their inability (or unwillingness) to act. It is the
Dove who forces the sisters finally to acknowledge their true selves by
biting Amelia on the breast and firing the pistol through the center of a
painting of two courtesans. Just before the curtain comes down, Vera
enters crying, "It is obscene! It is obscene!"

One could read "Djuna" for "The Dove," and the play as a wake-up
call to women who avoided truly living because of fear of exposure, their
own passivity, or obedience to society's conventions. Though the play
does not contain overt sexual encounters between women, as did the
New York productions of *The God of Vengeance* (1922) or *The Captive*
(1926), the sexually charged atmosphere leaves little doubt as to the lesbian content of the play. Yet critics, hesitant or unable to name the theme
in the absence of blatant action, retreated from *The Dove* under the guise
of misunderstanding the piece. The *New York Evening Post,* under the
headline "Pseudo-Freud, Neo-Shaw, Pre-Barrie in the Little Theatres,"
provided the following review:

All she [Barnes] achieves in *The Dove,* however, is a wearisome talk
orgy wherein the action is supposed to be reduced to the points of
Freudian symbolism. But one can't be constantly brushed up on
Freud, so that the reviewer is tempted to go along with others and
say that the performance was "over the heads of most of the audience." After one of the esoterically sensual sisters in the play has
voiced her strange ecstasies in a long, jumbled monologue, the girl
who is in love with her leans over and bites her shoulder. This
smashing climax is followed by two revolver shots. Then someone
appears with one of the pictures, saying:
   "It is obscene! It is obscene!"
And it probably is.
The play was acted with a strained intensity that irritated.[26]

The *New York Sun* seemed even less sure what the play was about:

There was . . . the . . . effort of the Studio Theatre, called *The Dove,*
perhaps because it had to be called something and doves had as
much connection with it as anything else. Save, perhaps, bats. It is,
one fancies, a study of inhibitions in the *fin de siecle* period and
shows, perhaps, what awful things inhibitions were in those days. It
gives an effect rather as one might obtain if, say, one were to read
Gertrude Stein on a merry-go-round, by candlelight. But so lamen-
tably few of us had had such experience.

The three women . . . in the cast act "The Dove" quite as though
they knew what it was all about. As, indeed, perhaps they did.[27]

Both critics imply, no less evasively than Barnes, the lesbian subject matter of the play, one by stating that "it probably is" obscene, the other by
comparing the play to reading "Gertrude Stein on a merry-go-round, by
candlelight." Yet it is these and other critics' refusals to name the
"taboo" subjects of Barnes's work and their determination to describe
the plays as inaccessible, muddled, or "wearisome" playwriting that condemned Barnes's career to obscurity.

The Dove marked the beginning of a hiatus in Barnes's playwriting
career. In the years immediately following *The Dove,* her contributions
to the theater came in the form of previews of upcoming performances,
interviews, and her own philosophical musings on the work of other theater artists. Her lack of critical recognition, as well the puritanical
restraints on writers, may be one reason why, when given the opportunity to live abroad on assignment for *McCall's* magazine in 1921, Barnes
abandoned Greenwich Village and the world of theater to spend much of
the next twenty years in less hostile foreign lands. The world of Paris in
the 1920s allowed Barnes to explore her lesbianism without censure or
the necessity of hiding, while receiving the acceptance and encourage-
ment of other women artists, as well as some of the most important male
writers of the twentieth century.

After her breakup with Thelma Wood in 1929, Barnes plunged into a
series of brief relationships with men. Traveling between the United
States and Europe, she began work on *Nightwood,* in an attempt to exorcize herself of Thelma's betrayal. Forced by the beginning of World War
II to return to New York, Djuna moved into what would be her final residence at 5 Patchin Place in 1940.

Between 1940 and 1958, Barnes rarely left the tiny apartment. Struggling to overcome her escalating alcoholism, her life in New York

was as far removed from the life at 9, rue St. Romain, as possible.
. . . That in old age Barnes became increasingly confined to her own

home, and that she preferred the monastic life of her tiny apartment to any alternative that New York City might offer, suggests a desperate need to establish control over her daily life.[28]

Alcohol was not the only demon that Barnes attempted to exorcize during this period. Her family history had provided background material for some of her earlier works. "The Biography of Julie von Bartmann," an unpublished full-length play completed in 1924, and *Ryder,* a novella published in 1928, contain incidents that bear strong resemblance to the people, events, and places of Barnes's younger years, focusing particularly on the sexual proclivities exhibited by her father, Wald Barnes. With Barnes's permanent return to the United States, the ghosts of her upbringing attained positions of prominence in her writing. As early as 1940, Barnes started work on a full-length play, *The Antiphon,* the last major piece she would ever publish. As its title suggests, *The Antiphon* is Barnes's response to her family and to the suffering, betrayal, and alienation that Barnes experienced.

Her estrangement from her family had grown in proportion to her reputation as a writer. Following the publication of *Nightwood,* and its very public acknowledgment of Barnes's lesbianism, the relationship between Barnes and her family deteriorated even further. Never comfortable with their sister's persistence in pursuing an occupation that was financially insecure, and which often left her dependent upon benefactors such as Peggy Guggenheim for basic necessities, her conservative brothers were doubly concerned that the reflected taint of Barnes's taboo sexuality might impinge upon their successful careers. Their attempts to have Barnes committed to a sanitarium to confront her problems with alcohol and her failing health resulted in what Barnes considered to be "yet another violation of her person."[29] With the publication of *The Antiphon* in 1958, and the airing of the family's incestuous laundry, Barnes succeeded in severing all relationship to her family.

Considered by Barnes to be her most autobiographical work, the play is set in England in 1939, on the occasion of a family reunion. Barnes's mother, uncle, and brothers are characterized, as is Barnes herself. It is a play of lust, jealousy, betrayal, and death, written in the style and language of a Jacobean revenge tragedy. Like most Barnes plays, *The Antiphon* baffled many critics, some of whom contended that the play was written "not for acting but primarily for the writer."[30] Certainly, both the subject matter and the struggles of Barnes's life suggest that the play had a cathartic purpose. Yet the play is eminently stageworthy, set in lavish detail among the ruins of Burley Hall. The discomfort that critics feel with the play is partially explained by Anne B. Dalton: "By writing about father-daughter molestation instead of the daughter's desire to seduce the father, and by portraying the father as the violator, Djuna was radically challenging the culture order of her time and ours."[31] Even more shocking, and perhaps less comprehensible to the critics, was Barnes's frank portrayal of the mother who both envied and betrayed her daughter.

Miranda, the play's protagonist, is a middle-aged woman who has been sexually victimized as a young woman by both her father and her brothers. The action of the play is the exposure, not only of the incest-laden past, but also of the complicity of the mother, Augusta, in allowing the rapes to occur. Fueled by a jealous need to live through her daughter while simultaneously condemning her, Augusta taunts her daughter by demanding, "Is it true that you had forty lovers?" while attiring herself in Miranda's rings, hat, and shoes.[32] Blaming Miranda for the loss of her sons' love, Augusta ends the play by killing her daughter with a blow from the ringing curfew bell.

Championed by Edwin Muir, T. S. Eliot, and Dag Hammarskjold, *The Antiphon* finally realized a full production at Sweden's Royal Dramatic Theatre in 1961. Though the play was a huge success translated into Swedish, it has never received a major production in English. Treated like royalty by the Swedish producers, Barnes continued to remain an enigma to the American dramatic critics. Estranged from her family, Barnes's final years were spent in the company of an increasingly smaller group of friends and literary acquaintances. Despite the fact that much of her writing had been devoted to purging the taboo sexuality that formed both her personality and her artistry, Barnes remained secretive and bitter about the facts of her life. Throughout her life, she had been caught in the double bind of needing to express her inner truth, yet also needing to disguise the reality of her formative sexual experiences. The resulting body of literature gives testimony to the complex, and often shocking, reality of Barnes's life. In a day and age when sexuality was rarely discussed openly, Barnes used difficult language, subtle innuendo, and artistic genius to both reveal and protect the secrets of her life. In choosing to write for the theater, Barnes acknowledged the theater's ability to communicate in words as well as by other means.

To Barnes's credit, she never relinquished her own idealistic vision of what art, and the theater, could and should be. There is a touch of bitterness in her reflections on what had become of the Provincetown Players, and the theater world, she had once admired:

The things that produced the Provincetown Players and made the group what it was, had not made them what they are. Therefore, we hear much talk of "lost atmosphere." People speak of those early days as if they were some sort of collar stud which, by diabolical mischance, had been mislaid by the injustice of God.

The French are otherwise. They, too, to be sure, are idealistic in youth; but they are also idealistic in age. They do not speak of the days "when." In their lives there is no mislaid stud of enthusiasm. They have, with the peculiarly economical spirit of their race, kept their stud where they can, at any moment, lay their hands on it. It is perhaps not the bright stud it used to be, it is indeed a little dulled, but it will be found in their dress shirt when they are laid out for their grave.[33]

For Barnes, France would always be the place of infinite possibility, where one could be whomever one chose to be. In Paris, Djuna achieved great passion, great friendships, and great literary success. There, she could walk hand in hand down the street with her woman lover, discuss literature with James Joyce, and be admired both as a woman and as a writer. By contrast, America, with its puritanical double standards, inelegant streets, and capitalist mentality, offered little idealism. One might view her later denial of friends, lovers, alcohol, and cigarettes, as well as her total dedication to eight hours of writing a day, as Barnes's attempt to create and control a world of her own making, one in which the true artist stands supreme and alone. She continued to write for the theater, regardless of whether or not her plays were produced. Like the French she so admired, Djuna Barnes chose to go to her grave with her collar stud firmly in place, never succumbing to the pressures of tawdry commercialism or fawning admirers.

NOTES

1. There are two unpublished full-length plays, *The Biography of Julie von Bartmann* and *Anna Portuguise,* both available in manuscript at the Barnes Collection, University of Maryland.

2. Letter to Natalie Barney dated May 31, 1963, Barnes Collection.

3. Djuna Barnes, "Playgoer's Almanac," *Theatre Guild,* January 1931, 34.

4. Mary Lynn Broe, "My Art Belongs to Daddy: Incest as Exile: The Textual Economics of Hayford Hall," in *Women Writers in Exile,* ed. Broe and Angela Ingram (Chapel Hill: University of North Carolina Press, 1989), 53. Phillip Herring, *Djuna: The Life and Times of Djuna Barnes* (New York: Penguin, 1995),

suggests that these letters be read as evidence of "good-natured fondling" and Zadel's attempt to make Djuna comfortable with her sexuality, regardless of what direction it took.

5. Herring, *Djuna*, 156.

6. Shari Benstock, *Women of the Left Bank: Paris, 1900–1940* (Austin: University of Texas Press, 1986), 258.

7. Judith Schwartz, *Radical Feminists of Heterodoxy: Greenwich Village, 1912–1940* (Norwich, VT: New Victoria Publishers, 1986), 75.

8. Herring, *Djuna*, 59.

9. Jan McDonald, *The New Drama, 1900–1914* (London: Macmillan, 1986), 1.

10. Robert Karoly Sarlos, *Jig Cook and the Provincetown Players* (Amherst: University of Massachusetts Press, 1982), 106–7.

11. Djuna Barnes, "The Songs of Synge. . . ," *New York Morning Telegraph Sunday Magazine,* February 18, 1917, 8.

12. Djuna Barnes, "Playgoer's Almanac," *Theatre Guild,* February 1931, 35.

13. Djuna Barnes, "Alla Nazimova, One of the Greatest of Living Actresses, Talks of Her Art," *Theatre Guild,* June 1930, 32.

14. Djuna Barnes, "Playgoer's Almanac," *Theatre Guild,* March 1931, 34.

15. Emily Coleman, letter to Djuna Barnes, October 27, 1935, Barnes Collection.

16. Benstock, *Women of Left Bank,* 245.

17. Hutchins Hapgood, *A Victorian in a Modern World* (New York: Harcourt, Brace, 1939), 393.

18. Djuna Barnes, letter to Natalie Barney, October 16, 1963, Barnes Collection.

19. S. J. Kaufmann, "Djuna Barnes Arrives," *New York Globe and Commercial Advertiser,* November 3, 1919, 22.

20. Alexander Woollcott, "Second Thoughts on First Nights: The Provincetown Plays," *New York Times,* November 9, 1919, sec. 8, p. 2.

21. Rebecca Drucker, "As We Were Saying," *New York Tribune,* November 16, 1919, 7.

22. *Smith College Weekly,* November 11, 1925.

23. Djuna Barnes, *The Dove,* in *A Book* (New York: Boni and Liveright, 1923), 147.

24. Barnes, *The Dove,* 155–56.

25. Barnes, *The Dove,* 161.

26. *New York Evening Post,* May 7, 1926, 14.

27. "And Yet Again: The Bayes Still Scene of One-Act Plays," *New York Sun,* May 7, 1926, 26.

28. Benstock, *Women of Left Bank,* 257.

29. Herring, *Djuna,* 249.

30. Louis F. Kennenstine, *The Art of Djuna Barnes: Duality and Damnation* (New York: New York University Press, 1977), 154.

31. Anne B. Dalton, "Escaping From Eden: Djuna Barnes' Revision of Psychoanalytic Theory and Her Treatment of Father-Daughter Incest in Ryder," *Women's Studies* 21 (March 1993): 164.

32. Djuna Barnes, *The Antiphon* (London: Faber and Faber, 1958), 110.

33. Djuna Barnes, "The Days of Jig Cook; Recollections of Ancient Theatre History but Ten Years Old," *Theatre Guild,* January 1923, 31.

George Kelly, American Playwright

Characters in the Hands of an Angry God

Billy J. Harbin

George Kelly (1887–1974) became one of America's most distinguished playwrights in the 1920s with *The Torch Bearers* (1922), *The Show-Off* (1924), and *Craig's Wife* (1925), for which he gained the Pulitzer Prize in 1926. Additional plays by Kelly continued to appear on Broadway throughout the next two decades, his last, *The Fatal Weakness,* in 1946. Although his best plays of the twenties have appeared on American stages for more than seventy years, critical assessments of Kelly's work virtually expired with his last produced play. Foster Hirsch's study of Kelly's plays, published in 1975, remains the only exception.[1] Hirsch offers a perceptive analysis of Kelly's craft and art, but he chooses not to consider two complex influences at work in Kelly's plays, and these are the focus of this essay: Kelly's rigid Irish Catholic upbringing, overseen by the stringent tutoring and domineering presence of his mother, Mary Kelly, and, secondly, his homosexuality.

Born in Ireland, Mary Costello (1852–1926) had come to America at the age of thirteen, married at seventeen John Henry Kelly, an Irish laborer, and gave birth to ten children (six boys) between 1872 and 1894. Some of the children left school in the fourth grade; none went beyond the eighth. One by one as they reached the employable age of nine, they went to work in the Dobson Carpet Mills, which employed and exploited the large Irish Catholic settlement in the Falls of Schuylkill area of Philadelphia.[2] Yet each of Mary Kelly's five sons (one had died at the age of ten) in adulthood achieved fame and fortune, three of them (Patrick, Charles, and John) in the construction business,[3] and two (Walter and George) in the theater. The Kellys, a family reared in poverty and with scant education, had become in the first quarter of the twentieth century one of the notable families of Philadelphia.

In an interview for *American* magazine (in 1925, one year before her death), Mary Kelly talked about her need to assume matriarchal roles of "doctor, nurse, preacher, and teacher," as the family moved through hard times. She emerges in the interview as a mother who allowed neither discussion nor debate about her rules, authority, or judgment; they were not negotiable: "I laid down the code of justice in the family; and I was the policeman that kept order, and the jury that decided the cases, and the judge that handed out the punishment." She also preached to her children, "There're always some folks that won't do their share—and there're always some that do two shares.[4] Mary Kelly clearly did "two shares," while her husband, "whose life she dominated until a heart attack leveled him in 1917," accepted a passive role, becoming a marginal household figure.[5] Unsentimental, stern in manner, she found it difficult, perhaps a sign of weakness, to be physically demonstrative; she disliked emotional display.[6]

But in biographical accounts Mary Kelly emerges, too, as an individual of uncommon intelligence and ambition.[7] With virtually no formal education, she was schooled instead by priests in the moral teachings of the Catholic Church and by herself (as an obsessive, voracious reader) in literature and politics: "I never stopped reading and studying! I've stood by the stove hundreds of times, a baby under my left arm and a book in my left hand, while I made pancakes with my right one. . . . I've sat at my sewing machine, with a cradle beside me, and a newspaper hung in front of me."[8] In the Irish Catholic settlement of the Falls of Schuylkill, the Kellys were poor and worked in the mills like everyone else, said a neighbor, but "they read . . . that's what set them apart; they were different."[9] Mary Kelly's stringent Catholicism and intellectual curiosity influenced all of her children, but only George left plays as his testaments, and these documents reveal how profoundly his mother's dominant presence and teachings affected him and his art.

George Edward Kelly, the ninth of the ten children, quit school in the fourth grade to work in the mills. In young adulthood, he worked for the Pencoyd Iron Works, learning to be a draftsman, but he longed to go on the stage, and "all his spare time was spent in reading and studying to fit himself for it."[10] His mother explained: "He would come into the house . . . snatch the cloth from the table, throw it around his shoulders and stalk up and down the room, acting a scene from some play or other." He stayed on at the ironworks, but he was unhappy, and his mother finally asked him what he wanted to do with his future. "Go on the stage," he replied. After taking a night course in "dramatic art" at a local school, he resigned his job and went to New York.[11] George's older brother, Walter, had gone into vaudeville at the turn of the century, became a headliner by 1905 as a monologist (known as "the Virginia Judge"), and toured abroad.[12] Undoubtedly, his brother's example as an international vaudeville star encouraged George to view the stage both as an escape route from home and as an adventurous future career for himself.

In 1910, Kelly secured an acting job in a touring production of *East Lynne,* and from 1911 to 1914, he performed leading roles in national touring companies of *The Virginian, Live Wires,* and *The Common Law.* In 1915, Kelly entered vaudeville, acting in Paul Armstrong's sentimental one-act sketch, *Woman Proposes.*[13] In the following year, after becoming dissatisfied with the contrived conventions of available vaudeville sketches, he began to write his own material.

Comedy sketches first began to appear in vaudeville in 1873 and dramatic sketches in 1890; by 1896 one-act sketches had become a conventional part of an evening's bill. Since most of the acts on the bill were specialty pieces presented "in one" (an area downstage in front of the curtain), sketches "broke up the monotony" because they used the full stage. Sketches were essentially miniature plays, staged with actors, furniture, and props.[14] Although respected authors such as David Belasco, Arthur Hopkins, George M. Cohan, and J. M. Barrie wrote pieces that were performed in vaudeville (often acted by headliners or stars), hundreds of sketches that fed the vaudeville circuits throughout the country were written by less skilled authors according to a generic formula. Joe Laurie Jr. includes the following types of sketches as among the most popular: "The Man and Woman Act," "The School Act," "The Double Dutch Act," "The Double Wop Act," "The Straight and the Jew," and "The Double Blackface Act."[15] George Kelly's early sketches departed from the conventional by addressing moral questions through the depiction of unexaggerated, average characters in a middle-class, realistic environment. Kelly rejected any temptation to gain attention through startling melodramatic or farcical effects. It is remarkable that at this initial stage of his writing career, Kelly's artistic choices came out of a conscious view of what he wanted his art to be. Kelly stated in an interview in 1927, "I kept my integrity . . . because in my sketches I never wrote down to the vaudeville audiences. I never made any cheap appeals to laughter or pathos. I never compromised."[16]

For his first one-act sketch, *Finders Keepers* (1916), Kelly created the role of the righteous husband, Eugene Aldrid, for himself. Aldrid challenges the moral transgression of his wife, who refuses to return to its rightful owner a purse she found containing four hundred dollars. In a dramatic pattern that came to characterize his art, Kelly created the male role to reflect innocence, moral strength, and generosity of spirit, and the female, to depict, on the contrary, a deceitful Eve in a domestic Eden. Aldrid confronts his wife and sees that justice prevails.[17] The domestic realism of the middle-class setting, the unsentimental, even cynical, depiction of a marital relationship, and the humorless, moral passion at work in the plot all signify the playwright's refusal to play down to vaudeville audiences and present, as well, motifs that will dominate his future work.

After acting successfully in *Finders Keepers* for two seasons on the Keith circuit, Kelly went into the army in 1917; discharged a year later, he returned to vaudeville and resumed writing and performing one-act sketches. Kelly had by now been away from the scrutiny and instruction of his mother and her church for eight years, trouping in vaudeville houses across the country, meeting, working, and socializing with a diverse population of theater folk, refined and vulgar, sophisticated artists and knockabout tumblers, who represented myriad religious and antireligious views, ethnic origins, educational and social backgrounds, and sexual proclivities. His plays reveal, from vaudeville (1916–22) to the Broadway years (1922–46), that while the moral fervency of his childhood instruction found voice in his works, an equally influential education from his vaudeville, social, and emotional experiences shifted and matured his perspectives, altering his view of himself and his art.

In his biography of the Kelly family, Arthur H. Lewis identifies George Kelly as homosexual on the basis of interviews with George's nephew Charles, among other evidence.[18] It is reasonable to assume that his initial sexual experiences with other males took place after he went into show business. "Historically," argues Laurence Senelick, "the theater has been a safe-house for unconventional behavior. Although its public nature has required it to endorse norms, its space is specially licensed to harbor unorthodox individuals and otherwise inadmissible conduct."[19]

In *The Virginian*, Kelly played the heroic title role, "an illiterate, big-souled cowpuncher," who woos and wins a puritanical, refined, eastern schoolteacher. Foster Hirsch claims that the role of the heroine is "closer to the Kelly persona" than the rough cowboy.[20] The roles Kelly began writing for himself in vaudeville support Hirsch's assessment. The dispassionate, scrupulously moral husband in *Finders Keepers* and the free-thinking, fastidiously groomed actor in *The Flattering Word* (1918) suggest that Kelly's view of himself had been shaped not only by the moral righteousness of his mother's teachings but by his artistic and emotional experiences in vaudeville.

Erving Goffman argues that those who wish to conceal a taboo identity may "present the signs of their stigmatized failing as the signs of another attribute, one that is less significantly a stigma."[21] With himself in mind as the model, Kelly created the role of the actor, Eugene Tesh, in *The Flattering Word*, knowing that he would perform it on the Keith circuit. He could depict Tesh's chosen bachelorhood, dandified costume, and histrionic gestures without risking an identity with himself. The play also indicates that Kelly, after nearly a decade in vaudeville, has turned away from the strictures of his Irish Catholic religion and found liberation in the more permissive world of the arts. Kelly's description of Tesh offers a reasonably accurate portrait of Kelly himself; it is, in fact, remarkably similar to his appearance in the 1924 photograph that illustrates this essay:

> He is tall and thin,—has a lot of soft-looking black hair and is rather austerely pale; [he exhibits] a certain charm of manner, and the suggestion of a twinkle in his eye. He wears a long, beautifully tailored coat of excellent black, with a high rolling collar; and, under it, a perfectly cut, double-breasted sack suit of the same material. He is quietly gloved and spatted; wears a gorgeous shawl scarf of steel-blue silk around his neck, and carries a snakewood cane, tipped with silver.[22]

Tesh, performing an engagement in Youngstown, stops by to say hello to an old school chum, Mary, now married to a pastor who, Tesh discovers, is strongly opposed to the theater. Tesh (i.e., Kelly) argues to the pastor that religion can foster intolerance in the guise of righteousness, but the theater has the power to enlighten closed minds. Already, at the beginning of Kelly's writing career, the theater has become his church and the script, his pulpit.

Kelly's unconventional one-act sketches deeply impressed Rosalie Stewart, who ran a vaudeville booking agency in New York. In 1918, she took over Kelly's career as his agent and producer, soon becoming, next to his mother, the most influential female in his life and career. Stewart believed that Kelly had exceptional potential as a developing writer, not only for vaudeville but for the legitimate stage, and she urged him to expand his sketch, *Mrs. Ritter Returns* (1916), into a full-length play.[23] This resulted in *The Torch Bearers* (1922), which marked Kelly's Broadway debut as playwright. He then developed another sketch, *Poor Aubrey* (1919), into *The Show-Off* (1924), and in the next year *Craig's Wife* established him as one of America's foremost dramatists (see fig. 5).[24]

Rosalie Stewart, to whom Kelly entrusted all business and managerial matters, produced all of his plays throughout the period of his best achievements, the decade of the 1920s. She relocated to Hollywood in 1932, became notable in the industry for her development of screenwriters, and sold at least four of Kelly's plays to film studios (*The Torch Bearers, The Show-Off, Craig's Wife,* and *Behold the Bridegroom*). She probably influenced Kelly to sign with Metro-Goldwyn-Mayer as a screenwriter in 1931. He had become disenchanted and angered by the New York failures of his plays *Maggie the Magnificent* (1929) and *Philip Goes Forth* (1931) and was ready to look creatively in other directions. Kelly worked as a consultant for several films, but "they weren't anything he wanted to put his name to." Ultimately, he received screen credit only for the 1935 film *Old Hutch,* which starred Wallace Beery.[25] Never happy with Hollywood's use of writers, after the completion of the Beery project Kelly left MGM to return to Broadway with his play *Reflected Glory* (1936). Hirsch accurately observes that Kelly's studio fate was similar "to that of other established writers imported to Hollywood in the 1930s" in that the uniqueness of his writing, which is why the studio hired him in the first place, "was never translated intact to the screen."[26]

Kelly and Stewart's professional and personal relationship, based upon mutual trust and respect, endured for over half a century. An articulate, confident, and successful woman in a man's business world, Rosalie Stewart, like Kelly, apparently had no interest in marriage, nor in presenting the conventional feminine image of delicacy or vulnerability. She smoked cigarettes, drank daiquiris, and could hold her own in conversation with anyone in the business, including cynical reporters.[27] Journalists seemed surprised to discover that she made good sense: "She talks differently from most women. . . . What she says, she knows."[28] An interviewer described her as an "out-spoken and matter-of-fact" woman, who "spells efficiency from the direct way she looks at you through her platinum chained pince-nez glasses to the tailored cut of her smart dark wool street clothes."[29] Her friends and traveling companions were women in the profession, such as Patricia Collinge and Pauline Lord.

Stewart's astute managerial skills nurtured Kelly's professional career, and her loyalty and services to him continued until she died in

FIG. 5. George Kelly and Rosalie Stewart on December 10,
1924, docking in New York upon return from producing *The
Show-Off* in London.

*(Courtesy, Billy Rose Theatre Collection, New York Public Library for
the Performing Arts.)*

1971. Even through the last decade of Kelly's life in California, and the
final few years of her own, Stewart entertained him and his companion,
William E. Weagly, made his travel reservations, and provided him the
services of her own secretary.[30] "Rosalie Stewart," Kelly confided in his
late years, "was a woman of great integrity. During all the years she rep-

resented me and produced my plays, we never had a contract in writing, merely her word and mine."[31]

George Kelly and William E. Weagly (1896–1975) probably became lifetime partners in the mid-1920s, although one source suggests that they may have met as early as 1919.[32] Weagly, nine years younger than Kelly, may have been a bellhop at New York's Concord Hotel, when Kelly, who had a suite there, presumably chose him privately as his lover and publicly as his valet/secretary/traveling companion.[33] Weagly, "slightly built, plain-looking [and] unsophisticated,"[34] became schooled by Kelly in the social graces (which Kelly himself had learned from others after leaving home), and he carried out myriad services to assist Kelly, including cooking and typing.

"The Kellys," observed a member of the family, "are essentially righteous, puritanical, moral people," who "are always [pronouncing] moral judgments."[35] George's Philadelphia family, after his mother died in 1926, consisted of his several siblings and their extended families. His older brothers Patrick and John had become wealthy building contractors, renowned throughout Philadelphia for their civic leadership and as inspirational representatives of second-generation immigrant Irish-Catholics who through intelligence and initiative had successfully exploited their American opportunities. George did not have a close relationship with any of his brothers, but he regularly returned to Philadelphia for family visits throughout his life; he was especially fond of his nieces (and later of his great nieces and nephews).

The Philadelphia Kellys refused to recognize Weagly's relationship with George Kelly as anything other than employee/employer. Lewis claims that when George and William Weagly visited in Philadelphia, Weagly was treated not as a guest but as George's valet/secretary, and he "ate in the kitchen with the hired help or didn't eat at all."[36] John Cain, a childhood neighbor and longtime friend of George Kelly, recalled, "When [George] came to Philadelphia . . . Weagly was passed off as [his] valet; the family would not accept him in any other way. That was in Philadelphia. Elsewhere, it was different."[37] All available evidence indicates that George Kelly acquiesced throughout his life to the Kelly family's judgmental treatment of Weagly. Presumably, George had a puritanical fear of scandal and of offending social propriety, as well as an inbred inability to challenge the Kellys' rules on their own turf.

Lewis, perhaps on the basis of John Cain's statement, argues that Kelly when away from his Philadelphia family made his own rules and controlled the observance of them: "Even though he may have prepared the meal, Bill Weagly's place [in their own home], regardless of who was present, was that of co-host, his seat at one end of the table." When they were invited out, Kelly expected Weagly "to be accepted as a social equal."[38] If members of the Kelly family visited George in California, they were expected to accept Weagly as a cohost; some accepted the conditions, others stayed away.[39]

However, from my interviews with a Kelly family member who spent considerable time with George Kelly (and who requested anonymity), I believe that Lewis's view of Kelly and Weagly as equal partners away from Philadelphia does not sufficiently suggest the ambiguities of their relationship. Like all intimate and lifetime relationships, theirs was profoundly complex, and it became even more enigmatic over the years as they both grew older, living many decades with the necessity for a public disguise of their private selves. My family source visited with George Kelly in California, in Philadelphia, and in Monaco on trips to see George's niece, Princess Grace, and believes that while George Kelly and William E. Weagly may have had a passionate relationship in their early years, in their older years, and as Kelly's celebrity and artistic demands diminished, the playwright shifted back to his Irish Catholic roots and increasingly became devoted to aesthetic and philosophic studies, intellectual pursuits in which Weagly could not participate.[40] John Cain observed: "Weagly was a very quiet fellow; nothing special about him and I don't know what the hell they talked about all those years. Bill was not intelligent; actually he was George Kelly's shadow."[41] By their late years, Weagly had become a marginal domestic figure, with Kelly very much the master of the household.[42] When Foster Hirsch interviewed Kelly in his Sun City, California, home in 1971, Weagly appeared briefly in the kitchen doorway, wearing an apron. Kelly ignored his presence and did not introduce him to Hirsch.[43] Dan McCormick, another childhood friend from the Falls, claimed, "When George came to Philadelphia and bought a house up in Mount Airy [an area adjacent to the Falls] John [Cain] and I would go there for dinner. Weagly would cook, come in and say 'hello,' then disappear upstairs. He never participated in our talks."[44] The evolution of Kelly and Weagly's private relationship from one of equity in the passion of their young manhood to inequity in their older years was not unlike the history of Mary Kelly's relationship with her husband.

Arthur Lewis suggests that George Kelly's homosexuality influenced his judgmental depiction of women, whose various sins against males or social codes permit him to condemn them. Lewis cites Joseph Wood

Krutch's critical essay on Kelly for support:[45] "Hate seems to be the real source of [Kelly's] inspiration, and one is almost inclined to suspect that behind the harshness of his attitude [toward his female characters] lies some personal experience which would have to be known before one could entirely understand [his] vehemence."[46]

One could argue that Kelly's public presentation of himself in his plays as artistic guardian of social morals and manners conflicted with his private homoerotic behavior or self-identity. Keeping his public mask in place required vigilance, and perhaps the necessity for doing so generated resentment that found release in his art through an austere judgment of his wayward female characters. Nevertheless, perhaps the most dominant influence upon his perception of females came from his Irish Catholic mother, who emasculated her husband throughout his lifetime, wielded absolute control over her children, and, in her late years, took pride in her stringent tutoring and public credit for her children's success. Mary Kelly, struggling to find some identity for herself, beyond the incessant couplings that produced child after child with a man whom she did not love, claimed the role of a ruling matriarch, with ten children to mold who would "respect me as their superior."[47] In an interview with Mary Kelly, the interviewer reports: "That she did make them what they are, not one of them would deny. . . . She would not deny it herself! She *knows* that she has been the most powerful factor in molding their lives."[48]

Women do not come off well in Kelly's first full-length play. *The Torch Bearers* satirizes the artistic pretentiousness that Kelly believed had begun to dominate the little-theater movement. He condemns those community members (primarily women) who love being *in* the art but have no knowledge of the art itself. They more profitably should be tending their husbands and homes. Kelly views these untalented dabblers, who take to the stage to gratify vanity, as sinners against both art and the home. But, in a moral stance that he was to assume in virtually all of his plays, his aloof condemnation of the naive players seems to exceed their crime. Kelly's nephew observed, "My Uncle George always *said* [of his aims in his works], 'I am not the judge . . . and I am not the law giver'" (expressing a negative version of his mother's own declarations). But, actually, "In all his plays," he is saying, "This is right; this is wrong; this is true; this is false; this is good; this is bad."[49] In art and in life, Kelly increasingly developed an austere, judgmental voice that seemed to replicate the stringent pronouncements of his mother, who "laid down the code of justice in the family" in the Falls of Schuylkill.[50]

Kelly's passion for guarding the theater arts from the tampering of pretentious pseudoartists found expression again in *Philip Goes Forth* (1931), his lecture to the untalented who "clutter the theatrical marketplace" rather than remain home to do the work for which they are qualified.[51] Young Philip Eldridge's romantic, delusional quest for success as a playwright is contrasted with the practical reality of his father's business world, where Philip's actual talents belong. Ultimately, his eyes are opened, his lesson is learned, and he returns to his father's firm. Critics distrusted Kelly's solemn sermon about a young man's exploration of his talents. Perhaps Kelly "intended to write about [a spiritual] 'going forth,'" but he failed to develop a protagonist of sufficient complexity to carry the theme.[52] Kelly's portrait of the confused young male, less harsh and more forgiving than his treatment of the ludicrous females in *The Torch Bearers,* demonstrates, some critics suggested, the playwright's gender bias.[53]

Reflected Glory (1936), the last of Kelly's plays about the theater, featured Tallulah Bankhead in her first major New York role, that of an actress torn between choosing a career and marriage. Muriel Flood, acclaimed in her art, longs also to fulfill herself in more conventional ways through marriage and children; ultimately, she realizes her acting gifts are responsibilities that she must bear, even at the sacrifice of romance. Muriel Flood is depicted sympathetically, but the male characters become marginalized as merely stereotypical suitors for Muriel's hand. It can be argued that Kelly's uncommon reversal in gender bias permits Muriel to represent himself in disguise, and the play serves to justify his own rejection of society's conventions (courtship, marriage, children) in favor of his art. Kelly uses Muriel Flood as a character through whom he may address issues of marriage and art without putting his own male persona at risk. Muriel confesses that she may not be "temperamentally suited" to marriage; a suitor replies that "there never was a woman in the world that wasn't temperamentally suited to marriage," but "there might be certain types of men."[54] Throughout his lifetime, Kelly was questioned about his chosen bachelorhood; his usual reply was given for the last time in 1967, when he was eighty: "I always felt I was temperamentally unsuited to marriage," virtually the same line that he had written for Muriel Flood more than thirty years previously.[55]

In *The Show-Off* (1924), Kelly began his dramatic explorations of the postwar generation, an increasing concern that found expression again in *Craig's Wife* (1925) and *Behold the Bridegroom* (1927). *The Show-Off* opened on Broadway on February 5, 1924, and was one of 196 plays in a

season that included premieres of Molnar's *The Swan;* Kaufman and
Connelly's *Beggar on Horseback,* Sutton Vane's *Outward Bound;*
Hatcher Hughes's *Hell-Bent for Heaven;* Eugene O'Neill's *Welded;* and
the Marx Brothers in *I'll Say She Is.* Other notable presentations of the
season included the Moscow Art Theatre in a repeat visit from the previous year; Eleonora Duse's final appearance in New York in *The Lady
from the Sea* (she died on this American tour later in Pittsburgh); Julia
Marlowe and E. H. Sothern in *Cymbeline;* Walter Hampden's *Cyrano de
Bergerac;* John Barrymore's *Hamlet;* Jane Cowl in Maeterlinck's *Pelleas
and Melisande* and Shakespeare's *Romeo and Juliet;* and the Theatre
Guild's production of *Saint Joan.*[56]

Named above are less than 20 productions, and the season included
more than 175 in addition. Among those were Vincent Lawrence's *Two
Fellows and a Girl* and *In Love with Love;* Myron C. Fagan's *Thumbs
Down;* Barry Conners's *The Mad Honeymoon;* Aaron Hoffman's *The
Good Old Days;* Harlan Thompson's *Little Jesse James;* Edward Laska's
Red Light Annie; Edward Childs Carpenter's *Connie Goes Home;* St.
John Ervine's *Mary, Mary, Quite Contrary;* Guy Bolton's *Chicken Feed;*
Winslow and Nyitray's *What's Your Wife Doing?* Sydney Rosenfeld's
Virginia Runs Away; and Lynn Starling's *Meet the Wife.* The list goes on
to include another 150 plays for the season. Thus, Broadway in the
decade of the 1920s, and even into the 1930s, presented nearly 200 plays
every season, a typical Broadway context in which Kelly presented his
works throughout his early career. That *The Show-Off, The Torch Bearers,* and *Craig's Wife* were singled out of a vast sea of plays to become
critical and popular successes testifies to the new playwright's unique
achievements as an emerging American dramatist of the first rank. *The
Show-Off* actually "won the vote of the Pulitzer Prize play jury for first
place," but the decision "was reversed by the advisory board," and the
award went to Hatcher Hughes for *Hell-Bent for Heaven.*[57]

Kelly's *The Show-Off* presents the domestic relationships of a middle-class Philadelphia suburban family, the Fishers. But Kelly's unsentimental, hard-edged appraisal of the setting and the characters prevents
the play from becoming merely another conventional Broadway domestic comedy. Kelly created two of his finest original characters for the play:
Aubrey Piper, a show-off braggart, liar, and buffoon, who drifts and
blusters through life, expecting fortune to drop in his lap; and Piper's
adversary, Mrs. Fisher (Kelly's memorable tribute to Mary Kelly), a
hardworking, no-nonsense, bluntly honest matriarch, who dominates the
household. Her contemptuous view of Piper (as well as, sometimes, of

her own two daughters) provides a moral commentary on the floundering, self-centered generation that wants something for nothing. The postwar youth represent, as Mary Kelly once said, "folks that won't do their share." They seek to profit from the labors of others. Essentially, the play is about Aubrey's struggle with the Fishers to maneuver his way into the family through marriage and make their home his home. By the play's end, he has succeeded, despite Mrs. Fisher's resistance; the younger generation push aside the older, taking possession of the space earned by others. The plot echoes Mary Kelly's lectures to her children in the Falls: "I taught them that 'tis not right to live on other people's labor; but that everybody ought to help earn what he gets."[58]

In the following year Kelly's award-winning play, *Craig's Wife*, brought him eminent respectability as a dramatist, but the unrelieved harshness of his depiction of the deceptive, predatory Harriet Craig, led critics, such as Joseph Wood Krutch, to raise questions about his gender bias, as well as his stringent moral judgments. In Kelly's plays, women invariably find suitable (often economic) places for themselves in marriage, but virtually never do they marry for love, and their generous-spirited, guileless husbands become easily duped by them. Walter in *Craig's Wife* provides a major example of an ideal Kelly male character; never worldly-wise, Kelly's vulnerable males become easy prey to cynical, dominant females. Harriet has married the morally responsible, financially successful Walter Craig for economic security and the possession of his beautiful home. Her design to gain absolute control of him and the household goes awry when Walter ultimately confronts her lies and deceptions. Kelly later claimed that he depicted Harriet as "the modern woman," who, faced with the realities of getting ahead in the world, has dropped any romantic notions about men and is now cynically regarding "marriage as a means of insuring . . . food, shelter, and clothes."[59] Kelly saw her as representative of the reckless and irresponsible postwar generation, who sought material comforts at the cost of others; furthermore, she typified for him the increasingly aggressive and invasive females of the new age, who were beginning to claim equitable places for themselves in all areas of social conduct, including the job market. *Craig's Wife*, originally subtitled, *A Drama of the Changing Social Order*, reflects Kelly's alarm and anger at what he perceives as a moral erosion of American (patriarchal) values.

Behold the Bridegroom (1927) continues Kelly's assessment of the postwar era and represents his view of human conduct at its most judgmental. The play depicts, as Joseph Wood Krutch noted, a Puritan sense of justice in which "the damned must be given one glimpse of paradise before they are plunged into hell forever."[60] Antoinette Lyle, a spoiled, morally adrift young woman of the licentious jazz age, has lived a loose life of pleasures and affairs, when she meets and falls in love with Spencer Train, an innocent, morally righteous, young man. But having "wasted her capacities on cheap loves, she was not ready when the bridegroom came," and has forfeited her right to unite with him.[61] Kelly, unwilling to soften his contempt for the hedonistic morality of the 1920s, permits no opportunity for the heroine's pardon or atonement. Self-condemned, she falls into sickness and dies, unable to redeem herself from past sins.

In his plays, Kelly often demonstrates less interest in exploring the complexities and ambiguities of human behavior than in identifying sins of omission or commission and passing sentence upon them. The playwright said in an interview in 1971 (at the age of eighty-four) that he wrote *Behold the Bridegroom* to demonstrate "the inevitability of the returning tide."[62] The unrelieved severity of Kelly's damnation of his wayward protagonist calls to mind Puritan Jonathan Edwards's fiery, hell-and-brimstone sermon from the eighteenth century, "Sinners in the Hands of an Angry God." Edwards meant to terrorize his congregation into seeking forgiveness and redemption; Kelly's sermon, however, permits no potential for reformation. Kelly's insistent, missionary zeal to advocate certitudes for behavior morally, socially, and legally beyond reproach, behavior that he as a sexual alien was at odds with (either in practice or in self-identity), raises the question of whether, even unconsciously, he employed his art to some extent to deflect public homophobic suspicions of his private sexual persona.

In *Daisy Mayme* (1926), Kelly developed variations upon major themes established in his previous plays: the opportunistic female predator versus the innocent and generous spirited male; the struggle for possessing a house, for displacing the rightful owner, who has earned the space; and the Mary Kelly maxim that there are always some people who "let the willing horse pull the load."[63] In this play, the predatory female, Laura Fenner, is sister to the head of the household, bachelor Cliff Ettinger; the brother and sister situation in the plot reflects Mary Kelly's testament to her children: Cliff is the one who has always done two shares in looking after family members. A Kelly ideal male, Cliff is morally decent, financially successful through his own labors, and responsible to others. Laura Fenner intends to keep Cliff from marrying so that she may eventually become the head of his handsome household, but she fails when Daisy Mayme visits Cliff and his niece-ward May, the daughter of Cliff's recently deceased sister, Lydy. Daisy, one of Kelly's most humane female creations, conveys a natural life-force of common sense and humor that challenges Laura's power within the household. In the play's resolution, Daisy and Cliff agree to marry, not because they love each other, but to provide a family home for May and to reject Laura's possessive claims upon the house.

At the close of the 1920s, Joseph Wood Krutch's response to Kelly's play, *Maggie the Magnificent* (1929), that it "commands respect without awaking enthusiasm,"[64] captures in a few words the critical reaction to Kelly's works that persisted throughout the thirties and forties. Kelly's austere, judgmental voice, raised in play after play, began to fall on deaf ears, and he never again in his career equaled the bright promise and remarkable success of his first three plays. Rosalie Stewart tried to persuade him to broaden his subject matter and soften his acerbic treatment of plot and character. In particular, she gave him a number of themes to consider, but he rejected any notion that he needed to make his work more appealing or commercial. He refused to compromise, and he grew bitter that critics and audiences no longer appreciated his plays.[65]

Kelly's last Broadway productions, *The Deep Mrs. Sykes* (1945) and *The Fatal Weakness* (1946), provide his final, cynical explorations of marital relationships. In the former play, father and son remain in loveless marriages out of a socially conditioned sense of duty, although each has loved or does love another woman. *The Fatal Weakness* featured the stylish actress Ina Claire as Mrs. Espenshade, the wife of a man who secretly is having an affair. The wife finds a delusionary romantic fulfillment in attending beautiful weddings of handsome young couples whom she does not know. Kelly suggests that the lovely weddings inevitably lead to disenchantment; monogamous and enduring love between two persons is an elusive ideal, a fantasy. Kelly, of course, could never depict a same-sex relationship in his plays, but his persistent rejection of loving relationships throughout his art, demonstrates his own disbelief in the viability of a committed, lasting relationship between two people, regardless of gender. Undoubtedly, his lifetime need to mask his sexual identity from homophobic detection, his increasingly dispassionate, even sterile, relationship with his companion, and, perhaps, above all, the critical and popular rejection of his plays on Broadway (more or less consistently from 1929 to 1946) contributed to his deepening cynicism.

Although Kelly had little interest in the work of other playwrights, he knew best the plays of Clyde Fitch (1865–1909), whose popular social comedies and dramas in urban settings at the turn of the century made him a national celebrity.[66] Kelly's working-class, Irish Catholic origins influenced his art in other directions than that of the university-educated Fitch, but Kelly recognized in Fitch a kindred spirit. Fitch, like Kelly, managed his plays as a legitimate outlet for his homoerotic persona; both discovered through their art opportunities for expressing secret selves in addressing social, sexual, moral, and artistic issues. Both Kelly and Fitch exerted absolute control over the productions of their plays by insisting upon directing their own work. Finally, both playwrights used rehearsals as apt occasions for displaying feminine behavior in the guise of acting demonstrations for their actresses. (For further discussion of Clyde Fitch, see Kim Marra's essay elsewhere in this volume.) Kelly even demonstrated acting scenes for friends: "he pulled the curtain apart a bit, then the whole curtain, and he walked into the room. He was no longer George Kelly, he was Ina Claire [and he assumed] all the postures of the woman in his play."[67]

Kelly's work as a director began in vaudeville with the staging of his own early pieces. Throughout his career, he directed all of his own plays, which his producer, Rosalie Stewart, fully supported, because Kelly seemed to possess an innate sense of appropriateness in the deployment of actors, settings, costumes, and props. Kelly had "a low opinion of the average director,"[68] and as playwright, he was concerned that directors (after the Broadway run, when the rights became available nationally) would not have the skills to translate his plays to the stage. Consequently, when writing the plays, he maintained control over the material (to the extent that he could), through extensive stage directions and detailed descriptions of the settings and costumes. For example, costumes are scrupulously described in all of his plays, especially for women. But note, too, his precise description (quoted earlier in this essay) for the costume of the male character, Tesh, in *The Flattering Word*. His plays reflect that he was as fastidious in his art as he was known for being in life, and as director he meticulously designed the flow and timing of the stage traffic to reflect the dramatic and comic rhythm of the text. Kelly instructed Helen Lowell, who played Mrs. Fisher in *The Show Off*, "when she was seated in a rocking-chair that, at a certain point, she was to laugh after she had rocked three times . . . Miss Lowell complained to him one evening that the laugh had not gone well with the audience." He replied, " 'That was because you rocked only twice before you laughed.' "[69]

In his final years, Kelly reclaimed his Irish Catholic religion, reflecting perhaps the playwright's reversion to his mother's moral codes that he had in younger years questioned. He reclaimed, too, his Irish Catholic roots in the Falls as one of Mary Kelly's own, as one of the Philadelphia Kellys. George Kelly at the age of eighty-seven, knowing he had not long to live, decided that he wanted to die publicly with his Philadelphia Kelly family and not privately with his companion of a lifetime, William E. Weagly. From California, Kelly took the train east to join the Kellys, leaving Weagly behind in their Sun City home. He died on June 18, 1974, under the care of a Kelly niece. At the Irish Catholic funeral, the Kellys maintained the public decorum they had long demanded of George by excluding his lifetime companion from the family group of mourners. Weagly "sat weeping in a back pew at St. Bridget's."[70]

NOTES

1. Foster Hirsch, *George Kelly* (Boston: Twayne, 1975).

2. William A. McGarry, "Oh, for a Million Mothers Like Mary Kelly!" *American Magazine*, September 1925, 19, 72, 74, 76.

3. Patrick and John, building contractors, erected many significant buildings in the Philadelphia environs in the early twentieth century; Charles was superintendent of construction for his brother Patrick. John, father of actress Grace Kelly, was also famed as a single and doubles sculler champion in the 1920 Olympics.

4. McGarry, "Million Mothers," 19.

5. Arthur H. Lewis, *Those Philadelphia Kellys: With a Touch of Grace* (New York: William Morrow, 1977), 31.

6. Lewis, *Those Philadelphia Kellys*, 90.

7. McGarry, "Million Mothers," 19; Lewis, *Those Philadelphia Kellys*, 30–33.

8. McGarry, "Million Mothers," 19.

9. Lewis, *Those Philadelphia Kellys*, 38.

10. McGarry, "Million Mothers," 76.

11. McGarry, "Million Mothers," 76.

12. Charles Kelly Jr., George's nephew, has said that "Uncle Walter got his start in vaudeville because he was a maverick, wouldn't obey his parents." When he was about twenty-two (in 1895), his parents locked him out of the house because he had not returned by the family curfew of 11 P.M. He then left home and soon entered vaudeville (Lewis, *Those Philadelphia Kellys*, 67). After his success, he reconciled with his parents. George, a more compulsively dutiful son, both resented and envied Walter's ability to walk away from the family; his relationship with his brother remained strained for the rest of their lives.

13. Hirsch, *George Kelly*, 17.

14. Joe Laurie Jr., *Vaudeville: From the Honky-Tonks to the Palace* (New York: Henry Holt, 1953), 48–50.

15. Ibid., 423ff.

16. Stephen Rathbun, "A Playwright-Director," *New York Sun*, December 3, 1927.

17. See George Kelly, *Finders Keepers* (New York: Samuel French, 1916–51, many editions). The play was copyrighted in 1916 as *The Lesson.*

18. Lewis's biography, *Those Philadelphia Kellys,* published in 1977 after the deaths of all of Mary Kelly's children, also discusses George Kelly's relationship with his companion William E. Weagly. Among other references, Lewis quotes Kelly's nephew, Charles: "Uncle George was a homosexual" (124).

19. Laurence Senelick, introduction to *Gender in Performance: The Presentation of Difference in the Performing Arts* (Hanover, N.H.: University Presses of New England, 1992), xi.

20. Hirsch, *George Kelly,* 17–18.

21. Erving Goffman, *Stigma: Notes on the Management of Spoiled Identity* (Englewood Cliffs, N.J.: Prentice-Hall, 1963), 94, 101.

22. George Kelly, *The Flattering Word* (New York: Samuel French, 1918–52, many editions), 13.

23. Lewis, *Those Philadelphia Kellys,* 101.

24. Rosalie Stewart revealed in an interview the production costs of Kelly's first three Broadway plays: *The Torch Bearers,* sixteen thousand dollars; *The Show-Off,* twenty-one thousand dollars; and *Craig's Wife,* twenty-two thousand dollars (Ward Morehouse, "Broadway after Dark," unidentified newspaper clipping, Billy Rose Theatre Collection, New York Public Library of Performing Arts).

25. Hirsch, *George Kelly,* 23.

26. Ibid.

27. Morehouse, "Broadway after Dark."

28. Anonymous author, "Theatre Needs Uniform Admission, Says Rosalie Stewart, Box-Office Portia," *New York Morning Telegraph,* December 5, 1926.

29. Helen Worden, "Unknown Authors Getting the Breaks in Hollywood, Says Rosalie Stewart, Most Successful Film Agent," *New York World Telegram,* n.d., Billy Rose Theatre Collection, New York Public Library for the Performing Arts.

30. Lewis, *Those Philadelphia Kellys,* 99.

31. Ibid.

32. Ibid., 128. Weagly's obituary, which appeared in his hometown newspaper, *Record Herald,* in Waynesboro, Pennsylvania, October 15, 1975, states that Weagly had been "employed by the late George Kelly [who had died in the previous year] as a personal secretary and traveling companion for 34 years." This would date their partnership from 1940, but according to Lewis's interviews with those who knew Kelly, the playwright and Weagly probably met over a decade earlier.

33. Lewis, *Those Philadelphia Kellys,* 126.

34. Ibid., 125.

35. Ibid., 67.

36. Ibid., 126.

37. John Cain, quoted in ibid., 128.

38. Lewis, *Those Philadelphia Kellys,* 126.

39. Ibid.

40. Anonymous Kelly family member, telephone interview with the author, January 9, 1998.

41. John Cain, quoted in Lewis, *Those Philadelphia Kellys,* 128.

42. Anonymous Kelly family member, telephone interview with the author, January 9, 1998.

43. Hirsch, interview with author, April 13, 1996.

44. Dan McCormick, quoted in Lewis, *Those Philadelphia Kellys,* 128–29.

45. Lewis, *Those Philadelphia Kellys,* 110–11.

46. Joseph Wood Krutch, "Drama: George Kelly," *Nation,* November 13, 1929, 564.

47. McGarry, "Million Mothers," 19.

48. McGarry, "Million Mothers," 72.

49. Charles Kelly Jr., quoted in Lewis, *Those Philadelphia Kellys,* 67.

50. McGarry, "Million Mothers," 19. For his biography of the Kelly family, Arthur H. Lewis held extensive interviews with George Kelly's many nieces and nephews, who knew Kelly well. That he could be a controlling martinet in life, as well as judgmental in his plays, is clear from their testimony of experiences (*Those Philadelphia Kellys,* 92–94).

51. Hirsch, *George Kelly,* 96.

52. Francis Fergusson, quoted in Hirsch, *George Kelly,* 97.

53. Hirsch, *George Kelly,* 97.

54. Quoted in ibid., 103.

55. Irving Drutman, "Anybody Here Seen Kelly?" *New York Times,* December 3, 1967. A Kelly family member said, "Tallulah Bankhead said that George Kelly was the only man she ever loved, but he wouldn't marry her" (interview with author, January 9, 1998).

56. Burns Mantle, ed., *The Best Plays of 1923–24, and the Year Book of the Drama in America* (New York: Dodd, Mead, 1942), 1–10.

57. "Professor Kelly Speaks," *Brooklyn Daily Eagle,* October 11, 1936, Billy Rose Theatre Collection, New York Public Library of Performing Arts.

58. McGarry, "Million Mothers," 74.

59. Interview with George Kelly, *Boston Transcript,* October 25, 1962, quoted in Hirsch, *George Kelly,* 62.

60. Krutch, "The Austerity of George Kelly," *Nation,* August 30, 1933, 241.

61. Ibid.

62. Quoted in Hirsch, *George Kelly,* 84.

63. Kelly, *Daisy Mayme* (New York: Samuel French, 1926–54, many editions), 85.

64. Krutch, "Drama: George Kelly," *Nation,* November 13, 1929, 563–64.

65. Anonymous Kelly family member, interview with the author, January 9, 1998.

66. Hirsch, *George Kelly,* 24.

67. Irwin W. Solomon, quoted in Lewis, *Those Philadelphia Kellys,* 97.

68. Stephen Rathbun, "A Playwright-Director," *New York Sun,* December 3, 1927, Billy Rose Theatre Collection, New York Library of Performing Arts.

69. Rathbun, "A Playwright-Director."

70. Lewis, *Those Philadelphia Kellys,* 129.

Let's Do It

The Layered Life of Cole Porter

Mark Fearnow

We have long taken for granted the presence of large numbers of gays and lesbians in the theater as well as in the other arts. Recent scientific research verifies the correspondence between homosexuality and artistic inclination, thus debunking the truism that gays and lesbians are as numerous in other professions as in the arts, but that they are simply more open about themselves in artistic professions and so more visible. The population studies conducted by Yankelovich Partners, Inc., show both a higher than average employment of gays and lesbians in artistic work and a high interest among gay and lesbian subjects in creativity and aesthetics in daily life. The Yankelovich study in some ways justifies a long-standing practice in psychological evaluation in which a "high aesthetic interest" as measured by standardized tests such as the Minnesota Multiphasic Personality Inventory was a primary indicator of homosexual orientation. In the words of brain researcher Simon LeVay in summarizing this aspect of the Yankelovich study, the "blurring of the boundary between life and art is a truly 'gay' characteristic."[1]

A simple organic explanation of this correlation seems unlikely. While the phenomenon of same-sex attraction may well have a basis in genetics, the tendency of gays and lesbians toward the aesthetic is a response to their social situation. Out of their experience of radical otherness comes a compelling need to compensate creatively, to imagine themselves and the world otherwise, to view the world as a kind of theater in which heterosexuals play out roles that might seem natural and automatic but that are really a kind of choreography.

LeVay, who has made his name in science as a researcher in the area of anatomical variance between homosexual and heterosexual subjects, chooses a behavioral explanation, emphasizing the role of the "outsidedness" of the gay child in establishing the tendency to perceive the world and human nature "in layers, as if the screen we call the observable world

FIG. 6. Cole Porter in Hollywood, a few months before his
accident in 1937.

(Courtesy, Theatre Collection, Museum of the City of New York.)

is but one of many screens on which reality plays itself out."[2] The theater
is an obvious corollary to the "screens" theorized by LeVay. The theater's
inherent projection of flexible and various "realities" and its cultivation of
the human capacity for enacted imagination would make it a natural mag-
net for "outsider" children who sense the lack of correlation between their
own feelings and the reality presented them by a heteronormative society.
As have so many other radically "other" children, Cole Porter found in
the theater both a refuge and a playground. LeVay seems to assume that
biology is unlikely to discover a "homosexualendum" lobe in the brain
that enables gay men and lesbians from the time of their birth to make

clever rhymes and spin out amusing stories or pretend to be other than who they are. Rather, LeVay would say with Karl Marx, "It is not the consciousness of people that determines their existence, but rather it is their existence that determines their consciousness."[3]

The consciousness of Cole Porter (1891–1964) and the lyrics that he wrote provide stunning examples of the layered reality theorized by LeVay. Multivalent, packed with meaning, Porter's life is a virtual manuscript of the gay "otherness" perceived at first naively in childhood and later, in adulthood, ironized and exploited for pleasure. Book-length biographical studies (especially by Schwartz, 1977, and McBrien, 1998) have documented the facts of Porter's homosexuality, but little connection has been drawn between the doubleness of his life and doubleness in his lyrics. For this essay, Porter's lyrics provide a continuous illumination to the manuscript record of his life. The lyrics represent a sly and complex relation with the world, a means of artistic expression that coincided with a mode of living. As in the case of so many pre-Stonewall homosexual writers who aspired to mainstream acceptance—Tennessee Williams and Hart Crane are obvious examples—Porter was driven to a level of "codedness" in his work. Far from an artistic flaw, the complexity afforded by this intellectual loop-the-loop became the distinguishing mark of his artistic accomplishment. Like the "something unspoken" that animates most of Williams's plays and the veiled core of pain embedded in Crane's poetry, Porter's double life propelled him to a high level of metaphor in his work. Unlike these other artists, Porter's enormous personal wealth insulated him from much of the suffering and humiliation that social pressure and persecution impressed on less economically advantaged homosexuals of his era. For him, his secret life was a source of guiltless pleasure, and the maintenance of a double life a delightful game. The wit and frivolity of his lyrics illustrate that life attitude and—in their riddles and double meanings—are games in themselves. It was an attitude far different from the tormented life of Lorenz Hart that Jeffrey Smart describes elsewhere in this volume.

Cole Porter was born in the small rural community of Peru, Indiana, on June 9, 1891, the only child of Kate (Cole) Porter, daughter of one of central Indiana's wealthiest families, and Samuel Fenwick Porter, the soft-spoken druggist whom she had married. Kate and her wealthy father, J. O. Cole, became the dominant influences in the young Cole Porter's life. J. O. Cole had built enormous wealth by returning to Indiana with his profits from the California gold rush and investing the money in farm and timber lands and, most productively, in the natural gas fields that underlie the rolling terrain of east-central Indiana. J.O. determined that his grandson would be raised in as practical and businesslike a manner as possible so that upon adulthood he would be well equipped to manage the family's properties and businesses.

Kate Cole had other ideas, and—despite her dependence on her father's money—she typically overcame his objections to her plans for Cole, either through persuasion or deception. Cole's father, by contrast, was a fairly absent figure in the boy's upbringing. Though Sam Porter lived until 1927, he spent the last ten years of his life as an invalid and rarely left his room, having suffered what the Peru newspapers described as a "prolonged nervous breakdown."[4] Late in life, Porter told an interviewer that he could remember almost nothing about his father, an especially striking statement considering that Porter was thirty-six years old at the time of Sam Porter's death.

As the result of Kate Cole's planning and J. O. Cole's money, Porter was raised in as regal an environment as rural Indiana could afford. With a public school education being out of the question, and there being no private schools in Peru or the surrounding area, Kate arranged for her son to be educated privately through a variety of tutors in literature, French, dancing, riding, piano, and violin. Determined that Cole would enter the world of the eastern elite, and despite his grandfather's objections, Kate sent Cole to the Worcester Academy in Worcester, Massachusetts, in 1905, where the boy became a star student.

His accomplishments were perhaps less impressive than they appeared to the school staff. When Cole was six years old, his mother had consulted a fortune-teller, who advised that her son would achieve greatness if his middle name were changed so that his initials spelled a common word.[5] It is a measure of the Cole family's importance in Miami County that when Kate marched into the courthouse and demanded the birth records, they were simply handed over, and she was allowed to do to them whatever she wished. Kate obliterated her son's original middle name and substituted "Albert," thus giving him the initials "C.A.P." While she had the records, she took the opportunity to change his year of birth, marking out 1891 and replacing it with 1893. Kate's exact motivation for this change cannot be known, but it seems likely that she wished to make Cole appear even more remarkable than he already was, a prodigy, in fact. So when Cole entered Worcester he was supposed to be a twelve-year-old and the youngest member of his class. In fact, he was a fourteen-year-old in disguise: layer 1.

After his enrollment at Worcester, Cole rarely returned to Indiana.

He graduated as valedictorian from the school in 1909 and, as a graduation present, was given a trip to Europe with a few of his prep school friends. The unescorted group of teenage boys headed directly to Paris (a city that Cole had dreamed of seeing since his childhood French lessons) and then spent several weeks touring France, Germany, and Switzerland. After a hectic August spent in mad shopping for Kate's and Cole's idea of an appropriate "college wardrobe," Cole entered Yale University in the fall of 1909.

The slender and gregarious freshman provoked attention upon his arrival in New Haven thanks to the expensive, if somewhat garish, wardrobe that he and Kate had ordered from tailors in Indianapolis and Chicago. An upperclassman described Porter's first appearance on campus in a checked suit and salmon tie, hair oiled and parted in the middle, "looking just like a Westerner all dressed up for the East."[6] Owing more perhaps to his musical talent and engaging personality than to his wardrobe, Porter rapidly became one of the best-known members of his class. He gravitated almost at once to a group of upperclassmen who were very much like himself: wealthy, homosexual, devoted to theater, music, and wit. Cole's lifelong friendships with Monty Woolley and Leonard Hanna date from this period. Charles Schwartz, who in 1977 published the first honest biography of Porter, speculates that Cole's homosexual activities may have begun in his first year at Yale, or that Porter may simply have continued and expanded a hidden way of life that he began at the all-male Worcester Academy.

The homosexual scene at Yale in the teens was typical of the situation in wealthy American circles: faculty, staff, and students knew that there were homosexuals on campus, but they were young men of some of the country's wealthiest and most influential families and so were fairly immune to criticism or harassment. One Yale alumnus from the time told Schwartz that while Porter spent much of his time with Leonard Hanna and Monty Woolley, who were "both clearly homosexual," there was nothing really to "confirm those suspicions" about Porter himself.[7] In spite of his companions, his taste in clothing, his effusive personality and slight lisp, Porter created an ambiguity about himself by appearing as frequently in public with attractive women as with his male friends. He also pledged in what was seen as one of the "best" Greek-letter fraternities (Delta Kappa Epsilon), and attended fraternity functions with the requisite female companion. In short, Porter took steps to cover his private life with a public veneer of conventional heterosexuality. This veneer, if not perfect, was good enough, since few were in a position to exert power over the wealthy and popular student. This ambiguity might have made possible what Schwartz sees as an important pattern in Porter's musical and social activities at Yale: the elaborate steps he took to insure proximity to the Yale football team. He was elected cheerleader, chairman of the football song selection committee, and composed five "fight songs" that have become Yale classics. While conducting a private life that included "fucking parties" organized by Woolley and held in one of the New York hotels owned by Woolley's father, Porter managed also to remain just one of the guys around the gridiron, the star of the pep rally: layer 2.

Porter wrote more than three hundred songs while at Yale, most of them for original musicals staged by Delta Kappa Epsilon or the Yale Dramatic Association and performed by entirely male casts—a common enough grounds for cross-dressing in the all-male colleges of the era before coeducation. Porter also acted in these productions, as did his friends Woolley and Hanna. Cast photographs collected in Robert Kimball's *Cole* and in his *Complete Lyrics of Cole Porter* show the young composer posing with fellow Yale men dressed as ballerinas, Mexican senoritas, and "prom girls" for the satirical farces devised largely by Porter, Woolley, and T. Lawrason Riggs. The manuscripts and scores for most of these shows are now lost, but many of Porter's lyrics survive. With titles like *And the Villain Still Pursued Her* (1912), *Paranoia* (1914), and a spoof of the Mexican revolution titled, *We're All Dressed Up and We Don't Know Huerta Go* (1914), the Yale shows display Porter's wit and his talent for clever rhymes to be nearly full grown. Though the topics of the songs are usually sophomoric in their restriction to college life (satirizing such local institutions as the Elizabethan Club or the varsity crew), the sharpness and style that would drive Porter's best work were already in dramatic evidence. An example is the lyric for Porter's "A Football King," written for *The Pot of Gold* in 1912, and subsequently revised and sung by the Yale Glee Club. As the rhythm of the lines suggest, the music has a thumping, mock-heroic, Gilbert-and-Sullivan quality:

> *Verse*
> Now I'm in an awful condition,
> Filled with a vaulting ambition,
> While I rave on deliriously,
> Please don't take me too seriously.
> I merely want to say,
> I'd like to shine in a physical way.

Refrain
If I were only a football King,
I'd go punting around all day,
Of every eye the apple,
When wearing my Y to chapel.
The girls would write for my autograph,
And all of that sort of thing,
Were I an oracular,
Very spectacular,
Regular football King.

Patter
Now I'm sure that I should find it heaven
If I had a chance to make the Yale eleven,
With my only stunt to go around and punt the afternoon away.
The cynosure of ev'ry eye, whenever I should pass men,
I'd open up and show my Y to all the underclassmen.
For my autograph I'd charge a dollar,
And I'd be the title of an Arrow collar,
Such a very muddy sort of very bloody sort of thing.
My opponents I should give a scalding
That would make me rival Captain Jesse Spalding,
If they'd only realize that I'm a football King.[8]

The lyric is especially telling in terms of the outsider position taken by the singer, who is not "regular" and imagines a little drama of what his life might be if only he were. This early song may even display an example of the pleasure Porter took in presenting sexual material through double entendre, in the provocative and odd image of the singer opening his clothing to display his "Y" to all the underclassmen (a *Y* being not just the first letter of *Yale*, but also a slang term for the human crotch). An earlier version of the song used somewhat more graphic language as the singer imagines his physical self as a football hero. In this version, he longs just to be a football "man" and not a "king":

If I were only a football man,
I'd go punting around all day,
Of every eye the apple,
When wearing my Y to chapel.
My talk would be so corpuscular,
My verbs would even be muscular,
And mine would be such downs

As to bring home the touchdowns
If I were a football man.[9]

In spite of a weak academic performance at Yale (the somewhat pre-
dictable result of Porter's continual immersion in social and artistic projects during his four years there), he did graduate in the spring of 1913.
Thereupon, Cole obeyed his grandfather and enrolled in Harvard Law
School, a step that J. O. Cole envisioned as putting the final touches on
the future captain of the natural gas industry. But without mentioning
the fact in his letters to his grandfather, Porter soon changed his registra-
tion to Harvard's Graduate School of Arts and Sciences and applied himself in a modest way to a program of courses in music theory and har-
mony. He spent most of his time continuing to write songs for shows
back at Yale, where he was being viewed as something of a necessity for
the continued social life of the university.

He was also making his first contacts in the world of New York theater and music publishing. These fields were closely allied in an era in
which the Broadway stage was the primary cradle of American popular
song. Songs typically had little narrative relationship with the show's
book and were valued more for their commercial potential as sheet music
products. In 1915, two songs that Cole Porter had written for Yale shows
were incorporated into the Broadway musicals *Hands Up* and *Miss
Information*. Though motion pictures had damaged live theater as a business on a national scale, the Broadway stage remained a vital showcase
for plays and musical shows. In fact, the teens were part of an arc of
growth in Broadway business that would reach its peak with 270 productions in the 1927–28 season. When Porter entered this world in the
1914–15 season, Broadway saw the staging of 157 productions in sixty-
one venues. Of these productions, twenty-one were musicals, two were
revues, and eight were operettas.[10]

Neither *Hands Up* nor *Miss Information* proved commercial successes, but Porter's work had by this time attracted the interest of Elisabeth "Bessie" Marbury, a wealthy socialite and lesbian who was influential in the Broadway scene as an agent and producer. Marbury arranged
for Porter to collaborate with his former Yale classmate T. Lawrason
Riggs on a Broadway musical called *See America First*—a satire of patriotic musicals and devised in the same rollicking, farcical style that had
delighted the Yale students. Marbury's production methods were
unorthodox. She arranged financing for the show not through the usual
"angels," but by enlisting support from her significant others: Elsie de

Wolfe (an actress who became famous as a decorator) and Anne Morgan, of the J. P. Morgan family, also a lesbian and a pioneering feminist.[11] Marbury cast in the show's leading role a young woman named Dorothie Bigelow. Bigelow had just arrived in the United States from England and, though she had no experience as an actress or singer, she did have an impeccable social background. Her aristocratic family having sent her to the States in 1915 as a safe haven from the war, Bigelow had at once been adopted as a protégée by Mrs. O. H. P. Belmont, a leading socialite and campaigner for women's rights. Bigelow gained a reputation as a potential stage star due both to her exceptional manners and physical attractiveness and to the fact that Mrs. Belmont had announced her intention of building around Bigelow a new musical play about women's suffrage.[12] When that project collapsed, Marbury seized upon Bigelow as a prepromoted public personality and cast her as the fresh young star of *See America First.*

The show opened on March 28, 1916, a near operetta with twenty-six songs (music and lyrics by Porter) arranged in a plot devised by Riggs. Porter's lyrics for the show are clever and ironic but, when compared to his later work, not yet sexually devious. An example is the song "Sweet Simplicity," in which the heroine sings of her "simple" tastes:

Some ladies live in extravagant style,
Doting on vain display.
Happy with little,
I cheerfully smile,
Isn't a pittance as good as a pile?
A string of pearls refined and chaste,
With one tiara in perfect taste,
For any young girl should suffice.
Why, I once wore a ball gown twice![13]

Critics found little to admire in the piece and, with the exception of the opening-night performance that was organized by Marbury as a gala society event, audiences were unenthusiastic. The show ran for only fifteen performances. Bigelow was described by a critic for the *New York Herald* as "pretty, but her singing voice was inadequate in volume, small in range, and not very beautiful in quality."[14] The show itself was criticized for being silly and unsophisticated, identified for what it was: a college play mounted on Broadway. The critic for the *New York Tribune* was one of several who suggested that the play's only chance for success would be the mass attendance of Yale alumni living in New York.[15]

Riggs, Porter's collaborator, made bitter comments to the press about the inadequacies of the show's star and declared his intention to leave dramatic writing forever. Riggs followed through on this statement, apparently shaken enough by this single failure to convert to Catholicism and join the priesthood, eventually becoming a chaplain at Yale.[16]

What happened to Porter after the failure of *See America First* provides a fascinating episode in gay biography. In addition to the deceptions about his age and sexuality, Porter had by 1916 established a pattern of telling deliberate, astonishing lies to the press and other persons who did not know him well. He seemed to take grand pleasure in spinning these tall tales and feeding them to a gullible public, as soon as there was a public who was interested. While an undergraduate, he told a reporter for the *New Haven Register* that he had spent several years "in the mountains of Rumania" and that while there he had the occasion to hear the strange calls of many exotic birds; these strange sounds, he confessed, and not his own imagination, formed the basis of the staccato opening ("Bingo! Bingo!—Bingo! Bingo! Bingo!") he conceived for his football song, "Bingo Eli Yale."[17] Porter had, of course, been to Europe only briefly (in 1909), and never to Rumania, but the New Haven reporter simply repeated the composer's claims and laid down another minilevel in the Porter mythology. What Porter actually did after the failure of *See America First* was to take a Manhattan flat and enjoy the social scene. Elsa Maxwell, the ultimate society hostess of the teens and twenties, described Porter's attendance at a series of glittering parties during this period of 1916–17, at which he drank heavily and entertained the other guests with his own songs as well as parodies of current favorites.[18] In July 1917, a year and a half after the closing of *See America First*, Porter sailed to France as part of a "relief mission" organized by socialite Nina Larre Smith Duryea, whom he served as personal assistant. During this time, Porter lived alone in Paris in a comfortably furnished home on the Place Vendôme.[19]

The myth of Porter's war years is far more glamorous. Porter told various versions of this story over the years, the main theme being that he was so distraught over the failure of his first Broadway show that he fled immediately to France and signed up with the French Foreign Legion. On other occasions, he told interviewers that he was a member of the regular French army or that he had been part of the American Aviation Forces in France.[20] Like the reporter back in New Haven, interviewers and editors for major newspapers and magazines, as well as two biographers, simply repeated Porter's claims throughout his lifetime, apparently never checking records to verify the composer's story. No account ever challenged Porter's supposed military heroism until Charles Schwartz published his biography in 1977. His search of French and American military records showed that Porter had never been part of any army anywhere, despite his frequent appearance on the streets of Paris in the uniforms of various branches of the military and at various ranks: layer 3.[21]

While in Paris, Porter met Linda Lee Thomas, a native of Louisville, Kentucky, a well-connected socialite, known for her exquisite taste and manners. Linda Lee Thomas had moved to Paris in 1912, following her divorce from Edward Russell Thomas.[22] At the time of the divorce, she became impressively wealthy in her own right, receiving more than a million dollars in cash, stocks, and other properties.[23] Thomas and Porter met at a society wedding reception and immediately struck up a friendship that was to last for the rest of their lives. On December 18, 1919, they were married in a civil ceremony in Paris.

Linda and Cole saw in one another the perfect match: Porter adored Linda's elegance and wealth at a time when he was still dependent on his grandfather's allowance; she found in Porter a witty and youthful companion (she was eight years his senior) who made no sexual demands. Brendan Gill, who knew them both, acknowledged the frequently voiced theory that Linda was a lesbian, but thought it more likely that Linda had simply had enough of "the sexual side of marriage" because of the sexual sadism of her former husband.[24] There is also the issue of Linda's acquisitiveness and her love of ornament. She was famous among her set for her exquisite taste in furnishings and jewelry. Acquiring Cole Porter as a husband can be seen as yet another of her wise selections. Among company that pleased him, Porter was an endlessly entertaining companion, making plentiful double-edged remarks that could be taken by those who preferred innocence as amusing silliness and by those who enjoyed wickedness as outrageous sexual innuendo. So their marriage was of mutual benefit: Cole gained access to the "rich-rich" (to describe those who controlled their wealth, as opposed to his own position in the teens, dependent upon an allowance from his family), and Linda gained a delightful companion who offered her sanctuary from unwanted sexual pressure. The two were devoted companions for the rest of their lives, practically symbiotic. After Linda's agonizing death from emphysema in 1954, Porter declined steadily into a seemingly paranoiac eccentrism.

Porter's sexuality was certainly no secret from his wife. Both were open-minded, sexually liberated people who enjoyed one another's company. Linda's many friends, a majority of whom were gay or lesbian, soon became Cole's friends and, beginning as early as 1920, the Porters spent much of their lives traveling around the world on their yacht or entertaining in one of their exquisite homes in the company of gay men such as Noel Coward, Jack Wilson, Howard Sturges, and Monty Woolley, and lesbians such as Elsa Maxwell, Anne Morgan, Elsie de Wolfe, and Elisabeth Marbury.[25] Though everyone "in society" knew about the nonsexual aspect of the Porter marriage, no word ever appeared in the media indicating that *Les Coleporteurs* (as the couple was known in Paris) were anything other than a conventional heterosexual couple, devoted to one another and endlessly entertaining: layer 4.

The pleasure that Porter seems to have taken in deceiving the public is emblematic of a tactic that he employed throughout his lifetime. As in his lyrics, so often built around a series of double entendres, Porter constructed his life with multiple realities: the private facts kept just for an insider's coterie, behind a public mask of conventionality and sentimental romance. Consider the lyric for one of Porter's most famous songs: "Let's Do It, Let's Fall in Love," which first appeared in the 1928 musical, *Paris*. The two-part title itself displays the pattern: the song is really about sex but pastes over this fact the treacly veneer of romantic love. The song begins with the line, "Birds do it, bees do it" and adds "up in Lapland little Lapps do it." The thought ends with the invitation, "Let's do it, let's fall in love." The song then takes the singer through an astonishing catalog of creatures who do it: Lithuanians and Letts do it, the Dutch, the Finns, folks in Siam do it ("think of Siamese twins"), nightingales, larks "k-krazy for a lark" do it, grouse, fowls, owls, penguins on the rocks and even cuckoos in their clocks do it. The list drives on for five refrains, exploring various animal kingdoms all doing it, and every third, sixth, and thirteenth line consisting of the mantra, "Let's do it, let's fall in love." Among many stunning rhymes and clever wordplays, perhaps the most devious is also the briefest: "Moths in your rugs do it, What's the use of moth balls?"[26] The song can stand as an emblem for Porter's entire way of living: reveling in the raw, erotic power that drives life, then slapping a token mask of convention over this truth before showing it to the world. The masking piece here is the token phrase, "Let's fall in love," stuck onto the ends of these long biological phrases as a kind of last-minute save, like a satin bow over the genitals of a naked dancer.

Gerald Mast, in his *Can't Help Singin'*, raises a fascinating issue when he points out the frequency with which Porter's lyrics refer to love as an "it" or a "thing." Among the songs that use this device are some of Porter's best-known works: "It's De-Lovely," "It's Bad for Me,"

"You've Got That Thing," "You Do Something to Me," "What Is this Thing Called Love?" and the doubly ambiguous "It Was Just One of Those Things." Mast sees in this tendency a reflection of Porter's cool, abstracted, calculating way of viewing the world, a radical contrast with the love lyrics of Lorenz Hart or Ira Gershwin, who describe love in more sensual and emotional language and figures. Porter's lyrics, says Mast, are certainly sexual, but not sensual. They have more the quality of delicious public gossip than of private longing, "drawing room dish," rather than bedroom confessional.[27]

Mast's point is a subtle one and surely makes sense. But there is also a more practical reason for Porter's use of all those pronouns: they allow the lyrics to be interpreted as either clean or dirty. All of those *its* and *things* can stand both for love and its sweet niceties or for sex acts ("You Do Something to Me") and even sexual organs ("You've Got That Thing"). Other songs use words that are safe enough in heterosexual culture, but are ripe with suggestion in a gay context. Prime among these are "Blow, Gabriel, Blow," and the inevitable, "You're the Top." Porter even devised parody lyrics for the latter song, adding among its gorgeous rhyming list of superlatives, "You're the breasts of Venus, you're King Kong's penis, you're self abuse." The parody ends with the lines:

I'm a eunuch who's just been through an op!
But, if baby, I'm the bottom,
You're the top![28]

The regular lyric is enough, in its title alone, to get a gay audience chuckling. With rhymes such as "steppes of Russia" with "the pants on a Roxy usher" and "dam at Boulder" with "moon over Mae West's shoulder," the list of attributes pushes on for seven refrains, each one ending with the declaration of one's own bottomness and the other's topness. Porter was well aware of this lingo—which refers to the positions of dominance and submission in homosexual intercourse—just as he was aware of the hilarity of Bianca singing (in *Kiss Me Kate*) of her desire for any "Tom, Dick or Harry." In the last verse, the names switch around, so that the song ends with her expression of longing for any Tom, Harry or Dick. Finally, she repeats the last words twelve times, wanting "a dicka dick" over and over again.[29] As Gerald Mast asks, when discussing this lyric, "How can you sing in the upper case?"[30] The songs are only mildly coated with propriety, maintaining a delicate doubleness. "Tom, Dick or Harry" can be heard simply as Bianca's desire for just any husband, or as her desire for a male sexual organ, or both. In essence, the song is a kind of lie: it pretends to an innocence that it does not possess. Porter must have enjoyed the mass public acceptance of these linguistic jokes just as much as he enjoyed putting over the tales about his travels in Rumania and his war record. He was one with Oscar Wilde in opposing the decay of lying. For both, lying was a vital creative activity, productive of both beauty and shelter, worthy of protection against a misguided moralism.

The participation in this duplicity by the press is especially telling, as the multiplicity was not simply facilitated by the media, but was forced on gays and lesbians before Stonewall. By the time Porter had achieved prominence as one of America's leading theatrical composers in the 1930s, virtually everyone in show business knew that he was a homosexual. Yet not one word was published or broadcast about Porter's actual sexual identity until Brendan Gill included the subject in a biographical essay in the *New Yorker* in 1971—seven years after the composer's death.[31] The hundreds of reporters who interviewed and wrote about Porter during his lifetime, the authors of two fantasy-filled biographies, and the creators of the bizarre "bio-pic" that purported to tell his and Linda's life stories were not only silent on the issue, but went to considerable lengths to mislead the public. It is difficult to interpret this massive media collusion as anything other than a conscious enforcement of heterosexuality—a deliberate stifling of reality and promotion of a fiction so as not to call into question the way things were supposed to be. Though some might argue that media professionals participated in this camouflage out of affection for Porter and concern for his well-being, I find this explanation unpersuasive. Of the hundreds of writers and editors, producers and directors involved in creating the media version of "Cole Porter: Heterosexual Composer," few would have known him well enough to wish to protect *him*. Moreover, Porter was not a particularly likable person once he had achieved success. He came to believe that other people existed solely for his amusement, and, when they began to bore him, he would look at them with disgust and walk abruptly from the room.[32] The explanation for the media collusion on Porter is no different than for other pre-Stonewall homosexuals. The object being protected was not the individual; it was heterosexuality as a compulsory and monolithic public structure.

The height of heterosexual media fantasy can be found, no doubt, in the bizarre spectacle of *Night and Day,* a 1946 Warner Brothers film "biography" that presented Cole as a wounded war hero, Alexis Smith portraying Linda Lee Thomas as a volunteer Red Cross nurse, and

Monty Woolley as himself, yet somehow transformed into a heterosexual law professor. The film is essentially the love story between Cole (Cary Grant) and Linda, whose devotion to one another overcomes many hardships. Cole's first Broadway show bombs, not because it had a terrible book and a lead actress who could not act, but because it happens to open on the same night as the sinking of the *Lusitania*. Hearing news of the disaster, the horrified audience rushes from the theater. Overwhelmed by patriotic feeling, Porter tells a distraught Linda that he must go to join the war effort. Gravely wounded as a member of the French Foreign Legion, Cole is nursed back to health by the saintly Linda, who has rushed to the front to volunteer as a Red Cross nurse. The couple finally marry and flourish amid Broadway success, and the film ends with Porter slowly mounting the steps in the Yale chapel to address wounded soldiers from the Second World War, and inspire them to courage and good humor.

Among the film's other absurdities, Cole is depicted as refusing to accept any financial help from his family. In real life, nearly all of his correspondence home before the time of his marriage to Linda included requests for ever larger allowances and advances on allowances. The idea of Linda serving as a nurse and later as a volunteer in an orphanage for refugee children is equally fantastic. In life, Linda was surrounded by an entourage of servants (housemaids, a personal maid, cooks, drivers, gardeners, and housekeepers) who performed every possible physical service for her, service that extended even—Cole's mother wrote home enviously—to putting on her stockings for her. The concern shown by the creators of *Night and Day* in projecting an unquestionable heterosexual world extended to Monty Woolley, who appears in the film as a grotesquely altered version of himself. The film takes elaborate care to answer any doubts that Woolley's long bachelorhood might arouse, by showing him ogling female flesh at every opportunity. In one scene, Woolley is shown leering at a group of chorus girls. When he attempts to follow them across a lawn, he is restrained by an indulgent Linda, saying, "Oh, no you don't. You're coming with me."

One accurate element in the film is the depiction of Porter's massive leg injuries sustained in a riding accident in 1937 (fig. 6). The injuries were so severe that he underwent more than thirty operations, none of which were able to relieve his chronic pain or restore full function. After the accident, Porter was forced to give up cruising and to rely almost exclusively on "call boys," a complication that Warner Brothers chose to omit from their motion picture.[33]

Though Porter feigned disgust with the supposed film biography, his valet told Schwartz that during Porter's later years, when it began to appear on television, he would roar with laughter at the film's absurdities. Still, Porter collaborated wholeheartedly in the project, approving the script and casting, as well as negotiating a three-hundred-thousand-dollar payment for the rights to what was supposed to be his life story.[34] Porter's private attitude toward the film at the time of its production might be divined from a reading of the grotesque caricature that is Woolley's performance. The two men chatted almost daily during filming, and if one knows a more accurate version of the lives of Porter, Thomas, and Woolley, it is hard to see Woolley's performance as anything other than a gigantic wink to the cognoscenti. He is the leering, bearded, middle-aged queen familiar to observant residents of any university town, *playing at* being a wise heterosexual, dedicated to leading the younger Cole and Linda to true love and marital bliss. Scattered among his sentimental utterances in counsel to the star-crossed lovers are moments when Woolley turns perceptibly toward the camera, rolls his eyes upward and enjoys a steady intake of breath, as if to say, "Bear with us, Miss Thing, they're paying us plenty for this."

By the time the film was released in 1946, Porter was at the top of his profession as a composer and lyricist for theater and film. His sophistication and skill developed greatly during the 1920s as he wrote songs for vaudeville-like reviews such as *Greenwich Village Follies* (1924) and *Paris* (1928). His reputation as a witty artist was bolstered by such songs as "Let's Do It" (1928), "Let's Misbehave" (1927), "I've Got a Crush on You" (1929) and "You Do Something to Me" (1929). Soon after, Porter began to prove his talent for ballads with songs such as "What Is This Thing Called Love?" (1929), "Love for Sale" (1930), and "Night and Day" (1932). Porter's first smash hit came in 1934, in his collaboration with Howard Lindsay and Russel Crouse on the Guy Bolton–P. G. Wodehouse story for *Anything Goes*. This show launched Porter's long association with Ethel Merman, whom he considered the outstanding stage singer of his time. In addition to the title song, which became something of a Porter signature tune, his score included such songs as "I Get a Kick Out of You," "You're the Top," and "Blow Gabriel Blow." The composer followed up this success with great songs for some forgettable shows: "Begin the Beguine" and "Just One of Those Things" for *Jubilee* (1935), "It's De-Lovely" for *Red, Hot, and Blue!* (1936), "At Long Last Love" for *You'll Never Know* (1938), and "My Heart Belongs to Daddy" for *Leave It to Me* (1938). During the 1930s, Porter also began his long relationship with Hollywood, completing scores for such films as *Born to Dance* (1936) and *Rosalie* (1937).

The income from Porter's songs, shows, and films added to his and Linda's already ample fortune. Porter had inherited income-producing forest lands, gas fields, and coal mines when his grandfather died in 1923. These multiple incomes allowed the Porters to live in very high style, dividing their time between a vast suite on the Lido, a series of fabulous Renaissance palaces in Venice, two adjoining apartments at the Waldorf in New York, and—beginning in the 1930s—a rented estate in Hollywood. The Porters were forced to give up their home in Venice as the result of a 1927 police raid on their home, the Palazzo Rezzonico, in which a group of local teenage boys was discovered dressed up in Linda's clothing and parading before Porter and several gay friends. The incident would have simply been overlooked, as were Porter's many other violations of public mores, except that one of the boys was the son of Venice's chief of police.[35]

This incident is misleading in regard to Porter's sexual preferences. He typically sought out mature, rugged-looking men, preferably sailors or truck driver types. Through confidential interviews with Porter's friends after the composer's death, Schwartz assembled a good deal of information about Porter's sexual activities. Though Porter obviously enjoyed the company of other wealthy gay men (Leonard Hanna, Monty Woolley, Howard Sturges, Noel Coward, Jack Wilson), he seems rarely to have developed sexual relationships with men of his own economic class. He was a regular customer of male brothels in the 1930s and, after his accident, he and Woolley made frequent use of pimps who supplied men of whatever race and type desired and who would appear at the door of the pair's hotel suite dressed as delivery men so as not to attract the attention of hotel detectives.[36]

William McBrien's 1998 biography downplayed Porter's casual sexual relationships, but did bring forward an abundance of new information—much of it documented through letters and diaries—about Porter's long-term romances with men such as the architect Ed Tauch in the 1930s, dancer-choreographer Nelson Barclift in the 1940s, and marine and later actor Robert Bray in the 1950s. Porter was, as McBrien's evidence shows, "in love" with these men; yet the relations bear a certain hint of Porter's habitual buying of "love"—his lovers and had far less wealth and power than did Porter—and so were inherently asymmetrical. His letters to them and the record of events that McBrien uncovered indicates a pattern of manipulation and enticement by which Porter sought to gain and maintain affection through the bestowing or beholding of financial and professional favors. This pattern extended even to Porter's final days, when he altered the terms of his will so as to exclude Robert Bray, who had disobeyed Porter in filing for a divorce from his wife.[37]

The hardest part of Porter's life began in 1937, when his legs were crushed in a riding accident. The damage was so severe that the composer was in constant pain for the rest of his life. The right leg was amputated in 1958. Porter also suffered through a string of failed Broadway shows in the 1940s, and show business insiders began to whisper that the accident and its aftermath had ruined Porter's talent. These rumors were put to rest with the gigantic success of *Kiss Me Kate* in 1948 and by the moderate successes of *Can-Can* (1954) and *Silk Stockings* (1955).

Porter was troubled by chronic depression from 1950 to 1951 and was treated with electrical shock therapy. After Linda's death in 1954, Porter found work difficult. He retreated in the later 1950s to his nine-room apartment on the thirty-third floor of the Waldorf Towers in New York, or to his country estate near Williamstown, Massachusetts. Porter and Woolley's friendship had faded by this time, leaving the composer emotionally isolated. Porter's main sexual outlet in his later years was found in the person of his masseur, who spent more than an hour per day with Porter behind a closed door.[38]

Porter's secretary began to keep a rotating list of dinner guests who were willing to go through an unpleasant evening alone with Porter out of loyalty. Guests described Porter in this late period as a host, immaculately dressed, who would drink to excess before dinner and then sit silent and staring, either into thin air or at the television set that was kept on throughout the evening. His valet would put him to bed at ten o'clock.[39] Porter died of the combined effects of emphysema and kidney failure on October 15, 1964.

The loneliness and ill-health of Porter's last years were in stark contrast to the conviviality and pleasure that had comprised the first fifty years of his life. The story of his life and that of his wealthy friends is a testament to the dominance of class over sexual politics. The freedom that he and his circle enjoyed in their time was purely the result of wealth. Money allowed them to live gay and lesbian lives that were relatively unrestrained by social mores. Only a thin veneer of heterosexuality, epitomized by the many "marriages" like that between Cole and Linda, was necessary to provide cover in the wider public sphere. In the same period, the 1930s, when Porter and Woolley cruised the streets of Manhattan in a convertible Rolls Royce in search of willing sailors, with little fear of arrest or harassment, gay men were being arrested daily, often on the flimsiest of charges and typically as the result of entrapment by plain-clothes police officers.[40] New cabaret laws forbade not only openly gay entertainment, but even comics who "pretended to be homosexual."[41] The role of money in social tolerance of homosexuals is exemplified in the case of William Eythe, leading man in Porter's 1950 show, *Out of This World*. Shortly before the show was to open, Eythe was arrested in a New York subway men's room, charged with soliciting sex from an undercover policeman. The charges were dropped and the story squelched thanks to cash payments, likely made by Porter himself, to the "right people."[42]

Porter's 1934 lyric for his song, "Anything Goes," suggests Porter to be a postmodernist ahead of his time:

> In olden days, a glimpse of stocking
> Was looked on as something shocking,
> But now, God knows, anything goes.

If moral standards are in flux, so are aesthetic ones, with "good authors, too, who once knew better words" now only using four-letter words. Economic and social standards have been shown to turn on their heads within one generation, with "that gent today you gave a cent today" who once "had several chateâux." An early draft of the song even declared the moral equivalence of "saying prayers" and having "affairs with young bears."[43] So striking is this lyric as a kind of anthem of impermanence, or at least subjectivity, that when the neopositivist philosopher David Stove wrote his vitriolic attack on Karl Popper and the French postmodernists, he began his lead essay by relating Popper's rejection of knowability to Porter's lyric.[44] He calls his essay, "Cole Porter and Karl Popper: The Jazz Age in the Philosophy of Science." Stove makes an important point. Porter's lyric is all about *glissement:* slippage between word and meaning, between sign and signified, between appearance and reality. If things can change so utterly and so rapidly, the lyric asks, how can it be that anything is permanently true?

As in the experience of Michel Foucault, Porter's view of life from a position of otherness led him to a rejection of "the way" things are supposed to be. Porter saw himself as the master of reality: like a camp queen, like Lypsinka in an Italian suit, Porter could be whomever he wanted to be; he could create any reality he wished. His life is a restatement of the elaborate development of irony in a gay life, of the pleasure of knowing secrets, a lifelong expansion upon the pleasure felt in making coded remarks in straight company. Porter's supreme pleasure was the pleasure of mockery. From the time of his Yale dramatic productions, Cole reveled in the delightful irony of pretending to satisfy cultural expectations of gender and sexuality, while at the same time doing just what he felt like doing behind a shield of what was called good taste and discretion. Like the framing devices that LeVay and Nonas find characteristic of gay art, devices that allow the author to arrange and observe the world as if in a toy theater, Porter manipulated his life and public perception of it.[45] Outside of the gigantic heterosexual play, he staged his own fictional life right next to it, modest in size, but quite polished, a toy theater inside a "theater" that believes itself to be real life. Like the miniature house inside the house in Edward Albee's *Tiny Alice*, the existence of the "toy" calls into serious question the "reality" of the "real" house and its inhabitants. The slippery lyrics and the multivalent life of Cole Porter find a synthesis here, in the territory of theater, and the revelation of the hidden life is the yanking down of the scenery. Ah! So that was illusion? Then anything goes.

NOTES

1. Simon LeVay and Elisabeth Nonas, *City of Friends: A Portrait of the Gay and Lesbian Community in America* (Cambridge: MIT Press, 1995), 351; Yankelovich Partners, *A Yankelovich MONITOR Perspective on Gays/Lesbians* (Norwalk, Conn.: Yankelovich Partners, 1994).

2. LeVay and Nonas, *City of Friends,* 353.

3. Karl Marx, *Critique of Political Economy* (1859), quoted in introduction to *The Communist Manifesto,* by Karl Marx and Friedrich Engels, ed. Samuel H. Beer (New York: Appleton-Century-Crofts, 1955), ix.

4. Charles Schwartz, *Cole Porter: A Biography* (New York: Dial Press, 1977), 88.

5. Ibid., 19.

6. Ibid., 22.

7. Ibid., 30.

8. *The Complete Lyrics of Cole Porter,* ed. Robert Kimball (New York: Alfred A. Knopf, 1983), 5–6.

9. Ibid., 6.

10. Glenn Loney, *Twentieth Century Theatre,* vol. 1, (New York: Facts on File, 1983), 77.

11. For information about the relationship of Marbury, de Wolfe, and Morgan see Jane S. Smith, *Elsie de Wolfe: A Life in High Style* (New York: Atheneum,

1982), 120–21; and Kim Marra, "A Lesbian Marriage of Cultural Consequence: Elisabeth Marbury and Elsie de Wolfe, 1886–1933," in *Passing Performances: Queer Readings of Leading Players in American Theater History,* ed. Robert A. Schanke and Kim Marra (Ann Arbor: University of Michigan Press, 1998), 104–28.

12. Schwartz, *Cole Porter,* 41.

13. *Complete Lyrics,* 41.

14. Quoted in Schwartz, *Cole Porter,* 42.

15. Schwartz, *Cole Porter,* 42.

16. Ibid., 43.

17. Ibid., 30.

18. See ibid., 44–45.

19. See Robert Kimball, *Cole* (New York: Holt, Rinehart, and Winston, 1971), 40.

20. For Porter's versions of his wartime service, see ibid., 38–39.

21. Schwartz, *Cole Porter,* 46–47.

22. See Kimball, *Cole,* 40–45; and Schwartz, *Cole Porter,* 50–55.

23. Schwartz, *Cole Porter,* 51.

24. Brendan Gill, "A Biographical Essay," which serves as introduction to Kimball, *Cole,* xv.

25. See Jean Howard, *Travels with Cole Porter* (New York: Harry N. Abrams, 1991).

26. *Complete Lyrics,* 72–73.

27. Gerald Mast, *Can't Help Singin': The American Musical on Stage and Screen* (Woodstock, N.Y.: Overlook Press, 1987), 186.

28. Ibid., 188.

29. *Complete Lyrics,* 275.

30. Mast, *Can't Help Singin',* 188.

31. The Gill essay was reprinted in Kimball, *Cole.* Interestingly, the honest but sensational Gill essay seems to have provoked little public reaction. Far more attention was drawn to the issue of Porter's homosexuality by the publication of a lurid story about Porter's paid sexual encounter with a handsome wine steward, written by Truman Capote and published in *Esquire* in November 1975, 110–18. This story, which Capote claimed as factual, was part of a piece called "La Côte Basque, 1965," one of the few chapters that Capote ever produced for his long-awaited, high-society tell-all "novel." The three chapters in existence at the time of Capote's death were published in 1987 by Random House (in an attempt to recoup a fraction of the advances they had paid Capote for the book over the course of nearly twenty years) under the title *Answered Prayers: The Unfinished Novel.* The Porter-and-the-wine-steward story appears there on pages 142–43.

32. See Schwartz, *Cole Porter,* 39, 100, 126.

33. For a detailed comparison of the film to real life, see Steven C. Smith and Sylvia Stoddard, "Night and Day: The Difference between Cole Porter's Life and the Movie about Him," *Show Music* 7, no. 4, (1991–92): 37–42.

34. Schwartz, *Cole Porter,* 215.

35. Ibid., 77.

36. Ibid., 114–15.

37. William McBrien, *Cole Porter: A Biography* (New York: Knopf, 1998), 154–55, 194–95, 237–38, 248–50, 361, 391.

38. Schwartz, *Cole Porter*, 264–65.

39. Gerald Clarke, *Capote: A Biography* (New York: Simon and Schuster, 1984), 340–41.

40. See George Chauncey, *Gay New York: Gender, Urban Culture, and the Meaning of the Gay Male World, 1890–1940* (New York: Basic Books, 1994), 331–54.

41. Ibid., 352.

42. Schwartz, *Cole Porter*, 243.

43. *Complete Lyrics*, 121.

44. David Stove, "Cole Porter and Karl Popper: The Jazz Age in the Philosophy of Science," in *The Plato Cult and Other Philosophical Follies* (Oxford: Basil Blackwell, 1991), 1.

45. See LeVay and Nonas, *City of Friends*, 353–54.

Lorenz Hart

This Can't Be Love

Jeffrey Smart

"I was one of his boys," says the anonymous interviewee; "When it came to sex, Larry [Hart] left an awful lot to be desired."[1] Evidence of Lorenz (Larry) Hart's homosexuality—or resistance to his homosexuality—can be seen in all spheres of his life. It undeniably shaped his personal life; it characterized and finally destroyed his partnership with Richard Rodgers; and it permeates his lyrics, whether in a few overt references or in assigning viewpoints and subjects to certain genders.

Lyricist Lorenz Hart (1895–1943) was born in New York City to German-Jewish immigrant parents. His collaboration with composer Richard Rodgers began in 1919, and over the next twenty-plus years produced such shows as *Dearest Enemy, A Connecticut Yankee, On Your Toes, The Boys from Syracuse,* and *Pal Joey,* and such songs as "Manhattan," "The Blue Room," "Ten Cents a Dance," "The Most Beautiful Girl in the World," "I Didn't Know What Time It Was," and "Blue Moon." Rodgers and Hart were among the premiere creators of musical theater of the day. Together, they created shows that were witty, tuneful, occasionally daring, and experimental in use of source material. Yet, in spite of his success, Hart experienced such self-loathing that he drank himself into an early grave. He died at age forty-seven from pneumonia contracted during a drinking binge.

This essay will reexamine Hart's personal life in light of George Chauncey's prize-winning study of gay life and patterns of homosexual/homosocial behavior in *Gay New York: Gender, Urban Culture, and the Making of the Gay Male World, 1890–1940.* To understand Hart's view of homosexuality, the essay collates gay and/or sexual references in his lyrics with his own social behavior. The resulting picture is then compared to psychiatric definitions of homosexuality iterated in Henry L. Minton's article "Femininity in Men and Masculinity in Women: American Psychiatry and Psychology Portray Homosexuality in the 1930's." A gender analysis of the themes in Hart's lyrics not only reflects Hart's experiences of the world, but also demonstrates how he recontextualized those experiences for a heterosexual public. Finally, the partnership, working methods, and dissolution of "Rodgers and Hart" are examined in light of social shifts highlighted in Chauncey and the Freudian dynamics of male-male collaboration elaborated in Wayne Koestenbaum's *Double Talk: The Erotics of Male Literary Collaboration.* Though Hart's homosexuality has long been acknowledged, it has not been examined except as one cause for the lifelong unhappiness expressed in his lyrics. Hart's homosexuality exists in biographies often as an unchanging fact; in this essay, the shifting attitudes toward homosexuality from the 1920s through the 1940s are presented as a backdrop to Hart's feelings toward himself, as well as others' feelings about him, especially Richard Rodgers's reactions. No previous attempt has been made to catalog thoroughly Hart's references to homosexuality in his lyrics, and none has shown the broader influence his homosexuality had on his artistic expression.

In retrospect, it seems unsurprising that Hart, a gay man, chose a career in musical theater, whose appeal so stereotypically marks a gay man today. But though the presence of effeminate chorus boys gave musical theater a gay appeal even in the teens of the twentieth century, Hart may have been attracted to writing for the stage for other reasons.

Hart was acclimated to the theatrical world. As children, he and brother Teddy were taken to the German-language theater and to vaudeville. For the amusement of their family they imitated the sketches they had seen. Performances continued at summer camp. Visitors to the home and family friends were from the theater, and Hart's peers—Oscar Hammerstein II, producer Mel Shauer—were also choosing show business as a profession.[2]

But Hart's ability to write may have been the strongest reason he chose the theater. His felicity with words—writing humorous essays, creating poems in German or English—was evident from the start.[3] His skill with words was one of the few ways Hart could stand above his peers. Theater in the teens and twenties was still a literate medium, its supremacy largely unchallenged by other entertaining media, and one capable of attracting attention from a very social smart set. Hart liked attention and he liked to show off for his groups of friends—how better than in the collaborative art form of musical theater? Unlike the lonely world of the solitary playwright typing out his nonmusical play in obscurity, the musical theater offered two audiences: collaborators (for Hart, the composer and book writer, then the production team as the show is revised on its path toward the opening) and the broader paying audience of New Yorkers. And don't forget that when you live constantly in public, you have no private life and no time for it. The theater had many attractions for Hart.

Anecdotes about Hart's sexuality from the 1920s are few.[4] For one, fewer people who knew him during that time lived to the more open 1970s to tell about it. But there is also the sense that he could manage his sexuality more discreetly when he was younger, and that only later did it compound his self-destructive unhappiness. At the same time, the most overt references to gay life are found in his earliest professional lyrics, which were written during the explosion of interest and visibility of gay life in the 1920s. This explosion can be seen in the "pansy" acts that flourished in cabarets and burlesque and the "problem plays" of homosexuality *(The Captive, The Drag)* that appeared on the legitimate stage.[5]

The earliest stories confirming Hart's homosexuality center on his life in Hollywood in the early 1930s. The repressed Hart ran wild when he got away from his hometown (even if that town were New York City). He frequented a "sleazy" movie theater in downtown Hollywood, attended parties with Tallulah Bankhead and William Haines, followed the nightclub career of pansy performer Jean Malin, and patronized the "Rocky Twins"—Paal and Leif—"wild" Norwegian female impersonators and "male courtesans." In his biography of Hart, Frederick Nolan notes that Hart liked Hollywood because his own leanings seemed mild compared to those of many around him. As one friend said, "It was easy for [Hart] to be led astray. He wanted to be led astray. There was nothing you could do about it. You couldn't ride herd on Larry Hart. Not in Hollywood." It is from Hollywood, too, that we have the report of Hart's only statement acknowledging his homosexuality. While there, Hart came under a brief blackmail threat when someone mailed information to his mother that intimated his homosexuality; Hart confided in one friend that "his mother would die if she thought her son was homosexual."[6]

Hart's underlying self-loathing stemmed from a handful of liabilities. Hart was short (at four feet, ten inches, he even wore lifts with his slippers), misshapen (his head was too large for his body), habitually late (due to late-night parties), an alcoholic, and a homosexual. Seeing himself in a mirror, he would make expressions of "outright disgust."[7] In bed, "He didn't know what to do or how to do it. But he wanted to, desperately," said one former male sex partner.[8] Hart's ineptitude at lovemaking is but one facet of his loathing of his homosexuality; more telling is the fact that he could not remain in bed with a sex partner: "you'd wake up and find him in the closet," continues the former sex partner; "He'd get up out of bed and go sleep in the closet. He had this complex about sleeping with someone."[9] In general, Hart could sleep through all sorts of racket, even friends on the phone beside his bed, so this action says much about Hart's rejection of and discomfort with his homosexuality.[10] Already suffering from short stature, Hart saw his homosexuality as only another, compounding debit. The majority of gay men during the period were faced with the "loss of jobs, family, and social respect" because of their homosexuality and subsequently internalized antihomosexual attitudes.[11] These attitudes and other circumstances formed a series of stumbling blocks in Hart's life.

During the 1930s, American scientists studied the causes and conditions of homosexuality, but, as Minton shows, they merely confirmed what society already believed. Society held that one set of predisposing factors toward homosexuality was "an effeminate father and an aggressive masculine mother." Hart's parents more closely matched the "ideal circumstances" for raising properly gender-identified children: "the father should be an understanding, tolerant but virile and decisive male. The mother should have . . . gentleness, patience and passivity."[12] Thus one reason some of Hart's friends denied his homosexuality may have stemmed from the belief that nothing in his home life suggested it.[13]

Hart's German-Jewish background was another stumbling block. Talmudic law is strict in its prohibition of homosexual acts.[14] The Hasidic movement had "enlightened" German Jews and assimilated them into bourgeois society—a society where family was "based on notions of sexual modesty and restraints." Thus, "the Jewish middle class is doubly cursed by the repressive Jewish tradition and by nascent bourgeois respectability."[15] Hart's parents had both emigrated with their large families intact, and thus continued Old World traditions in America.[16] Chauncey notes that the stability of Jewish families and community life impeded the expression of homosexuality.[17] The family's cultural pride in things German could have meant that the message of Magnus Hirschfeld may have crept into Hart's consciousness.[18] However, the two-year Eulenberg affair—the revelation of homosexuals near the kaiser, threatening the German family, which filled the domestic and foreign press—may have done more to impress the young Hart (who would have been between the ages of twelve and fourteen) with a disapproving opinion of homosexuality.

Society's attitude at large toward homosexuality also hampered its expression. "In those days it wasn't an open and acknowledged thing. . . . [Hart] felt permanent guilt because he was a homosexual," states one acquaintance. Interestingly, Richard Rodgers's wife Dorothy demonstrates the strength of the veil when she writes about her father (Benjamin Feiner) and his bout of depression. There was a heavy stigma attached to mental illness in 1931—and it should be remembered that homosexuality was also considered a mental illness. "Nervous breakdowns," she states, "like cancer, sex and venereal disease, were never spoken of out loud. Friends tactfully avoided asking questions." When these attitudes are considered in conjunction with the gay code to "honor other men's decisions to keep their homosexuality a secret," it is easy to see why Hart and his associates tried to render such an influential part of his life invisible.[19]

The models visible to Hart were also less than fitting and encouraging. "Given the centrality of the fairy to gay New York," says Chauncey, "many more homosexually active men refused (or saw no reason) to identify themselves as queer at all." Aside from the typical drag roles of the college stage, there is no evidence that Hart, like the pansies of the day, enjoyed wearing women's clothing or behaved in an effeminate way.[20] Another friend remembered, "Homosexuality in that period had two levels: One, it was held in major contempt, and the other was that among his kind it was the most exclusive club in New York"—of course, the signal examples were the more glamorous ones of Cole Porter and Noel Coward, not that of swarthy, dwarfish Larry Hart.[21] (Mark Fearnow's essay on Cole Porter in this volume reveals clearly the contrast between the two.)

The period's definition of an "invert"—"the homosexual with the inappropriate gender identity, mentality, and emotionality"—corresponded to the era's central image of the homosexual as fairy.[22] Hart understood homosexuality to mean the infusion of a female spirit inside a male body, a tenet of 1930s psychiatry.[23] Though Hart himself loathed psychiatry and psychiatrists, Freudian ideas of sexuality were seeping into American culture and Hart's consciousness.[24] In one number he wrote entitled "Reincarnation," the male singer gets his feminine charm from Marie Antoinette. In another number, Sir Galahad asks, "Who put the gal in Galahad" and is psychoanalyzed to discover, "I'm neither a sister nor a brother." Even while dismissing psychiatry, Hart repeated the notion: "Psychoanalysts are all the whirl. / Rich men pay them all they can. / Waking up to find that he's a girl / Is too good for the average man."[25] Even though Hart's exterior could not be characterized as feminine, he probably suspected femininity in himself in his "dependence upon a more aggressive male," that is, Rodgers.[26] Still, the match was not a close fit; other models were available.

The complementary category to "invert" is "pervert": "the homosexual whose gender characteristics were 'appropriate,' but who by chance, possibly flavored with curiosity, turned to a form of sexuality that went against his or her natural gender adjustment," as Minton sums up. Beyond the stigmas of immorality and sickness heaped upon homosexuality, the category of pervert, and thus Hart, was most open to cure, reflexively reinforcing notions of immorality and sickness and Hart's loathing of psychiatrists. Within this "masculine" category, Hart's behavior most closely matches that of the "wolf"; he kept control-dominance in his male-male relationships through use of power: money, status, and intelligence. Hart was attracted to tall, handsome, slim, stupid, young blond men. Hart's friend Milton Bender, usually culled these men from chorus boys looking for work—men inferior to Hart in earning power, status, and the ability to carry on a conversation. Hart would overwhelm them with gold cigarette cases and watches. Hart's reliance on Bender for contacts and need to impress them with gifts make Hart far less predatory than the image of "wolf" connotes. With the inequality existing between Hart and the men he chose as sexual partners, there is no basis for a long-lasting, mutual relationship—though he desired such. He was so lonely that when a friend agreed to go for a middle-of-the-night carriage ride, Hart proposed that he and the friend should share living quarters.[27]

Several other facets of then-current views on homosexuality correspond with Hart's character—and must have rankled Hart as well. The first is homosexual as failure, "a person who has failed to achieve and maintain adult heterosexual modes of sexual expression . . . [and is unable] to meet the responsibility of establishing and maintaining a home which involves the rearing of children."[28] This notion of failure must have been reiterated in his mother's continual belief and suggestion that he get married.[29] Freud further clarified the equation of heterosexuality with adulthood by asserting that "homosexuality was an immature form of sexuality."[30] Much of Hart's life was lived under the shelter of an extended childhood: the irresponsibility of much of his behavior, bunking with his brother most of his adult life, the Peter Pan collars on his pajamas, living with his mother. His height figured into this as well: Rodgers refers to him as a kid and a little brother and claims to have taken him shopping for clothes in the children's section of a department store.[31] Minton reports the notion that "the so-called well adjusted homosexual is not without conflict which he may learn to conceal by bravado or express in his defiance or his contempt for conventionality." This description may have been aimed more precisely at the transvestite fairies, but an expression of this behavior can be seen in Hart's obsessive check-paying and his dislike of anything mundane or middle class, whether it be keeping regular hours or adhering to standards of middle-class prudishness.[32]

Lorenz Hart's adult life careened between the licentious and the respectable. On the licentious side, he had as his friend, agent, and pimp, Milton "Doc" Bender, a dentist by trade, who was loathed by those who protected Hart. The puffy-faced Bender appointed himself Hart's shadow. Bender hosted orgies, where Hart was always an invited guest, and connected Hart with a series of anonymous male sexual partners.[33] Hart's licentiousness was also served by a number of drinking partners, including John O'Hara, the author of the "Pal Joey" stories. Those who kept Hart in line include his mother, his brother Teddy, his maid Big Mary, and Richard Rodgers (fig. 7). Hart's ties to his family were strong. He always lived with his mother when in New York and even brought her out to Hollywood for a time in the 1930s. Her rigid schedule of meals and seasonal cleanings never accounted for Hart's irregular schedule and may have earned her Hart's soubriquet of "The Cop." He allowed his mother to become "his anchor and his grip on life," as she had been to his father. When brother Teddy was home from his vaudeville tours, he slept in the same room with Hart, in adjoining beds, until Teddy's marriage in 1938. His maid, Big Mary, constantly badgered and belittled Hart over his lateness and apparent lack of work.[34]

Upon his return to New York in the mid-1930s, Hart discovered a changed New York. The frivolity of the 1920s was over and Broadway was a sober place; the number of productions was down and so were the opportunities to display gay life except in the most closeted circumstances. In 1937, the Catholic Church, which had helped "clean up" the movies with the Production Code, set its sites on Broadway with the Dunnigan Bill, which would have given the commissioner of licenses censorship powers not unlike the lord chamberlain's in Britain. The bill was vetoed, but the spirit of the times was apparent.[35]

Yet Hart's attraction to men could not be stifled as it once had and became fairly common, if unspoken, knowledge.[36] His increasing wealth made him a frequent party-giver and easy touch. He took care to protect his mother, installing a steel door between his quarters and hers to muffle the sounds of his parties.[37] Yet even while surrounded by festive hangers-

FIG. 7. **Lorenz Hart and Richard Rodgers at work on *Pal Joey*.**

(Courtesy, Billy Rose Theatre Collection, New York Library for the Performing Arts.)

on, Hart was an intensely lonely man. Singer Mabel Mercer said, "He was lonely in the crowds that he demanded, sought, and collected around him. He was the saddest man I ever knew."[38] The easy access to alcohol and joyless anonymous sex often interfered with his work, the only aspect of his life in which Hart took pride.

Hart dated several women during the 1930s and 1940s, even though he was convinced that he was too ugly to be loved by any woman.[39]

There were three women to whom he proposed. One was Frances Manson, a story editor for Columbia Pictures, who turned down Hart's proposal because of his drinking. Another was opera singer Nanette Guilford. Guilford was taller than Hart, buxom, elegant, talented, and intelligent. When Hart proposed, she turned him down because of her previous bad experience in marriage. Vivienne Segal was another elegant, intelligent woman whom Hart adored. She recalls that Hart proposed marriage to her without ever having kissed her. Neither Guilford nor Manson relates any kind of physical relationship with Hart.[40] The women Hart admired—including Rodgers's wife Dorothy and his brother Teddy's wife Dorothy—were elegant, intelligent women who fit the ideal of the time. They become an image and useful vessel in his lyrics and librettos. Gay men's adoration of "ideal" women is common; for Hart it reflected his conflicted feelings about his sexuality and his desire to fit in with society.

During all these years, Hart remained close to his family, who were obligated by blood ties to take care of him. His opportunistic acquaintances took care of his sexual needs. Yet Hart continued to return to the one person who meshed least well with him and was least obligated to become part of his life: Richard Rodgers. What did Hart receive from that relationship?

Rodgers—the songwriter who behaved like a stockbroker—was Hart's antithesis: solidly middle to upper middle class in his upbringing and outlook, Rodgers was stability to Hart's restlessness, sobriety to Hart's excess, and method to Hart's inspiration as he was melody to Hart's lyrics. Hart's relationship with Rodgers seems to be summed up in one neat couplet: "You're careful, clever, virtuous and sensible, / I'm carefree, foolish, naughty, reprehensible." To Hart, Rodgers became known as "General," "Teacher," or "Professor"; to Rodgers, Hart became "a partner, a best friend, and a source of permanent irritation."[41]

Rodgers and Hart's professional lives are inextricable. Rodgers was sixteen when he met Hart—seven years his senior. Rodgers confessed to his "reverence" for the erudite, energetic Hart.[42] One hypothesis has been put forth as to what twenty-three-year-old Hart made of the talented, earnest family friend. Musical theater historian Gerald Mast suggests that Hart's "deepest unrequited love" may have been for Rodgers.[43] Nolan quotes one friend of Hart's saying, "Poor Larry. What a shame he had to fall in love with Dick."[44] Whether these feelings were overt, covert, acknowledged or not, their personal lives became as intertwined as their professional ones. Much of their writing was done in each other's homes,

and both families became known to each other.[45] Together they survived
six years of struggle and amateur shows before becoming "overnight"
successes with *The Garrick Gaieties* in 1925. Rodgers looked after the
business side of "Rodgers and Hart" soon after this, accepting job offers
and ensuring that Hart was present for work. When the call came from
London to write *Lido Lady,* they traveled together, vacationed together,
and rented a flat together.[46] When Rodgers married in 1930, he brought
his six-week bride to London to another flat shared with Hart; Hart and
Bender even joined them on the French Riviera during the honeymoon.[47]
Work in Hollywood in the early 1930s was no different: Rodgers, his wife,
and Hart traveled together and lived in the same house upon arrival.[48]
Even as late as 1942, Rodgers, his wife, and Hart traveled together and
shared the same accommodations.[49] Hart usually had his own floor
and/or entrance during these periods of cohabitation, and Rodgers could
easily excuse sharing living space as an easier way to work with and keep
track of his partner. The times treated men's associations differently, but
even Hart's sister-in-law refers to their "very special relationship."[50]

Though the amount of guidance and protection Rodgers gave Hart
makes their relationship seem one-sided, Rodgers also benefited from the
association. The young Rodgers learned about theater from Hart's expertise. Reviewers and commentators discussed the style and content of
Hart's lyrics in the newspapers, bringing Rodgers's songs added luster.
Hart even affected the composition of the songs. Soprano Helen Ford,
star of *Dearest Enemy* and *Peggy-Ann,* could never get Rodgers to write
in a flattering key for her; neither would Rodgers write low enough for
"Moanin' Low" singer Libby Holman—he always wrote for Hart's
range.[51] Moreover, he also wrote for Hart's penchant for complicated
rhymes; Rodgers often composed with repeated phrases and patterns that
"dictated relentless rhyming."[52] Hart's absences and disinterest forced
Rodgers to write melodies that were interesting for their own sake.[53]
Music analyst Alec Wilder tacitly acknowledges this, devoting six out of
his seven sections on Rodgers's work to the songs he wrote in collaboration with Hart, dismissing his work with Hammerstein as "bordering on
musical complacency."[54]

Only a handful of quotations reveals Rodgers's affection for Hart.
He once said, "I think Larry and I were very sensitive to each other
immediately, and yes, had a genuine liking for each other." In a public
address in 1973, Rodgers admitted, "I loved working with him and I
loved him. I miss him terribly." Otherwise, one has to look at his actions:
Rodgers's affection can be seen in his willingness to search for Hart, to

defend him to other collaborators, and to accept him back after his many disappearances.[55]

This acceptance was accompanied by Rodgers's anger, which he had learned to express in one of three ways: "bickering, yelling or unnatural silence."[56] Rodgers's anger toward Hart is evident in many anecdotes. He recalls their fights over their professional work were "furious, blasphemous and frequent," making "noise [that] could be heard all over the city."[57] When Hart appeared with a cigar at breakfast, nauseating Rodgers's pregnant wife, Rodgers yelled, "Will you, for God's sake, get that damn cigar out of here!"[58] Rodgers answered the phone, thinking he was tricked by Hart, with "Listen you bleeping son of a bleep . . ."[59] On more than one occasion Rodgers resorted to locking Hart in rooms to get work out of him.[60] Even after Hart had been dead twenty years, the mention of his name could send Rodgers into a furniture-pounding fit.[61]

The combination of acceptance and anger became addictive. "When you're not around to scold me, / Life's a bitter cup," sings one of their characters. Hart's lyrics reflect the need for abuse in love. This mixture of closeness and distance turned their later relationship toxic. During their successes of the late 1930s, Hart became more careless—increasingly drunk or absent—while Rodgers gained in confidence. In general, Rodgers was impatient to write; not finding Hart when he needed him— as increasingly became the case—only frustrated him further. Rodgers grew angrier; his attitude changed; he became "snide and critical." Finally, he sought new creative partners. Rodgers approached both Ira Gershwin and Oscar Hammerstein II while he still worked with Hart. Hammerstein, of course, took Rodgers up on the offer when Hart nixed the idea that became *Oklahoma!* For Hart, the descent continued. The death of his mother one month after the opening of *Oklahoma!* loosened Hart's ties with the respectable people holding him together.[62] By the end of the year, he was dead.

Rodgers sweeps Hart's homosexuality and his own personal feelings toward him under the carpet in his mostly ghostwritten autobiography *Musical Stages;* Hart is noted by his disappearances, most frequently to the bar.[63] However, Rodgers's wife indicates that he knew: "Although I don't think the public was aware of Larry's sexual preferences, . . . it was pretty generally accepted by all who knew him that he was a homosexual."[64] In *Musical Stages,* Rodgers obliquely hints of Hart at Ralph's Bar and at the Luxor baths, but does not explain that these places had "mixed" clientele.[65] The only reference in which Rodgers acknowledges Hart's homosexuality comes secondhand; during "a burst of pique,"

Rodgers called Hart "that drunken little fag."[66] Why did Rodgers so aggressively silence Hart's homosexuality? The answer lies in the very collaboration between them.

In his Freudian study of male-male collaboration, Wayne Koestenbaum states that "men who collaborate engage in a metaphorical sexual intercourse," that "collaboration is always a sublimation of erotic entanglement," that men working together "were enacting if not feeling homosexual desire, and that collaboration between men still carries that charge."[67] This, I suggest, was unacceptable to Richard Rodgers. Rodgers's homophobia turned into action as he covered up two suspect "flaws" in his relationship with Hart: weakness and aggression.[68]

Clearly, Hart's homoerotic desires did not bother Rodgers for a good many years. Koestenbaum remarks, "When two men write together . . . they rapidly patter to obscure their erotic burden"; the speed of Rodgers and Hart's writing kept this "erotic burden" hidden, as did perhaps their arguments.[69] Also, their work served as the interface between them; Koestenbaum states that the work produced is "alternately the child of their sexual union, and a shared woman" (the text takes on "feminine properties").[70] The problem in the 1930s and 1940s was that Hart turned away from the work but still turned to Rodgers for the kind of interaction they usually shared during collaboration. Hart became—consciously or no—more drunk, more absent, forcing Rodgers (and others) to care more, to do more, to love more. He overstepped Rodgers's personal boundaries. Rodgers, though talented, is never characterized as a generous man; Stephen Sondheim succinctly accuses him of having "limited soul."[71]

Yet Rodgers reacted to more than Hart's transgression; he reacted to something in himself. Of two collaborators, one "keenly feels lack or disenfranchisement, and seeks out a partner to attain power and completion." In their early years, Hart had the seniority, skill, knowledge, and connections to make them successful. Even so, this was not uppermost in Rodgers's mind after his initial meeting with Hart; Rodgers went bubbling home under the powerful emotion of "I have a lyricist! I have a lyricist!" "A writer turns to a partner," Koestenbaum elucidates, "not from a practical assessment of advantages, but from a superstitious hope, a longing for replenishment and union that invites baroquely sexual interpretation."[72] Such a revelation of "superstition" would have been unthinkable to Rodgers. He wanted to wipe out that early expression of need—feminine need—that did not coincide with his mature persona and career with Hammerstein.

What may have upset Rodgers more is his perception that, contrary to the feminine position of need, he took an active, aggressive part in the relationship. Rodgers wrote his melodies to "seduce" Hart into working.[73] It is not difficult to site this collaboration. Freud posited the anus as "secondary to sexual reproduction"; however, in homosexual theory, precedence is given "to the symbolic 'anus,' the place where men conceive when they write together." Rodgers once told Alan Jay Lerner "that if he didn't compose regularly, he actually became physically constipated."[74] By possessing the reproductive site and seducing Hart, Rodgers takes on an aggressive "female" role, making him more gender-confused than Hart. To Rodgers, being the aggressive partner was worse.[75] After Rodgers had won Hammerstein into partnership—his most obvious dismissal of his collaboration with Hart—Rodgers's method of composition changed: no longer did he write the melody first and attempt to coax lyrics from his partner. Now Hammerstein provided the text that Rodgers set to music.

Rodgers's renunciation of Hart occurred during a period of two important changes: a growing antigay movement and a shift in the definition of homosexual. The late 1930s and the 1940s saw "a powerful campaign against gay life"—shutting down gays' meeting places and decreasing their visibility except as sex deviants and criminals. By the 1940s, the definition of "homosexual" shifted from focusing on the role of insertee or effeminate character to a larger one wherein any man engaged in homosexual acts—even metaphorical ones—was classified as homosexual. Chauncey describes the concurrent spread of the idea of heterosexuality during this period, noting the growing fear of being "implicated" as homosexual.[76]

Rodgers set about to wipe out the homosexual context of his association with Hart entirely. After Hart's death, "Rodgers treated his own early career like some faintly embarrassing youthful fling." Yet the songs of Rodgers and Hart—"to what was often Rodgers's intense annoyance"—became increasingly popular. Says Koestenbaum, "Books with two authors are specimens of a relation, and show writing to be a quality of motion and exchange, not a fixed thing." Rodgers could not allow these songs—his music, interweaving and dallying with Hart's text—to exist outside an approved framework. When Hart's will was contested because of the large percentage it gave to his financial advisor, Rodgers argued for the will, stating that Hart was in full control of his faculties in the last six months of his life. One friend said, "Dick perjured himself on the stand. All he wanted was to control the copyrights."[77] Rodgers firmly controlled the rights to these songs, editing the first anthology.[78] Today, the Rodgers and Hammerstein Organization remains "indifferent" to Rodgers's work with Hart and has allowed their properties "to languish."[79]

No matter the control Rodgers sought over their songs, the evidence of Hart's homosexuality—and Hart's enduring influence on theater— remains within them. The most overt references are found in songs dating from the 1920s and early 1930s Hollywood. In "Manhattan" (1925), Hart has the couple singing that they will "starve together, dear, / In Childs." George Chauncey identifies several Childs restaurants in the theater district that were established meeting places for gays in the 1920s and 1930s. In the second edition of *The Garrick Gaieties* (1926), Hart has Sir Galahad running around to Childs. The couple in "Manhattan" were undoubtedly going to Childs to view the "show" of gay men acting in campy ways, as did many tourists in Stewart's and the Life Cafeteria in Greenwich Village. The reference to starving refers to the fact that a nickel cup of coffee could be purchased to support hours of mixing and conversation.[80] Thus the couple takes on the double role of observer and participant—echoing Hart's own position.

In *The Girlfriend*, from 1926, the number "What Is It?" asks explicitly the gender role question of the day: "A she or he?" Noting that men and women are behaving as the opposite sex, the lyric follows one female. Now that her hair is short, "She fits right in a nest of boys, / For the rest of boys / Are girls." An illustration of the original production of this number shows, significantly, mannish women being upstaged by a chorus line of effeminate men (fig. 8). To top it off, the caption misquotes the song to read "The best of boys are girls." Concerning this gender confusion, Hart later (1940) has a Gypsy Rose Lee stand-in state: "I don't like a deep contralto / Or a man whose voice is alto. / Zip! I'm a heterosexual."[81]

Hart was aware of the real life of gay men behind their screen images in silent films: "He-men who suggest a lot / When they bare their chest a lot / Do fancy needlework at home." He notes that "Sheiks may be effeminate," a fairly clear reference to Valentino. Once sound came in, "Hercules and young Ulysses / All talk like sissies." A female transvestite number written during Rodgers and Hart's Hollywood days in the early 1930s has the singer declaring, "I'm one of the boys . . . / I go to the tailor Marlene [Dietrich] employs."[82]

There are a few references to lesbians in his lyrics as well. There is a purposely misapplied quote displaying posed young women as "The Children's Hour." In *By Jupiter* (1942), an effeminate male complains to the woman who ignores him that "you'll let my well of loneliness run

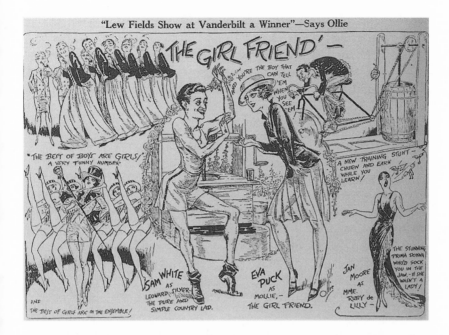

FIG. 8. Ollie from *Zitz,* a society gossip tabloid, illustrating the first night of *The Girl Friend.* Note the figures in the upper-left-hand corner.

(Collection of the author.)

dry," a topsy-turvy reference to the title of Radclyffe Hall's 1929 lesbian novel.[83]

Hart's few mentions of cruising sites are so bound in heterosexual context, it seems he is writing from hearsay rather than direct experience. He knew of Central Park as a "rendezvous for lovers" in the song "A Tree in the Park" and later bemoaned Mayor LaGuardia's moral cleanup of the city with "No dark park to kiss your girl in."[84] More directly, Hart's lyric kids one marine because he supposedly hangs around "the piers that are on the East River"; the waterfront was a known cruising area for gay men, where gays and sailors easily mixed.[85] There is only one reference in his lyrics to Greenwich Village ("Where modern men itch / To be free"). In other lyrics, Hart mentions many streets in the nearby Soho area but never includes even veiled references to the Village.[86] Again, this more directly reflects Hart's experiences. An intensely private man, he didn't swan in public with other gay men but relied on private parties or contacts in mixed bars for his gay life, as did many other men during the period.[87] The club in *Pal Joey* may have been patterned on one such bar. In the opening scene, the bar manager asks after Joey's vices, warning him that "the drummer is just a boy." Joey later makes a joke of this while introducing the acts, telling a story where one patron overlooks the physical beauty of a specialty dancer because "he was waiting for the drummer." The sudden noise from the band betrays the drummer's nervousness.[88]

Hart was familiar, too, with the signs that would identify gay men. Plato, one of the standards of the gay reading list, is mentioned three times. One man still chasing women after they've refused him states that "Plato and I can't agree." One man uninterested in sex with his wife is reading Plato. The female in "My Heart Stood Still" reads Plato as well before falling in love. A sunflower spied on one man's lapel provokes the viewer to exclaim "Swish, swish, swish!" One song recalled an incident when a man accidentally idling in the lingerie section of a store is accosted by "So that's the kind of guy you are, huh? / A chemise fancier—a twiddle twa— / Me a twiddle twa! / That meant a fight!"[89] Both of these comments also reveal the hostility toward gay men.

However, these references to gay life are usually found in the secondary rank of Hart's songs and form a small portion of the more than six hundred songs he wrote. Hart's professional life and artistic output more subtly reflected his homosexuality. Unlike Cole Porter or Noel Coward, Hart did not surround himself with homosexual artists onstage or behind the scenes. This is not to imply that there were not homosexuals around him. There were chorus boys, of course—Richard Rodgers made sure there were no effeminate young men as the chorus of marines in *Present Arms*—and backstage personnel—Herb Fields, their stateside librettist during the 1920s, "was part of the gay scene, too," and choreographer Busby Berkeley, who worked on two early Rodgers and Hart shows, was as "sexually ambivalent toward women" as Hart.[90] Still, Hart never sought—or disapproved of—these associations. Only rarely does Hart write a line that subverts heterosexual expectations with gay subtext. Even when he does, these lines are sung by women, masking the threat. An Amazon in the gender-reversed *By Jupiter* sings out "a sailor has a boy in every port," hinting at the understood relations between sailors and gay men. An abandoned young woman sings, "I was a queen to him. / Who's goin' to make me gay now?"[91] Significantly, this is the only time Hart used the word *gay* when a homosexual subtext could be posited; all other uses rely on conventional meanings of merry, quick, or colorful. At other times Hart uses *pansy* or *fairy,* but more as a reference to urban life than as an indicator of subtext. Hart's references are never as bold or blunt—or even given to males—as those of Cole Porter, who, in 1919, had one man singing of "My Cozy Little Corner in the Ritz" where he could see the kings "And let the queens see me."[92] Hart never sought the coterie audience that belonged to Porter.[93]

Previous studies of Hart's lyrics note three qualities: triple rhymes, polysyllabic rhymes, and risqué humor. Those who knew him personally also note the speed with which he worked. The common thread uniting these qualities is the desire to show off, reflecting the bravado of the gay man. Hart was aware of his showing off and attempted to break away from it: "They said all I could do was triple rhyme. . . . I could have said, 'I took one look at you, / I threw a book at you,' but I didn't." His later lyrics show more directness than earlier ones, but he never abandoned his ability to dazzle. At the same time, Hart's complicated rhyme schemes, which call attention to surface cleverness rather than reveal character (e.g., "Beans could get no keener re- / Ception in a beanery"), may have reflected a fear of exposure. Hart's risqué lyrics also reflect a conflicted nature. Director Josh Logan noted, "I found that Larry loved to 'put something over' on the censors; he was constantly a naughty boy, but an innocently naughty boy." Hart's sense of humor was never injurious, but reflects an immature, omnipresent awareness of sex. A good example comes from the rejecting husband in *By Jupiter:* "Off to bed we will creep / Then we'll sleep and sleep and sleep . . . / I'll give you plenty of nothing."[94]

Hart's perceptions of life were filtered through his experiences as a homosexual and found expression in his lyrics.[95] Corresponding to Hart's almost pathological need to be surrounded by people was an equally intense need for privacy.[96] Musicals of the period frequently feature characters who long to escape the city's bustle or the intrusions/obstacles of others. Two lovers alone on the physical stage openly cherish their privacy ("Do, do, do / What you've done, done, done / Before, Baby" sings the leading couple in the Gershwins' *Oh, Kay!*).[97] Time and again in the musicals of Rodgers and Hart, two characters alone on stage long for even more distance between themselves and other prying people (either other characters offstage or, by extension, from the theater audience). One couple yearns for a year "On a Desert Island with Thee"—"with thy mama many miles away." Other couples sing of disappearing to their "Mountain Greenery"—"Beneath the eyes of no ma and no pa"—heading upstairs to "The Blue Room," rendezvousing beneath their little "Tree in the Park," or checking into a small hotel—"Not a sign of people. / Who wants people?"[98] *By Jupiter* imagines an entire land without spying eyes: "Maybe there's a place where you're afraid to kiss; / You could only do it if you hid . . . Not here!" Hart's homosexuality comes into play as a subversive element, reversing musical comedy tradition by implying lovers need a separate place to do more than sing—suggesting a coarse physical reality to beautified stage heterosexuality. Generating this need for privacy must be Hart's own need to express his physical desires away from disapproving eyes—where even a kiss is taboo. Another source of this unease with the public is expressed through an introspective number cut from *Pal Joey*—interesting especially because the Joey of O'Hara's stories never gives way to self-reflection: Joey sings, "I can't be sure of girls, / I'm not at home with men— / I'm ending up with me again."[99] This privacy is both a desire and a result of homosexuality.

Hart's lyrics—like his life—never reflect an ongoing, stable, mature relationship. Partly this is due to the musical comedy genre wherein there are obstacles to be overcome as boy gets/loses/gets girl or vice versa. There are moments, however, when heterosexual couples confess a love for one another that is untainted by the bites and fights of Hart's more physically based lyrics. Rodgers's melodies for these tunes usually proceed with restricted intervals over their octave-plus range, breaking into jumps of fourths or fifths during the release. Of one such song, Wilder writes that it has "a tranquility achieved by great spareness and, but for the climax of sudden brilliance, complete simplicity."[100] Hart turns to wordplay to find lyrics for these songs, specifically to extended metaphors. "Moon of My Delight" ends with the couple gaining "a satellite or two." "Yours Sincerely" explores the way devotion is expressed at the end of a letter: "very truly," "Ever your humble servant / Faithfully, I remain." "With a Song in My Heart" examines love as a song that "soon is a hymn" "when the music swells." Two martial lovers (Greek and Amazon) who first express their love in soldierly terms—"I'm at your command"—later learn that love is a "Careless Rhapsody" that has "chords that will bind us." One couple in *The Boys from Syracuse* sings: "The shortest day of the year / Has the longest night of the year / And the longest night / Is the shortest night with you."[101] In these songs, Hart skillfully plays with an image, teasing it apart and not letting it settle until the song reaches its conclusion, but says very little. The artificiality of the construction in the resulting lyric prevents any heartfelt connection. The melody is needed to give any emotional depth; a sense of beauty is the most the two combined can hope for. In these lyrics, Hart substitutes surface for substance, revealing that, given the assignment "this is for the boy and girl to sing," he was at a loss to define, explore, or plumb heterosexual love or, indeed, any enduring love beyond the lustful or bitter.[102]

For Hart, love hurts—from the first look that infatuates, to ongoing symptoms so severe they could send you to a doctor. Of forty-three songs describing the physical impact of love, sixteen (37 percent) are sung by men alone, compared to five (12 percent) for women alone (three are unascribable to gender). Of the nineteen duets, twelve (63 percent) are initiated by males, while the females echo the sentiment in a repeated chorus. Thus of the forty references ascribable to gender, twenty-eight (70 percent) are wholly male or initiated by men. The notion "I took one look at you, / That's all I meant to do, / And then my heart stood still!" is echoed by many men. "It happened—I felt it happen" sings the man in "Have You Met Miss Jones?"; in the release section (set to Rodgers's jumping tune), he further describes it: "And all at once I lost my breath, / And all at once was scared to death, / And all at once I owned the earth and sky!" The physical sensation only continues in love. The male singer of "You Took Advantage of Me" has fallen, been slayed, killed, shaken down, had his goose cooked, is "hot and bothered," suffers "something awful" whether his sweetheart is far or near, and finally caves in with "So lock the doors / And call me yours." Hart recognized this theme in his songs and kidded himself about it by exaggerating the notion into physical illness. If you've been love-stung, then "the doctor can't help you." "How's Your Health?" advises the man, "Love's the only barometer / For all your pains and aches." In "This Can't Be Love," Hart reverses himself by having the male character plead it can't be love "because I feel so well / No sobs, no sorrows, no sighs / . . . I get no dizzy spells / . . . My heart does not stand still."[103] Giving these physical bouts with lust to male characters reveals Hart's understanding of "male" characteristics.

Hart's experience with stupid men becomes a thread in his lyrics. Of thirty-four references to stupid people, eighteen (53 percent) are men (the number rises to twenty-six—76 percent—when including references to men and women as stupid). As one female sings, "I guess that I like you / 'Cause you have no I.Q." Even though a male may be "a sap" and "a half-wit," he has redeeming virtues: "you're ev'ry inch a man, / Tall and slender, strong and tan." More bluntly, Pal Joey "has no head to think with," "And yet where it counts / He's adept enough."[104] The overall picture of men in love—not too bright, but decidedly corporeal—reflects a distinct homosexual underworld of brief sexual encounters where good looks are desired and conversations are limited.

Beyond the comic physical impact love had on Hart, Mast notes another possible type: bruisings from the rough trade found in some of the bars he ventured to—"The furtive sigh, / The blackened eye" not being randomly rhymed.[105] Aside from possible physical abuse, there was certainly petty thievery. One male singer asks, "Did a glamorous skirt / Ever pilfer your shirt and tie?" Though a woman might take a shirt and tie as a trophy, it is more likely that an impecunious male lover would steal the higher-quality shirt and tie of Hart. Also, Pal Joey notes that, when he comes home drunk and alone at night, "My wallet is all right"; Hart's drunken, accompanied homecomings must have put his wallet in danger.[106] The contrast between Hart's need to control his lovers and the petty abuses he may have taken from them further highlights the opposing extremes operating in his life.

If the often rough physicality of love is expressed through male characters, the emotional pain of love is expressed primarily through females. The overlapping ideas that a lover is a fool, that one is unrequited or lonely without love, that the beloved is too good, that love is unreal, that loving is giving in to weakness are expressed by female characters alone in twenty-five out of fifty-three cases (47 percent compared to thirteen—25 percent—for men alone); the total rises to thirty—56 percent—including female instigations of same. The lonely "Little Blue Girl" asks only that "somebody send a tender / Blue boy, to cheer a / Little girl blue." When love comes, it is often met by disbelief: "Do you love me? I wonder . . . can it be true?" sings one young woman. One female revels in abasement by singing: "I'm not so pleased with myself, / My attractions are few, / But I'll be pleased with myself, / If I'm pleasing you." More often, love comes unbidden and remains unrequited: Morgan le Fay sings, "Can't you do a friend a favor /Can't you fall in love with me?" This exposure leaves the singer feeling a fool. One female declares bluntly, "I'm a fool, little one, / For I wouldn't love you if I were wise." An unrequited female sings, "Fools rush in, so here I am, / Very glad to be unhappy."[107] The male and female of "I Wish I Were in Love Again" ask for "The self-deception that believes the lie." Self-deception is tied to foolishness when the jilted female sings, "Falling in love with love / Is falling for make believe. / Falling in love with love / Is playing the fool."[108] Vera Simpson, perhaps the most self-aware of all of Hart's creations, asks, "Must I want the one [man] who's not for me? / It's just my foolish way." She is also, of course, "Bewitched, Bothered, and Bewildered" by Joey. Finally, she sings of her relationship with Joey: "Take it away, it's too good to be true."[109] Hart's loneliness, self-abasement, and self-pitying sentiments are funneled most directly through female characters. By channeling his experiences and feelings into "appropriate" staged representations (following the "male" and "female" characteristic patterns widely believed of the day), Hart's understanding of his divided nature becomes overt even as he buries it in a too careful heterosexual context.[110]

Larry Hart is generally acknowledged for his brilliant contributions to, and standards of, lyric writing, while his homosexuality has been little discussed. Hart's earliest lyrics easily touched on gay themes during the openness of the 1920s and early 1930s, though his own ease came only amid the larger debauchery of Hollywood. His return to his repressive home environment, New York, in the 1930s and 1940s was matched by a growing antigay movement; Hart's sexuality became part of a tawdry demimonde, while his overt lyric references came only during appropriately "daring" subject matter such as in the gender-reversed *By Jupiter*. Against the increasingly repressive social background came Richard Rodgers's reaction to the Freudian implications of his collaboration with Hart, which ended in their partnership's dissolution. Finally, Hart's understanding of the coexistence of male and female natures in the homosexual reflects 1930s psychiatric beliefs; the result is the bifurcation of sentiments in his lyrics into male corporality and female emotional suffering. Clearly, Hart's homosexuality influenced his life and work far more pervasively than has been previously documented.

NOTES

1. Samuel Marx and Jan Clayton, *Rodgers and Hart: Bewitched, Bothered, and Bedeviled* (New York, G. P. Putnam's Sons, 1976), 224.

2. Frederick Nolan, *Lorenz Hart: A Poet on Broadway* (New York: Oxford University Press, 1994), 8–11.

3. Ibid., 9.

4. Nolan suggests that Hart's initial sexual forays took place while a counselor at summer camp (ibid., 20). Though this sounds plausible, Nolan provides no evidence.

5. George Chauncey, *Gay New York: Gender, Urban Culture, and the Making of the Gay Male World, 1890–1940* (New York: Basic Books, 1994), 310–12.

6. Dorothy Rodgers writes of Hart's homosexuality in a chapter entitled

"Hollywood," in *A Personal Book* (New York: Harper and Row, 1977), 107; Marx and Clayton, *Rodgers and Hart,* 186–87, 170–71; Nolan, *Lorenz Hart,* 192, 172, 193; Marx and Clayton, *Rodgers and Hart,* 190–91.

7. Gerald Nachman, "Lorenz Hart: Little Boy Blue," *Theater Week,* May 8, 1995, 35; Marx and Clayton, *Rodgers and Hart,* 200, 19; Dorothy Hart, *Thou Swell, Thou Witty: The Life and Lyrics of Lorenz Hart* (New York: Harper and Row, 1976), 122.

8. Nolan, *Lorenz Hart,* 238.

9. Marx and Clayton, *Rodgers and Hart,* 224. Frederick Nolan's biography, *Lorenz Hart,* quotes interviews collected in earlier books, notably *Rodgers and Hart* and *Thou Swell, Thou Witty;* occasionally he has quoted the source more fully than earlier books did. Citations of more than one source here should not be taken to imply that there is more than one original source.

10. D. Hart, *Thou Swell, Thou Witty,* 23.

11. Chauncey, *Gay New York,* 25, 280–81.

12. Henry L. Minton, "Femininity in Men and Masculinity in Women: American Psychiatry and Psychology Portray Homosexuality in the 1930s," *Journal of Homosexuality* 13, no. 1 (1986): 2. Hart's father had an open-handed attitude toward guests in his home, personal habits, and the legality of business dealings; Hart's mother, though she had her patterned ways, remained quietly in the background of Hart's life.

13. Nanette Guilford is one who denies Hart's homosexuality, but she acknowledges "he was led into things" (Marx and Clayton, *Rodgers and Hart,* 191). Henry Myers was another denier (Marx and Clayton, *Rodgers and Hart,* 74).

14. Michael Kauffman, *Love, Marriage, and Family in Jewish Law and Tradition* (Northvale, N.J.: Jason Aronson, 1992), 138–40.

15. David Biale, *Eros and the Jews: From Biblical Israel to Contemporary America* (New York: Basic Books, 1992), 150–51, 169.

16. D. Hart, *Thou Swell, Thou Witty,* 13.

17. Chauncey, *Gay New York,* 73.

18. Marx and Clayton, *Rodgers and Hart,* 16; D. Hart, *Thou Swell, Thou Witty,* 15–16.

19. Marx and Clayton, *Rodgers and Hart,* 190; D. Rodgers, *A Personal Book,* 102; Chauncey, *Gay New York,* 276.

20. Chauncey, *Gay New York,* 24; Nolan, *Lorenz Hart,* 15.

21. Marx and Clayton, *Rodgers and Hart,* 238.

22. Minton, "Femininity in Men," 12; Chauncey, *Gay New York,* 16.

23. Chauncey, *Gay New York,* 49.

24. Hart flew into a "rage" when he heard the word *psychiatrist;* his sister-in-law states he had an "old-fashioned" prejudice against psychiatry (D. Hart, *Thou Swell, Thou Witty,* 160). Hart's resentment may also have stemmed from the fact that those around him—Rodgers, his brother, and his wife—tried to get Hart committed (D. Hart, *Thou Swell, Thou Witty,* 159). Josh Logan may also hit upon a cause when he notes that Hart's loneliness and drinking, combined with his ugliness, made him a Romantic figure, subject to pointing and pity—"an emotion that causes writers to write" (D. Hart, *Thou Swell, Thou Witty,* 111); Hart

may have believed that examining and dispelling that nexus of emotions would have meant killing what made him a good writer, a fear common enough in early views of psychiatry. Hart revealed in "Where or When" that "the things you think / Come from the dreams you dream," acknowledging the subconscious (*The Complete Lyrics of Lorenz Hart,* ed. Dorothy Hart and Robert Kimball [New York: Alfred A. Knopf, 1986], 228). The entire plot of *Peggy-Ann* acknowledges it as well—it is the dream of the title character.

25. *Complete Lyrics of Lorenz Hart,* 198, 74, 222.

26. Minton, "Femininity in Men," 6.

27. Ibid., 12, 8; Chauncey, *Gay New York,* 88; Marx and Clayton, *Rodgers and Hart,* 236, 116; Nolan, *Lorenz Hart,* 193; Marx and Clayton, *Rodgers and Hart,* 168–69.

28. Minton, "Femininity in Men," 5.

29. Richard Rodgers, *Musical Stages: An Autobiography* (New York: Random House, 1975), 204–5; Marx and Clayton, *Rodgers and Hart,* 155, 166.

30. Minton, "Femininity in Men," 8.

31. D. Hart, *Thou Swell, Thou Witty,* 121; Marx and Clayton, *Rodgers and Hart,* 89; Nolan, *Lorenz Hart,* 129, 266.

32. Minton, "Femininity in Men," 6; Marx and Clayton, *Rodgers and Hart,* 220; D. Hart, *Thou Swell, Thou Witty,* 73. Josh Logan stated Hart "hated anything he considered too ordinary. Respectable, proper, was not only repulsive but stupid and dull" (Marx and Clayton, *Rodgers and Hart,* 205).

33. Marx and Clayton, *Rodgers and Hart,* 116. One guest described these orgies later in mock horror: "kissing with the lights on! Shocking!" (Nolan, *Lorenz Hart,* 237).

34. Marx and Clayton, *Rodgers and Hart,* 235; D. Hart, *Thou Swell, Thou Witty,* 119, 22; Marx and Clayton, *Rodgers and Hart,* 18; D. Hart, *Thou Swell, Thou Witty,* 121; Marx and Clayton, *Rodgers and Hart,* 114–15.

35. Kaier Curtin, *"We Can Always Call Them Bulgarians": The Emergence of Lesbians and Gay Men on the American Stage* (Boston: Alyson, 1987), 210–11.

36. D. Rodgers, *A Personal Book,* 111.

37. Marx and Clayton, *Rodgers and Hart,* 238.

38. Nolan, *Lorenz Hart,* 222.

39. Marx and Clayton, *Rodgers and Hart,* 191.

40. D. Hart, *Thou Swell, Thou Witty,* 84, 70; Marx and Clayton, *Rodgers and Hart,* 207. This lack of reportage is in part a reflection of behavior expected for women who lived through that era. Neither does Dorothy Rodgers mention a physical relationship with her husband.

41. Marx and Clayton, *Rodgers and Hart,* 229; *Complete Lyrics of Lorenz Hart,* 204; Marx and Clayton, *Rodgers and Hart,* 86; R. Rodgers, *Musical Stages,* 28.

42. R. Rodgers, *Musical Stages,* 27.

43. Gerald Mast, *Can't Help Singin': The American Musical on Stage and Screen* (Woodstock, N.Y.: Overlook Press, 1987), 169.

44. Nolan, *Lorenz Hart,* 19. However, Nolan does much to show the time, distance, and attitudes that kept their relationship more professional than intimate.

45. Hart's father thought Rodgers's family was "beautiful but dead" (Marx and Clayton, *Rodgers and Hart*, 117); Rodgers thought Hart's father "never learned to behave himself" (R. Rodgers, *Musical Stages*, 29).

46. R. Rodgers, *Musical Stages*, 84.

47. D. Rodgers, *A Personal Book*, 67, 116.

48. Ibid., 86, 108–9. Hart finally moved away from Rodgers and his young family into new quarters shared with boyhood friend and movie executive Mel Shauer (D. Hart, *Thou Swell, Thou Witty*, 73). Though Shauer later married, it is interesting to note that Shauer was a tall, blond swimmer who invited the 1932 Olympic swim team plus Hollywood stars to their home for the "party of the year" (D. Hart, *Thou Swell, Thou Witty*, 73).

49. R. Rodgers, *Musical Stages*, 209; Nolan, *Lorenz Hart*, 292.

50. *Complete Lyrics of Lorenz Hart*, xiv.

51. D. Hart, *Thou Swell, Thou Witty*, 170; Marx and Clayton, *Rodgers and Hart*, 82; R. Rodgers, *Musical Stages*, 62.

52. Philip Furia, *The Poets of Tin Pan Alley: A History of America's Great Lyricists* (New York: Oxford University Press, 1990), 96. Rodgers usually wrote the music first in their collaboration; occasionally he would take a phrase/title from Hart and set it to music (D. Hart, *Thou Swell, Thou Witty*, 36). Mast is alone in averring that more complicated lyrics would be set to music after they were written (*Can't Help Singin'*, 171).

53. Marx and Clayton, *Rodgers and Hart*, 89.

54. Alec Wilder, *American Popular Song: The Great Innovators, 1900–1950* (New York: Oxford University Press, 1972), 164.

55. Nolan, *Lorenz Hart*, 22; D. Hart, *Thou Swell, Thou Witty*, 185, 184; Nolan, *Lorenz Hart*, 274, 296.

56. R. Rodgers, *Musical Stages*, 8.

57. Richard Rodgers, introduction to *The Rodgers and Hart Song Book* (New York: Simon and Schuster, 1951), 3.

58. D. Rodgers, *A Personal Book*, 72. In *Musical Stages*, Rodgers recalls the incident differently: "Once I'd explained to him, as diplomatically as I could, that Dorothy and I preferred privacy at this time of day, Larry good-naturedly left us alone" (136–37). The discrepancy highlights the caution that must be used in reading Rodgers's book.

59. Mary Rodgers, interviewed on *Larry King Weekend,* CNN, August 20, 1994.

60. D. Hart, *Thou Swell, Thou Witty*, 41; Nolan, *Lorenz Hart*, 206.

61. Marx and Clayton, *Rodgers and Hart*, 148. Rodgers is careful to state in his autobiography that he doesn't thrive on antagonism: "I cannot conceive of being in any kind of a personal relationship based on conflict, . . . [including] partner-partner" (Rodgers, *Musical Stages*, 47). His further iteration, "I could be angry with what he [Hart] was doing to himself and what this was doing to our relationship, but I never reached the point of issuing ultimatums or expressing my displeasure in a direct manner" (206) begins to sound defensive, responding to an unrecorded accusation. While it may be true that his breakup with Hart before *Oklahoma!* was the "first time ever" he was "brutal" with him (216), Rodgers's silent disapproval must have made for tense working conditions.

62. *Complete Lyrics of Lorenz Hart,* 150; Nolan, *Lorenz Hart,* 219–20;

Marx and Clayton, *Rodgers and Hart*, 268, 223, 184, 212, 247–48, 257; Nolan, *Lorenz Hart*, 304.

63. *Musical Stages* was written in 1975, Marx and Clayton's book in 1976, Dorothy Hart's *Thou Swell, Thou Witty* in 1976, and *A Personal Book* by Dorothy Rodgers in 1977. Rodgers's book and Dorothy Hart's fail to acknowledge Hart's homosexuality, though Dorothy Hart cannot avoid the "nondescript characters," "so-called friends," and "hangers-on"—undoubtedly homosexual—who breezed through Hart's life (*Thou Swell, Thou Witty*, 161, 171, 172). Rodgers's book is a complete wipe (see *Musical Stages*, 86, 139, 158, 178, 204). Hart is never characterized as anything but a drunk, "the same sweet, self-destructive kid I had always known" (78).

64. D. Rodgers, *A Personal Book*, 111.

65. R. Rodgers, *Musical Stages*, 205; Mast, *Can't Help Singin'*, 168. Neither is mentioned explicitly in Chauncey's exhaustive look, *Gay New York*.

66. Nachman, "Lorenz Hart," 43.

67. Wayne Koestenbaum, *Double Talk: The Erotics of Male Literary Collaboration* (New York: Routledge, 1989), 3, 4, 8.

68. Rodgers's friend and drama critic George Oppenheimer noted that "he hates homosexuality" (Craig Zadan, *Sondheim and Co.* [New York: Harper and Row, 1986], 104). On the whole, these conjectures do not apply to conscious awareness or decisions made on Rodgers's part, but to subconscious or unarticulated—certainly unrecorded—feelings.

69. Koestenbaum, *Double Talk*, 3.

70. Ibid. Ann Douglas notes the number of male collaborators writing songs and plays during the 1920s and 1930s as an example of the era's stress on craft, the art needed to turn out a professional "object" (*Terrible Honesty: Mongrel Manhattan in the 1920s* [New York: Farrar, Straus and Giroux, 1995], 298). This "object" takes the receptive female place in the collaboration. George S. Kaufman's observation, "A collaboration is like a marriage without sex," becomes enlightening (D. Hart, *Thou Swell, Thou Witty*, 169).

71. Zadan, *Sondheim and Co.*, 102.

72. Koestenbaum, *Double Talk*, 2; Nolan, *Lorenz Hart*, 19; Koestenbaum, *Double Talk*, 4.

73. "I would try to have a tune ready to play him," said Rodgers, "because this was one way to seduce him" (Marx and Clayton, *Rodgers and Hart*, 89). Another way was drink (R. Rodgers, *Musical Stages*, 206).

74. Koestenbaum, *Double Talk*, 7; Nolan, *Lorenz Hart*, 286.

75. In his introduction to the *Song Book*, Rodgers tries to wipe out his aggression by stating that he had "to examine [Hart's] words and work with them," implying that Hart wrote text first and then Rodgers wrote the music—the reverse of their usual method of collaboration (1).

76. Chauncey, *Gay New York*, 148, 340, 359, 21, 118–21.

77. Nachman, "Lorenz Hart," 43; Nolan, *Lorenz Hart*, 314; Koestenbaum, *Double Talk*, 2; Nolan, *Lorenz Hart*, 314.

78. Rodgers wrote the introduction, selected the songs, secured the copyrights, approved the arranger, and chose the illustrator, literally embedding the songs in a context of his design (*Song Book*, 244).

79. Nachman, "Lorenz Hart," 43. Nachman adds that "in its defense, they

only partially control his work. Also, the relationship between the Rodgers and Hart estates is as fragile as the one between the original partners" (43).

80. *Complete Lyrics of Lorenz Hart,* 33; Chauncey, *Gay New York,* 163–68; *Complete Lyrics of Lorenz Hart,* 74.

81. *Complete Lyrics of Lorenz Hart,* 67, 274.

82. Ibid., 83, 84, 143, 201.

83. Ibid., 218, 285.

84. Ibid., 87; Chauncey, *Gay New York,* 182–83; *Complete Lyrics of Lorenz Hart,* 262.

85. *Complete Lyrics of Lorenz Hart,* 119; Chauncey, *Gay New York,* 142, 189; also Mast, *Can't Help Singin',* 168. One picture in D. Hart, *Thou Swell, Thou Witty,* 26, shows Hart amid an anonymous group of five men during World War I. On one end is a soldier; on the other, a burly sailor.

86. *Complete Lyrics of Lorenz Hart,* 33. However, Mel Shauer noted that Hart "knew the verbal expressions that were being used in Greenwich Village, on Park Avenue, or anywhere" (D. Hart, *Thou Swell, Thou Witty,* 75).

87. Marx and Clayton, *Rodgers and Hart,* 202–3; Mast, *Can't Help Singin',* 168; Chauncey, *Gay New York,* 278.

88. John O'Hara, *Pal Joey* (novel, libretto, and lyrics) (New York: Popular Library, 1976), 112, 134. Though pinning this reference on Hart is difficult, it is certainly possible. No similar story is found in O'Hara's Pal Joey short stories. Two sources state that, after the first draft of the libretto, O'Hara left much of the revision of the text to Rodgers, Hart, and director George Abbott (Mast, *Can't Help Singin',* 175; also R. Rodgers, *Musical Stages,* 199); however, George Abbott and June Havoc both state O'Hara helped with revisions on the road (Nolan, *Lorenz Hart,* 276). Nevertheless, Gene Kelly, the original Joey, demonstrates how invested in the musical Hart was: when Brooks Atkinson queried in relation to the show, "can you draw sweet water from a foul well?" Hart "burst into tears" and locked himself in his room (D. Hart, *Thou Swell, Thou Witty,* 147).

89. Chauncey, *Gay New York,* 285; *Complete Lyrics of Lorenz Hart,* 47, 252, 105, 181, 216. For no particular reason I can detect except his familiarity with all kinds, both of these latter references are sung by Jimmy Durante.

90. R. Rodgers, *Musical Stages,* 115; Frederick Nolan, *The Sound of Their Music: The Story of Rodgers and Hammerstein* (New York: Walker and Company, 1978), 115; Nolan continues that Fields maintained "a fiction of straightness" by escorting chorus girls (106). Dorothy Rodgers tells a story of Hart's punching the nose a dance director who threatened to fire a chorus boy who wouldn't go out with the dance director (*A Personal Book,* 115).

91. *Complete Lyrics of Lorenz Hart,* 285, 152. This construction also hints that Hart may have believed that being gay was only something that occurred in relationship to someone else (making it easier to deny). Though this notion was common enough at the time of the song's composition (1930), it is controverted by his simultaneous references to inversion.

92. Where Rodgers and Hart created "Ten Cents a Dance" about a taxi dancer, Porter created "Love for Sale" about a prostitute. Robert Kimball, ed., *The Complete Lyrics of Cole Porter* (New York: Alfred A. Knopf, 1983), 45.

93. Chauncey, *Gay New York,* 288.

94. D. Hart, *Thou Swell, Thou Witty,* 36; *Complete Lyrics of Lorenz Hart,* 71; Marx and Clayton, *Rodgers and Hart,* 205; *Complete Lyrics of Lorenz Hart,* 285.

95. In the subsequent discussion, the tallies are subjective to lyric interpretations and may be described as thorough rather than exhaustive.

96. R. Rodgers, *Musical Stages,* 176; D. Hart, *Thou Swell, Thou Witty,* 158.

97. George and Ira Gershwin, *Oh, Kay!* (Nonesuch [Roxbury Recordings] 79361–2, 1995), booklet, 38.

98. *Complete Lyrics of Lorenz Hart,* 109, 71, 87, 222. Mast tells that this particular hotel was a none too savory establishment for illicit trysts in New Jersey (*Can't Help Singin',* 171). Rodgers, typically, writes of an "idealized country inn" and speaks of Hart's ability to "write longingly about quiet pleasures" (R. Rodgers, *Musical Stages,* 175).

99. *Complete Lyrics of Lorenz Hart,* 281, 275.

100. Wilder, *American Popular Song,* 199, 207, 213, 201.

101. *Complete Lyrics of Lorenz Hart,* 129, 132, 133, 283, 286, 253.

102. Rodgers also speaks of these songs as a given in the genre (R. Rodgers, *Musical Stages,* 72).

103. *Complete Lyrics of Lorenz Hart,* 104, 233, 118, 245, 268, 253.

104. Richard Rodgers and Lorenz Hart, "I Feel at Home with You," *A Connecticut Yankee* (original cast recording of the 1943 Broadway production, recorded by Decca Records on December 22, 1943) (AEI 1138 Mono, 1982); *Complete Lyrics of Lorenz Hart,* 165, 275, 273.

105. Mast, *Can't Help Singin',* 168; *Complete Lyrics of Lorenz Hart,* 228. Mast's information seems to come from generalized information about the bars during the period (257 n. 2); Chauncey also notes physical abuse from trade (*Gay New York,* 60). Rodgers relates one story of Hart's being severely beaten by a drunken houseguest who refused to leave (R. Rodgers, *Musical Stages,* 179; Nolan, *Lorenz Hart,* 289), but no other source corroborates or suggests Hart's being subjected regularly to physical abuse.

106. *Complete Lyrics of Lorenz Hart,* 245, 275.

107. Ibid., 217, 52, 193, 295, 121, 224. When asked if Hart really was glad to be unhappy, Rodgers replied, "He most emphatically was not! In fact he was very unhappy about it" (Nolan, *Lorenz Hart,* 211).

108. *Complete Lyrics of Lorenz Hart,* 228, 252.

109. Ibid., 272, 275. The character also uses the initials of, and was played by, Vivienne Segal.

110. Minton, "Femininity in Men," 9.

Dorothy's Friend in Kansas

The Gay Inflections of William Inge

Albert Wertheim

"I want my plays only to provide the audience with an experience which they can enjoy . . . and which shocks them with the unexpected in human nature, with the deep inner life that exists privately behind the life that is publicly presented." So wrote William Inge (1913–1973) in *Theatre Arts* (1953) discussing his recently opened and successful *Picnic*.[1] Although at the time, Inge's words probably seemed like authorly generalities, today, thinking through *Picnic* and other Inge plays, we can see that Inge was cuing the perceptive viewer or reader of his plays to look beneath the surfaces for what is closeted within the characters and even within the audiences and readers themselves. Inge went on to say, "I shall try to recommend the play [*Picnic*] as I would a short trip, to be enjoyed not for the hope of its destination but for what one sees along the way." In other words, Inge stressed once more that we are not to look for some large uplifting theme but for what the work reveals about its characters and us.

Listening to Inge's advice will quickly open up a play like *Picnic* in ways in which it has not previously been discussed. For the most part, Inge's plays have been viewed as C. W. E. Bigsby has characterized them: they are "about the suffocating determinism of small-town life" and a depiction of "the world which lay behind the *Saturday Evening Post* covers."[2] Robert Brustein writes that "Inge is regarded as Broadway's first authentic Midwestern playwright who "seems to have restored to Midwesterners their privilege to be as traumatized by life as any other Americans represented on Broadway."[3] Likewise, R. Baird Shuman explains that *Picnic* "consisted initially of little more than character sketches of five women living humdrum existences in a small Kansas town" into whose "female microcosm" Inge introduces a virile male, Hal Carter, so that "The play deals with the unsettling effect Hal's presence has on the women and on the society of which they are a part."[4] Coming closer to the truth is a more recent article that contends that Inge is subverting conventional assumptions and stereotypes of male and female behavior.[5] These characterizations are not false, but they overlook, perhaps deny, the sexuality and significant homoeroticism from which Inge's plays spring (figs. 9 and 10).

It is no secret that William Inge was gay, but most discussions of the connection between his homosexuality and his plays are like that of Inge's biographer, Ralph Voss, who eschews that connection except in regard to those works in which an overtly gay man appears.[6] It is only in two recent gay studies of theater and film that the homoeroticism of *Picnic* is pointed out. Revealingly, it is done so as an aside and as something we all know. John Clum, in his book on modern gay theater, writes in passing of the hunky men in *Picnic* and *Come Back, Little Sheba* noting, "Straight men could fantasize about the sexual attractiveness and power these male characters had, and women in the audience could identify with the women in the play, but gay men knew what these plays were about."[7] Again in a passing remark in his essay on gay men and film, Al LaValley says of the film version of *Picnic* that "today the homoerotic content of stud William Holden's dance seems hard to miss."[8]

The dissonance and disparity between the conventional wisdom and the *selbstverständlich* attitude of Clum and LaValley are a remarkably fine example of what David Van Leer argues in his chapter on gay writers of straight fiction:

> Most social intercourse involves not coherent conversations, but densely coded improvisations between groups barely conscious of their own identities or of the difference between them. And often minorities speak most volubly between the lines, ironically reshaping dialogues the oppressor thinks he controls or even finding new topics and modes of speaking to which the oppressor himself lacks access.[9]

He goes on to say that "gay writers found in certain linguistic strategies a voice of their own long before sexuality was spoken of openly. And . . . straight readers responding to this voice can unintentionally find themselves speaking someone else's language." Much the same point is made by Alan Sinfield, who posits that until recent years "gay men [i.e., writers] courageously and inventively sustained a private subculture under the noses of the censor."[10] In the theater, however, Van Leer's astute insight must be expanded from the linguistic level to include the physical and gestural as well as the spoken presentation of the dialogue. To take an obvious example, the gay/straight doublespeak in Oscar Wilde's *The Importance of Being Earnest* is not just there in the "linguis-

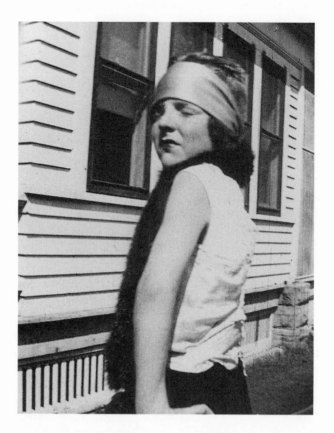

FIG. 9. Billy Inge, about ten, costumed as a young girl.

(Courtesy, William Inge Collection, Independence Community College, Independence, Kansas.)

tic strategies" that create the discussions of Bunburying and cucumber sandwiches but in the semiotics of the over-the-top bearing of Ernest and Jack, and in the spoken manner (tone of voice) of their courtships. In the major plays of Inge, and especially in *Picnic*, as Inge hinted, much is going on beneath a surface that seems merely to depict some repressed women and a virile man against the background of the American heartland, a Kansas reminiscent of Dorothy's dreary town in *The Wizard of Oz*. What *Picnic* is really about is not so much Inge's women and their conventional small-town lives as it is about Hal Carter, the sexually desirable phallic man who descends from nowhere amid the Kansas cornfields, and about the effect he has on all the characters, *male* and female.

FIG. 10. Dressed as a little old lady with a monocle,
Billy completely fooled his mother and sister.

*(Courtesy, William Inge Collection, Independence Com-
munity College, Independence, Kansas.)*

Using the homoerotic inflections of *Picnic,* Inge bears out Van Leer's
assertion, for he compels his straight audience members unintentionally
to speak and understand his subversive "language," the gay texture of
the play. Discussing Tennessee Williams, who was Inge's friend, mentor,
inspiration, and possibly lover,[11] David Savran incisively writes that "his
homosexuality is both ubiquitous and elusive, everywhere in his work
and yet nearly impossible to pin down. . . . Williams's homosexuality is
endlessly *refracted* in his work: translated, reflected, and transposed."[12]
Much the same can be said of William Inge.

Writing as he did in the 1950s, when fears of political subversion
were at an unprecedented high in postwar America and when, as Martin

Duberman reminds us, American homophobia was in one of its high-voltage phases,[13] Inge was surely aware that plays openly about sexual transgression would be seen as subversion of another kind, and would unquestionably not be acceptable or tolerated in the United States at that time. One must remember that Inge was writing during the heyday of the House Un-American Committee investigations and the army-McCarthy hearings. This is the period of politically charged plays like Maxwell Anderson's *Barefoot in Athens* (1951), Sidney Kingsley's dramatic adaptation of Koestler's *Darkness at Noon* (1951), Arthur Miller's *The Crucible* (1953) and *A View from the Bridge* (1955), and the revivals of James Thurber and Elliott Nugent's *The Male Animal* and of Lillian Hellman's *The Children's Hour*.[14] It was a period when the now seemingly tame *Seven Year Itch* (1952) and *The Moon Is Blue* (1951) were considered quite risqué. And potentially transgressive offerings were guarded, circumspect, and equipped with heterosexual dust to throw into the eyes of censorious and homophobic audiences. Certainly such is the case of *Gentlemen Prefer Blondes* (1949), *Tea and Sympathy* (1953), and Tennessee Williams's *The Rose Tattoo* (1951), *Camino Real* (1953), *Cat on a Hot Tin Roof* (1955), *Sweet Bird of Youth* (1958), and *Suddenly Last Summer* (1958).

Like Williams, Inge knew that the presentation of an overtly homosexual character or theme and Broadway success was an oxymoron. All the same, a gay sensibility informs his major plays, is refracted in them, and most importantly permits him special insights, insights derived from his personal experience of gay alterity, that allow him to write movingly and knowledgeably of his characters. To read Inge's plays without acknowledging their gay inflections is to see them as less than they are. Nevertheless, except for Clum's and LaValley's already quoted parenthetical asides, critics have been profoundly silent about the homoerotic tones in Inge's work. Perhaps they do not see them. Perhaps they do not wish to see or discuss them.[15] The aim of this essay, then, is to bring hitherto unacknowledged gay matters to the fore and thereby evince an enhanced understanding of, and esteem for, Inge as a dramatist.

The clearest example of the ways in which Inge's gay sensibility inform his dramatic works can be found in *Picnic*. Challenging as it will heterosexual hegemony, *Picnic* is appropriately located in a quintessentially American town, a Grovers Corners transported from New Hampshire to Kansas. The script calls for a set providing "the panorama of a typical small Midwestern town, including grain elevator, a railway station, a great silo and a church steeple." Onto that set of American conventionality steps the well-built Hal Carter, an outsider, an other, who is characterized as "an exceedingly handsome, husky [euphemism for "hunky"?] youth dressed in T-shirt, dungarees and cowboy boots."[16] Having drifted into town, he has found work doing chores for Mrs. Potts, a lonely woman of sixty who has spent her life caring for her bedridden, shrewish mother. Furthermore, Inge pointedly has Hal enter bearing a loaded trash can on his shoulders in order to have Hal tense his muscles and reveal his impressive masculine physique. And, of course, Inge knew that it is not usually women but gay men who were turned on by beefcake bodybuilders like Hal. To Inge's Kansas town—and perhaps to sectors of Inge's audience—Hal is a dangerous, attractive outsider who threatens social stability and conventional sexual mores.

After Hal's initial entrance, the stage is flooded by women: Mrs. Potts; Millie Owens, the sixteen-year-old tomboy and budding intellectual; Madge, her extraordinarily beautiful eighteen-year-old sister; Flo, their middle-aged mother; and their boarder, Rosemary Sydney, a middle-aged, spinsterish high school teacher. The women, who are on stage, all notice and react to an offstage Hal, whom they see with his T-shirt removed. Playfully, Inge here titillates his audience, male and female, who wish they, too, could catch a glimpse of the now bare-chested and remarkably well-muscled hunk.

In contrast to Hal, the object of both the hetero- and homoerotic gaze is Alan Seymour, Madge's boyfriend and the man her mother hopes she will marry and who will presumably transport Madge from her lower-middle-class world to the small-town high society of the country club. But Alan is contextualized in terms of low sexual voltage. Flo remarks, "Alan is the kind of man who doesn't mind if a woman's bossy"; and her statement is ironically juxtaposed to a train whistle and Madge's subsequent romantic, phallic fantasies about trains, "Whenever I hear that train coming to town, I always get a little feeling of excitement—in here. (*Hugging her stomach*)" (79). Flo then questions Madge about Alan's sexuality:

> *Flo.* Does Alan ever—make love? . . . Do you let him kiss you?
>   After all, you've been going together all summer.
> *Madge.* Of course I let him.
> *Flo.* Does he ever want to go beyond kissing? . . .
> *Madge.* Well—yes.
> *Flo.* Does Alan get mad if you—won't?
> *Madge.* No.
> *Flo.* He doesn't . . .

Madge. Alan's not like *most* boys. He doesn't wanta do anything
   he'd be sorry for.
Flo. Do *you* like it when he kisses you?
Madge. Yes.
Flo. You don't sound very enthusiastic. (80)

With these comments as its preamble, the entrance of Alan is not one
awaited with bated breath by the audience, whereas they do eagerly hope
to see Hal reenter with his shirt off and his body on display.

When Alan enters, he seems a rather bland figure, uninteresting even
to the playwright, for Alan is, tellingly, the only character in the play for
whom Inge provides no description in his stage directions. Soon there-
after and to the at last satisfied prurient curiosity of the audience, Hal
enters "bare-chested now, wearing his T-shirt wrapped about his neck"
(90). His entrance is pointedly preceded by a "sudden explosion" and Flo
Owens's risible phallocentric line, "He must have a gun!" (90). At that
moment, the tepid Alan suddenly recognizes Hal as his college friend and
is propelled into an animated, enthusiastic physical action, far more
immediate and natural than his stilted advances toward Madge or his
restrained and well-mannered behavior among the female characters.
The spirited homosocial greeting between the two men noticeably crosses
the borders into the homoerotic. Alan mounts onto Hal's back and the
two of them, moving like bucking broncos, powerfully suggest the gay
coloration of their relationship, allowing Inge simultaneously to
acknowledge and parody the gay imaginings of the play's male audience.
The moment is one ablaze with homoeroticism:

Alan. Hal Carter!
Hal. I was comin' over to see you a little later.
*Alan. (Recalling some intimate roughhouse greeting from their col-
   lege days)* How's the old outboard motor?
Hal. (With the eagerness of starting a game) Want a ride?
Alan. (Springing to Hal, *clasping his legs around* Hal's *waist,
   hanging by one hand wrapped about* Hal's *neck, as though riding some sort of imagined machine)* Gassed up? *(With his finger,
   he twists* Hal's *nose as if it were a starter.* Hal *makes sputtering
   noise of an outboard motor and swings* Alan *about the stage,*
   Alan *holding on like a bronco-buster. They laugh uproariously
   together)* Ahoy, brothers! Who's winkin', blinkin', and stinkin?
   (90–91)

Theirs is a special dance that casts a thin veil of homosocial acceptability
over patently homosexual transgressive vitality. This is, moreover, the

first of several hetero- and homoerotic dances Hal will perform in the course of the play.

Another most important gay strain in the play is encoded in Inge's characterization of Millie Owens, a persecuted intellectual who is sexually "othered" by the town's conventionality, fear of difference, and implicit homophobia. Not surprisingly, she is initially paired with Hal, whose otherness is likewise an object of fear and attraction. Later she is, revealingly, paired with Alan. In terms of gender and class expectations Millie is an unruly young woman. She carries herself like a boy and is usually presented on stage, as she was in the film version of *Picnic*, dressed in jeans, a man's shirt, and a baseball cap. At the heart of her altercation with her nemesis, the newsboy Bomber, is Millie's gendered otherness:

> *Bomber.* It's no fun lookin' at you. I'm talkin' to *you* goonface!
> *Millie. (Jumping to her feet and tearing into* Bomber *with her flying fists)* You take that back, you ornery bastard. You take that back.
> *Bomber. (Laughing, easily warding off her blows)* Listen to goonface! She cusses just like a man. . . . Lookit Mrs. Tar-zan! Lookit Mrs. Tar-zan! (76–77)

Her plans are to go to college, read books that college men like Alan read, and leave Kansas for New York. These mark her defiance of class as well as sex roles. "Madge," she says, "cooks and sews and does all those things that women do" (99). Millie clearly intends to cross the sexual and class boundaries that her sister embodies.

Bomber's scornful nickname for Millie is not "Miss Tar-zan" but "Mrs. Tar-zan," with the indicator of a married woman. This puts a finger on the gender confusion or conflation inherent in Millie. She is turned by Bomber's expression at once into a married woman but also into a female manifestation of Tarzan, an epitome of butch maleness. A gay-sensitive reading of Millie, however, rapidly reveals that her otherness is not, finally, lesbian, but the otherness of gay men that David Bergman articulates so well.[17] Indeed, Millie seems very much like some drag version of Inge himself, replicating the otherness he must have felt growing up gay within the narrow confines of social and sexual acceptability in Independence, Kansas. Inge's biographer, Voss, guardedly and circumspectly writes, "Billy Inge was different, then—a 'speckled egg' no doubt at times bewildered by his hormones and his environment."[18] To be sure, Inge's Millie, like the playwright himself, is indeed a most peculiarly "speckled egg." On the one hand, Millie's tomboy or butch bearing is a female obverse of male effeminacy; yet on the other hand, she is a curious example of what David Van Leer calls "queening," that is, "the ways in which gay men and to some extent women shape dominant cultural forms by silently importing into heterosexual plots rhetorics and motifs more common to their own homosexual community."[19] At radical odds with Millie's masculinized, tomboy surface is the fact that she writes poetry, an endeavor in small-town America given to overly romantic spinsters and effeminate young men (e.g., Alma Winemiller and her poetry circle in Tennessee Williams's *Summer and Smoke*). Likewise, the book Millie is reading is one that had already become a gay camp classic, Carson McCullers's *The Ballad of the Sad Café*. Consequently, the cues for her otherness here are gay, not lesbian. Her attraction, moreover, to Hal (and his tacitly acknowledged kinship with her) is at least in part gay inflected. Theirs is a tacit bonding between two victims of alterity in the face of hegemonic class and gender oppression.

The big festival in *Picnic*'s small Kansas town is Neewollah, Halloween spelled backwards. In recent years, Halloween, the night when the spirit world holds sway, has been claimed in many American cities by gays as the night when gay inner spirits are released and celebrated.[20] Ahead of his time, perhaps, Inge formulates a Neewollah town in which much seems sexually reversed, subverted, and bent. Along those lines, then, it seems appropriate that two gay-inflected characters, Alan and Millie, find a kinship. It is Alan who supports Millie's reading *The Ballad of the Sad Café*, which, the homophobic Rosemary Sydney has informed Millie's mother, is a filthy book that the Daughters of the American Revolution has banned from the public library. The final moments of the play make still clearer the notion that Alan and Millie are gay-inflected kindred spirits.

> *Millie.* I . . . I always liked you, Alan. Didn't you know it?
> *Alan. Like* me?
> *Millie.* It's awfully hard to show someone you like them, isn't it?
> *Alan.* It's easy for *some* people.
> *Millie.* It makes you feel like such a sap. I don't know why.
> *Alan.* I . . . I'm glad you like me, Millie.
> *Millie.* I don't expect you to do anything about it. I just wanted to
>   tell you. (136)

Inge, writing in the years before Stonewall, shrewdly throws sand in the eyes of his straight readers and audience members while guardedly implying to his gay ones the nature of the communication between Millie and Alan.

What does Inge gain by his homoerotic dramaturgy? *Picnic* is hardly a Wildean send-up of the well-made plotting of conventional straight plays. Inge's achievement, however, begins to come clear through the play's dances of desire, foreshadowed by the gay-charged roughhouse of Alan and Hal. With the music of the picnic in the background, the subsequent sexual choreography of the play begins. Rosemary Sydney's date, the middle-aged businessman Howard Bevans, does not care to dance with her, so she dances with Millie, whom Hal has escorted to the picnic. Two seemingly straight women dancing together is socially acceptable and hardly unconventional, but when Howard dances with Hal, their comically transgressive behavior brings on a quick and offended homophobic response from Rosemary:

> *Howard.* S'posin' Hal and I did that.
> *Rosemary.* Go ahead for all I care. (Howard *turns to* Hal *and, laughing, they start dancing together,* Hal *giving his own version of a coy female.* Rosemary *is irritated by this.*) Stop it! (117–18)

Hal's phallic charisma has its effect on Howard Bevans. But Howard, like many primarily straight men made uncomfortable by a recognition of their own male-male desires, deals with such dangerous feelings by parodying them.

What follows is an evocation of Hal's phallic sexuality enacted through a dance essentially celebrating his male sexual vitality, a dance during which Hal will replace Howard with female partners: Millie, Rosemary, and Madge. With Millie, he is a kindly teacher helping her to locate her sexuality. She learns to stop taking the man's role by leading and to identify with an icon of female (though also camp) sexuality as she exclaims, "I feel like Rita Hayworth!" (118). Rosemary's raw desire overcomes her surface of censorious schoolteacherly propriety to reveal her underlying unfulfilled lust. Vulgarly she grabs Hal's body and comes close to raping him:

> *Rosemary.* Now it's his turn to dance with *me.* I may be an old-maid schoolteacher, but *I* can keep up with you. Ride 'em cowboy! (A *little tight, stimulated by* Hal's *physical presence, she abandons convention and grabs* Hal *closely to her, plastering a cheek next to his and holding her hips fast against him. One can see that* Hal *is embarrassed and repelled.*) . . . Dance with me. I can keep up with you. You know what? You remind me of one of those ancient statues. There was one in the school library until last year. He was a Roman gladiator. All he had on was his shield. *(She gives a bawdy laugh.)* A shield over his arm. That

was all he had on. All we girls felt insulted, havin' to walk past
that statue every time we went to the library. We got up a peti-
tion and made the principal do something about it. *(She laughs
hilariously during her narration)* You know what he did? He got
the school janitor to fix things right. He got a chisel and made
that statue decent. (121)

Rosemary's is a compelling ambivalence, for she simultaneously positions herself so that Hal's penis is pressed against her body while she narrates the dismemberment of the classical statue resembling Hal. When
Hal repulses her aggressive advances, Rosemary holds on to his shirt and
tears a piece of it off, italicizing her fleshly desire and revealing once
again for the audience Hal's impressive, muscular, "Roman gladiator"
physique. Inge thus includes the audience in the unsettling eroticism of
the scene.

This carries over into the scene's central action, the extended, largely
silent, highly charged, erotic dance sequence between Hal and the beautiful Madge. When one reads the text, it is essential to remember that the
dance takes considerable time and that it is clearly arousing to all who
watch, on both sides of the proscenium arch. Inge thus constructs around
Hal a semiotics of desire: those watching on stage and those in the audience watching from their seats are affected by the homoerotic and heteroerotic fragrances that emanate from the dance. The play, thus, at once
stages both male-female and male-male desire. In the closeting darkness
of the theater, men, straight and gay, as well as women have the permission to fantasize about Hal; and consequently, Hal's dance with Madge
is provocative for all sexual orientations. Indeed, what Inge manages to
craft by writing a play that is on one level about the sexual awakenings
of underdeveloped or repressed females and on another level about
homoeroticism is no mean feat, for *Picnic* ultimately provides a representation of sexuality that transcends gender and orientation. As they
come to understand both these aspects of *Picnic,* straight playgoers will
find themselves unintentionally, but nevertheless ineluctably, forced to
speak and understand the language of gay desire.

Gay inflections, like those of *Picnic,* can also be found in Inge's three
other seemingly straight major plays: *Come Back, Little Sheba* (1950),
Bus Stop (1955), and *The Dark at the Top of the Stairs* (1957). In *Come
Back, Little Sheba,* which preceded *Picnic,* the bodybuilder, Turk, who
poses for Marie's drawing class assignment and is her sexual partner, is,
like Hal, the object of both the hetero- and homoerotic gaze on the part
of both the audience and the other characters. Explaining his function on

the college track team, Turk's phallicism is as comically obvious as that of Shakespeare's Mercutio:

> They got me throwing the javelin. . . . It's a big long lance. You hold it like this, erect—then you let go and it goes singing through the air, and it lands yards away, if you're any good at it, and sticks in the ground, quivering like an arrow. I won the state championship last year. (15)

Inge forces his audience, however, to regard Turk with conflicted feelings. Turk has a near-perfect body and the unsubtle suggestion in this passage of his large, erect, prizewinning phallus are meant to be attractive and arousing. Indeed, his speech is the verbal analogue of outlined genitals beneath the clothes of male models in soft-core pornographic magazines. At the same time, Turk's swaggering masculinity and coarse sex drive are repugnant, for he is devoid of sensitivity and driven merely by lust. Love, affection, tenderness are not in his vocabulary; and he becomes, like Williams's Stanley Kowalski, a sexually attractive enemy.

To Turk, Inge juxtaposes Marie's fiancé, the dependable, conventional, sexually colorless Bruce, who comes from an affluent family, works for a company, and will marry Marie when "he feels he can support a wife and children" (13). When Marie characterizes Bruce with "he's got a wonderful personality," a code phrase for "sexually uninteresting," we understand why Marie chooses Turk as a sexual partner (13). The contrast between Turk and Bruce helps Inge frame and bring into focus the play's central male character, Doc, who "Treats women like they were all beautiful angels" (48). When Doc's wife, Lola, narrates his history, it will doubtless sound archetypal and familiar to a wide sector of gay men in the audience (including Inge himself):

> Doc was sortuva Mama's boy. He was an only child and his mother thought the sun rose and set in him. Didn't she, Docky? She brought Doc up like a real gentleman. . . . Did you ever notice how nice he keeps his fingernails? Not many men think of things like that. And he used to take his mother to church every Sunday. . . . Treats women like they were all beautiful angels. We went together a whole year before he even kissed me. (47–48)

Clearly, Lola was Doc's momentary rebellion from his mother's hold and his role as an exemplary, virtuous son. That rebellion brought a lifelong penalty, for he had been forced to marry the frowzy Lola and abandon his medical studies to become a chiropractor. Compulsively neat and morally prudish, Doc is now yoked to a slattern and is a recovering alcoholic. He is, moreover, a character drawn by a dramatist who brings his knowledge of gay lives, gay neuroses, and alcoholism to bear, employing that knowledge to create a moving and tragic portrait. And it is not just Doc but Lola as well who bears the stamp of Inge's gay understanding.

The once sexy Lola set her cap in high school for the shy, effeminate Doc. She became pregnant, miscarried, and as a result could not afterwards bear children. Nevertheless, she and Doc, spurned by their families for their premarital sex, were cast out from Green Valley, like Adam and Eve from Paradise, to settle and reach sad middle age somewhere east of Eden in the nameless midwestern city where *Come Back, Little Sheba* takes place.

What rings false in the expositional background given of Lola and Doc's youthful indiscretion is that they were irrevocably exiled for their premarital sex and Lola's pregnancy. More often than not, such transgressions in a small town are smoothed over by a quick marriage ceremony. And Lola and Doc's exile seems especially harsh since they did, indeed, get married and their offending fetus miscarried. These events would add up more understandably were the protagonists both male. This is not to say that Inge's characters are gays disguised for Broadway as straights, but rather that in *Come Back, Little Sheba,* Inge can, through what Van Leer calls queening, channel his knowledge of othering and family rejection, experiences so well known to gays, in order to give depth and feeling to the portrayals of Lola and Doc. He thus effectively brings to bear a gay discourse on a heterosexual one, colonizing the space between them. Gay audience members or readers are likely to be on immediately familiar ground with Doc and Lola, and with their domestic and personal problems. Straight audience members or readers will understand Lola and Doc as well but will do so by unconsciously learning the foreign language of gay experience. One might also say, borrowing terminology from postcolonial discourse, that Inge's playwriting artfully forges a hybridity based on the abrogation of the language or narrative of the heterosexual center and reconstituting it through the homosexual language or narrative of the periphery.[21]

This happens again in rather more clear yet more complicated ways in *Picnic*'s successor, *Bus Stop,* which R. Baird Shuman calls "an anatomy of love."[22] Indeed it is that, but not quite the way Shuman and other heterosexist critics might have us believe. *Bus Stop* is one of those plays in which the location is, in a sense, the inanimate main character, for the place serves as a unifying setting for several separate but thematically related plots. It is thus in a class with modern plays like Eugene

O'Neill's *The Iceman Cometh,* Arnold Wesker's *The Kitchen,* Tennessee Williams's *Camino Real* and *Small Craft Warnings,* Peter Nichols's *The National Health,* or such popular vehicles as Neil Simon's *Plaza Suite* and *California Suite.*²³

In Inge's play there are what appear to be three distinct couples who come together somewhere between Kansas City and Topeka at a snow-bound Kansas bus rest stop: the hard-boiled Grace, the rest stop owner, and Carl, the bus driver; Elma, the teenager who works as a server at the rest stop and Dr. Gerald Lyman, an alcoholic college professor with an alleged taste for young girls; and Bo, an untamed cowboy, infatuated with Cherie, a dance hall "chantoosie." As the play progresses, Grace and Carl go upstairs for some casual sex that provides an unseen but important backdrop for the other two plots. Lyman "comes on" to the impressionable, underage Elma; but, after suggesting they meet in Topeka, he is struck by his conscience and backs off. In the course of the evening, Elma learns about the dangerous charms of lecherous older men and grows up. Bo, a Montana cowboy, has gone to an urban inferno, a Kansas City dance hall, for his first spree in a big city (one remembers with amusement the "Everything's Up to Date in Kansas City" lyrics in Rodgers and Hammerstein's *Oklahoma!*). Bo is brought there by the aptly named Virgil, an older cowhand and his mentor/guardian. At the dance hall, Bo mistakes the professional flirtation of Cherie for affection, is smitten, and kidnaps her with the intention of taking her back to Montana and marrying her. In the course of the night, Bo is tamed and learns how a man must treat and love a woman.

All this sounds like a dramatic panorama of complementary, straight-forward heterosexual love narratives. But looking at *Bus Stop* more closely, reading it gay, one can clearly recognize that two of those narratives are a form of "queening," an Inge smokescreen for examining gay relationships and male-male desire. To what seem like three straight discussions in Inge's "anatomy of love," two more gay ones must be added.

The heavy-drinking Dr. Lyman, we sense throughout *Bus Stop,* is on the bus moving westward across state lines because of some indiscretion probably related to alcohol or sex. Toward the end of the play, those suspicions are confirmed by Carl, the bus driver:

> Hey, know what I heard about the perfessor? The detective at the bus terminal in Kanz City is a buddy of mine. He pointed out the perfessor to me before he got on the bus. Know what he said? He said the p'lice in Kanz City picked the perfessor up for *loiterin'* round the schools. . . . Then they checked his record and found he'd

been in trouble several times, for gettin' involved with young girls.
(213)

But the effeminate, affected, campy, gay-coded style of Lyman seems
almost heavy-handed in signaling that Carl's description of Lyman's past
is probably correct except for the gender to which he is attracted. When,
moreover, Lyman, at the play's beginning, is singled out and othered by
the bus driver as an "easterner," the term reverberates with suggestions
of homophobia. Indeed, it seems very much like that other midwestern
euphemism, "He's a New York type," signifying a Jew. Lyman's
groomed response, "Come, come now. Don't scold," followed immediately by his initial affected address to the teenage waitress, Elma,
"'Nymph, in thy orisons be all my sins remembered!'" should make it
plain just what "easterner" means (161).

Lyman courts and attracts Elma by quoting from Shakespeare's sonnets, and convincing her to enact with him the balcony scene from
Romeo and Juliet. Possibly remembering that Shakespeare's sonnets were
likely addressed to a man and that Elizabethan boy actors played female
roles, Inge may have been ahead of his time, queering the Renaissance
before it was fashionable to do so. And, although no one has ever mentioned it in print, it seems clear that *Elma,* hardly a common name, is an
anagram for *male* even as Dr. Lyman's name not only marks him as a liar
but punningly suggests the sex with which he prefers to lie. This is Inge
brilliantly inscribing a gay text within the margins of a straight one.
Despite the fact no critics have commented on Inge's strategy, no gay-
alert audience member would nowadays fail to perceive it.

The Lyman-Elma plot of *Bus Stop* is significant for the method by
which Inge subversively introduces an examination of one form of homoerotic love, but it is significant still more for Inge's sensitive treatment of
Lyman's longings, their connections to his drinking, and of the nascent
sexual desire in Elma. It is likely that the portrait of Lyman draws upon
Inge's cynical view of himself: sometime professor, alcoholic, Shake-
speare-quoting aesthete, homosexual, fancier of teenage boys. *Bus Stop*'s
"anatomy of love" is, consequently, subversively and importantly
extended beyond the conventional limits permissible in a 1950s drama.
And a recognition of Inge's gay strategies provides a basis for a revalua-
tion of his reputation and of his place in the canon of American drama.

Bus Stop's anatomy of love is extended as well in another direction.
This otherwise comic play ends on a disturbingly sad note. The snow-
storm abates; the bus takes Dr. Lyman, Bo, and Cherie westward; Elma
goes home, and Grace closes the rest stop. Bo's friend, Virgil, however, is

left behind, and, as Grace closes her doors, he is literally left alone and in the cold:

> *Grace.* There'll be a bus to Kanz City in a few minutes. I'll put the
> sign out and they'll stop.
> *Virgil.* No, thanks. No point goin' back there.
> *Grace.* Then I'm sorry, mister, but you're just left out in the cold.
> *Virgil. (To himself)* Well . . . that's what happens to some people.
> (219)

These are the closing lines of the play; and in more ways than one, Virgil is Inge's "odd" man out.

The combination of Bo and Virgil seems at first a strange one. Why is Bo, who is slightly more than twenty, traveling in the company of a man twenty years older than he? What is the nature of their relationship? On Virgil's part, it seems at first glance one based on homosocial desire. An ersatz parent and a friend to Bo, who was orphaned at age ten, Virgil is a man at home in male society. Asked by Bo whether he was ever in love with a woman, Virgil answers in the affirmative but explains why it came to naught:

> Well, I was allus kinda uncomfortable around the gal, 'cause she was sweet and kinda refined. I was allus scared I'd say or do somethin' wrong. . . . It was cowardly of me, I s'pose, but ev'ry time I'd get back from courtin' her, and come back to the bunkhouse where my buddies was sittin' around talkin', or playin' cards, or listenin' to music, I'd jest relax and feel m'self so much at home, I din wanta give it up. (185)

Virgil's preferences as indicated here suggest that his relationship with Bo falls somewhere on what Eve Sedgwick would argue is the continuum between homosocial and homosexual.[24] Theirs is more than an avuncular relationship, though there is nothing to suggest that they have been sexual partners.

In his discussion of *Where's Daddy?* (1966), R. Baird Shuman explains, "Inge's plays of the 1960s deal openly with homosexuality, whereas his plays of the 1950s could not. . . . Not only had the times changed to the point that Inge could now be more open about homosexuality than he was in the past, but the psychoanalysis he had been through by this time helped him to understand human sexuality, particularly homosexuality, better than he had a decade earlier."[25] Whether Inge understood homosexuality better in the 1960s than he had in the 1950s is a moot point, but his relative openness in the 1960s—particularly in

Where's Daddy?—provides a basis for assessing the Virgil-Bo relationship through hindsight.

In *Where's Daddy?* the relationship between Pinky and Tom nearly parallels that of Virgil and Bo. As a fifteen-year-old hustler in a gay bar, Tom was taken home by Pinky, a gay man thirty years his senior, and raised by him.[26] There seems little question that they have enacted roles of parent and child, of friends, and of lovers. But in *Where's Daddy?* Pinky must cast off his lover-friend-son, so that Tom can enter the heterosexual world as Teena's husband and proper father of their child. Pinky and Tom are a replication of their closeted 1950s forebears, Virgil and Bo. As it is Pinky's responsibility, it is the responsibility of Virgil, the homosocial/homosexual older man, to leave his protégé, Bo, and send him off to Montana and marriage. The end of *Bus Stop,* with Virgil as the friendless lone figure on stage and with Lyman's departure alone on the bus, is, then, a moving portrait of the loneliness and solitude of gay men in a society where happy endings seem exclusively to be reserved for heterosexuals, and where the gay men either travel alone or are left out in the cold.

When seen as a play revolving around the analogous actions of three heterosexual love plots, *Bus Stop* appears a well-constructed but conventional comic drama. When seen, however, as a play containing two additional homoerotic plots, it becomes a daring and profound piece worthy of far more attention than it has in the past received. Indeed the melancholic gay-inflected plots add depth to and enrich our understanding of the straight ones, and vice versa, so that Inge enables his audience to enlarge the range of their understanding of love and its hetero- and homosexual forms through his artful subversive dramaturgy.

In the course of writing *Come Back, Little Sheba, Picnic, Bus Stop,* and *Dark at the Top of the Stairs,* Inge becomes increasingly clear— though never unambiguously explicit—about homoerotic issues and about his use of them to make his audiences and readers more humane. The last and most autobiographical of his major plays, *Dark at the Top of the Stairs,*[27] comes nearest to doing so. Among the critics there seems to be a consensus that *Dark at the Top of the Stairs* suffers from a divided emphasis, with an unruly subplot threatening to overwhelm a main one.[28] But the critics' discomfort with the stress laid on what they would deem a secondary plot seems little more than a homophobic response to an essentially homoerotic plot's failing to be contained and demanding to be heard. In this regard, Robert Brustein's comments on the play are the most stunning. He never mentions the play's second plot or the striking young man whose suicide is so central to the play's meaning.[29]

Set in the Oklahoma of the early 1920s, only fifteen years after the Sooner State entered the Union, *Dark at the Top of the Stairs* foregrounds a heterosexual plot about the dashing, virile, and patently heterosexual Rubin Flood. Inge creates in Flood a character who captures the anxieties of a new way of life that threatens what was once the freewheeling Oklahoma Territory. Flood's own untrammeled individualism is threatened by his wife's attempts to domesticate him, by the capitalism and parvenu manners that have come to Oklahoma with oil fortunes and with statehood, and by the new technological age of the automobile, which is fast making Rubin's agrarian harness business obsolete. On various levels, Rubin clearly fears the emasculation evident in his uxorious brother-in-law, Morris, whom Inge describes as "a big defeated-looking man of wrecked virility" (251). Like so many plots of heterosexual anxiety, this one ends in compromise, with Rubin's reconciliation to change, and a grudging submission without loss of masculinity to the responsibilities of a paterfamilias. Indeed, the play ends with Rubin's asserting, "Just don't get the idea you can rearrange *me* like ya do the house, whenever ya wanta put it in order," with his going upstairs to bathe, and then with his impatiently shouting down to his wife to come upstairs to the coital bed. The play ends on an extraordinarily heteroerotic note, for Cora, "like a shy maiden, starts up the stairs, where we can see Rubin's naked feet standing in the arm light at the top." Then, with a hint of orgasms to come, she calls to him as the curtain falls, "I'm coming, Rubin. I'm coming" (304).

Juxtaposed to this (parody of?) conventional heterosexuality, and often overwhelming it, is the play's far more powerful, dangerous, homoerotically subversive plot. The most arresting figure in the Flood household is not Rubin but his son, ten-year-old Sonny Flood, whose characterization is loaded with queer coding. A mama's boy and avid collector of movie star photos, Sonny lacks all interest in the male-bonding games and activities of his peers. For this he receives their othering taunts and scorn:

> Sonny Flood! His name is mud!
> Sonny runs home to Mama!
> Sonny plays with paper dolls!
> Sonny Flood, his name is mud!

(231)

The audience quickly understands the coding and recognizes Sonny as nascently gay. His mother seems to understand this as well, telling him:

> People distrust you if you don't play the same games they do, Sonny. It's the same after you grow up. . . . You're a speckled egg, and the old hen that laid you can't help wondering how you got in the nest. (234)

The alterity of Sonny, the "speckled egg," the gay outsider, is clear. He simply does not belong in the monochromatic nest, that site of hetero-sexuality.[30]

It is appropriate, then, that one of Sonny's prize Hollywood photos is of another outsider, the Italian and sexually ambiguous Rudolph Valentino, whose gaiety is implied by Aunt Lottie's reaction to the legendary lover's photo, "You know, it scares me a little to look at him. Those eyes, that seem to be laughing at you, and all those white teeth. I think it's a sin for a man to be as pretty as he is" (260). These comments are almost immediately followed by the entrance of a teenage Valentino, Sammy Goldenbaum, a Jewish boy whose Semitic good looks and atypical family situation mark him as still another outsider and a kindred spirit to Sonny. He steps onto the stage looking very much like a young Valentino and the embodiment of a homoerotic sexual fantasy:

> He is a darkly beautiful young man of seventeen, with lustrous black hair, black eyes and a captivating smile. Yet, something about him seems a little foreign, at least in comparison with the Midwestern company in which he now finds himself. He could be a Persian prince, strayed from his native kingdom. But he has become adept over the years in adapting himself, and he shows an eagerness to make friends and to be liked. (262)

By far the most striking and strikingly handsome person in the play, Sammy visually dominates the stage, drawing the eyes of all the other characters and of the audience. Furthermore, the connection between Sammy and Valentino is obviously made, for during part of the scene "The Sheik of Araby" is heard from a piano in the background. Like Sonny and like Valentino himself, Sammy is a "speckled egg." It is not merely that the aura of homosexuality hovers over him but also that in conventional and Christian Oklahoma, he stands out as a Jew and as the child of a single parent, a bit-part blowzy Hollywood actress who has placed him in several military boarding schools while she changed husbands and lovers.

The bonding between Sammy and Sonny, the two socially peripher-
alized boys, is immediate and astonishingly erotic. It is reminiscent of and
more openly sexual than the horseplay between Alan and Hal in *Picnic*.
Sonny first provocatively straddles Sammy's back, and then grabs
Sammy's sword from his military uniform. It is a moment, verbally and
semiotically, of unmistakably phallic performance:

> *Sonny. (Jumping up and down)* Can I have a sword? I want a
> sword.
> *Sammy.* Do you, Sonny? So you want a sword? Here, Sonny, I'll
> give you *my* sword, for all the good it'll do you. . . . What do
> you want a sword for, Sonny?
> *Sonny. (With a lunge)* To *show* people. . . .
> *Sammy.* And what do you want to show people, Sonny?
> *Sonny.* I just want to *show* 'em. *(He places the sword between his
> arm and his chest, then, drops to the floor, the sword rising far
> above his body, giving the appearance that he is impaled.* Lottie
> *is horrified)*
> *Lottie.* Oh, darling—put it down. Sonny, please don't play with
> that nasty thing any more. (267–68)

Clearly, Sonny feels Sammy's homoerotic magnetism and romances the
stranger by offering to show him a gay treasure, an icon of his homosexuality, his movie star collection, and reciting, like Dr. Lyman before him,
a Shakespearean soliloquy. The message is not lost on Sammy, who picks
up Sonny and carries him "on his shoulders like a triumphant hero"
(269). It is totally understandable, then, when Sonny throws a tantrum in
hope that Sammy will take him and not his sister, Reenie, to the party at
the country club. And the erotic charge of the scene is, further, emphasized by having Reenie's friends, Flirt and Punky, petting in the background while all these things are transpiring. The interplay between the
heteroerotic and homoerotic in this scene captures the spirit of the play
as a whole, for in inscribing the one upon the other, Inge presents such
powerful gay flirtation that it makes the straight foreplay seem intensely
dull.

Similarly, the play's unseen homoerotic climax greatly overshadows
its unseen heteroerotic bedroom conclusion. In his conflation of Jewish
and gay, Inge engineers a climax in *Dark at the Top of the Stairs* that
trades on the interchangeability of anti-Semitism and homophobia.
Sammy commits suicide after he is publicly humiliated, "outed," as a
Jew. But for alert readers, the incident echoes Blanche Dubois's outing of

Alan Gray (which also ends in suicide) in Williams's *A Streetcar Named Desire*. The events preceding Sammy's suicide are narrated by Flirt:

> But one thing did happen at the party. He was dancing with Mary Jane Ralston . . . and Mrs. Ralston . . . she'd had too much to drink . . . comes out in the middle of the floor and stops them. . . . Anyway, she came right out in the middle of the floor and gave Sammy a bawling out. . . . She said she wasn't giving this party for Jews, and she didn't intend her daughter to dance with a Jew, and besides, Jews weren't allowed in the country club anyway. And that's not so. They are too allowed in the country club. Maybe they're not permitted to be members, but they're certainly allowed as guests. (291–92)

This description and commentary richly evoke the commonality between the alterity and peripherization of Jews and gays.

What Inge does once again in *Dark at the Top of the Stairs* is not, as the critics mistakenly assert, to dramatize two discrete, disjunctive plots. Instead he creates a thoughtful play that makes its point by overlaying a gay plot onto a straight one. Rubin Flood is out of step with his society. So are Sammy and Sonny. Sammy's humiliation and subsequent suicide, however, are employed by Inge to help him underline the great difference between possible heterosexual and homosexual resolutions. In *Bus Stop*, Inge contrasts the comic union of Bo and Cherie with the melancholy isolation of Lyman and Virgil. Likewise in *Dark at the Top of the Stairs*, Rubin Flood's situation is a matter of phallic and patriarchal adjustment. The phallus is the instrument of order; for Rubin it is both domestic and coital scepter. For Sammy and Sonny, the gay inflected characters, however, the phallus is the site of their difference, deviance, and disgrace. "Don't play with that nasty thing," they are told.

Sammy, like Rubin, resolves his difference in a bedchamber, but for him it is a lonely hotel room that does not contain a marriage bed but a window from which he leaps fourteen stories to his death. He does not, like Rubin, land on a soft conjugal mattress inside a house, but outsider that he is, he is splattered on the pavement outside the hotel. This is the lonely fate that the play holds out for speckled Humpty-Dumptys. For Sammy, who does not belong in the nest, suicide is his escape, even as it was to be for Inge himself.

Learning of Sammy's suicide, Sonny reacts violently. Symbolically, his prior restraint and repressed hedonism give way; and he smashes his piggy bank to yield to childish sybaritic propensities played out in movies and candy. The lonely, gay life of *The Glass Menagerie*'s Tom Wingfield, whose passions are movies and drink, seems destined to be Sammy's future. And Inge, too, loved men, movies, and alcohol. *Dark at the Top of the Stairs* is surely autobiography written with the mauve ink of the playwright's gay knowledge.

In his later 1960s plays, Inge comes to write openly about homosexuality. Beside *Where's Daddy?* two other short plays, *The Boy in the Basement* (1962) and the wonderfully titled *Tiny Closet* (1959), present moving portraits of gay men. These late plays, however, were not successful and lack the artistry of the four major plays, which, I would argue, derive their power precisely through their *in petto* gaiety. The homoerotic inflections of *Dark at the Top of the Stairs, Bus Stop, Picnic* and *Come Back, Little Sheba* are used by Inge subversively to enable and even force his audience to overcome its innate homophobia and find its humanity, a humanity capable of embracing and understanding all of his characters, male and female, gay and straight.

NOTES

1. William Inge, "*Picnic*: From 'Front Porch' to Broadway," *Theatre Arts,* April 1954, 34.

2. C. W. E. Bigsby, *Modern American Drama, 1945–1990* (Cambridge: Cambridge University Press, 1992), 153–54. See also Ralph F. Voss, *A Life of William Inge* (Lawrence: University of Kansas Press, 1989), 274.

3. Robert Brustein, "The Men-Taming Women of William Inge," *Harper's* (November 1958): 52.

4. R. Baird Shuman, *William Inge*, rev. ed. (Boston: Twayne, 1989), 33.

5. Jeff Johnson, "Gendermandering: Stereotyping and Gender Role Reversal in the Major Plays of William Inge," *American Drama* 7 (spring 1998): 33–50.

6. Voss, *Life of William Inge*, 200–201.

7. John M. Clum, *Acting Gay: Male Homosexuality in Modern Drama* (New York: Columbia University Press, 1992), 23.

8. Al LaValley, "The Great Escape," in *Out in Culture: Gay, Lesbian, and Queer Essays on Popular Culture,* ed. Corey K. Creekmur and Alexander Doty (Durham, N.C.: Duke University Press, 1995), 68.

9. David Van Leer, *The Queening of America* (New York: Routledge, 1995), 19.

10. Alan Sinfield, *Cultural Politics—Queer Readings* (Philadelphia: University of Pennsylvania Press, 1994), 64.

11. Voss, *Life of William Inge*, 81–84.

12. David Savran, *Communists, Cowboys, and Queers* (Minneapolis: University of Minnesota Press, 1992), 82.

13. Martin Duberman, *About Time: Exploring the Gay Past,* rev. ed. (New York: Penguin, 1991), 177–85.

14. See Albert Wertheim, "The McCarthy Era and the American Theatre," *Theatre Journal* 34 (1982): 211–22.

15. Robert Brustein's *Harper's* essay, 52–57, is a good example, for it strongly posits the high sexual charge of the typical Inge man, who "proclaims his manhood in much the same way that Jayne Mansfield proclaims her womanhood." Brustein argues that the effect of Inge's Stanley Kowalski imitation is that Inge's women attempt to tame and emasculate him. Brustein, however, eschews any mention of the Inge male sex symbol's possible effect on the other males in the play.

16. William Inge, *Four Plays* (New York: Grove Press, 1958), 75. All quotations from *Picnic; Come Back, Little Sheba; Bus Stop;* and *Dark at the Top of the Stairs* are taken from this edition; subsequent references are given in the text.

17. David Bergman, *Gaiety Transformed: Gay Self-Representation in American Literature* (Madison: University of Wisconsin Press, 1991), 30–36.

18. Voss, *Life of William Inge,* 25.

19. Van Leer, *The Queening of America,* 66–67.

20. See for example, "Homosexuals Unmask on Night of Costumes," *New York Times,* October 31, 1988, A-12; "In San Francisco, Big Halloween Bash Is Becoming a Drag," *Wall Street Journal* (October 29, 1995), A1; "Halloween Unmasked: It's an Adult Rite," *San Diego Union-Tribune,* October 31, 1996, E-1; "San Francisco's Monster Bash Moves to the Civic Center: Annual Party Outgrows Castro Haunt," *San Francisco Examiner,* October 30, 1996, C-1; "Devil in a Blue Dress; Dupont Circle Area Becomes Halloween's Main Drag," *Washington Post,* October 31, 1996, B-1; "A Crossover Success: Halloween," *Los Angeles Times,* October 30, 1995, B-1.

21. See e.g. Bill Ashcroft, Gareth Griffiths, and Helen Tiffin, *The Empire Writes Back: Theory and Practice in Post-colonial Literatures* (London: Routledge, 1989), 38–44.

22. Shuman, *William Inge,* 43.

23. One form of this genre is explored in Carol Rosen, *Plays of Impasse: Contemporary Drama Set in Confining Institutions* (Princeton: Princeton University Press, 1983).

24. Eve Kosofsky Sedgwick, *Between Men: English Literature and Male Homosocial Desire* (New York: Columbia University Press, 1985).

25. Shuman, *William Inge,* 99–100.

26. William Inge, *Where's Daddy?* (New York: Dramatists Play Service, 1966).

27. Voss, *Life of William Inge,* 169, 172.

28. John Gassner, *Theatre at the Crossroads* (New York: Holt, 1960), 167–73; Gerald M. Berkowitz, *American Drama of the Twentieth Century* (London: Longman, 1992), 101; and Shuman, *William Inge,* 52–54.

29. Brustein, "Men-Taming Women," 53. In the presentation of Sonny, the nascent gay son, in the Inge-Kazan production, Brustein sees only Oedipal subtextuality: "Where Inge indicates a tight bond between mother and son, Kazan

slammed home all the incestuous implications." The rather clear gay implications, Brustein seems not at all to see.

30. In an interview, Inge admitted, "Yes, I guess I was the little boy [Sonny]." See Walter Wager, ed., *The Playwrights Speak* (New York: Delacorte Press, 1967), 133. Likewise, Voss, *Life of William Inge,* 21, notes that the "speckled egg" euphemism also appears in Inge's first play, *Farther Off From Heaven;* and Voss makes the connection to Inge's own childhood situation.

Critics and Audiences

"Appealing to the Passions"

Homoerotic Desire and Nineteenth-Century Theater Criticism

Lisa Merrill

> True criticism is the proper estimate made of the works of art
> and of letters. . . . [It] makes true merit blossom in the sun-
> shine it throws around it. It is the rain to give life and vitality
> to the early seed, the light to consummate its growth. . . . A
> true critic is one who examines closely his own feelings
> before he grasps the pen.
> —James "Colley Cibber" Rees, 1874

> Any work of literature or art, of poetry or oratory, as well as
> the drama, must, to produce the finest effect, appeal to the
> passions.
> —Adam "The Vagabond" Badeau, 1859

Critics, like other spectators, react to those public figures who are the
objects of their gaze through beliefs about gender and sexuality that are
constructed in a given historical moment. Thus their aesthetic perceptions and expressions of desire are informed by the historically contingent concepts that shape what and how they see. In Barbara Herrnstein
Smith's terms, critics operate as "metonymic representative[s]" for the
communities that inform or motivate their judgments, standing in for the
values and beliefs of what I have elsewhere called a virtual community of
spectators and readers.[1] Unlike other spectators, however, by choosing to
publish their reactions, reviewers and critics set themselves up as arbiters
of the representations they have witnessed, and their own texts become
part of the discursive frame through which performers are perceived.

Nineteenth-century American theater criticism was written by a
range of writers with vastly different backgrounds, purposes, and passions. In the second half of the century, a burgeoning periodical press in

the United States provided both a place of employment and a public site for the arts criticism of established editors and critics, such as Henry Clapp Jr. of the *Saturday Press* and the *Leader* and William Winter of the *Albion* and the *Tribune*.[2] However, throughout the century, but particularly in the decades from 1820 to 1860, countless others wrote arts criticism sporadically, publishing anonymously or under pseudonyms. I have found that homoerotic passion informed the aesthetic and critical responses of a number of those theater critics and reviewers who "grasped their pens," in James Rees's terms, and seized upon the periodical press as a venue in which they might promote, dismiss—in essence, "perform"—their reactions to stars such as Edwin Forrest, Edwin Booth, and Charlotte Cushman. These articles and notices set the tone for the responses of antebellum audiences who read them and so helped lay the critical ground for the development of the American theater. In the period before 1860, cultural critics, essayists, and journalists such as James "Acorn" Oakes, James "Colley Cibber" Rees, and Adam "Vagabond" Badeau contributed to what Denise Quirk has called "the cultural work performed by periodicals,"[3] through their passionate advocacy for those public figures who served as objects of their desire.

This connection between homoeroticism, cultural criticism, and the nineteenth-century periodical press has not been explored previously. In researching this essay I have been engaged in the detective work of decoding pseudonyms, matching up the unpublished letters of little-known writers with the articles they wrote, finding clues about relationships previously hidden. Yet the rewards are considerable. I have discovered that public reception of Edwin Forrest and Edwin Booth—the two foremost nineteenth-century male actors in the United States and the "matinee idols" of their times—was shaped at a nascent point in their careers by critical reviews and articles authored and authorized by men with deep personal attachments to and love for these performers. Examining the depiction of Forrest and Booth by male critics, reviewers, and biographers reveals the role played by an economy of homoerotic desire in the anonymous and pseudonymous theatrical notices and reviews published in the nineteenth-century American periodical press.

One of Forrest's earliest and most consistent supporters was his "beloved friend" James Oakes. In her essay, "My Noble Spartacus: Edwin Forrest on the Nineteenth-Century Stage" in *Passing Performances,* Ginger Strand discusses the passionate attachment between Forrest and Oakes.[4] Strand's interesting work has opened the door for further investigation more appropriate to this volume and its focus on writers and critics. I have determined that in addition to providing Forrest with emotional support and professional advice, for decades Oakes seized upon the possibilities offered through his platform as "Acorn," the drama correspondent to Porter's *Spirit of the Times* (and occasional contributor to numerous other periodicals), to function as an unofficial press agent for Forrest and so contribute to the critical construction of the tragedian's career. Similarly, like Oakes, Adam Badeau, a *Sunday Times* arts critic who wrote under the pseudonym "Vagabond," met actor Edwin Booth early in Booth's career and became simultaneously a champion of Booth's talent and, for a time, the actor's most intimate friend. "Acorn's" representations of Forrest from the late 1830s onward and "Vagabond's" depiction of Booth in the late 1850s and early 1860s provide a window into changing constructions of masculinity and same-sex desire.

Although considerable unpublished personal correspondence attests to the affectional and homoerotic connection between America's two leading male actors and the men who were their closest friends as well as two of their earliest and strongest advocates in the press, this "queer reading" of Forrest's and Booth's critical reception does not attempt to establish the (homo)sexuality (in the modern sense of the term) of either actor or of his critics. Rather, I wish to consider how same-sex attraction factored into the critical reception each actor received, particularly in accounts written, published, and authorized by his most intimate male friends.[5] In their articles reviewers and critics provided potential audiences with strategies for "reading" performances and responding to performers.[6] Thus, those reviews and memoirs that stressed the "manly" beauty critics found in Forrest's muscular physique or Booth's "soulful" face helped establish ways these actors and their bodies functioned symbolically for the public at large and implied other spectators—men as well as women—might also take pleasure in seeing them.

Because constructions of sexual behavior, gender, and sexual identity had different interpretations in earlier eras than they do today, the intense same-sex attachments between the actors and critics I am examining here were subject to different constellation of "meanings" than they would be for modern readers. On the one hand, in the early and middle nineteenth century, emotional expressions of same-sex intimacy and attachment were not incompatible with accepted discourses of sentimental friendship and loving comradeship. So, while certain sexual acts and behaviors between same-sex partners were subject to vigorous, punitive legislation—particularly for male partners—the emotional and even romantic expression of love between them was often celebrated. In fact, as Eve Sedgwick has suggested, nineteenth-century men's preference for the company of other men could, in this earlier age, be seen as *evidence of* their masculinity, rather than a cause to question it.[7] This discourse of manly attachment underscored the intense bonds reviewers such as "Acorn" and "Vagabond" felt for their subjects, and informed the articles they published.

Forrest and Oakes: Playing upon "the Manliest Sympathies" in the Press

In the early decades of the nineteenth century, the development of the popular cultural institutions of the American theater and the American press were closely interrelated. Both served as platforms for representations of the young nation; in doing so both inevitably helped produce the various "publics" they addressed, and each built upon the visibility and accessibility of the other. In the period from 1825 to 1850, there were few special theatrical journals in the United States, and dramatic criticism was, for the most part, left to the general periodicals and newspapers.[8] Newspapers and periodicals reported on noteworthy theatrical events and personages, thereby helping to build an audience, while theatrical events and celebrities were considered news, and mention of them would often help sell newspapers. Moreover, the same individuals frequently held a pecuniary interest in each, so that proprietors and editors of periodicals who were or had been actors, playwrights, managers, or lessees of theaters had a personal economic stake in theatrical reportage that either filled houses or kept the paying audience away.

With the line not clearly drawn between reviews and arts criticism on one hand, and public relations "puffery" on the other, articles about actors published on the pages of early-nineteenth-century American periodicals were unstable sites: as advertisements for evolving aesthetic values, they were as likely to be placed in the press by any (often anonymous) individual with a vested financial interest in the success or failure of a particular work as by a journalist or essayist exploring in print the meanings and value he or she derived from a given performer, production, or aesthetic text. In 1846, poet and *Brooklyn Daily Eagle* editor and critic Walt Whitman railed against this practice. Whitman charged that "most of the 'criticisms' in the metropolitan press are written *before the plays are played*—and paid for by the theatre, or other parties. Of those which are not paid for, the majority are the fruits of solicitation, favoritism, and so on."[9] Many "amusement-mongers"—as journalist Charles T. Congdon called the Boston theater managers he encountered in the 1850s—seemed to believe that, as repayment for the reviewer's free admission or for advertising in the paper, a manager was "entitled to the occupation of as many columns as he cared to fill," presumably with a positive review.[10] Moreover, as a general practice, in the early decades of the century, payment for journalists and freelance contributors was sporadic and meager, so "most writing in newspapers was done by lawyers and other men of education as a labor of love or of political fealty."[11] For successful Boston salt merchant James Oakes, the "labor of love" that fueled much of his writing for the press was the opportunity to effectively publicize the career of his beloved friend Edwin Forrest.

Theater reviews in the early and middle nineteenth century frequently functioned as an advertisement for an artist, but, because a published review of a cultural text or performance was presented as a critical evaluation, it did more than report on a performance; it inevitably "generate[d] the effect of describing the value it actually helped create."[12] In Forrest's case, reviews helped set the terms for the aesthetic value of Forrest's muscular form of masculinity. From the outset of his career, reviewers commented on Forrest's virility, his manly physique, and the national character he was believed to represent. Forrest's remarkably successful public image was constructed and reinforced by theater reviews, many of them written by cultural critics impelled by their own homosocial passions such as Forrest's friends James Oakes and James Rees and illustrations and photographs created by his close friend (and later biographer) Gabriel Harrison.

Forrest's earliest characterizations of the gladiator Spartacus, the Native American Metamora, and Shakespeare's Othello and Coriolanus, among other roles, afforded him opportunities to display his assiduously cultivated athletic physique.[13] As early as 1837 a critic asked rhetorically whether anyone but Forrest "can so powerfully depict, as his [Forrest's] strong lineaments and muscular proportions do, the terrific contortions of the human face and form when convulsed by . . . fierce and coarse passions."[14] And the physicality of Forrest's portrayals, contemporaries claimed, "played upon the manliest sympathies" of theatergoers as no actor had previously.[15] What were the "manly sympathies" present in Forrest's presumptively male spectators, and how did his performances and critical writing about them provide access to these feelings? Kirk Fuoss, in his work on "Performance as Contestation," has written of the importance of attending to ways in which a given performance "engage[s] in communal identity politics"; exploring how a performance functions rhetorically, "argu[ing] for particular construals of categories such as 'us' and 'them,' 'insider' and 'outsider,' 'ally' and 'opposition,' 'community' and 'other.'"[16] It is my contention that by conflating Forrest's heroic characters, the actor's own physical prowess, and his patriotic self-identification, critiques of Forrest's performances set the terms for contested notions of masculinity, and the class and national interests his particular form of masculinity would serve.

Throughout Forrest's career, reviews of his performances became a rallying cry for a particular "communal identity" of physically powerful, virile American men whose homosocial attachments to each other could be seen as a glorification of manly bonding and class-inflected democratic principles. As Bruce McConachie has noted, Forrest's representation as a heroic, self-made man "of the people" inspired his largely male audience of worshipful fans.[17] In fact, critical support for and appreciation of Forrest's hypermasculine working-class bravado was so imbricated in presumptions about national identification that those critics who disparaged Forrest's acting style were at pains to explain their position. Thus journalist Charles T. Congdon warranted, "As an American, I am under constitutional obligations to declare Mr. Forrest the finest tragic actor of this or of any age; but as a man and a critic, I resolutely refuse to say anything of the sort."[18] Although in 1880 Congdon wrote dismissively of Forrest's "mastodian [*sic*] muscularity," he noted that the climate of the earlier era in which he and Forrest had lived was such that "with such a frame, and a good costume, it would have been strange if he [Forrest] had altogether missed dignity."[19]

Forrest's construction as the masculine icon of the nation—indeed his excessive performance of virility and physical prowess—was partially generated by James Oakes, who along with others constructed, "sculpted," and reinforced Forrest's hypermasculine persona and interpreted the iconic American star for contemporary readers. Edwin Forrest and James Oakes first met on February 5, 1827, during the nearly twenty-one-year-old actor's first performance in Boston. Forrest was playing Damon in John Banim's *Damon and Pythias*. Sitting in the audience, James Oakes, a year Forrest's junior, remembered being moved to tears by this depiction of the deep, ennobling love between the male protagonists. According to William Rounseville Alger (who, at Oakes's suggestion, fifty years later became Forrest's official biographer and knew both men), "After the play Oakes went behind the scenes and obtained an introduction, his heart yet shaking from his eyes the watery signals of profound emotion awakened in him by the performance."[20] For the remainder of their lives Forrest and Oakes would consider their relationship a similarly intimate, consistent attachment. Alger described Oakes as "the true Pythias in the real life of this Damon" and wrote that from the time of their first acquaintance Forrest and Oakes "flowed harmoniously together as if they had been foreordained for each other by being set to the same rhythm."[21]

As Ginger Strand has observed, the unself-consciousness of Alger's account of what he described as Forrest and Oakes's "half-century of unfaltering love" illustrates the range of homoaffectional bonds acceptable between nineteenth-century men. Forrest's early biographers wrote openly about the passionate attachment between Forrest and Oakes, and Alger quoted directly from Oakes's letters, including his fervent and embodied assurance to Forrest, "I am, from top to bottom, inside and out, and all through, forever yours."[22] That America's first great male actor—whose on- and offstage performance of hypermasculine virility was read by many as metonymic of physical, vigorous democratic American identity—was intimately attached to another man may at first surprise contemporary readers accustomed to associating men's passion for each other with effeminacy. Yet, in an era in which a construction of masculinity was often based upon a negation of any association with femininity, men's same-sex passion could be seen as a heroic attachment, reinforcing each man's virility. For some, the celebration of male bonding and appreciation of men's bodies represented a valuing of physical health, a refutation of "femininity" associated with domesticity and weakness. But others no doubt sensed erotic possibilities in the cult of physical fitness and manly comradeship.

Forrest was large, powerful, and muscular. Oakes was similarly muscular; in fact, they strongly resembled each other. Both men identified with and strove to embody a particular ideal of masculinity that they were drawn to in each other and that they claimed was representative of their nationality as Americans. Both men were committed to a regimen of physical exercise they maintained throughout their lives. In fact, Forrest died of a stroke at the age of sixty-six, with a barbell in his hand. The letters between these men are replete with mentions of strenuous hiking trips, various exercise programs, and their common appreciation for the muscular male physique. They wrote to each other about their respective health, diet, and exercise practices, such as bodybuilding, bathing rituals, and their practice of pounding or flagellating their bodies with rubber balls attached to elastic cords.[23]

The virile "manliness" Forrest and Oakes admired in each other matched the public display of Forrest's body on stage, and both were infused with potential or actual homoeroticism. Hypermasculine athletic men like Forrest and Oakes glorified what Richard Wagner described as a "Spartan" model of male comradeship, signaling the ideal of physical prowess and love between men in ancient Greece. Wagner believed that "the spirit of comradeship which pervade[d] and shape[d] the whole economy of the Spartan state" arose from "genuine delight in the beauty of the most perfect body—that of the male."[24] In the United States, Walt Whitman similarly celebrated the "adhesive love" of male comrades and claimed that "emotional, muscular, and heroic" love between men was a vital component of the American democratic ideal.[25]

Throughout the 1840s Whitman was a steady contributor to New York newspapers and magazines, publishing fiction, journalism, theater criticism, and editorials. In his early years Whitman (who, like Oakes, favored muscular men) had been particularly moved by his aesthetic response not only to Forrest, but even more strongly to an earlier starring actor, British-born Junius Brutus Booth. Whitman relished being in the company of other male spectators, brawny "full-blooded" men who sat with him in the gallery of the Bowery Theater, their "emotional nature . . . roused by the power and magnetism" of actors like Edwin Forrest and Junius Booth.[26] Although Junius Booth was small in stature, Booth's passion onstage influenced Whitman, who later claimed that "his [Junius Booth's] genius was to me one of the grandest revelations of my life, a lesson of artistic expression. The words fire, energy, *abandon,* found in him unprecedented meanings."[27] While it is impossible to fully determine the precise complex and often contradictory understandings of same-sex attraction that underlay the aesthetic perceptions of an earlier age, attitudes like these espoused by Wagner in Europe and Whitman in the United States equated manliness, physical prowess, and nationalism, and were part of the critical currency that informed public reaction to Forrest and Booth.

Criticism and biographical accounts of Forrest by his contemporaries frequently fetishized his muscular body, treating the male body as erotic spectacle, an object the critic clearly gazed at with pleasure. The visual display of Forrest's body suggested a range of meanings for nineteenth-century critics and spectators. For some, the celebration of men's bodies—

especially what Yvonne Tasker, discussing modern film action heroes, has termed "over-developed and over-determined" bodies—was in keeping with a discourse that valued masculine markers of physical health and exclusively male athletic pursuits as emblematic of male bonding and comradeship.[28] Yet the athletic manliness that Forrest embodied could also serve as an available source of voyeuristic or narcissistic pleasure. In his biography of Forrest—for which Oakes supplied much of the background—William Rounseville Alger depicted the pleasures offered by the display of Forrest's body in the youthful years, when Oakes first knew him:

> What a grand form he had! What a grand face! What a grand voice! . . . As he stepped upon the stage in his naked fighting-trim, his muscular coating unified all over him and quivering with vital power, his skin polished to a smooth and marble hardness, conscious of his enormous potency, fearless of anything on the earth, proudly aware of the impression he knew his mere appearance, backed by his fame, would make on the audience who impatiently awaited him—he used to stand and receive the long, tumultuous cheering that greeted him, as immovable as a planted statue of Hercules.[29]

And Forrest selected roles in which his well-developed musculature would be displayed; thus, Forrest can be said to have used his body to shape the American stage into a potential male homoerotic public space, as male spectators and critics like Oakes responded enthusiastically to the spectacle of Forrest's enormous calves and muscular arms in the costume of the bare-chested Spartacus or the Native American warrior, Metamora—roles that Forrest commissioned and that journalist Charles T. Condon claimed were "specially written for his [Forrest's] private legs and larynx."[30]

Shortly after their first meeting, Oakes "began scribbling criticisms" of Forrest's performances that Oakes "often gave to the regular reporters and dramatic critics of the newspapers, and sometimes sent them directly in his own name to the editors" of "several leading journals in the east and the south."[31] Thus, Oakes served as an arbiter of representations of his intimate friend's body. In later years he arranged for the commissioning of a colossal heroic statue of Forrest and was instrumental in selecting Alger as Forrest's "official" biographer, believing Alger would understand the two men's impassioned attachment and value it. And, most significantly for this essay, Oakes deployed all of his considerable contacts in the press to publicize the talent and character of his beloved friend, tirelessly advocating for Forrest, negotiating with managers on

Forrest's behalf, and then writing "notices" and reviews of Forrest's performances.

> Oakes made it his study to do everything in his power to aid and further his honored friend alike in his personal status and in his professional glory. For this end he wrote and moved others to write hundreds and hundreds of newspaper notices, working up every conceivable kind of item calculated to keep the name and personality of the actor freshly before the eyes of the public.[32]

Oakes's unabashedly "heroic adhesion and indefatigable attentiveness to all whom he admires and loves,"[33] as Alger described it, prompted Oakes to express his admiration and love for Forrest in countless articles and reviews placed in various Boston papers as well as in those periodicals edited by his close friends, George W. Kendall and A. M. Holbrook of the *New Orleans Picayune,* John W. Forney, editor and proprietor of the *Pennsylvanian,* and, most notably, William T. Porter, editor of the *Spirit of the Times* (New York).[34] Porter's *Spirit of the Times* was a weekly broadsheet, founded in 1831 to cover sporting events, literature, and theater. "As an object of lively interest, *The Drama* demands our best interests and will continue to be a prominent feature in this paper," the paper announced regularly in the 1830s, advertising the use of freelance contributors like Oakes. "The *Spirit of the Times* finds its way into every Green Room in the Union, and has so many correspondents among the profession, as to have acquired a character for authentic, exclusive, and early *Green Room Intelligence,* not exceeded by any journal whatever."[35] Oakes became a regular contributor to *Spirit of the Times* and frequently published sporting and theatrical notices anonymously and under his pseudonym, "Acorn." Although not a professional journalist, Oakes's short articles, often written in the form of letters to "P[orter]," earned him a steady readership. An article in 1848 identified "Acorn" as *Spirit*'s "well-known and witty Boston correspondent" and covered his travel adventures just as they did Oakes's accounts of Boston politics, sports, and theater.[36]

Unlike the lofty goals for drama criticism later expressed by established critics like William Winter, who maintained that by writing about the theater a critic would "contribute to the improvement of the public taste and therein he will benefit society,"[37] Oakes used the press primarily as a venue to advance the work of his beloved friend. While Winter stated explicitly that "personal feelings have not influenced my praise, neither have they prompted my censure,"[38] as a reviewer Oakes clearly made no such attempt at objectivity, nor did he claim one.[39] As Forrest's devoted friend, Oakes put forth such articles as were calculated to present his hero in a positive light. Yet, as intimately as he knew Forrest personally, Oakes's reviews and articles exposed readers to his critical and aesthetic evaluations without disclosing the passionate private relationship that motivated and framed many of his perceptions. Unbeknownst to readers, then, early descriptions of what was considered good acting and desirable American character traits were informed by what might today be considered a gay male aesthetic.

Describing Forrest's Othello, Oakes/"Acorn," wrote, "No man, excepting one possessing great genius, coupled with diligent and patient research into every chamber of the human heart and mind, is capable of giving such portraiture." And, after having compared Forrest favorably with Edmund Kean, whose performance Oakes had witnessed in his youth, Oakes/"Acorn" informed the *Spirit*'s readers, "The writer has now no desire to witness any other actor in this great character, but is content that the impression made on Friday evening past, remain unaltered and undimmed, as a model picture for future reference."[40] Of Forrest's Macbeth, Oakes announced, "There are such a variety of passions and impulses to be portrayed that it requires mighty intellectual strength, as well as great physical powers . . . all of which Mr. Forrest possesses in an eminent degree." Refuting in the press other reviewers who were critical of his beloved Forrest, "Acorn" asserted that "notwithstanding the writer has heard many persons decry the Macbeth of Mr. Forrest, he has never yet seen a man possessing a mind unswayed by prejudice who was not willing to acknowledge the superiority of portions of this great tragedian's interpretation of the character."[41]

In his attempt to counter any bad press Forrest received, recasting it as "prejudice" against the actor, Oakes published reviews of individual performances he witnessed and routinely reported the enthusiasm of Forrest's audiences, characterizing Forrest as a star who performed "with greater power" at each ensuing engagement. "I have so often before spoken of this great tragedian's ability," "Acorn" wrote on January 17, 1853,

> that I will not now enter into a critical analysis of any of his impersonations, but suffice for the present by saying, that all his portraitures are marked by deep thought and original and bold conception; while in execution they are artistic and finished, and never have I seen his characters rendered with greater power than during his present engagement.[42]

As further evidence of his beloved Forrest's popularity, and of his own access to private information about the star, "Acorn" informed *Spirit*'s

New York readers that "a manager of one of the New Orleans theatres was in town and offered Forrest Two Thousand Dollars per week to act a series of weeks at one of the Crescent City theatres. It would seem by this that his popularity was on the increase in other cities as well as in Boston."[43] Oakes was privy to all aspects of Forrest's professional life and freely publicized those pieces of information that would be advantageous to Forrest's career.

At the same time, Oakes's coverage of other theatrical personages was calculated to support Forrest's efforts as well. For example, as early as 1839 in a *Spirit* review of Forrest's "absolutely perfect" representation of Richelieu (a part originally written for British actor William Charles Macready), Oakes commended "the completeness with which Mr. Forrest executes any point, nay, every passage." Although noting that the role "is a favorite part of Macready," Oakes claimed that Forrest played the part "as perfectly as possible," and found it incredulous that any other opinion of Forrest's "genius" might be expressed.[44] When in 1848 Macready—by then Forrest's acknowledged rival—arrived in the United States for a third American tour, "Acorn" sarcastically displayed his biases against his friend's competitor, announcing in the pages of the *Spirit of the Times* that "Mr. Macready, the tragedian, and in his own estimation, the embodiment of the entire British stage, arrived here in the Acadia."[45]

In the intervening nine years, the long-standing cultural competition between England and the United States festered in the rivalry between Forrest and Macready, largely carried out, as Macready claimed, in Forrest's chosen "battle-ground . . . the American Press and from thence he [Forrest] flung his aspersions on me."[46] Press reportage of Macready's prior American tour in 1843–44 had been marked by class interests and nationalist versus pro-British sentiment, with more privileged, cultivated, and pro-British supporters favoring Macready's interpretations, while the largely working-class, democratic, and patriotic American audiences preferred Forrest.[47] In fact, James Rees later bragged that during Macready's 1843 engagement in Philadelphia "it is a well known how we [Rees writing as "Colley Cibber"] defended Mr. Forrest against those who were advocates of the English actor." "Colley Cibber's" pro-Forrest, anti-Macready articles were so vehement that "the result of our labors," Rees acknowledged, "was the removal of our name from the free list" by theater manager E. A. Marshall.[48] During Macready's 1843–44 tour, American actress Charlotte Cushman costarred with the famous British tragedian on American soil and received such positive reviews in the American press that she traveled to England to try her talents before British audiences. Arriving in London at roughly the same time as Forrest, the powerful, androgynous Cushman performed for a time with her fellow American.

Critical response to Forrest, Cushman, and Macready was shaped by and in dialogue with the elision between gender and nationality that critics and theatergoers associated with each of these starring performers, carried out in the pages of the press. In England as in the United States, reception of Forrest was complex, motivated in part by criticism of Forrest's performance of a form of masculinity that departed from British models of manly reserve, and in part by partisan notions of national and class allegiances. For the most part, the London press vilified Forrest's articulation, interpretation, and understanding of canonical Shakespearean roles. Significantly, the *London Examiner*'s editor and drama critic was Macready's close friend, John Forster. Conflating gender, class, and national markers of identity, the *Examiner* had claimed that Forrest "cannot appreciate, even if he understands, the language . . . of the bard of Avon." In an explicit display of classist anti-American sentiment, the *Examiner* claimed that Forrest had been "flattered and encouraged by his own ignorant, ill-judging countrymen, who know no more of Shakespeare than of Hebrew or Sanskrit, and who mistake rapt and outrageous gestures for expression and feeling."[49] However, Forrest's American costar, Charlotte Cushman, was lauded by the same British critics who disparaged him and was frequently associated in print with Forrest's British rival, Macready, whom she was said to resemble. Although Oakes and other advocates in the American press attributed Forrest's poor reception in England to anti-American partisans, the enthusiastic reaction Cushman received for her extremely androgynous portrayals complicated the argument. While Forrest was largely unsuccessful with London critics, Cushman was lauded by the British press. Moreover, the recourse to language of "Americanness" that was used to praise Cushman's "masculine" "intelligence and force" and at the same time invoked to criticize Forrest further heightened the competition and inflamed the rivalry between Forrest and Macready.[50] Forrest—whose performance of masculinity embodied what Mary Poovey has described as the mid-nineteenth-century "model of a binary opposition between the sexes"—was enraged by positive reactions to Cushman's forceful characterizations.[51]

For years after Cushman's performances with Forrest in London, James Oakes's published criticism of Cushman continued to reflect the tenor of his and Forrest's disapproval; in addition to charging Cushman with "Macreadyism," Oakes's reviews of Cushman in the *Boston Atlas* and *Spirit of the Times* praised her power but raised the possibility that Cushman's portrayals were aberrantly "masculine," "excit[ing] wonder, instead of commanding admiration." For example, "Acorn" complained that Cushman's Lady Macbeth "bullied Macbeth" into committing the murder of Duncan. Oakes suggested that in Cushman's interpretation the lack of "all those little womanly characteristics which is [*sic*] innate to the nature of the gentler sex" should have provoked Macbeth "rather to have turned such a shrew out of doors, and lived alone in peace!!" Moreover, Oakes continued to associate Cushman in print with Macready: "There is, through all Miss Cushman's acting, a taint of those peculiarities, and mechanical clap-traps, and mannerisms . . . not a few of which can be traced to the Macready and Charles Kean school of acting."[52]

In London, Macready had his own advocates in the press, most notably the *Examiner*'s John Forster. As with Forrest and Oakes, Macready expected Forster to find occasions for "keeping my name before the public, " and regarded it as a slight upon their friendship if Forster "allowed six or eight weeks to pass over" without a mention of Macready in the *Examiner*.[53] Oakes's apparent recognition of the extent to which reviews of theatrical practice could be fueled by homoerotic bonds between actor and critic led him to associate Macready with Forster's criticism of Forrest. In a lengthy article in the *Boston Mail*, Oakes blamed Macready for the negative reviews Forrest received during his tour of England, alleging that Macready "possesses the body and soul" of Forster, and implied that this intimacy led Forster to do "all kinds of dirty work for his master."[54] By implication, Forrest was not subject just to anti-American feeling; his masculinity was set at odds with British masculinity (personified by Macready) by a rival national homoerotic aesthetic.

In Edinburgh, shortly after his disastrous London performances with Cushman, Forrest attended a performance of Macready's *Hamlet* and hissed his British rival. Explaining what was to the British a most ungentlemanly violation of professional decorum, Forrest claimed in a letter he sent to the *Times* that he was merely expressing his disapprobation of the "abuse of the stage" Macready committed by introducing into his performance of Hamlet a "fancy dance" in which Macready waved his handkerchief and pranced across the stage.[55] For Forrest, Macready's "desecration" had effeminate overtones, and Forrest's public claim that he was, in effect, policing the boundaries of appropriate masculine gender display underscored specific classed and national performances of

gender.[56] Haunting the margins of excessive or inappropriate performances of "masculinity," "femininity," or "effeminacy" was the unarticulated awareness of the possibility of transgressive sexual behavior. In
Forrest's construction, Macready—English, cultured, educated—was
accused of acting like an effete "fop" at a time when American notions of
masculinity were increasingly modeled on muscular displays of manly
vigor.

Paradoxically, this was an age so open to the spectatorial pleasures
leading actors offered to same-sex viewers that British actor John Coleman could remark unself-consciously in his memoir of his pleasure in seeing Edwin Forrest, "I am pure Pagan, and always have been of the opinion that physical beauty in man and woman is a thing to stir the heart
and thrill the brain."[57] Forrest's "robust virility" had impressed the
young Coleman, who met Forrest in Edinburgh at the time of the "hiss-
ing" incident. Coleman remembered that Forrest's disdain for Cushman
(and the gender conventions she traversed) was as vehement as his dislike
of Macready. Conflating the "masculine" American actress Cushman
with the British male costar she so strongly resembled, Forrest was out-
spoken about the degree to which positive responses she received from
British audiences fueled his rage. "When the conversation turned upon
Macready and Miss Cushman," Coleman recounted, "it was evident that
we had alighted on a sore place. That an 'epicene thing' (for woman he
would not concede her to be) whom he regarded as an imposter, an
intriguante whom he stigmatised as being 'hideous as Sycorax' or
worse—a 'Macready in petticoats,' should succeed where he failed, he
regarded as an outrage upon common sense and his nationality."[58]

While years of reportage of the cultural conflict between Forrest and
Macready highlighted the various performances of nationality and class
each of the leading male tragedians represented, and the various class
identifications of the spectators who favored either the forceful, "democratic," brawny Forrest or the genteel, "aristocratic," English Macready,
the tension between the two men was also played out on the axes of
stereotypes about gender and sexuality then current. In short, the competing notions of masculinity each actor embodied were imbricated in the
other qualities championed or denigrated by their respective advocates in
the press. It would seem, then, that the specter of transgressive gender performance underlay the American-British cultural competition that erupted
so fatally in New York in the spring of 1849. Forrest and Macready were
both performing the same roles at different theaters. Reviews, articles, letters to the editor—all forms of press coverage of the leading actors—were

the ground upon which competing notions of sexuality, gender, class, and national identity were played out. The overt rivalry between Forrest and Macready reached its apogee on May 10, 1849, when a riot ensued as Macready's performance of *Macbeth* at the Astor Place Opera House was disrupted by fans of Forrest protesting English cultural claims of "superiority." The militia, called out to quash the riot, fired into the crowd and killed more than twenty people. The sexual and gender tensions that were constructed and inflamed by criticism such as that by Oakes, Rees, and Forster had contributed to the violent public performance of protest that culminated in the Astor Place Riot. And articles in the periodical press continued to be the sites in which these conflicting positions were constructed, shored up, and represented.

"Towering Specimens of Impassioned Manhood"

For decades Oakes's anonymous and pseudonymous criticism of Forrest and his competitors continued to set the stage for Forrest's critical reception. In an attempt to keep his beloved friend before the eyes of readers and spectators, Oakes published a wide range of articles about Forrest, drawing attention to the larger-than-life-size heroic sculpture of Forrest as Coriolanus that Oakes had arranged to be commissioned, presenting to the public Forrest's side of his acrimonious divorce suit, and discussing in print the beauty of Forrest's curtain speeches—even those delivered when Oakes was not physically present.[59] Repeatedly Forrest consulted his "dearest friend Oakes" on business affairs and financial arrangements and acknowledged Oakes's role in his career, thanking him for sending along such articles as "the timely and graceful notice in the Boston *Post.*"[60] Writing from Philadelphia thanking Oakes for a letter that "made my heart beat quicker and freer," Forrest remarked that an article Oakes had published "in the Boston *Express* was well done and well timed" and informed Oakes that he had arranged to have it reprinted in a Philadelphia paper.[61]

Throughout their lives the two men lived in separate cities, and so their letters are filled with arrangements to see each other. In addition to annual lengthy vacations together and long visits whenever Forrest performed in Boston, Forrest repeatedly wrote how much he wanted to see Oakes, and often asked Oakes to come to Philadelphia to be with him—mentioning that his Philadelphia home "when adorned by your [Oakes's] presence, needs no other embellishment"[62]—or to come to New York to see him perform. When Oakes joined Forrest during these engagements or saw him perform in Boston, Oakes's subsequent articles in the press were calculated to further Forrest's career. Gratefully, Forrest acknowledged after receiving an article Oakes published about Forrest's performances in Boston that "your article on the performances at the Boston theatre was one of the best you ever wrote—brief and complete."[63]

Although both men were married, their letters reveal that their most passionate connection was unquestionably to each other. After his very public separation and bitter divorce from British actress Catherine Sinclair, Forrest wrote to Oakes of marriage as "an invention of the Devil." And, although Oakes remained married, his emotional life seems to have been lived completely apart from his wife, centered instead on Forrest and on the small circle of close male friends they knew in common. In fact, Forrest congratulated Oakes when Oakes retired and moved in with his sister, and Forrest continued to propose ways the two men might spend more time together. When Oakes considered taking a trip to Europe with his daughter, Forrest mused how he would like to come along, as Oakes's companion: "Wouldn't we let the world wag—and a fig for care."[64] Ardently, Forrest wrote Oakes "how much I long to see you, to talk over what we alone can feel and know" and assured Oakes that he was "as ever, yours in heart and mind."[65] Forrest was thankful that "Almighty God . . . has quickened [their] two hearts . . . with unselfish and unwavering devotion to each other"[66] (see fig. 11).

When around this time James Oakes met and befriended Reverend William Rounseville Alger, he recognized that Alger had "just the right spirit" to serve as Forrest's official biographer and arranged for Forrest and Alger to meet. Alger was a writer and lecturer who devoted much attention to same-sex relationships; in 1868 he published *The Friendships of Women*,[67] in which he discussed in positive terms the romantic and ardent homoerotic attachments of the Ladies of Langollen, Sappho, Anna Seward, and Margaret Fuller among others. Alger planned a similar, though never completed, volume about pairs of male friends. Once he met Alger, Forrest concurred with Oakes's suggestion, assuring Oakes that "we could not have selected a better man than Mr. Alger," and commending Alger's "manly reason, and his entire freedom from sectarian taints."[68] In his subsequent biography of Forrest, Alger attested to the role Oakes played in selecting Alger to memorialize Forrest: "Oakes had long felt that the life of his friend . . . eminently deserved to be recorded

FIG. 11. James Oakes, around 1865.

(Courtesy, Harvard Theatre Collection, Cambridge, Massachusetts.)

in some full and dignified form. He was seeking for a suitable person to whom to intrust the work. With the assent of Forrest he [Oakes] urged me to assume it."[69]

Alger was not the only contemporary biographer of Forrest who acknowledged the intimate lifelong attachment between Forrest and Oakes, and the shaping influence of the latter on the career of America's first great male actor. Gabriel Harrison, an artist and photographer who did etchings of Edwin Forrest in all of his major roles, had seen Forrest act more than four hundred times and framed his account of Forrest's life along with a pictorial record. With his "artist's eye" and an apparent appreciation for the muscular male physique, Harrison also described Forrest's "wonderful physical being" particularly as the homoerotic character Damon. Conflating Forrest's body type, the roles he portrayed, and men's same-sex emotional bonds, Harrison wrote that Forrest's "grand massy figure was more than equal to Damon's broad and generous quality of democratic mind and devoted friendship."[70] In Harrison's eyes, Forrest was "a wonderfully male man; indeed he was a gladiator in physique."[71] Harrison revealed that James Oakes "knew more of the secret nature of Forrest than any other associate" and published Oakes's letters recounting Forrest's last months.[72]

Actor Lawrence Barrett also acknowledged the importance of "the manly affection and enduring trust of James Oakes" in Forrest's life, as well as the role played by theater critic and historian James Rees in forwarding Forrest's career.[73] Rees and Forrest had been boy actors together in Philadelphia, but the two young men lost touch in 1822 when the sixteen-year-old Forrest went off to Cincinnati to perform. Rees, several years Forrest's senior, shortly turned to writing. Under the pseudonym "Colley Cibber" Rees published dramatic criticism, compilations of early American theater history, and numerous plays and dramatizations of contemporary novels.[74] Later in the lives of Rees and Forrest, their mutual friend, John W. Forney (for whom Rees had written much criticism), reintroduced the two men.

For years Rees had followed and written about Forrest's career, although the actor "had not the least idea" that critic "Colley Cibber" and his boyhood companion of the Apollo Theater days were the same person. Afraid of Forrest's reputation for brusqueness, and concerned that unsolicited overtures at friendship might be rebuffed, for thirty-five years Rees remained unknown to Forrest, claiming that "as an actor we admired him, and felt more real pleasure in speaking of him than we imagined we should enjoy in speaking to him."[75] As fond as he was of Forrest, Rees attempted to appear neutral in print. Noting that many of the flattering articles he wrote about Forrest were published before they resumed their relationship, Rees (using the plural "we") claimed that "our readers will understand that we have never praised nor spoken in commendatory terms of Mr. Forrest unless he came up to our notion of how and in what manner a part should be played." Yet as a barometer for distinguishing "a proper appreciation for true art," Rees, like many others who were moved by Forrest, relied not only on his critical judgment but on "the effect good acting has on us *physically* as well as mentally."[76] In his review of an 1864 performance of Forrest's *Coriolanus* at the Philadelphia Academy of Music, Rees was moved to comment on "the Roman manliness of his [Forrest's] face and figure, the haughty dignity of his carriage." Later, as a personal friend, Rees attested to Forrest's great power to literally "act upon a body weaker than his own," claiming that Rees's nervous headaches were relieved "under the manipulating power exercised upon him by Mr. Forrest."[77]

After Forrest's death, Rees was eager to establish in print his close friendship with the celebrated tragedian. Rees rushed to complete his biography of Forrest before Alger's "official" authorized biography was published, and Rees publicized the fact that in the last years of Forrest's life, Rees—who lived near Forrest in Philadelphia—oversaw the care of Forrest's home whenever the actor was on tour. Rees's articles and book about Forrest led fellow actor Lawrence Barrett to note that Forrest and Rees's reacquaintance led to the "renewal of an old boy-love begun in their earlier thespian days in Philadelphia" and to comment that James Rees "as 'Colley Cibber' has given us an estimate of his dead friend, true and invaluable."[78]

Yet despite describing himself as Forrest's "constant companion" in the latter part of the actor's life,[79] Rees in his biography of Forrest ultimately confirmed Oakes's primacy in Forrest's emotional life, as had Alger, Harrison, and Barrett. Oakes was so closely connected with Forrest that it is he who was wired when Forrest died, and nothing was done with Forrest's body until Oakes arrived from Boston. As the closest person to Forrest, and the architect of Forrest's career, Oakes had arranged for Forrest's funeral just as he had scripted and overseen such other public representations as Forrest's critical evaluations, publicity, commemorative statue, and official biography. After Forrest's death, Oakes's proprietary relationship with the body of the man he loved was such that he was able to give another friend, James Lawson, a lock of Forrest's hair.[80]

To many of Forrest's critics, both admirers and detractors, Forrest *was* his body, and his body signified the nation. Ironically, perhaps, to modern readers, given the overt homoeroticism in so much of the reportage about Forrest, those nineteenth-century spectators who *resisted* the appeal of "the robust and towering specimens of impassioned manhood which he [Forrest] exhibited, teeming with fearless energies" were regarded as "persons of a feeble and squeamish constitution and sickly delicacy who could not stand the powerful shocks he administered to their nerves." In short, in the misogynist terms of the day, they were either women or effeminate men. Conflating those groups, Alger claimed,

"Faint ladies, spruce clerks, spindling fops, and perfumed dandies were horrified [by Forrest and] vented their own weakness and ignorance of virile truth in querulous complaints of his [Forrest's] coarseness and ferocity."[81] In essence, Forrest's excessive masculinity as described, desired, and admired by Oakes was largely embraced because homosociality reinforced the beliefs in gender difference so adamantly proscribed in their era. Yet the "impassioned manhood" and "virile truth" that had so engaged Alger, Rees, and Oakes—and had been, to a large extent, constructed for the public by their critical efforts—was not the only model of masculinity available to spectators. Not long into the second half of the nineteenth century another competing construction of American masculinity would claim attention of theatergoers, and it, too, would be largely the result of a passionate connection between a male critic and the leading actor he adored.

Midcentury Manly Love

The middle to late 1850s to 1860s witnessed a watershed in the public articulation of male homoerotic desire in print and the ways men's love for and attraction to each other might be read. In 1850 English poet laureate Alfred Tennyson published *In Memoriam,* a long, passionate tribute to his deceased friend, Arthur Hallam. In the poem Tennyson lovingly commemorated in undeniably romantic terms the "gentleman[ly]" Hallam's "manhood fused with female grace."[82] And in 1855 American poet and journalist Walt Whitman glorified "the manly love of comrades" in the first edition of his poetry collection *Leaves of Grass.*[83] Tennyson explicitly equated his love for Hallam to love between men and women, and Whitman went so far as to assert that fervid companionship between men was at the root of American democracy. Men were writing about loving men, and the pleasure of seeing and being seen. As Whitman asked in *Song of the Open Road:* "Do you know what it is as you pass to be loved by strangers? / Do you know the talk of those turning eyeballs?"[84] The appearance of these texts excited considerable uproar and contributed to a complex and contradictory discourse then circulating as critics debated whether such poems merely celebrated the same-sex romantic friendships so prevalent in the nineteenth century or whether they depicted (and advocated) "inappropriate" or "immoral" passions.

With these debates as a backdrop, men onstage also continued to serve as the object of desire for other men, although often in ways that are hard to recognize from this distance in time. As Joseph Roach suggests, "Historians might . . . profitably ask by what methods the performance signified, how its meanings came to be shared with its audience, and why its success or failure seemed to be rooted in the particular ideological and aesthetic contingencies of the moment."[85] Theater criticism reflecting the homoerotic desire of popular male critics was one of the ways in which the shifting meanings of masculinity at this historical moment were rendered legible in American society as male cultural critics shared with readers their particular aesthetic and erotic responses to men they admired.

Booth and Badeau: "The Vagabond" and His Prince

In the spring of 1857, theatergoers witnessed the first New York starring engagement of the late Junius Booth's twenty-three-year-old son, Edwin—whom Booth had named after Edwin Forrest. A more different physical type than Forrest can hardly be imagined. Lawrence Barrett, Edwin Booth's costar at New York's Metropolitan Theatre, described Edwin as "a slight pale youth, with black, flowing hair, soft brown eyes full of tenderness and gentle timidity, and a manner mixed with shyness and quiet repose."[86]

In the audience for Booth's New York engagement was Adam Badeau, the twenty-five-year-old cultural and arts critic for the *Sunday Times* and *Noah's Messenger* (see fig. 12). Under the pseudonym "Vagabond," Badeau had made a practice of "prying into all sorts of places" and publishing critical essays about performances, persons, and arts events as disparate as concerts at the Academy of Music, black prayer-meetings, speeches by suffrage orators. Like Whitman, who in his journalism and poetry took readers on tours of the city and its people in an attempt to define an American aesthetic, "Vagabond" promised readers of his collected criticism: "I will sometimes tell you what I have seen behind the curtain, and sometimes discuss the merits of a favorite actor on the stage. Pictures and parties, beaux and bores, all I study; art and life, in all their phases, I like to contemplate. . . . I am likely to find out whatever there is of queer, quaint, or passing strange in this metropolis."[87] Badeau rejoiced in the innovative and avant-garde arts of the day and wrote articles about the impassioned emotionalism he found in the poetry of Tennyson, the novels of George Sand and Charlotte Brontë, and the paintings of Frederick Church. To Badeau artistic expressions that were impulsive, earnest, erratic, and original were the most appropriate archetypes for American art.

When Badeau first saw Edwin Booth perform, Badeau was "struck at once with [Booth's] dramatic fire, his grace, his expressive eye and mobile mouth,"[88] and in May 1857 "Vagabond" announced in his weekly *Sunday Times* column that "Edwin Booth has made me know what tragedy is. He has displayed to my eyes an entirely new field; he has opened to me the door to another and exquisite delight; he has shown me the possibilities of tragedy."[89] Badeau responded immediately and intensely to Booth, coming to see every night of his New York performance run and advising *Sunday Times* readers to do likewise. For Badeau, Edwin Booth's performances were the harbinger of a new type of American art—every bit as meaningful and life-changing to him as the elder Booth's performances had been to Whitman. In keeping with the changing times, Badeau favored a different and more refined construction of American masculinity than did Whitman. Unlike the "entirely physical" heroic style of Forrest, whom Badeau declared in print "moves us but does not inspire us," the beautiful, young, soulful Booth offered viewers moments of "divine fire." Badeau's critical essays about the American theater in general and Booth specifically shaped the terms by which Booth subsequently would be known to spectators (fig. 13).

When Booth's run ended in June, Badeau wrote Booth an impassioned letter and enclosed his published reactions to the actor. Identifying himself as "so warm an admirer, let me say, so sincere a friend," Badeau (whom Booth biographer Gene Smith has described as "an intellectual newspaper essayist of ambiguous sexual orientation") offered Booth more than the admiration of a critic or fan; Badeau offered to tutor the largely unschooled Booth in theater history, literature, and the arts, to help Booth achieve the "absolute mastery" of his art. Acknowledging his "infatuation" with Booth (in all of the ambiguous nineteenth-century meanings of the term), and his own potential influence as a critic, Badeau suggested in this first introductory letter, as though to ward off any objections on Booth's part: "I can possibly have no interest to subserve by thrusting my friendship upon you, for though I have a connection and influence with the press, I am independent of it as a means of support. I shall be most happy on your return, to exhibit my earnestness by serving you in any way in my power, by introductions, *by public notices*" (emphasis added).[90] In the summer of 1857, just months after

FIG. 12. Adam Badeau.

(Courtesy, Hampden-Booth Theatre Library at the Players Club, New York City.)

they met, Booth accepted Badeau's invitation, and together the two men visited museums, libraries, and literary salons, read criticism and biographies of great actors, and discussed interpretations of Booth's Shakespearean roles. And, as with freelance critic James Oakes's efforts on Forrest's behalf, Badeau continued see to it that "public notices" of Booth's talent found their way into print.

Bruce McConachie has discussed the growth of a movement toward an ideology of respectability in the American theater after the midcentury

FIG. 13. Edwin Booth as Hamlet.

(Courtesy, Hampden-Booth Theatre Library at the Players Club, New York City.)

and notes that "no other actor was as sanctified by the American bourgeoisie in the 1860s as Edwin Booth," who was constructed by critics as "the bourgeois answer to the plebeian but still mighty Forrest." McConachie cites an 1863 article by George William Curtis, editor of *Harpers,* comparing Forrest's "biceps aesthetics" and the "coarse" theatergoers who applauded him with the thin, intellectual, long-haired and dark-eyed Booth and his more "cultured" audience.[91] But what has been largely overlooked in this construction is Adam Badeau's hand in the initial shaping of Booth as the sensitive, tasteful, "intellectual" American actor and the profound effect Badeau's relationship with Booth had on the transition then under way in the American theater.

For the next three years, until Booth's marriage and Badeau's subsequent entrance into the Union army, Badeau later claimed "we were as intimate as it is possible for two young men to be."[92] Badeau involved himself in every aspect of Booth's career, eagerly "hunt[ing] up books and pictures about the stage, the finest criticisms, the works that illustrated his scenes, the biographies of great actors, and we studied them together."[93] Their intense friendship grew swiftly into a passionate homoerotic connection that Badeau himself described as their "peculiar intimacy." In print in later years, Badeau remarked, "I had a good deal of leisure and could pass my days as well as nights in his company, and I knew no greater pleasure than he gave me, either on or off the stage."[94] Badeau addressed some of his private letters to Booth "My Prince," complained when Booth did not write frequently enough, "fretted" if "anyone [else] should think themselves preferred, even though I knew they were not," and wrote him, "pray stay a god."[95]

Badeau was aware of his embodied response to Booth, and used his criticism to explore his visceral and visual reaction to "the man I love best in the world."[96] For example, the last act of Booth's *Richard III* revealed "the poetry of the stage, the realization of your ideas of the Richard of Shakespeare," Badeau informed his readers in the late 1850s, using the second-person form to elide other spectators' responses with his own. Meanwhile, in their private correspondence, both men continued to enact the erotic and performative potentialities of representation. When Booth sent Badeau as a gift a picture of himself as Hamlet, Badeau thanked him, announcing, "I am going to do what you told me—'look at and talk to the picture while you are awa[y].' I hope soon to have you in person to look at and talk to."[97] Throughout the early years of Badeau's intense affection and worshipful devotion to Booth, Badeau continued to publish critical essays expounding "the manifestation of the divinity of poetry in the flesh"; finding in Booth's acting "what otherwise is intangible and unnatural, only perceptible to the eyes of the soul, actually vivified to the *bodily* sense." Combining the aesthetic, sensual, and spiritual feelings that Booth evoked, Badeau pronounced to his weekly *Sunday Times* readers, "My soul is reached through the medium of my senses,"[98] and so eroticism and spectatorial pleasure together served a higher moral purpose.

But so rhapsodic were Badeau's published accounts of Booth's bodily effect on him, that in a *Sunday Times* column titled "My Unknown Correspondents," Badeau acknowledged that one of his readers "who read my praise of young Booth's beauty, was sure it was written by a woman." While his public use of a pseudonym afforded Badeau a degree of anonymity, it both raised and masked the gender ambiguities implicit in his presentation of Booth's aestheticized male body and the possibilities of homoerotic desire.[99] "Vagabond" never definitively identified himself to his readers. Yet the playful tenor of his "open secret" when publishing fervent accounts of the man he loved is apparent, and thus supports Martin Duberman's assertion that the "standard view of the history of male homosexuality in this country as an unrelieved tale of concealment and woe needs revision."[100]

As "Vagabond," Badeau had written, "Any work of literature or art, of poetry or oratory, as well as the drama, must, to produce the finest effect, appeal to the passions."[101] While Booth undoubtedly appealed to Badeau's passions, it is more difficult to determine precisely what Booth felt for his intimate friend, confidante, and critic. For the first few years of their friendship, the closeness between the two men seems to have been reciprocal. Booth wrote to "Ad" (as he called Badeau) regularly while on tour, confiding details of his notorious exploits. In October 1858, as Badeau read over "some fifty of your letters (I've got them all)," he remarked, "what pleased me more than the badinage or the ease" was that nearly everyone contained "proof of [Booth's] regard" for *him*.[102] Despite whatever degree of heterosexual desire Booth experienced or enacted on- and offstage, nonetheless for the rest of his life Booth elected to save scores of Badeau's letters to him. Years later Badeau made an effort to distinguish in print between Booth's well-known early promiscuous heterosexual escapades and the primacy of the two men's relationship, claiming that, in those early years while "hundreds [of women] flung themselves" at "Ned" Booth, Booth "cared nothing for any of them. Sometimes they amused, but more often disgusted him."[103] Badeau's articles about Booth reinforced the belief, commonly held in that era, that an individual's homoaffectional bonds and casual heterosexual encounters were not mutually exclusive. Thus, Booth's occasional alcohol-induced dissolute adventures while on the road posed no real threat to the emotional intensity of his attachment to Badeau. While Badeau hoped to curb Booth's occasional drunken "sprees, " his major concern about Booth's carousing was to complain to Booth that "you might have waited until I could take care of you."[104]

When Badeau and Booth were in the same city, Badeau would

accompany Booth in the actor's dressing room before a performance, and watch as his adored "Prince" would sit, stripped to the waist, applying stage makeup. In an article he published in *McClure's* magazine after Booth's death, Badeau revealed that on at least one occasion, in a playful display of intimacy and gender transgression, Badeau had pulled open Booth's robe as the two men sat together backstage between the acts of *Richelieu*. Badeau reported that Booth shrieked in falsetto, "'How dare you, sir?'" in what Badeau described as "a shrill tone, exactly like a woman," and marveled that a moment later, "he was the stately cardinal again."[105]

Yet in the second half of the nineteenth century, as now, undoubtedly male same-sex desire took multiple forms. Walt Whitman, for one, preferred less "genteel" men and did not respond to Edwin Booth as his embodiment of a manly ideal. "Edwin had everything but guts," Whitman professed to his confidant Horace Traubel many years later. Regarding Booth through his own aesthetic and erotic preferences, Whitman claimed that "if he [Edwin Booth] had a little more that was absolutely *gross* in his composition he would have been altogether first class instead of just short of it." Whitman had preferred to watch Edwin's father, whom Whitman maintained had "had more power and less finish."[106] But Whitman was, perhaps, influenced by the tastes of an earlier moment in theatrical performance styles as well as his own predilection for muscular working-class rather than refined bourgeois men.

Throughout the first few years of Badeau and Booth's intimate association, Badeau continued to publish weekly articles that helped shape and solidify Booth's professional reputation, and he usually sent Booth copies "of the article I wrote *à cause de vous*." In one "Vagabond" article, titled "Off the Stage," published on September 13, 1859, Badeau wrote of his backstage adventures with Booth and the extraordinary volumes of fan mail Booth received, which Badeau helped Booth answer, thus giving readers a further glimpse of "Vagabond's" intimacy with the new star he had helped create. By this time Booth was so frequently heralded in Badeau's columns that although Badeau declined to mention the name of the actor whose correspondence he quoted in this article, Badeau noted, teasingly, that any of his regular readers would be sure to know the actor's identity.[107]

Without question, Badeau's most remarkable—and explicit—"Vagabond" article was entitled "A Night with the Booths." This was a moving account of a night the two men spent alone together rummaging through theatrical mementos in Booth's childhood home, Tudor Hall outside Baltimore. In 1859, Badeau's published essay virtually brought his *Sunday Times* readers along on the adventure, as Badeau repeatedly invoked Booth's celebrated characterizations.

> The young actor and I started from Baltimore at noon, and drove about twenty-five miles before reaching the farm. We neither of us were particularly conversant with the management of horses under difficulties; and when the harness broke, as it did once or twice, Romeo and the Vagabond were in a quandary indeed.[108]

Once inside Tudor Hall, Booth and Badeau "sat on the floor together, in a closet, and reveled in our treasures."[109] For hours they poured over the old costumes, playbills, letters, and books of Edwin's late father, Junius Booth, and some of Edwin Booth's properties as well. Carried away by their enjoyment, the two men "had made no arrangements for sleeping," and so Badeau detailed in print the intimate contrivances they devised. To make a bed, "We put two sofas together." For a blanket "Roscius got into the old wardrobe of his father, pulled out an ermine cloak that belonged to Macbeth, and some of the trappings of Shylock or Lear, and tossed them to me. I made a pillow out of the very mantle of Caesar through which the envious dagger ran, and slumbered quietly enough, though Macbeth had murdered sleep in the robe that kept me warm."[110] In this article the intimacy the two men shared was rendered palpable: "We talked away long after our candles had burned out; previous to which I induced Hamlet to read me some funny stories, and when he got tired of reading, to tell me more; so I fell into a doze, with his voice ringing in my ears." Describing, for *Sunday Times* readers, his sleep in the arms of the man he loved, Badeau sardonically noted some of the gender implications in their intimacy: "I warrant you, some of his fair admirers would not have slept, so long as he talked, and doubtless they envy me my snooze on his arm. But 'twas dark, and I couldn't see his eyes; besides, I had seen them all day."[111] As a man who exclusively loved other men, Badeau engaged in some self-policing in print. While Badeau clearly indicated his romantic attachment to Booth, he both likened and differentiated between his own responses and those of Booth's "fair admirers." Bragging about the two men's intimacy and inferring that his unique access to the man he loved—the actor whose celebrity he had helped establish—exceeded that of anyone else, Badeau explained, "Next morning we rose late; the bed was so good, that not till eleven did I hear the tragedian rouse me." Offsetting and compounding the men's tenderness and familiarity with each other, Badeau identified Booth by his roles when describing for readers Booth's performance of private tasks. "This breakfast equipage was disposed on a garden table, and Hamlet did the honors very gracefully," "Vagabond" reported, and followed with "you should have seen Lear washing a tea-cup, and Romeo making the beds. However, he had a way of doing even these that was worth looking at."[112] And Badeau—the critic who first formulated Booth for other spectators—clearly enjoyed looking.

Shortly after this article was published, Booth's relationship with his future wife, Mary Devlin, threatened the intense bond between Booth and Badeau. Devlin was a young actress who had played Juliet to the impassioned Romeo of lesbian actress Charlotte Cushman and was apparently cognizant of the possibilities of same-sex passion. Aware that Badeau was "not like other men," at times during her engagement to Booth Devlin found Badeau an "intolerable bore, a second *Boswell,*" to Booth's Jonson. But she recognized that Badeau's "only fault" was in loving Booth too much, and that Badeau's love for Booth had motivated Badeau to do all he could to further Booth's career.[113] Acknowledging the homoerotic dynamics between Badeau and Booth, Devlin wrote Booth in the months before their wedding, "I sometimes feel as though he [Badeau] were a love-sick school girl I am consoling—for I am sure he is much more inclined that way than I am," and implored Booth, "[D]o not neglect him I pray you."[114]

Nonetheless, Badeau experienced the prospect of Booth and Devlin's marriage as a profound loss. As the date of Booth's marriage approached, Badeau wrote to Booth on black-edged mourning paper that he was "frightfully jealous" since he had "seen for some time evidence" of Devlin's "growing importance" to Booth and "of my own eclipse."[115] Attempting to mask his pain with wit, in one of his "Vagabond" columns Badeau had described marriage as an illness, protesting that "tis doleful, this rage for marriage. Half of my friends are affected by the epidemic." In an interesting gender reversal, where the implied "beauty" refers to a male rather than a female beloved, Badeau wrote prophetically—in anticipation of Booth's wedding—"Some of the pleasantest houses in town are now closed to me—that is the chief charm is gone; the beauty is married. . . . My confidences are over; there can be no more intimacies. . . . I can't discuss love anymore with such provokingly loveable people."[116] There was no question that Booth's marriage would "disturb the intimacy which I valued and enjoyed so highly," Badeau later acknowledged in print: "No man could be so intimate with two people at once as he [Booth] had been with me."[117]

Nevertheless, Badeau agreed to be the "best man" at Booth and Devlin's wedding in July 1860 and went along for two weeks of their honeymoon with them. Throughout the next year Badeau spent as much time as possible with Booth, who, Badeau claimed, "was most anxious to show me that his marriage made no difference in his feeling toward me."[118] For a time Badeau continued to attend and write about Booth's performances. During Booth's New York engagement, in autumn of 1860, Badeau "was with him [Booth] almost as much as ever. We sat up late into the night as of old," Badeau recounted in an article thirty years later. "And Mrs. Booth was often so good as to leave us together."[119] But when the Booths planned a tour of England in 1861, Badeau protested that accompanying the married couple would be like "waiting for the crumbs" whenever Booth "could spare a moment or a thought now or then."[120] Rather than settle for this inferior position, Badeau joined the Union army, first as aide to General Sherman, and later as secretary to Ulysses Grant.

From this point on, Badeau's career writing arts criticism came to a halt, and he spent many years out of the United States, in an ambassadorial position. Initially Booth and Badeau remained in close communication with each other. In fact, when Mary Devlin Booth died suddenly, in February 1863, Booth wrote to Badeau, confiding his grief, and Badeau noted that Booth had "turned to me in his bereavement." Several months later, Badeau was seriously wounded and was brought to Booth's home for his convalescence. However, Badeau's military responsibilities took his time and attention. Most of Badeau's subsequent writing focused on Grant and his Civil War experiences, while Badeau's emotional life centered on a soldier-companion, James Harrison Wilson, whose "new affection gives me real and exquisite happiness," Badeau confided to Booth. Yet, reminiscing about what he described as his "peculiar relationship" with Booth, Badeau plaintively remarked, "I can't root out all traces of what was once so firmly plait around my heart strings. Can you?"[121] And Booth, having benefited from Badeau's advice and intellectual companionship, as well as their emotional attachment, cultivated the friendship of another dramatic critic, the eminently respectable William Winter, with whom he corresponded largely about theatrical affairs for the remainder of his life.[122]

In August 1893, shortly after Booth's death, Badeau published a final revealing article about Booth in a popular periodical, *McClure's*, expressly calculated to enable readers to "think more highly and tenderly of the nature" of the man he had loved so passionately in his youth.

Badeau, now writing in his own name after a distinguished military and ambassadorial career, claimed in these "Personal Recollections" that as a result of the intimacy he had shared with Booth, "I have the right, therefore to tell what I shall unfold, for he gave it to me, and I have a further right in the certainty that nothing I can tell will depreciate his fame."[123] Using another article in the periodical press to bid farewell to the "beloved spirit" who had captivated him so personally, Badeau's hagiographic memoir detailed much of Booth's career and the emotional attachment the two men had shared.

By the twentieth century, however, the attachment and comradeship that had been so revered in Forrest and Oakes, as well as in Booth and Badeau, came to be read, when seen at all, through an increasingly homophobic lens. Hovering on the edge of public visibility, the recognition of same-sex attraction that animated Oakes's writing about Forrest and Badeau's criticism of Booth was increasingly rendered suspect. As Ginger Strand discusses, Richard Moody, in his 1960 biography of Edwin Forrest, noted the overt expressions of passion between Forrest and Oakes, and then refuted the possibility of a homosexual attachment between them with the assertion, "Except for the extravagant expressions of their affection, there are no grounds for believing that their relationship was unnatural."[124] Similarly, in a biographical study of Booth written in 1969, theater historian Charles H. Shattuck registered his discomfort with the homoerotic nature of Booth and Badeau's relationship, describing dismissively the "downright sexual possessiveness" Badeau felt for Booth. Rendering as pathological the love Badeau expressed for Booth, and discounting any possibility that such feelings might have been reciprocal, Shattuck asserted, "Discount as we will the queer turns of mid-century sentimentalism and neo-romantic codes of male friendship, many passages in his [Badeau's] letters make troublesome reading."[125] Citing Badeau's passionate acknowledgment, in a letter to Booth, "It's a frightful thing to live out of one's self; to be buried alive in somebody else. To depend upon that body for your happiness," Shattuck registered his disbelief "[t]hat Booth put up with such nonsense . . . but he did so, and we must adjust our preconception of his character enough to include the fact." Noting the numerous letters Booth and Badeau wrote to each other, dozens of which Booth saved for decades, the gifts Booth gave to Badeau, and other examples of their intimacy, Shattuck—incredulous that "year after year he [Booth] tolerated him [Badeau]"—speculated that "perhaps in those years Booth was not altogether beyond vanity, and enjoyed the 'conquest' of this brilliant young man of the world. Perhaps in his preoccupation with himself he was callous to Badeau's 'suffering,' and simply used him because he was useful."[126]

Certainly, Badeau *was* useful to Booth's career, but rendering as "unnatural" or "troubling" the same-sex passion that informed responses to these leading tragedians—casting such desire as an uncomfortable *effect* of celebrity to be "tolerated" or exploited (rather than enjoyed or celebrated)—occludes a crucial aspect of American theater history. What has escaped the attention of theater historians such as Shattuck and Moody is not only the potential pleasure and reciprocity of such feelings, but the fact that it was, to a significant extent, homoerotic-inflected passion that figured prominently in the public construction of Forrest and Booth as serious theatrical figures in the first place. It was the early critical accounts by "Acorn," "Colley Cibber," and "Vagabond" that paved the way to the future fame and fortune of Booth and Forrest and, in so doing, shaped the changing masculinities accepted as laudable in the American theatrical tradition. Theatrical notices in the periodical press provided a unique cultural venue for homoerotic musings, as the critics I have discussed in this essay, operating from their own experience of desire, performed their passions in the press and set the tone for ways in which their subjects would be received by others. And while nineteenth-century theatrical performances offered a range of "masculinities" to which male and female spectators could potentially respond, the "excess" meanings such critical writing made available opened up a potential space for male spectators' and readers' recognition and expression of homoerotic desire.

NOTES

1. On critics as "metonymic representatives" see Barbara Herrnstein Smith, "Value without Truth Value," in *Life after Postmodernism: Essays on Value and Culture*, ed. John Fekete (New York: St. Martin's Press, 1987), 10. On spectators as "virtual communities" see Lisa Merrill, *When Romeo Was a Woman: Charlotte Cushman and Her Circle of Female Spectators* (Ann Arbor: University of Michigan Press, 1999).

2. Tice L. Miller has discussed the roles played by Henry Clapp Jr. in establishing a mid-nineteenth-century society of journalists and critics and William Winter as Clapp's protégé and later as New York's "first and foremost" dramatic critic. See Tice L. Miller, *Bohemians and Critics: American Theatre Criticism in the Nineteenth Century* (Metuchen, N.J.: Scarecrow Press, 1981).

3. Denise P. Quirk, "Gender and Empire in the Mid-Victorian Women's

and Feminist Periodical Press," paper presented at the Research Society for Victorian Periodicals, September 1999, Yale University.

4. See Ginger Strand, "My Noble Spartacus: Edwin Forrest on the Nineteenth Century Stage," in *Passing Performances: Queer Readings of Leading Players in American Theater History,* ed. Robert A. Schanke and Kim Marra (Ann Arbor: University of Michigan Press, 1998).

5. For a different approach to questions of homoeroticism, twentieth-century constructions of sexuality, and critical practice, see Daniel-Raymond Nadon's essay on Eric Bentley in this volume.

6. Marvin Carlson makes a related point when discussing nineteenth-century theatrical reviews in France in "Theatre Audiences and the Reading of Performance," in *Interpreting the Theatrical Past: Essays in the Historiography of Performance,* ed. Thomas Postlewait and Bruce McConachie (Iowa City: University of Iowa Press, 1989), 95.

7. See for an extensive discussion of this claim see Eve Kosofsky Sedgwick, *Between Men* (New York: Columbia University Press, 1985), 207–13, and *Epistemology of the Closet* (Berkeley and Los Angeles: University of California Press, 1990); and John D'Emilio and Estelle B. Freedman, *Intimate Matters: A History of Sexuality in America* (New York: Harper and Row, 1989), 121–30.

8. Some special publications appeared for brief periods of time: the *Theatrical Censor and Music Review* was published in Philadelphia for a short time in 1828; John S. Wallace published *Opera Glass* briefly in the same year in New York. In 1841 the *Dramatic Mercury* was published in New York, edited by A. D. Patterson, who had been writing about the theater in *Albion,* and for nine months in 1841–42 the *Dramatic Mirror and Literary Companion* was published weekly in New York and Philadelphia. However, according to Fran Luther Mott, *A History of American Magazines,* the best theatrical criticism of the times was found in such New York–based general periodicals as the *New York Mirror,* Leggett's *Critic,* Porter's *Spirit of the Times, Arcturus,* Park Benjamin's *American Monthly,* Snowden's *Ladies' Companion,* the *New World,* and the *Knickerbocker.* Mott also cites the Boston-based *New England Magazine* and Nathaniel Parker Willis's *American Monthly,* and in Philadelphia, William E. Burton's *Gentlemen's* and the *Philadelphia Monthly.*" Frank Luther Mott, *A History of American Magazines* (Cambridge: Harvard University Press, 1957), 427.

9. Walt Whitman, *Brooklyn Daily Eagle,* October 7, 1846, cited in Whitman, *A Gathering of the Forces,* ed. Cleveland Rogers and John Black, 2 vols. (New York: G. P. Putnam's, 1920) 2:341.

10. Charles T. Congdon, *Reminiscences of a Journalist* (Boston: James R. Osgood, 1880), 312. Although Congdon protested these unethical practices, he was not above bragging about his own ingenuity in reviewing the 1855 Boston performances of French-speaking actress Mademoiselle Rachel—a feat most noteworthy since Congdon did not speak a word of French. Claiming that "A really good journalist never betrays his ignorance of anything," Congdon revealed that he had read English translations of the plays before the performance, and that with the aid of his French-speaking proofreader, Mr. Goodrich, he was able to produce "all manner of profound and acute critical observations"

as well as to save the money it would cost to hire "a really competent critic." Congdon, *Reminiscences of a Journalist,* 315–16.

11. Congdon, *Reminiscences of a Journalist,* 126.

12. Mary Poovey has made this point about nineteenth-century book reviews in *Uneven Developments: The Ideological Work of Gender in Mid-Victorian England* (Chicago: University of Chicago Press, 1988), 108.

13. Charles H. Shattuck makes this point as well in *Shakespeare on the American Stage* (Washington, D.C.: Folger Shakespeare Library, 1976), 65.

14. "Things Theatrical," *Spirit of the Times: A Metropolitan Gazette of the Sporting, Literary, and Fashionable* (New York) September 23, 1837, 1.

15. William Rounseville Alger, *Life of Edwin Forrest, the American Tragedian,* 2 vols. (Philadelphia: J. B. Lippincott, 1877), 1:179.

16. Kirk W. Fuoss, "Performance as Contestation: An Agonistic Perspective on the Insurgent Assembly," *Text and Performance Quarterly* 13 (October 1993): 337.

17. Bruce McConachie, *Melodramatic Formations: American Theatre and Society, 1820–1870* (Iowa City: University of Iowa Press, 1992), 84–85.

18. Congdon, *Reminiscences of a Journalist,* 190.

19. Congdon, *Reminiscences of a Journalist,* 191.

20. Alger, *Life of Edwin Forrest,* 1:164. Forty years later Oakes would insist that watching Forrest perform in this tale of heroic male loyalty and love could still cause him to "blubber out loud"; Forrest relished the "grand moral" of the tale and only wished that Shakespeare had selected it as one of his subjects. See Edwin Forrest to James Oakes, Baltimore, March 8, 1867, CO 721, folder 5, Forrest Collection, Manuscript Division, Department of Rare Books and Special Collections, Princeton University Library (hereafter Forrest Collection). This and other citations from the Forrest Collection published with the permission of Princeton University Library. I am grateful to Margaret M. Sherry, Archivist of Rare Books and Special Collections, for her assistance.

21. Alger, *Life of Edwin Forrest,* 1:164.

22. Alger, *Life of Edwin Forrest,* 2:637, 2:626. Ginger Stand has explored the relative acceptance of Forrest and Oakes's relationship by Forrest's early biographers, and the increasing circumspection and editing of the relationship in later years. See Ginger Strand, "My Noble Spartacus: Edwin Forrest on the Nineteenth Century Stage," in Schanke and Marra, *Passing Performances,* 26.

23. See, for example, Edwin Forrest to James Oakes, Philadelphia, October 30, 1867, Forrest Collection, CO 721, folder 5. Here Forrest questions "*how* much [pounding] is *too* much" given "the labour we delight in." This practice was suggested by a physician friend of Oakes's as a method to improve the circulation.

24. Quoted in Alan Sinfield, *The Wilde Century: Effeminacy, Oscar Wilde, and the Queer Moment* (London: Cassell, 1994), 115. Sinfield discusses the misogyny implicit in Wagner's statement as well as sexologist Edward Carpenter's deployment of Wagner to support Carpenter's theories about manliness and homosexuality. Sinfield also discusses the homoeroticism implicit in the "comradely ideal" in Walt Whitman's writing.

25. Walt Whitman, *Leaves of Grass: Facsimile Edition of the 1860 Text*

(Ithaca, N.Y.: Cornell University Press, 1961), 342, and Walt Whitman, "Democratic Vistas," in *Collected Writings*, vol. 9, in two parts, *Prose Works*, ed. Floyd Stovall (New York: New York University Press, 1964), 2:414. Whitman's importance to gay and lesbian history is discussed in Jonathan Katz, *Gay American History: Lesbians and Gay Men in the U.S.A.* (New York: Thomas Y. Crowell, 1976), 337–65. On Whitman and his use of the phrenological term "adhesiveness" to refer to same-sex love, see Michael Lynch, "Here Is Adhesiveness: From Friendship to Homosexuality," *Victorian Studies* 29 (autumn 1985): 84.

26. Walt Whitman, "The Old Bowery," in *Complete Poetry and Selected Prose and Letters*, ed. Emory Holloway (London: Nonesuch Press, 1938), 842. Yet by the 1840s even Whitman, with his well-professed love for the common man, found the Bowery Theatre increasingly vulgar and wished for a higher standard of American drama.

27. Whitman, "The Old Bowery," 844.

28. See Yvonne Tasker, *Spectacular Bodies: Gender, Genre, and the Action Cinema* (London: Routledge, 1993), 109.

29. Alger, *Life of Edwin Forrest*, quoted in Shattuck, *Shakespeare on the American Stage*, 65.

30. Congdon, *Reminiscences of a Journalist*, 192. Of course, women spectators and costars responded on many different registers to Forrest's body as well. Although it is beyond the purview of this essay, a broader study of the role of theater criticism in the construction of sexed and gendered bodies on the nineteenth-century stage would be fruitful. For a fascinating analysis of Forrest and class identifications, see Bruce A. McConachie, *Melodramatic Formations: American Theatre and Society, 1820–1870* (Iowa City: University of Iowa Press, 1992). For a discussion of the implications of a very different imbrication of class, race, gender, and homoeroticism in a later historical moment, see James Wilson, "'That's the Kind of Gal I Am': Drag Balls, Lulu Belles, and 'Sexual Perversion' in the Harlem Renaissance," in this volume.

31. Alger, *Life of Edwin Forrest*, 2:615.

32. Ibid., 2:615.

33. Ibid., 2:620.

34. Ibid., 2:621.

35. *Spirit of the Times*, March 4, 1837, 24. Tice L. Miller discusses the significance of dramatic criticism in *Spirit* under a later editor, Wilkes, who assumed editorship of the paper after Porter, however I have established that it was originally under Porter's stewardship more than two decades earlier that *Spirit* first covered dramatic events and personages.

36. *Spirit of the Times*, February 24, 1844, 613.

37. William Winter, *The Wallet of Time, Containing Personal, Biographical, and Critical Reminiscence of the American Theatre*, 2 vols. (1913; rpt. Freeport, N.Y.: Books for Libraries Press, 1969), 1:8.

38. Ibid., 1:xxii.

39. "Sayings and Doings in Boston, by 'Acorn,'" *Spirit of the Times*, August 19, 1848. While Oakes covered all the Boston theaters and claimed to wish "success to all of them," as "Acorn" he made special mention of those managed by friends such as Thomas Barry, whom Oakes often advised. On Oakes's serv-

ing as Barry's "right hand man" and advising him on what productions to put on, see Joel Myerson, Daniel Shealy, and Madeline B. Stern, eds., *Selected Letters of Louisa May Alcott* (Boston: Little, Brown, 1987), 24.

40. "Acorn," "Our Boston Correspondence: National Theatre," *Spirit of the Times,* February 5, 1853, clipping in Robinson Locke Collection of Dramatic Scrapbooks, series 2, no. 184, New York Public Library for the Performing Arts (hereafter Locke Collection).

41. "Letter from 'Acorn,'" *Spirit of the Times,* article dated Boston, December 3, 1855, clipping in Locke Collection, series 2, no. 184.

42. "Acorn," "Theatricals in Boston," *Spirit of the Times,* article dated Boston, January 17, 1853, clipping in Locke Collection, series 2, no. 184.

43. [James Oakes], "Theatricals in Boston," *Spirit of the Times,* article dated Boston, January 26, 1853, clipping in Locke Collection, series 2, no. 184.

44. [James Oakes], "The National," *Spirit of the Times,* September 7, 1839, clipping in Locke Collection, series 2, no. 184.

45. "Theatricals in Boston, by 'Acorn,'" *Spirit of the Times,* September 30, 1848, 373.

46. *Diaries of William Charles Macready, 1833–1851,* ed. William Toynbee, 2 vols. (1912; rpt. New York: Benjamin Blom, 1969), 2:412.

47. Similarly, Forrest's most hostile critic in the United States was Irish-born reviewer and manager William Stuart, while accolades came from those like Oakes and Rees, whose support for Forrest was infused with a pro-American fervor. "William Stuart" [also spelled Stewart] was the name used by Edmund O'Flaherty, critic for the *New York Tribune,* and later manager for the Winter Garden Theatre. Stuart's vitriolic reviews of Forrest are attributed to a range of motives. Gabriel Harrison describes him as "an Englishman," a "vampire of a critic" who bragged that he had really never seen Forrest act when he attacked him in the press. See Gabriel Harrison, *Edwin Forrest: The Actor and the Man: Critical and Reminiscent* (Brooklyn: Brooklyn Eagle Printing Dept., 1889), 160–61. Pecuniary motivations may also have been at the heart of Stuart's disapprobation. Actor Joseph Jefferson claimed that Stuart was paid expressly to write negative reviews of Forrest. Cited in Alan S. Downer, *The Eminent Tragedian: William Charles Macready* (Cambridge: Harvard University Press, 1966), 372. Stuart's advocacy of Edwin Booth, with whom he was engaged in theater management, may also have figured in Stuart's negative reportage of Forrest.

48. James Rees, *The Life of Edwin Forrest, With Reminiscences and Personal Recollections* (Philadelphia: T. B. Peterson and Brothers, 1874), 224. In his own diaries for the period, Macready recorded Colley Cibber's repeated "abuse" of him in the Philadelphia papers (*Diaries,* 2:233).

49. [John Forster], "Princess's," *Examiner* (London), February 1845, clipping in Charlotte Cushman Scrapbook, Charlotte Cushman Papers, vol. 20, Library of Congress, Washington, D.C.

50. I discuss Cushman's and Forrest's critical reception in England and the conflation of notions of nationality, gender, sexuality, and class in greater detail in *When Romeo Was a Woman,* chap. 4.

51. Mary Poovey, *Uneven Developments: The Ideological Work of Gender in Mid-Victorian England* (Chicago: University of Chicago Press, 1988), 8–9.

52. "Letter From 'Acorn': Theatricals in Boston" *Spirit of the Times,* December 8, 1849; "Letter From 'Acorn': Theatricals in Boston," *Spirit of the Times,* June 12, 1858. In her personal correspondence Cushman complained about the influence of Forrest and "Jim" Oakes, whom she described as "the man who wrote those letters to the *Atlas* from Boston against me." Charlotte Cushman to "Fred" [William Fredericks], September 15, 1850, in Extra-illustrated copy of Clara Erskine Clement, *Charlotte Cushman,* 2 vols. (Boston: Osgood, 1882), 2:150, Harvard Theater Collection.

53. Macready, *Diaries,* 2:419.

54. [James Oakes], "More about Macready," *Boston Mail,* October 30, 1848, quoted in *Account of the Terrific and Fatal Riot at the Astor Place Opera House on the Night of May 10, 1849: With the Quarrels of Forrest and Macready, Including All the Causes Which Led to that Awful Tragedy!* (New York: H. M. Ranney, 1849), 11. This article is attributed to Oakes in Alan S. Downer, *The Eminent Tragedian: William Charles Macready* (Cambridge Harvard University Press, 1966), 291.

55. Quoted in *Terrific and Fatal Riot,* 11–12.

56. Ginger Strand makes this point as well in "My Noble Spartacus."

57. John Coleman, *Fifty Years of an Actor's Life* (New York: James Pott, 1904), 334.

58. Ibid., 336.

59. For example, on November 11, 1864, Forrest acknowledged receiving from Oakes "the printed extract from my speech in Albany. Thank you for giving it to the public with your graceful preface." At the time he delivered the speech, Forrest had remarked to Oakes that while he "was sorry at the time you were not in the theatre to hear my utterance of it—had you been there, *I am sure* I should have heard your voice, in commendation of the feeling which prompted it." Days earlier Forrest had sent Oakes a copy of the speech, which Oakes then fashioned into another article about Forrest. Edwin Forrest to James Oakes, Philadelphia, November 11, 1864, Forrest Collection, CO 721, folder 2.

60. Edwin Forrest to James Oakes, Philadelphia, November 13, 1865, Forrest Collection, CO 721, folder 3.

61. Edwin Forrest to James Oakes, Philadelphia, December 13, 1866, Forrest Collection, CO 721, folder 4.

62. Edwin Forrest to James Oakes, Philadelphia, September 14, 1864, Forrest Collection, CO 721, folder 2.

63. Edwin Forrest to James Oakes, Portland, Maine, January 3, 1869, Forrest Collection, CO 721, folder 7.

64. Edwin Forrest to James Oakes, Portland, Maine, January 18, 1867, Forrest Collection, CO 721, folder 5.

65. Edwin Forrest to James Oakes, Philadelphia, April 11, 1865, Forrest Collection, CO 721, folder 3.

66. Edwin Forrest to James Oakes, Philadelphia, January 6, 1866, Forrest Collection, CO 721, folder 4.

67. William Rounseville Alger, *The Friendships of Women* (Boston: Roberts Brothers, 1868, 1879). In letters about Alger's writing, Forrest suggested Alger write about the love between "old Michael Angelo and his young votary

Cavalieri" as emblematic of male same-sex love. See Edwin Forrest to James Oakes, May 24, 1869, Forrest Collection, CO 721, folder 7.

68. Edwin Forrest to James Oakes, May 24, 1869; July 16, 1869, Philadelphia; 18 August 1869, Boston, Forrest Collection, CO 721, folder 7.

69. Alger, *Life of Edwin Forrest,* 1:16.

70. Harrison, *Edwin Forrest,* 131.

71. Ibid., 163.

72. Ibid., 137.

73. Lawrence Barrett, *Edwin Forrest* (Boston: J. R. Osgood, 1881), 76.

74. Rees's most notable play was an adaptation of Dickens' *Oliver Twist* in which Charlotte Cushman achieved much early success.

75. Rees, *Life of Edwin Forrest,* 94.

76. Ibid., 170.

77. Ibid., 183.

78. Barrett, *Edwin Forrest,* 76.

79. Rees, *Life of Edwin Forrest,* 22.

80. Harrison, *Edwin Forrest,* 154.

81. Alger, *Life of Edwin Forrest,* 177.

82. Alfred Tennyson, *In Memoriam,* in *The Poems of Tennyson,* ed. Christopher Ricks (London: Longmans, 1969). See Alan Sinfield, *Alfred Tennyson* (Oxford: Blackwell, 1986), chap. 5.

83. In this and in the subsequent 1856 and 1860 editions Whitman championed the love between men most explicitly and was subjected the much condemnation as a result. In editions published after 1860, Whitman increasingly censored *Leaves of Grass* in the course of revision. See Gary Schmidgall, *Walt Whitman: A Gay Life* (New York: Dutton, 1997).

84. Emory Holloway, ed., *Walt Whitman: Complete Poetry and Selected Prose and Letters* (London: Nonesuch Press, 1938), 140.

85. Joseph R. Roach, "Power's Body: The Inscription of Morality as Style," in *Interpreting the Theatrical Past: Essays in the Historiography of Performance,* ed. Thomas Postlewait and Bruce A. McConachie (Iowa City: University of Iowa Press, 1989), 107.

86. Cited in Mary Caroline Crawford, *Romance of the American Theatre* ([1913]; New York: Halcyon House, 1940), 314–15.

87. Adam Badeau published a collection of his criticism in *The Vagabond* (New York: Rudd and Carleton, 1859), x.

88. Badeau published this account of their first meeting thirty-six years later. See Adam Badeau, "Edwin Booth. On and Off the Stage. Personal Recollections," *McClure's Magazine,* August 1893, 258.

89. Badeau, *The Vagabond,* 287.

90. Adam Badeau to Edwin Booth, June 15, 1857, Hampden-Booth Library at the Players Club, New York; Gene Smith, *American Gothic: The Story of America's Legendary Theatrical Family—Junius, Edwin, and John Wilkes Booth* (New York: Simon and Schuster, 1992), 66.

91. Bruce A. McConachie, *Melodramatic Formations: American Theatre and Society, 1820–1870* (Iowa City: University of Iowa Press, 1992), 239.

92. Badeau, "Edwin Booth," 255.

93. Ibid., 259.

94. Ibid., 259.

95. Adam Badeau to Edwin Booth, October 7, 1858, Hampden-Booth Library at the Players Club; "Pray stay a god" quoted in Charles H. Shattuck, *The Hamlet of Edwin Booth* (Urbana: University of Illinois Press, 1969), 29, and Smith, *American Gothic,* 67.

96. Quoted in Shattuck, *Hamlet of Edwin Booth,* 29, and Smith, *American Gothic,* 67.

97. Adam Badeau to Edwin Booth, November 12, 1859, Hampden-Booth Library at the Players Club.

98. Badeau, *The Vagabond,* 292.

99. Ibid., 166. An intentional deployment of gender ambiguity can be observed in other critics writing at this time; for example, "Ned" Edwin G. P. Wilkins occasionally wrote cultural criticism for the *Saturday Press* in the voice of a somewhat frivolous society woman.

100. Martin Duberman, "'Writhing Bedfellows' in Antebellum South Carolina: Historical Interpretation and the Politics of Evidence," in *Hidden From History: Reclaiming the Gay and Lesbian Past,* ed. Martin Duberman, Martha Vicinus, and George Chauncey Jr. (New York: Penguin, 1989), 161.

101. Badeau, *The Vagabond,* 72.

102. Adam Badeau to Edwin Booth, October 7, 1858, Hampden-Booth Library at the Players Club.

103. Badeau, "Edwin Booth," 259.

104. Quoted in Eleanor Ruggles, *Prince of Players, Edwin Booth* (New York: W. W. Norton, 1953), 93.

105. Badeau, "Edwin Booth," 260.

106. Horace Traubel, *With Walt Whitman in Camden,* 9 vols. ([1905]; New York: Rowman and Littlefield, 1961), 1:355.

107. Adam Badeau to Edwin Booth, November 12, 1859, Hampden-Booth Library at the Players Club; [Adam Badeau], "The Vagabond. Off the Stage." *Sunday Times,* September 13, 1859.

108. While the Booth family home was obviously replete with memories of Junius Booth's career and the life of other members of this extraordinary family as well, there were no other "Booths" present during the adventure. It is clear from the article that "Vagabond" and Booth were alone; I suspect that plural "Booths" in the *Sunday Times* title was used strategically to offset the overt homoerotic content in the article (rpt. in Badeau, *The Vagabond,* 348).

109. Ibid., 350.

110. Ibid., 352.

111. Ibid.

112. Ibid., 353.

113. Mary Devlin to Edwin Booth, October 11, 1859, New York Public Library Theater Collection, published in *The Letters of Mary Devlin,* ed. L. Terry Oggel (New York: Greenwood, 1987), 18.

114. Mary Devlin to Edwin Booth, December 28, 1859, Player's Club, New York, published in *Letters of Mary Devlin Booth,* 27.

115. Adam Badeau to Edwin Booth, 22 April 1860, Hampden-Booth Library at the Players Club.

116. [Adam Badeau], "Vagabond," *Sunday Times and Noah's Weekly Messenger,* January 16, 1859, 1.

117. Badeau, "Edwin Booth," 263.

118. Ibid.

119. Ibid.

120. Shattuck, *Hamlet of Edwin Booth,* 29.

121. Adam Badeau to Edwin Booth, December 4, 1862, Hampden-Booth Library at the Players Club.

122. See *Between Actor and Critic: Selected Letters of Edwin Booth and William Winter,* ed. Daniel J. Watermeier (Princeton: Princeton University Press, 1971).

123. Badeau, "Edwin Booth," 255.

124. Richard Moody, *Edwin Forrest: First Star of the American Stage* (New York: Alfred A. Knopf, 1960), 345. See Strand, "My Noble Spartacus," on the historiography of Forrest and Oakes's relationship in nineteenth- and twentieth-century biographical accounts.

125. Shattuck, *Hamlet of Edwin Booth,* 28.

126. Ibid., 28–29.

"That's the Kind of Gal I Am"

Drag Balls, Lulu Belles, and "Sexual Perversion" in the Harlem Renaissance

James Wilson

Flaming youth, tiger tooth,
That's the kind of gal I am;
But when I'm in love with someone,
I can be a soft, sweet lamb—
When I'm through, "Toodle-oo"—
That's the kind of gal I am:

Wilder than a wild, wild rose
And smoother than the Jordan flows,
I'm just a mad-cap baby, called Lulu Belle;
Everyone in dark-town knows
I'm fickle as the wind that blows,
But how they crave this baby, called Lulu Belle.
—"Song of Lulu Belle"[1]

"Flaming Youth"

In March 1928, *Variety* reported a rather shocking situation: New York's homosexual community was getting so large that it could no longer accept any new members. Those refused entry into this "queer elite" naturally retaliated and waged out-and-out insurrection. The article, titled "Battle on among Broadway Elite of the 'Third Sex,'" begins: "New York's sex abnormal males have developed caste and it threatens to break up this, the biggest colony of its kind, in the world. It is because of its increasing numbers that the trouble has arisen, the old guard refusing to recognize newcomers, with the new arrivals subsequently causing trouble by supplying information to the police, false as often as not." According to the *Variety* reporter, the brouhaha first erupted when the organizers of a drag ball at Harlem's Rockland Palace were forced to limit the number of tickets to participants and spectators because the semiregular event had recently filled the hall to dangerous capacities. "It has left the homo-sexuals in a panic," the reporter explains, "with discussions nightly over the matter in a Fifth avenue restaurant near the park. Sometimes one of them even faints in excitement."[2]

As intimated in the article, the Rockland "drag" was one of Harlem's grandest occasions and had all of the flourishes of a genteel society affair. Typically, the men frequenting one of these balls, whom the *Variety* author identifies as "from all walks of life," spent several weeks planning and sewing the most extravagant and fashionable gowns, which were intended to elicit cheers and rapturous gasps from the several thousand in attendance. Likewise, conspicuously on view at the Rockland Palace were "certain women also of their own queer class" wearing the latest in stylish men's clothing. Apparently, for a novitiate to the gay and lesbian subculture of 1920s New York, exclusion from the Rockland drag was the equivalent of social homicide.

As evident by *Variety*'s sensational account, gay men and lesbians were prominent in Harlem of the 1920s, and they enjoyed an ambivalent tolerance both in the press and in public. Recent studies, including those of George Chauncey, Lillian Faderman, and Eric Garber, have shown that white tourists were especially intrigued by the exoticism Harlem represented, and cross-dressed men and women added to the allure.[3] Nightclub acts, catering to predominantly white audiences, often included transvestites, openly gay performers, and extremely ribald material, and reflected a fascination for performances that challenged white, middle-class decorum. This fascination, as countless newspaper articles from the period indicate, was motivated in large part by a lurid Broadway play about a black sexual siren called *Lulu Belle* (1926). The hugely successful play wasn't precisely about the "third sex," but it soon became identified with homosexuality and Harlem's drag subculture.

As Lisa Merrill documents elsewhere in this book, nineteenth-century theater reviews of Edwin Forrest and Edwin Booth forcefully "constructed and reinforced" popular images of physical virility, hypermasculinity, and Americanness. These representations helped forge a national character, and the discourse of homosocial attachment contributed to the shaping of a "glorification of manly bonding and class-inflected democratic principles." But by the 1920s, new images seeped into the cultural consciousness and threatened the supremacy of the idealized white American heterosexual male. Cross-dressed gay men, independent working-class black women, and "manly" women appeared with great regularity on the streets and stages of New York City and riled conservative social critics. In particular, entertainment articles and theater reviews reflected the highly charged and hotly contested debates around race politics and "sexual perversion."

For this reason, the responses to Harlem's drag balls and the controversial reception that greeted *Lulu Belle*'s opening are particularly meaningful. Previously little has been written about *Lulu Belle* and the play's connection to the drag subculture in the late 1920s, but the circulation of the title character within Harlem's gay community is significant in American theater history. The "flaming youth, tiger tooth" Lulu Belle became a symbol of defiance against the repressive middle-class ideals of the era, and as evidenced in the public discourse surrounding the play, she epitomized the transgressive sexual spirit that the Jazz Age represented.

"Fickle as the Wind That Blows"

On February 9, 1926, two years before the tumultuous ball described in the *Variety* article, Charles MacArthur and Edward Sheldon's controversial *Lulu Belle,* a play about Harlem life, opened at the Belasco Theatre. David Belasco's production, one of Broadway's biggest hits of the 1920s, packed audiences into the theater for more than two seasons, and it had tremendous success on the road as well. The play, which was written, produced, and staged by white men and starred white actors in blackface and black actors in supporting roles, is particularly notable in that it sent whites scurrying in droves to experience "authentic" Harlem nightclubs and to witness events like the Rockland ball firsthand. And although the play does not contain any visible homosexual characters—it is more concerned with representations of race and class—the gay male community in Harlem adopted the title character as its mascot and named a speakeasy after her. At Lulu Belle's, a drag club, black and white gay men and lesbians congregated nightly, and like the behavior at the Rockland drag ball, they parodied formal upper-class society functions.

Reactions to *Lulu Belle* in the press are particularly generative to a queer reading of the play. The white press generally disparaged it for its immorality, and the black press, while pleased that the production used so many black actors, regarded the sexually out-of-control title character (played by white actress Lenore Ulric) as a reminder to black women to remain pure for the sake of the race. As we see in the *Variety* description of the Rockland drag ball participants (references to "caste," "queer elite," and the "old guard," for instance), the hypersexual Lulu Belle is controversial not for her erotic desire, but for her representations of class and race. As Chauncey argues, the visible homosexual (that is, the cross-dressed man or woman) and the sexually unrestrained black woman, both associated with the working class, were particularly contentious figures to the African-American communities in the Harlem Renaissance. They posed a perilous threat to the advancement of the race because of their "low class" morality, and mocked the ideals of the middle-class family toward which the communities strove.[4]

Lulu Belle is also noteworthy for its use of a racially integrated cast, which was a rarity on Broadway in the 1920s. The production boasted a cast of 115, of whom 100 were black. While white actors played the major parts in blackface (there are also a few minor white characters), African-Americans took on the supporting and supernumerary roles. Both white and black critics singled out the white actors for their ability to pass for black. Arthur Hornblow in *Theatre Magazine* wrote, "Lenore Ulric outdid herself as the dusky wanton," and according to black author, lyricist, and statesman James Weldon Johnson, "The role of George Randall, the principal Negro male character, was finely played by Henry Hull, a white actor, whose make-up and dialect were beyond detection."[5] As Freda L. Scott explains, many of the black critics objected to the base depiction of Harlem life, but they applauded its efforts to provide greater theatrical prospects for Blacks in the theater. For instance, Hubert H. Harrison wrote in the Urban League's journal, *Opportunity,* that the production "makes it easier for the next step—an all Negro cast in a serious presentation of some other and more significant slice of Negro life."[6]

As Arthur Dorlag and John Irvine, the editors of Charles MacArthur's plays, point out, *Lulu Belle* stands very little chance being revived today.[7] Besides its often offensive references to Blacks ("real nigger style," "ascetic negresses," "young bucks," "darkies," and other derogatory expressions), it is a really dreadful play. In performance it runs more than three hours, the melodramatic plot is confusing and meandering, and the characters exhibit little development in the course of the four acts. When it opened in 1926, the production did have, in addition to an exciting performance by Ulric, a striking visual design that one came to expect from Belasco. Brooks Atkinson, reviewing the play in the *Times,* wrote that Ulric "vibrates like a taut wire," and he paid tribute to the "precise and accurate photography" of the scenography. Atkinson contrasted the extreme attempts at reality of Belasco's mise-en-scène to the highly stylized "new stagecraft" then in vogue. Whereas Belasco

sought to re-create the visual minutiae of a play in his design, practitioners of the "new stagecraft," including Robert Edmond Jones, Lee Simonson, and Norman Bel Geddes, attempted to capture a text's "spirit" by
using iconic objects, such as masks and imposing geometric shapes, as
well as atmospheric lighting. Atkinson wrote:

> Not for [Belasco] the esthetic spurs to the imagination now prac-
> ticed by our newer scenic designers and directors. Not for him the
> bewildering symbolism of masks and ominous shadows. To Mr.
> Belasco, "seeing is believing"; he leaves nothing out. At any rate,
> nothing except plot and story.[8]

In brief, the play's *Carmen*-like plot involves a scheming black woman
who betrays the affection of her devoted lover and moves from Harlem
to Paris to become a wealthy (white) count's mistress. Several years later,
her rejected beau, now released from prison after a fight over Lulu Belle,
tracks her down, confronts her, and strangles her. A few of the key
moments from the play demonstrate why the play was taken up by the
drag subculture.

The play opens in a black neighborhood on West Fifty-ninth Street in
New York's "San Juan Hill" neighborhood. As the stage directions
inform, "Everything is gay and lively and black." Flickering bar signs,
"dingy tenements," fire escapes, a high-class, "pretentious" apartment
building, and a movie theater currently showing Glory Champagne in *A
Lovely Sinner* set the scene; crap games, singing drunks, and arguments
about a prizefight create the mood. As the play opens, final preparations
for a "Society" wedding are under way, and the hero of the play, the
dashing George Randall (the best man in the wedding), is visiting from
White Plains, New York, with his wife and two children. An evangelist,
Brother Staley, accompanied by Sister Sally and Sister Blossom, emerges
from the crowd and begins leading the gathered families in prayer and
song. Enter into this admixture of wealth, squalor, and religious fervor,
Lulu Belle.

From her initial appearance, Lulu Belle stands outside of traditional
morality and middle-class values. As the evangelist leads the crowd in
"The Old Time Religion," she makes her first entrance through the pro-
cessional shouting, " 'Lo, boys! Whoopie! Le's all git religion." And as
the stage directions state: "Lulu Belle is young and beautiful and bad.
Her hair is bobbed, her clothes are the last word in negro elegance. At her
side to left of her is a little black hunchbacked creature, shabbily dressed,
who looks up at her like an adoring dog."[9] When the preacher scolds her

for her sinful dancing and tells her she is going to go to hell, she mockingly replies:

> Yo' bet I'm goin' t' hell, brothah . . . goin' t' hell in a bandwagon! An'when I git theah, I'm gonna walk right up t' dat ole debbil, jes like I'm doin' now . . . (She approaches the minister.) . . . an' I'm gonna jiggle mah hippies dat way.[10]

Lulu Belle then publicly humiliates him by exposing his hypocrisy. She announces that Brother Staley himself is no stranger to Harlem's nightlife, having encountered Lulu Belle at the Elite Grotto, where she is a hostess and dancer.

Later in the act, immediately before she seduces George Randall, causing him to leave his respectable life as husband, father, and barber in White Plains, Lulu Belle proves that the law poses no threat to her either (fig. 14). When a white police officer breaks up a fight Lulu Belle has started, she taunts him too:

> Policeman. (with conviction) Yer a wise-cracker, aincha?
> Lulu Belle. (virtuously) I'm a li'l widow mothah, dass whut I am, as anybody but a slewfoot h'ness bull could see by lookin' at me . . . (Glancing at her wrist watch) My, my, time to go home an' nurse th' baby! How time flies talkin' wid a charmin' unifo'm man! S'pose yo' could walk a piece wid me an' finish th' convusation as we go along?
> Policeman. (suddenly) Let's see yer hands. (He seizes them.)
> Lulu Belle. Quit ticklin' my wrist!
> Policeman. (Still holding one) Soft as dough . . . you don't work!
> Lulu Belle. Suttinly I wu'k!
> Policeman. Where?
> Lulu Belle. In de Brownskin Bakin' Comp'ny.
> Policeman. (sourly) Whadda y' bake?
> Lulu Belle. (Triumphantly) Jelly rolls! (She executes a shimmy. A window full of darkies and the ones at the back howl at this.)[11]

Because the officer does not want to have to go to court the next day, his day off, he lets her go with a stern warning (not to mention exposing his own hypocrisy): "If I find ya hangin' 'round here again I'll throw ya in th' hoosegow, day off or not! (He enters the bar.)"[12]

From a feminist standpoint, the exchanges between Lulu Belle and the evangelist and police officer enact a familiar narrative of the degenerate urban black woman in the 1920s. In "Policing the Black Woman's Body in an Urban Context," Hazel V. Carby traces this developing per-

FIG. 14. Lulu Belle vamps a police officer: "Off'cah, it'd be a pleasuah t' be pinched by anybody as handsome as yo'!" Edward Nannery and Lenore Ulric in David Belasco's production of *Lulu Belle* (1926).

(Courtesy, Billy Rose Theatre Collection, New York Public Library for the Performing Arts.)

ception prevalent not only among whites, but also of the black intelligentsia and the black middle class.[13] Beginning at the turn of the century, northern cities saw a huge rise in migration of African-Americans from the South. The anxieties associated with "social displacement and dislocation" produced a host of "moral panics," which were then transposed on to black women's bodies. These "moral panics," as she documents with essays and autobiographies from the turn of the century through the 1920s, were responses to single, jobless black women who turned to vice and depravity because of their "increasing inefficiency and desire to avoid hard work."[14] The difficulties Blacks faced in the cities were presumably rooted in the unpoliced, undisciplined, and unemployed bodies of single black women, which endangered "the success of the emergent black middle class." Black women were often viewed, argues Carby, "as signs of various possible threats to the emergence of the wholesome black masculinity necessary for the establishment of an acceptable black male citizenship in the American social order."[15]

In this context, Lulu Belle's "soft as dough" hands are particularly significant. Because she works in a nightclub and not (ironically) in a subordinate menial position, her body betrays her as not belonging to the "respectable" middle class. Even worse, her effrontery to middle-class values—represented above in terms of motherhood, and respect for the church and law—is embodied. That is, to show her contempt at efforts to reign her in, Lulu Belle demonstrates the extent of her *un*disciplined body ("jiggl[ing] [her] hippies" and "executing a shimmy," for example). To black middle-class communities of the 1920s, Lulu Belle personified the tremendous barriers Blacks faced in cultural advancement and securing approbation from white society.

It is important to remember the central irony of Lulu Belle as representative of a problem to her race: The play was written by two white men and performed by a white woman in blackface. Also, the audiences attending the Belasco Theatre would have been predominantly white. Generally, working-class Blacks did not frequent Broadway theaters, but they would have read about *Lulu Belle* in black newspapers such as the *New York Amsterdam News*. Indeed, "dirt" plays like *Lulu Belle,* which depicted the sexual exploits of loose women, were not particularly uncommon on Broadway in the 1920s. In 1922, for instance, *Rain*, John Colton and Clemence Randolph's adaptation of Somerset Maugham's short story and starring Jeanne Eagles, caused a sensation in its portrayal of the prostitute Sadie Thompson. *White Cargo* (1924), starring Annette Margulies as the South Pacific enchantress Tondalayo, Roland Oliver's

Night Hawk (1926), about a self-sacrificing prostitute, and *Shanghai Gesture* (1926), featuring Florence Reed as the ruthless Chinese madam, Mother Goddam, all dealt with similar themes. *Lulu Belle,* however, struck a nerve in the black community. The black press was quick to respond to the danger that women like Lulu Belle posed to the race and viewed the play as a morality tale. In March 1926, a month after the show opened on Broadway, the *Amsterdam News* printed an article by Ruth Dennis called "Lulu Belles—All?" An editorial statement frames the article and registers full support for the issues Dennis raises: "We have never aimed to assume a position of moralist or to preach morality, but there are certain truths which we, as a race, must recognize if we hope to attain those heights which we so blatantly tell the world we are aiming for."[16]

Ruth Dennis's exposé of the "unvarnished truth" poses the question: "Is 'Lulu Belle' based on the life of the average Negro girl?" She believes that it is. The crux of the problem, as she defines it, is that single black women spend all of their time concentrating on their appearance when they should be out working. Their preoccupation with fashion causes a "passionate discontent" with their economic caste, and they can focus only on how they can acquire "social recognition." In order to obtain such finery, they often resort to "all sorts of reprehensible follies," or "even crime." She writes, "The majority of Negro women are evading honest toil to live in licentious ease. 'Clothes, clothes, more clothes' is their one ambition."

This obsession with dress, "which [Negro women] parade with shameless audacity . . . before their envious and less successful friends," has much in common with the Rockland Palace ball (male) participants. The balls were competitive in spirit, as the main purpose for gathering was to show off the exquisite creations, and prizes were awarded for the most stunning. In the *Variety* article, the reporter claims that "the well-to-do votaries of the 'drags,' or the one who is being supported by a man of means will plan weeks in advance on a gown to wear, and will spend hundreds of dollars on the creation."[17] Similar to the Lulu Belles that Dennis describes, the men in drag display all the visible signs of belonging to the upper class, but they have not earned the distinction through honest labor. The central characteristic of the "male abnormals" is not their sexual attraction to other men but their obsession with drags and dresses. In both the *Variety* article and Dennis's, images of class subsume the representations of a deviant or rampant sexuality. The immorality or the "perversion" of the individuals is marked more by transgressing one's class (without having to work in the conventional sense), than by the sexual exploits they pursue. As with the Lulu Belles that Dennis describes, the participants' parade of tremendous wealth also belies the fact they do not work. The most successful drag participants, the article mentions, are unemployed, but they are backed by rich men. Lulu Belle's relationship with her French count embodies this goal.

According to Dennis, middle-class decorum and respect for motherhood have also been assaulted by the "Lulu Belles" of the black community. Proper, feminine behavior has been replaced by a passion for gambling, drinking, and dancing, and other activities inspired by "questionable novels and rotten theatricals."[18] She prophesies that if the Lulu Belles, who are "conspicuous everywhere" in the community, are not rooted out and reformed, the race will perish. She explains: "So great a responsibility rests upon Negro womanhood that it is imperative that serious consideration be given the condition of things as they stand in reference to her. The moral status of a race is fixed by the character of its women. If 'Lulu Belle' is typical, then the Negro is doomed." The future of the race, therefore, is dependent upon the unceasing and righteous work of the "anti–Lulu Belles," or those black women who have not yet succumbed to the temptations of vice and folly. In an earnest plea to cherish the few upstanding black women in the community, Dennis writes:

> These heroines [the anti–Lulu Belles] must realize that between good and evil conduct there is a great gulf. They must be God fearing teachers of truth and righteousness. They shall lead the Lulu Belles into chaste living and the race will forever call them "blessed."

The "chaste living" here refers to preserving black women's roles as wives and mothers. She claims it is the principal duty of black women to serve as the "custodians of the souls as well as the bodies of their children."[19]

The greatest crime Lulu Belle commits in the play is breaking up George Randall's family. In one of the excessively melodramatic moments of the play, the extent of this is evident. While sitting in a Harlem nightclub, George realizes he cannot go back home to his wife even after he has been told that his son Walter has died. The young boy, in an effort to support his mother and sister by selling newspapers in the rain, caught and succumbed to pneumonia. A letter from George's wife imploring him to go home, along with her apology for not being a "better wife," cannot persuade him. Lulu Belle has long since tired of George and commands him to go back (she tells him, "Ev'ry daddy has his day an' yo've had six months!"), but he cannot leave her. Inexplicably,

George cannot escape Lulu Belle's charms; it turns out that he loves her more than he does his whole family, "put t'gethah."[20] Like the "little black hunchbacked creature," Skeeter, who follows Lulu Belle everywhere, fetching her cigarettes and taking her insults, George's manhood has deteriorated. By act 3, Lulu Belle has destroyed a man and his entire family.

"Everyone in Dark-Town Knows"

Within conservative circles, the visible homosexual and the lascivious black woman such as Lulu Belle were often linked because of their "moral depravity," and the criticism hurled at the fictional character echoed similar arguments that lesbians and gay men encountered regularly. Just as heterosexual, single black women would inevitably bring about the downfall of the race, homosexual men and women threatened the stability of Harlem's two strongest institutions: The church and the family. As Steven Watson argues, on the one hand Harlem provided a measure of tolerance for lesbians and gay men, but on the other, the powerful Harlem churches were "strictly anti-homosexual."[21] George Chauncey charts a religious campaign in the 1920s, which was directed at homosexuals, focusing on the threat they posed to black communities. The crusade was fought primarily in the white press and led by Harlem's most renowned minister, Adam Clayton Powell. On November 16, 1929, the *New York Age* printed the following headline: "Dr. A. C. Powell Scores Pulpit Evils: Abyssinian Pastor Fires a Broadside into Ranks of Fellow Ministers, Churches . . . Denounces Sex Degeneracy and Sex Perverts." In a well-publicized sermon, Powell railed against the evils infiltrating society as a result of the activities in which many young people were engaging in Harlem's nightclubs and dance halls. Continuing the trend to lay the predicament of the race on women, he said he was particularly troubled by the rise in "sex perversion" among females, claiming it "has grown into one of the most horrible, debasing, alarming and damning vices of present day civilization, and is . . . prevalent to an unbelievable degree."[22] In a sermon the following week, he stated that the Negro family was particularly vulnerable to sex perverts because they induce "men to leave their wives for other men, wives to leave their husbands for other women, and girls to mate with girls instead of marrying."[23] Homosexuality was not just a moral problem, but it signaled doom for the propagation of the race.

Although this public attack on "sex perversion" occurred three years after *Lulu Belle* opened, the church's antihomosexual position was familiar to lesbians and gay men. In 1926, Edward Bourdet's play about lesbianism, *The Captive,* opened on Broadway, and it was met with fiery protest from the press and church for its immorality.[24] Certainly, when the black minister tells Lulu Belle she will go to hell if she does not alter her lifestyle, lesbians and gay men could identify with this vilification. Further, Lulu Belle's subversive impudence in the face of the minister must have registered a vicarious joy for those who saw or heard about the moment in the play. She does not cower when he criticizes her lifestyle; instead, she remains defiant and continues her quest for greater wealth and more fabulous clothes. Her attitude toward the law undoubtedly had the same effect on the subculture.

As indicated in the *Variety* article about the Rockland drag ball, the relationship between the homosexual community and the law was tenuous at best. On one hand, permits for such occasions could be obtained, but on the other, gay men and lesbians knew that the police might turn on them at any moment. A police report for the same ball described in *Variety* reflects the careful watch the police maintained:

> About 12:30 A.M. we visited [the Rockland drag ball] and found approximately 5,000 people, colored and white, men attired in women's clothes, and vice versa. The affair, we were informed, was a "Fag (fairy) Masquerade Ball." This is an annual affair where the white and colored fairies assemble together with their friends, this being attended also by a certain respectable element who go here to see the sights.[25]

The report mentions that because of the large number of officers, inside and outside the club, uniformed and in plainclothes, the three men filing the report stayed only a short time. They witnessed a number of intoxicated guests, but saw no reason to make any arrests. They conclude: "Prior to leaving [officers] B and 5 questioned some casuals in the place as to where women could be met, but could learn nothing."[26] The "women" here refers to prostitutes (one would assume that their prospects for making any money at an event populated mostly by gay men would be slim), and the report points to the cultural connection between whores and "fairies." Ethically and legally, prostitutes and homosexuals stood outside the boundaries of respectability. To middle-class Blacks, both groups were regarded as "low class" in terms of their morality and their social standing.[27]

Just as Lulu Belle's impertinence toward the evangelist probably aroused satisfaction from the gay and lesbian community, so too would her coy taunting of the white police officer and her ability to avoid arrest. An impudent young black woman or defiant cross-dressed black man on the streets of New York in the 1920s would not nearly have been so fortunate. This is reflected in an amusing *Variety* story dated April 21, 1926. The brief article states that Gene Mosely, a twenty-six-year-old "female impersonator" of 337 West Fifty-ninth Street (coincidentally, the same street as the setting for the first scene in *Lulu Belle*), was arrested for disorderly conduct. Like Lulu Belle, Mosely apparently infuriated the police officer with his inappropriate sexual advances.

> Policeman George Meyers, West 17th Street Station, said he was passing in front of the 59th street address early one morning when Mosely stepped up to him, threw his arms around his neck and tried to kiss him. Meyers said he pushed him aside and then recognized him as a man who had been arrested last December for a similar act.[28]

Mosely refuted the accusation, but when he could not provide "a satisfactory answer" why he was on the street at that time, the judge found him guilty. Mosely's punishment further demonstrates the perceived conjunction between charges of immoral behavior and indolence: He was sentenced to sixty days in the workhouse.

The most profound and well-documented effect Belasco's production had in the 1920s was its onstage presentation of "authentic" Harlem atmosphere, which was characterized by a raucous nightlife. At the same time *Lulu Belle* opened on Broadway, *Nigger Heaven,* by white author and socialite Carl Van Vechten, was a national bestseller. Van Vechten's novel, like *Lulu Belle,* depicted an exotic, thrilling world of jazz and bootlegged liquor and a life infinitely more exciting than the one whites endured below 125th Street. The two works created an insatiable desire among whites to experience the "real thing," and they traveled en masse to Harlem where they could take a vacation from their everyday middle-class morality. Press coverage of the goings-on in Harlem perpetuated the appeal and often credited *Lulu Belle* and *Nigger Heaven* for initiating the vogue.

In particular, act 3 of Sheldon and MacArthur's play attempts to recreate the wild abandon that people expected from Harlem's nightlife. The act takes place in the Elite Grotto, a fictional "black-and-tan" nightclub where Lulu Belle performs. The lengthy set description reflects

Belasco's careful attention to detail, and he made every effort to replicate a basement speakeasy with all of its characteristic "evil and exotic charm."[29] Numerous tables line a small, circular dance floor; there is a small bandstand with a piano and several chairs for the small orchestra; and an old pool table is upstage left. Covering the wall are pictures of Lulu Belle, and signs that warn, "No Improper Dancing or Actions Will Be Tolerated," "No Shimmie," and "Profane Language Not Permitted" (fig. 15). As one would expect (and hope), all of these rules are violated in the course of the act. Harlem's appeal for whites was its promise that all regulations of polite society would indeed be broken.

Of particular interest is a not very subtle reference to the liberated atmosphere of Lulu Belle's world. Belasco strategically placed a reminder on his set indicating that the defiance of rules takes on many different forms in New York's "Black Belt." A prominently displayed advertisement on the wall publicizes the active gay and lesbian subculture. It says: "Sheiks, Flappers and Dapper Dans! The pleasure of your company is requested at 14 Karet Boys Masquerade Ball and Dance at the Harlem Casino, January 26. Admission 75 cents. Boxes $3." Those familiar with the city's gay and lesbian subculture would have immediately recognized the allusion to the drag balls. The reference to "14 Karet Boys," for instance, is no doubt code for the young gay men in their expensive and glittering creations.[30] The sign may be taken to signify that while the activities in Lulu Belle's Elite Grotto are emancipating, they represent only a small part of the exhilarating possibilities in Harlem.

Jazz music, sultry singing, and wild, pulsating dancing punctuate the act. At one point the waiters break into a routine during which they balance their trays above their heads and "undulate" with the music. A few moments later the entire cast breaks into a feverish dance, trying to outdo each other with impressive new dance steps. In between Lulu Belle's arguments with George, there are fist fights, crap shoots, and more songs. But the high point of the act is Lulu Belle's Charleston, which she uses to entice the Vicomte de Villars, the playboy aristocrat who takes her with him back to Paris. The onstage crowd begs her to do an encore, and she obliges.

The effect that *Lulu Belle* had on white pleasure seekers was almost immediate. The *Pittsburgh Courier* reported in March 1926 that Anita Handy, in response to the newest vogue, edited a new magazine called *A Guide to Harlem and Its Amusements* and planned to lead tours to the most popular attractions. When her idea was denounced for focusing on the lurid side of Harlem, she responded that "she meant only to take

FIG. 15. Lulu Belle double-crosses George: "Ummmm! Weah yo' git dat wondahful haih tonic? Smells like about a hundred million lilies o' de valley! How about a little dance?" Henry Hull, John Harrington, and Lenore Ulric in David Belasco's production of *Lulu Belle* (1926).

(Courtesy, Billy Rose Theatre Collection, New York Public Library for the Performing Arts.)

advantage of the publicity given colored Harlem through *Lulu Belle* and Van Vechten's latest novel, which has caused a great number of people, especially white people, to visit Harlem, and many of them not knowing how to see the community intelligently."[31] Handy's tour would most surely lead to the epicenter of this thriving nightlife, a stretch known as "Jungle Alley," which was located between Lenox and Seventh avenues on 133rd Street. Many of the nightclubs, such as Barron's Exclusive Club, one of Harlem's oldest (it opened in 1915), Connor's, and the Clam House, were found on this block. She also promised that she would not show just the "night side life," but also "the better side of Harlem," including its churches, schools, and modest homes. Admittedly, she indicates that "the night side life is the only side the white tourists care to see, as it is the only side they have heard about."[32]

The attention whites lavished on the seamier side of Harlem, however, aroused the consternation of many in the black community and press. They viewed with dismay such works as *Lulu Belle* and its depiction of Harlem as a "paradise for cheap sport." They felt these works perpetuated stereotypical images of African-Americans as morally corrupt and scandal driven. This was a small element of Harlem life, they argued, and the more dominant "good" and "decent" side of their neighborhoods were ignored. Reverend William Lloyd Imes, a pastor of St. James' Church, asked: "Would white folk like to be judged by their cheapest and vilest products of society? Do they feel flattered by the sordid, degrading life brought out in the courts?"[33] And in an amusing and ironic piece for the *Messenger,* George S. Schuyler wrote that Harlem had very recently earned a degree of respect for its growing number of intellectuals, writers, and poets. He claims these achievements have been nearly forgotten due to the interest in the vulgar nightlife. Facetiously, he states that Carl Van Vechten and David Belasco would soon be participating in a public debate to determine who is "most entitled to be known as the Santa Claus of Black Harlem, a community described as the Mecca of the New Negro but lately called 'Nigger Heaven.'" Poking fun at Belasco and Van Vechten's capitalization on black life and their self-serving "support" of black literary and cultural life, he concludes, "both contestants are well known for their contributions to the Fund for the Relief of Starving Negro Intelligentsia and for their frequent explorations of the underground life north of 125th Street."[34]

In response to the black protest that *Lulu Belle* generated, some in the white press felt that African-Americans were being far "too sensitive." They did not think that it should be discussed as anything more than what it was: a piece of popular theater (and a not very good one at that). The *New York Herald Tribune,* for example, published a rebuttal to the claims of African-Americans that the play was a "libel on their race," and "an unfair indictment of an entire people." The unnamed author concedes that, yes, black people have been oppressed, but they have made great strides in their artistic and cultural accomplishments in which they rightly take "modest pride." He adds that they are not without help in their pursuits either: "Aiding them in their endeavor to justify themselves is a band of New York white folks, who, led by Carl Van Vechten and other intrepid abolitionists, clasp them hand in hand and help them over the rough places."[35] He also agrees that the portrait of black life as represented by Lenore Ulric is not "pleasant propaganda." On stage at the Belasco Theatre, "she is a smart viper, weaving her cankerous way from Harlem to Paris. . . . 'Lulu Belle' is not a pretty picture of a lady of color, or of the circles in which she wiggles." But this is no reason to protest, he says, for the history of the world's stage is filled with unpleasant images of every race, religion, and ethnic group. He cites several examples, including *The Cradle Snatchers* (1925), which "exceeds in its traduction of blonde life"; *The Shanghai Gesture,* "a bitter, unjust lampoon of the Chinese character and practices"; and "the Scandinavians may well consider themselves insulted by *Hamlet* and *Hedda Gabler,* and the Jews and Irish by *Abie's Irish Rose*"; and so on. He closes with the following rejoinder: "So the Negroes, like other persons, should take the abuses of the drama laughingly, and not waste their time in protest."[36]

The most vocal objections to *Lulu Belle* did not involve the play's unfavorable representations of African-Americans; the greatest concern in the press was its blatant immorality. Some say this was exacerbated by the integration of Blacks and whites on the same stage, and similarly, in the same nightclub. Conservative opponents of the Harlem nightclubs cited the immoral sexual behavior that seemed to result from the intermingling of the races. Black and white critics and moralists suggested that by allowing the two races to mix socially would invariably lead to any number of possible couplings between races and genders. Issues of purity of race usually delineated the arguments, but just below the surface were concerns that racial intermingling might lead to deviant sexuality. In their reasoning, interracial desire, a form of sexual perversion, was only one step removed from same-sex desire. Out of control and unregulated, Harlem became the arena in which whites experimented with such activities, and *Lulu Belle* metaphorically reflected this trend.[37]

This is evident in the most vitriolic response to *Lulu Belle,* Arthur Hornblow's review in *Theatre* magazine (April 1926). Aligning it with two other controversial plays on Broadway, *The Glass Slipper* (1925) and *The Shanghai Gesture* (the three of them together forming "an unholy trinity of theatrical filth"), Hornblow rants: "All the ordures of brutal concupiscence, the noisome scrapings of the sexual garbage can, the shameless, abandoned jargon of the brothel, raucous ribaldry, rape, lewdness, the whole gamut of depravity and lechery—such is the putrescent drama served to-day for the entertainment of your sons, and daughters, not secretly, furtively in some obscure East Side dive, but openly, brazenly in Broadway theaters of the first class."[38] He singles out *Lulu*

Belle as particularly reprehensible amid the other "erotic exhibitions of its kind." At least previous "bawdy" shows had casts "confined to white players," so "if indecencies of dialogue or situation were committed, at least it was among one's own, in the family so to speak." "But now," he says, "emulating the example of certain cabarets, where black-and-tan performers draw the midnight pleasure seekers, an added thrill is sought at the Belasco by mixing the colors."[39]

The most popular nightclubs as well as the most extravagant, however, did not actually encourage a commingling of the races. The three largest, the Cotton Club, Small's Paradise, and Connie's Inn, were mob-owned and strictly segregated except for the black waiters, kitchen staff, and entertainers. These clubs offered gaudy, nightly floor shows centered around a featured performer, such as Ethel Waters, Cab Calloway, or dancer Earl "Snakehips" Tucker, and a chorus line of light-skinned black women (or as they were sometimes referred to, "light, bright, and damn-near white").[40] Wealthy white patrons could watch a "Ziegfeldesque" show and eat overpriced fried chicken or barbecued spareribs in an ersatz jungle atmosphere, all the while maintaining a comfortable distance from the social reality outside. The more intrepid tourist might go to one of the hundreds of basement speakeasies, such as the Sugar Cane, which attracted a primarily black working-class clientele. Tucked away on one of the side streets, this "lap joint" catered to fewer white patrons, and the music was less refined than in the more extravagant clubs.

These were the venues that chiefly riled social and religious conservatives. As the press reported, committees were formed and social scientists were interviewed to determine the long-term social effects these cabarets might have. The *Hartford Times,* for example, analyzes the trend in the article, "Harlem Negroes Run Dives for White Folks" (July 23, 1927). It contends that because of plays like *Lulu Belle,* "cabarets, with a suggestion of abandoned wickedness" have sprung up in astonishing numbers. And worse, "These places have multiplied so rapidly that they are virtually unregulated and unsupervised, which cites grave social evils as a possible result of this haphazard mingling of races."[41] The "grave social evils" are not mentioned by name (perhaps because they are unmentionable), but prostitution and sexual deviance are the implied outcome of whites interacting with African-Americans. This moral depravity that unsegregated clubs caused was thought to stem from the "primitive" or "savage" urges that Blacks released in whites. While mixing with African-Americans and taking part in their "Dionysian" dances, Caucasians discarded their layers of civilization and social constraints. As James Weldon Johnson noted, Harlem was a place where whites took a "moral vacation."

> At these times, the Negro drags his captors captive. On occasions, I have been amazed and amused watching white people dancing to a Negro band in a Harlem cabaret; attempting to throw off the crusts and layers of inhibitions laid on by sophisticated civilization; striving to yield to the feel and experience of abandon; seeking to recapture a taste of primitive joy in life and living; trying to work their way back into that jungle which was the original Garden of Eden; in a word, doing their best to pass for colored.[42]

Harlem became a playground in which whites could indulge their passion to experiment with racial taboos. The nightclubs offered the possibility of transcending the socially codified barriers of race and class, and this experimentation resulted in the arousal of sexual pleasure.

Magnus Hirschfeld, "the Einstein of Sex" and cofounder of the World League for Sex Reform with Havelock Ellis, forwarded this argument in the press. In an interview with journalist George Sylvester Vierick, he discussed the reasons for white patrons attending black clubs and the erotic desire they stimulated. Unsurprisingly in his Freudian analysis, he does not mention black erotic desire. As is typical of the attitudes of the time, Blacks are the objects upon which whites cast their fantasies and are not in control of their own sexuality:

> The white man or the white woman who seeks love beyond the border line of color is thrilled by the sense of being subjugated by the more savage passions, the more dynamic life urge of a primitive race. In the man who thus surrenders his race pride it bespeaks a somewhat feminine attitude toward love. In a woman it is clearly an exaggeration of the normal desire for subordination.[43]

Within this framework, sexuality is intricately linked to race and gender. Hirschfeld equates black and female with the "primitive" (i.e., subordinate), and associates white and male with the "civilized" (i.e., superior).[44] He classifies sexual desire as either active (civilized/white/male) or passive (primitive/black/female). If one extends this formula to the Harlem nightclubs, then it becomes clear as to how a mixing of the races leads to moral depravity. Because whites submitted to their "primitive" and "feminine" urges (compare this to the earlier discussion surrounding the presumed weaknesses and uncontrollability of single black women), "grave social evils" were sure to follow. Interest in sexual perversion was a natural corollary of whites' rejection of middle-class morality. And to satisfy this curiosity, the more adventurous whites frequented clubs that featured gay and lesbian acts or ones that accommodated the "pansy trade" (i.e., female impersonators).

There were several such places in and around Jungle Alley, and these often attracted mixed crowds (i.e., hetero-/homosexual, black/white). The most notorious haunt for lesbians and gay men was Harry Hansberry's Clam House, "a narrow, smoky speakeasy" in Jungle Alley. *Vanity Fair* described it as "a popular house for revelers but not for the innocent young," and it was a gathering spot for well-known personalities. As Steven Watson reports, "Downtown celebrities went on bisexual sprees—among them were Beatrice Lillie, Tallulah Bankhead, Jeanne Eagels, Marilyn Miller, Princess Murat from Paris, and—dressed in matching bowler hats—came chanteuse Libby Holman and her heiress lover Louisa Carpenter du Pont Jenney."[45] One of the chief attractions at the Clam House was Gladys Bentley, who also played such Harlem hot spots as the Mad House, Connie's Inn, and the Ubangi Club. A 250-pound black blues singer, Bentley was notorious for wearing a tuxedo onstage and off and publicly marrying a woman in a New Jersey civil ceremony.[46] Although she was a talented piano player and balladeer, she is generally remembered for her "ad-libbed" lyrics of Broadway and popular songs. That is, she converted the sweet words of a love ballad into the filthiest song imaginable. One of the lyrics, a lampoon on "Sweet Georgia Brown" and "My Alice Blue Gown," familiar Broadway show tunes of the day, survives. Fusing and enhancing the original lyrics, Bentley's version became a tribute to anal sex:

And he said, "Dearie, please turn around"
And he shoved that big thing up my brown.
He tore it. I bored it. Lord, how I adored it.
My sweet little Alice Blue Gown.[47]

Although reactions to the version are not available, it seems fairly clear why such a song would be the catalyst for a raid of the club, an effect Bentley's performances often had, according to New York historian Wilbur Young. Young wrote in 1939, "Gladys, not content with merely singing them herself . . . would encourage the paying guests to join in on the chorus which they did willingly. At this stage, it was just a matter of time before the house got raided."[48]

Female impersonator Gloria Swanson (née "Mr. Winston"), famous for his rendition of "Get 'em from the Peanut Man (Hot Nuts)," could also be seen performing most nights in a Harlem basement speakeasy. Tastefully dressed in sequins and net, entertaining with his risqué song parodies and coyly demure dancing, Swanson often fooled unknowing audiences of his male gender. In his tight corset, which gave him a "swelling and well-modeled bosom," he was also loud, buxom, and the favorite of the underworld set. People generally referred to him with the feminine pronouns *she* and *her,* and as Bruce Nugent wrote, it was rare indeed that anyone ever saw Winston in male attire: "Seldom coming on the street in the daytime, breakfasting when the rest of the world was dining, dining when the rest of the world was taking its final snooze before arising for the day, his public life was lived in evening gowns; his private life in boa-trimmed negligees."[49]

Within Harlem's world of drag balls and gay nightclubs, the title character, or in the words of the hit song from the show, the "mad-cap baby, called Lulu Belle," deserved a special tribute. In homage to her, the gay community named the Lulu Belle Club on 341 Lennox Avenue, near 127th Street in Harlem after her. Black poet, artist, and actor Bruce Nugent, one of the few openly gay black intellectuals of the period, described the club as a hangout for "female impersonators," which catered to a primarily working-class clientele.[50] Carl Van Vechten visited the club on at least three separate occasions in 1928, which is evident in his diaries. The club apparently shut down for a period that year, perhaps because of numerous raids. On August 16, Van Vechten went to the "reopened Lulu Belle" with Louis Cole, a black entertainer who sometimes appeared in drag, and found it as "spirited as ever."[51]

A story on the front page of the *Amsterdam News* in February 1928 explains that within a two-week period, more than thirty men in drag had been arrested at the Lulu Belle Club. One particular evening, two undercover police detectives were dining at the club when five men dressed as women approached them and invited them to "take an auto ride." The detectives agreed and "told the 'girls' they knew a 'nice place' at 152nd street and Amsterdam Avenue." When the group arrived there, "the 'girls' were horrified to learn they had driven to the police station." With an amusement typical of the press, the reporter explains: "[The five defendants] confronted the Lieutenant in silk stockings, sleeveless evening gowns of soft-tinted crepe de chine and light fur wraps."[52] Unlike the character Lulu Belle, the five men were unable to use "feminine wiles" and avoid the inevitable: They were sent to jail because they could not pay the twenty-five-dollar fine. And in a notable corollary, Blair Niles's 1931 fact-based novel *Strange Brother* contains a brief account of prison conditions that men convicted of homosexual-related crimes like those arrested at Lulu Belle's might have faced. Near the end of the book, "Lilly-Marie," a young man who had been arrested for wearing women's clothing, describes his experiences. He states that on Welfare Island the men with such proclivities are segregated from the other male convicts. Among this group of "girls," the prisoners adopt the names of Broadway show characters, movie actresses, and opera singers. One of the "girls," he informs the protagonist, was called "Lulu Belle."[53]

Lulu Belle's status as a gay icon is not hard to imagine, and her place in American theater history needs to be reclaimed. The gay community's appropriation of the character demonstrates the manner in which the subculture reinterpreted elements from the dominant culture and used these to bolster their position in that world. Just as imperious screen star Gloria Swanson was a popular figure for parody in the 1920s (as Joan Crawford and Bette Davis would become in the following decades), Lulu Belle's parodic appeal to the drag subculture stemmed from her defiance in the face of attempts to make her conform to religious and social expectations. The critical denunciation of the play on the grounds that Lulu Belle posed a moral threat to society surely added to her popularity, as did Lenore Ulric's portrayal. Indeed, as a white actress playing a black working-class single woman who is also sexually liberated and wears gorgeous frocks, Lenore Ulric gave the ultimate drag performance.

Unfortunately, *Lulu Belle*'s notoriety, like the title character's, was short-lived. Perhaps it was inevitable that Lulu Belle would be punished and destroyed for violating convention and assaulting middle-class ideals—just as Harlem's nonstop party and white experimentation with black exoticism would die with the depression—but she remains obstinate to the end. Immediately after George chokes her, the stage directions in the play state: "Lulu Belle screaming ha-ha, crawls out of bed, picks flowers up from floor and throws them at George, then drops dead."[54] In her demise, she is remorseless, brazen, and—bedecked in ermine and diamonds—exceedingly glamorous. And as the participants at the Rockland drag and patrons at the Lulu Belle Club would have agreed, that is exactly as it should be.

NOTES

1."Lulu Belle," words by Leo Robin and music by Richard Myers (Authorized by David Belasco and dedicated to Miss Lenore Ulric), sheet music in Music Collection, New York Public Library at Lincoln Center.

2. "Battle on among Broadway Elite of the 'Third Sex,'" *Variety,* March 7, 1928, 45, 47.

3. See George Chauncey, *Gay New York: Gender, Urban Culture, and the Making of the Gay World, 1890–1940* (New York: Basic Books, 1994); Lillian Faderman, *Odd Girls and Twilight Lovers: A History of Lesbian Life in Twentieth-Century America* (New York: Columbia University Press, 1991); and Eric Garber, "A Spectacle in Color: The Lesbian and Gay Subculture of Jazz Age Harlem," in *Hidden from History: Reclaiming the Gay and Lesbian Past,* ed. Martin .Duberman, Martha Vicinus, and George Chauncey Jr. (New York: Penguin, 1989).

4. Chauncey, *Gay New York,* 253.

5. Arthur Hornblow, "Mr. Hornblow Goes to the Play," *Theatre,* April 1926, 15. James Weldon Johnson, *Black Manhattan* (New York: Da Capo Press, 1930, 1991), 205. *Variety* (April 28, 1926) reprinted black intellectual W. E. B. DuBois's praise for the white actors from the black journal *The Crisis:* "I knew, of course, that Miss Ulric was white. The exaggerated dialect fixes the racial status of the doctor, I was in doubt as to the prizefighter, and the lover absolutely deceived me. I was sure he was colored." The *Variety* reporter added: "The 'lover' is played by Henry Hull. This tribute coming from Dr. DuBois as to Hull's characterization is without a precedent among white theatricals" (72).

6. Quoted in Freda L. Scott, "Black Drama and the Harlem Renaissance," in *Theatre Journal,* December 1985, 432.

7. References to the play and the editors' introduction come from *The Stage Works of Charles MacArthur,* ed. Arthur Dorlag and John Irvine (Tallahassee: Florida State University Foundation, 1974), 3–75.

8. "Wages of Sin in Four Acts," *New York Times,* February 10, 1926.

9. *Lulu Belle,* 20.

10. Ibid., 21.

11. Ibid., 28.

12. Ibid.

13. The essay appears in *Critical Inquiry* 18 (summer 1992): 738–55.

14. Ibid., 741.

15. Ibid., 747. In *Ain't I a Woman,* bell hooks also outlines the historical basis for the portrayal of black women as degenerate and threats to the race. She points out the "competition" engendered between black and white women entering the work arena early in the century. According to hooks, white women workers enforced segregation so that they wouldn't catch a "private," "Negro" disease, which was a result from black women's sexual promiscuity. See bell hooks, *Ain't I a Woman: Black Women and Feminism* (Boston: South End Press, 1981), 131–33.

16. Ruth Dennis, "Lulu Belles—All?" *Amsterdam News,* March 24, 1926, 5.

17. "Battle On," 45. Of course, in many ways, Lenore Ulric's in the role of Lulu Belle had all the marks of a drag performance. Although hers was primarily a "trans-raced" rather than "transgendered."

18. The connection Dennis makes to "rotten theatricals" is a familiar argument. Throughout history, the theater has been considered a repository of sin and vice, and dramatic literature is viewed as the instigator. Actresses have traditionally taken a great deal of reproach for they have often been regarded as whores

who offer their bodies up for display (and sometimes more) to the paying public. See Jonas Barish's *The Anti-theatrical Prejudice* (Berkeley and Los Angeles: University of California Press, 1981), and Kristina Straub's *Sexual Suspects: Eighteenth-Century Players and Sexual Ideology* (Princeton: Princeton University Press, 1992).

19. Dennis, "Lulu Belles—All?" 5.

20. *Lulu Belle*, 51.

21. Steven Watson, *The Harlem Renaissance: Hub of African-American Culture, 1920–1930* (New York: Pantheon, 1995), 134.

22. Quoted in Chauncey, *Gay New York*, 254.

23. Ibid., 255.

24. See *Variety* front-page article, "Lukor Stops 'Captive,'" February 16, 1927, which details the events surrounding the arrest of the show's twelve cast members on indecency charges. Faderman mentions this in *Odd Girls and Twilight Lovers* (66), and Kaier Curtin discusses the play in his *"We Can Always Call Them Bulgarians": The Emergence of Lesbian and Gay Men on the American Stage* (New York: Alyson, 1987).

25. "New York City Police Report: Commercialized Amusement, February 24, 1928," in *We Are Everywhere: A Historical Sourcebook of Gay and Lesbian Politics*, ed. Mark Blasius and Shane Phelan (New York: Routledge, 1997), 228.

26. Ibid.

27. Chauncey develops this comparison quite fully in *Gay New York*. He explains that the two groups also had in common an ability to be "sexually exploited" by men without compromise to their manhood. He writes: "The belief that fairies could be substituted for female prostitutes—and were virtually interchangeable with them—was particularly prevalent among men in the bachelor subculture whose opportunities for meeting 'respectable' women were limited by the moral codes, gender segregation, or unbalanced sex ratios of their ethnic cultures" (83).

28. "Colored Impersonator Tries Kiss Cop—60 Days," *Variety*, April 21, 1926, 11.

29. *Lulu Belle*, 44.

30. Chauncey reprints two advertisements for Harlem drag balls that bear a striking resemblance to Belasco's mock notice. In both cases, the wording of the invitations imply that the festivities would be gay in nature: "Reunion and Costume Ball of the Tom Boys and Girls" in one, and "come over and be merry with the WE BOYS" in the other (*Gay New York*, 270).

31. "Her Idea Criticized," *Pittsburgh Courier*, March 20, 1926, Carl Van Vechten Scrapbooks, New York Public Library. David Levering Lewis acknowledges the rush to Harlem *Lulu Belle* caused in *When Harlem Was in Vogue* (New York: Oxford University Press, 1981): "If the sociology of vogues teaches that single events have complex antecedents, it was, with this qualification, *Lulu Belle* that sent whites straight to Harlem in unprecedented numbers for a taste of the real thing. Their arrival was so sudden that Harlem had to gallop in order to live up to its expectations" (164).

32. "Her Idea Criticized."

33. Lester Walton, "Harlem Resents Emphasis on Its Vice," *New York*

World, October 27, 1927, Carl Van Vechten Scrapbooks, New York Public Library.

34. "Literary Note," *Messenger,* October 1926, Carl Van Vechten Scrapbooks, New York Public Library. The black community had rather conflicted feelings toward white champions of African-American art, literature, and causes. Their rather dubious and sometimes exploitive support earned them the nickname "Negrotarians," to use Zora Neale Hurston's tongue-in-cheek term. While these white sponsors supported Blacks in their artistic endeavors, the recipients recognized that the reasons for support were not always so noble. Wallace Thurman wrote, "The Negrotarians have a formula, too. They have regimented their sympathies and fawn around Negroes with a cry in their heart and a superiority bug in their head. It's a new way to get a thrill, a new way to merit distinction in the community" (quoted in Watson, *The Harlem Renaissance,* 97).

35. "Oddments and Remainders," *New York Herald Tribune,* February 21, 1926, Carl Van Vechten Scrapbooks, New York Public Library.

36. Ibid.

37. As Mel Watkins explains ironically, "Even as they violently suppressed black efforts to advance in education and employment, and exercise their lawful rights, whites turned to the black community as a model for their rebellion against puritanical rural values." *On the Real Side* (New York: Simon and Schuster, 1994), 207.

38. Hornblow, "Mr. Hornblow Goes to the Play," 15.

39. Ibid.

40. *Brown Sugar,* Matthew Pook, producer, and Donald Bogle, screenplay, Ebony Productions, 1986.

41. "Harlem Negroes Run Dives for White Folks," *Hartford Times,* July 23, 1927, Carl Van Vechten Scrapbooks, New York Public Library.

42. Quoted in Watkins, *On the Real Side,* 209.

43. "Harlem's Emotional Beauty Charms 'Einstein of Sex,'" *Chicago Herald and Examiner,* December 3, 1931, Carl Van Vechten Scrapbooks, New York Public Library.

44. This follows a very similar argument that Rebecca Schneider develops in *The Explicit Body in Performance* (New York: Routledge, 1997).

45. Watson, *The Harlem Renaissance,* 129.

46. In his first autobiography, Langston Hughes writes: "For two or three amazing years, Miss Bentley sat, and played a big piano all night long, literally all night, without stopping—singing songs like 'The St. James Infirmary,' from ten in the evening until dawn, with scarcely a break between the notes, sliding from one song to another, with a powerful and continuous underbeat of jungle rhythm." *The Big Sea,* quoted in *Voices of the Harlem Renaissance,* ed. Nathan Irvin Huggins (New York: Oxford University Press, 1976), 371.

47. Quoted in Eric Garber, "Gladys Bentley: The Bulldagger Who Sang the Blues," *Out/Look,* spring 1988, 55.

48. Wilbur Young, "Gladys Bentley," in *Biographical Sketches: Negroes of New York* (WPA Writers Program, 1939), 1, Schomburg Collection, New York Public Library.

49. Bruce Nugent, "Gloria Swanson," in *Biographical Sketches,* 1. I am indebted to Thomas Wirth, the executor of Nugent's papers, for sharing this with me.

50. Referred to in Garber, "A Spectacle in Color." Bruce Nugent explained that homosexuality was generally tolerated within the Harlem Renaissance. In an interview with Thomas Wirth, he said: "There was a great admixture—the mixture of blacks and whites during that particular two or three years. Whites making p-i-l-g-r-i-m-a-g-e-s to black Harlem, doing the cabarets or Clinton Moore's private parties. Whites being able to mingle freely in every way, including sexual, with blacks. Blacks suddenly having the freedom to have white sex partners. . . . Blacks [were] very sought-after for everything, from cabarets, to everything" (interview in "Richard Bruce Nugent: Gay Rebel of the Harlem Renaissance," ed. Thomas H. Wirth, typescript, 1998).

51. Van Vechten also records going to drag balls, and he frequently went to the Clam House to see Gladys Bentley perform. Giving a sense of the exhausting night life he led here is a rather typical entry from February 15, 1929: "I went to a drag in Harlem . . . and went to the Lenox Ave Club where I danced with Louis Cole in drag. And then to Pods and Jerrys. Home at 7:30 A.M.—Saw millions of people I know" (Carl Van Vechten Papers, New York Public Library).

52. "Citizens Claim That Lulu Belle Club on Lenox Avenue Is Notorious Dive," *New York Amsterdam News,* February 15, 1928.

53. Blair Niles, *Strange Brother* (Rpt. London: GMP, 1991), 272.

54. *Lulu Belle,* 75.

The Gay Man as Thinker

Eric Bentley's Many Closets

Daniel-Raymond Nadon

In a tribute to Eric Bentley (b. 1916) in honor of his seventieth birthday, critic James McFarlane praised his many accomplishments, including his nine volumes of dramatic theory and criticism, nine plays, and countless books edited. McFarlane concluded, "Yet this breadth of interest is emphatically not at the expense of depth of penetration."[1] If, as Lisa Merrill has posited earlier in this volume, the professional critic provides discursive frameworks through which audiences view productions, then those provided by the distinguished, prolific Bentley have been among the most influential of the last sixty years. Given his iconic status in the field of dramatic literature and criticism, the multiplicity of forces informing his vision warrant particular scrutiny. Yet McFarlane, in keeping with standard tributes, omits key forces from this figure's personal life, especially his sexual orientation. Bentley began writing during World War II, when discussion of homosexuality was still taboo, and has continued through the virulently homophobic 1950s, the sexually liberating 1960s, into the age of AIDS and the new millennium. Unlike nineteenth-century predecessors James Oakes and Adam Badeau and older contemporaries such as William Inge, Bentley was able to undergo a personal coming out that coincided with the Stonewall Riots and the beginning of the gay rights movement (see fig. 16). But before as well as after this turning point, his sexual orientation powerfully shaped his style and point of view and prompted some of his most penetrating insights. This essay examines the dynamics by which Bentley, for decades, closeted himself through indirect and coded expression and containment of his identity and then gradually came out in plays as well as essays. Factoring the workings of subaltern desire into a reading of the full span of Bentley's career enlarges our understanding of the influential discursive frames he created and thus of his contributions to American theatrical and cultural history.

Looking back on his youth in the preface to his play *The Fall of the*

FIG. 16. Eric Bentley at the piano.

(Courtesy, Billy Rose Theatre Collection, New York Public Library for the Performing Arts.)

Amazons (1982), entitled "On Hating the Other Sex," Bentley acknowledges the profound effect of the closet on his life. He chronicles his emotional struggle with another male student, Fred. He was confused about his attraction to Fred, but was unwilling, at the time, to concede that it was rooted in sexual desire. His feelings were apparent enough that he was cautioned by Yale's dean of freshman (Bentley does not disclose the dean's name), for lavishing unwanted affection on one of his peers. In this incident, he sees the beginning of his life as a gay man, his closet, his theories and politics of homosexuality. He realized at that time how deep the taboos against homosexuality would run and that his longings, however powerful, should remain closeted. "ONE SIMPLY DOES NOT LOVE PERSONS OF THE SAME SEX: if it had taught me nothing else, Yale did seem to have taught me this."[2] He discovered that to become successful, one must assimilate. This was the prevailing mode of living he adopted for more than thirty years.

By contrast, Bentley has been less self-reflective about the effect of the closet on his writing. In a telephone interview I conducted with him in 1997, he questioned the value of "queer" readings of his earlier works. "Originally, I was not for the gay studies, gay theater mentality." In fact, he expressed his distaste for the word *queer*. Though skeptical of my project, he made an allowance: "I find this is better left to those who will follow me."[3]

In taking up the task Bentley leaves, it is appropriate to begin by invoking his adopted mentor, Oscar Wilde, infamously accused of "posing as a somdomite [*sic*]." Like Wilde, the closeted Bentley created and maintained many poses. He was, among other things, a gay man posing as straight and married, a gay activist posing as a conservative, an oppressed individual posing as a power figure, a rebel posing as a dutiful man, and most significantly, in terms of his early writing, a playwright posing as critic. The vast majority of Bentley's work before his coming out fell into the category of criticism. The act of criticism, instructing playwrights on how to write their plays effectively, creates in essence a closeted playwright. Bentley criticized the content, themes, structure, and character development of the best playwrights of the twentieth century. The passion and precision with which he criticized plays reveal his desire to rewrite the great authors. In the act of criticism, Bentley exhibited a hidden desire and a subjugated identity.

Bentley first established himself as a critic and thinker during the 1940s, when he began writing volumes covering practical, aesthetic, and philosophical aspects of theater. His first treatise, *A Century of Hero Worship: A Study of the Idea of Heroism in Carlyle and Nietzsche* (1944), was expanded from his doctoral dissertation completed at Yale University. He then published the following theoretical and critical works: *The Playwright as Thinker: A Study of Drama in Modern Times* (1946), *Bernard Shaw: A Reconsideration* (1947), *In Search of Theatre* (1953), *What Is Theatre?* (1956), *The Life of the Drama* (1964), *The Theatre of Commitment and Other Essays on Drama in Our Society* (1967), and *Theatre of War: Comments on 32 Occasions* (1974). In Bentley's opinion, the most profound of these works was one of the earliest, *The Playwright as Thinker*.[4] In the 1950s, Bentley also began writing dramatic reviews and criticism for various periodicals, especially the *New Republic,* where he was a drama critic from 1952 to 1956, and he continued to publish several books.

The critical stance Bentley adopted in *The Playwright as Thinker* can be related to his understanding of the dynamics of the closet. Much of his discussion centers upon investigating the hidden aspects behind playwrights' lives and work that he believes have been ignored by lesser critics. He sees the means by which the greatest playwrights carefully guarded "secrets" as effective modes of creativity and probes for deeper meanings in their texts and in their stylistic and philosophic proclivities.

Speaking of Henrik Ibsen, whom he covers first and most thoroughly, Bentley explains, "For if there is anything that the general run of critics cannot understand, it is that an artist should be secretive and difficult."[5] He argues that Ibsen was never a champion of realism. Ibsen's was a stylistic and philosophical closet. The author of *A Doll's House* and *Ghosts* merely attempted to gain acceptance and popularity by hiding behind the guise of naturalism and the "well-made play."

> Ibsen did not reject poetry when he rejected verse. He had no illusions about the French drama or about the middle-brow public. If he seems to write at the level of that drama or that public, it is because we choose to read him at that level.[6]

Underneath the modernist and realist traditions in which he had conventionally been placed, Ibsen, in Bentley's view, was "even more a romanticist."[7]

Setting up a counterpoint, Bentley, in effect, puts Wagner in an opposite closet. He claims that while on the surface Wagner seemed passionately against realism, he was at heart a "crude realist." Bentley rejects the notion of the confining stylistic labels that limit the freedom of expression necessary to the creation of great works of art. Great artists, he believes, are not simply categorized. They are not what they seem.

In another essay, he describes what we can view as Chekhov's "naturalist" closet. Although Chekhov's form appeared to be "slice of life," in reality his works were more "spatial" than "linear." Bentley claims that Chekhov's plots, while satisfying the critics and crowds with a realistic structure, ran much deeper. "The purpose of Chekhov's pretense to naturalism resembles the purpose of Ibsen's pretenses: Chekhov wishes to establish an ironic relation, a tension, between the surface and the substratum of his art."[8] Thus, Chekhov wished to set up a closet of sorts, presenting a surface meaning and a subjugated deeper meaning to be seen only by the trained critical eye.

Brecht's closet, according to Bentley, was more political than structural:

> The political Brecht is a socialist. Beneath the socialist is what we might call the Confucian—by which I mean that Brecht's economic

interpretation of human life, his materialism, is at the service of a finely humane, ironic, salty appreciation of normal experience.[9]

He accents the "democracy" of Brecht's text while downplaying the usual "socialist interpretation." Brecht, like Ibsen and the others, maintained stylistic and philosophical levels that, according to Bentley, are ignored by average critics.

The dynamics of the closet and repressed subaltern passion inform Bentley's criticism in other ways as well. As critics James "Acorn" Oakes and Adam "Vagabond" Badeau were enamored, respectively, of actors Edwin Forrest and Edwin Booth in the nineteenth century, so Bentley was enamored of director Elia Kazan. Throughout his career, he wrote passionately of Kazan's work, influence, and talent. In fact, he attributed the success of many of America's greatest playwrights to Kazan's direction:

> We are told that Mr. Kazan was virtually co-author of *A Streetcar Named Desire* and *Death of a Salesman* even to the extent of changing the character of the leading persons; it is arguable that both plays would have failed without his changes.[10]

Later in the same essay, Bentley continues his paean:

> Even if I knew I was to witness a hateful interpretation of a hateful play, I would await any Kazan production with considerable eagerness. For Mr. Kazan's name in the program guarantees an evening of—at the very least—brilliant theatre work at a high emotional temperature.[11]

While Bentley attributes the success of other plays such as *Tea and Sympathy* and *Camino Real* to Kazan's direction, he blames what he calls the "awkwardness" in *The Crucible* to Kazan's absence from the helm: "Mr. Kazan would have taken this script up like clay and re-molded it. He would have struck fire from the individual actor, and he would have brought one actor into much livelier relationship with another."[12]

Bentley addresses Kazan's public confession of Communism and subsequent incrimination of many of his theater colleagues, but falls short of chastising Kazan for naming names. Rather, he criticizes Miller for abandoning his professional affiliation with "the director that did so much to make him famous."[13] Bentley, who later confessed to having "socialist leanings" at the time, chooses to defend Kazan on the basis of his professional talents and credibility.

Unlike the cases of Oakes and Forrest and Badeau and Booth, there is no evidence of a personal relationship between Kazan and Bentley. Bentley's admiration for the director seems to have remained platonic and veiled behind professional flattery. Kazan, in fact, seemed awkward accepting Bentley's praise, stating in a letter that he had not written a line of either *Death of a Salesman* or *Streetcar*. Bentley replied: "But it seems to me that if a director helps to create the very idea of a character—changing it from what it was in the author's original script—he is co-author."[14]

Bentley peppered his criticism of other male artists with erotic commentary on the male form. In each case, he described in detail the erotic display of actors or characters and then, in a return to the closet, decried the exploitation of the male actor/character as shameful and indicative of a lack of artistic development. In a discussion of Marlon Brando's portrayal of Brutus in *Julius Caesar,* Bentley calls him "the most beautiful young man of the American stage, and in this film like enough to a classic statue."[15] He then criticizes the director, Joseph Mankiewicz, for ignoring the holes in Brando's acting technique and instead concentrating on displaying his "handsome body." In an essay entitled "Pathetic Phalluses," Bentley discusses the erotic display of the character Stanley Kowalski in *Streetcar Named Desire* and, as Albert Wertheim discusses in this volume, of Hal Carter in William Inge's *Picnic*. Bentley criticizes the lack of character development given to these "beautiful men":

> There is of course no denying that a hero has a body and that it is a male body. What is remarkable in certain plays of Tennessee Williams and William Inge is that so much is made of the hero's body and that he has so little else.[16]

From the closet, Bentley repeatedly signals his underlying interests by dedicating many pages of his critical writing to gay authors and playwrights. Just as playwrights before him substituted straight for queer characters and framed their plots in heterosexual contexts, Bentley substituted the experiences of "out" gay playwrights and critics for his own. While he could not disclose his own repressed desires, at least he could acknowledge and validate those in other writers. His opinions on gay-themed art, gay political movements, and so on could be masked behind the facade of a liberal heterosexual onlooker.

Bentley's writings on homosexuality began in 1944 with his first treatise, *A Century of Hero Worship*. One of these other nineteenth-century "hero-worshipers," Stefan George, is candidly described by Bentley as "homosexual." Bentley's description of George could easily be a description of himself, his closet, and his own works.

> He was also a homosexual. The doctrine of the New Love—*Das neue heil kommt nur aus neuer liebe* (the new salvation comes only from new love) is the direct product of a homosexual mind. Whether George (or, for that matter, Walt Whitman who preached the New Love in *Calmus*) would confess to homosexuality is irrelevant except insofar as unconscious homosexuality is subtler in its manifestations than the conscious sort.[17]

He defends George's choice to remain closeted and philosophizes about the nature of George's sexuality.

> It may very well be that George seldom thought how unusual was his indifference to women and his passionate attachment to men. He may have considered these attachments in terms of religion and philosophy. Probably his was in the proper sense Platonic love, such love as Socrates felt for Alchibiades.[18]

While the essay is primarily focused on Nietzsche's influence on George, the importance of his homosexuality and the notion of a gay aesthetic becomes an important subtheme of Bentley's evaluation. It is important to remember that this essay was written while Bentley was living an ostensibly heterosexual life, nearly ten years prior to his second marriage.

In his conclusion to the essay, Bentley describes George's position, which was similar to his own at the time. "George was an outsider. His sexual constitution, reinforced by his position as an artist, made him so. He called on his disciples to leave house and home. He hated the mores [of the nineteenth century]." Bentley goes on to describe the contradictory forces in George's character that render him an outsider:

> Catholicism, Hellenism, nobility, pride, egoism, Bohemianism, illiberalism, homosexuality, diabolism—the mind and art of George is a strange compound. In its wilful inconsistencies, its arrogant gestures, and its anti-social attitudes, it bears witness to the failure of nerve in European culture which weakened the intelligentsia and postponed or undermined democracy.[19]

Bentley, in many ways, could again have been describing himself. The closet, in which George lived, resembled Bentley's. He, too, expressed his homosexuality in code in his work. He, too, could not yet publicly define himself as homosexual.

Another of Bentley's early works, *The Dramatic Event*, includes a lengthy discussion of homosexuality prompted by his attendance at Ruth and Augustus Goetz's dramatic adaptation of Andre Gide's novel *The Immoralist*. Written in 1954, his critique rather daringly champions the homosexual cause. In describing the nature of homosexuality in drama, he states:

> The goal the Goetzes were making for was the open presentation of homosexuality and the open advocacy of a humane attitude to it. Up to now, as Gide told them in an interview, homosexuality in the theatre has been an accusation. Its standard form at present is, in fact, the unjust accusation; for our public has reached the point where it will allow the subject of homosexuality to come up, provided that the stigma is removed before the end of the evening. Our public motto is: tolerance—provided there is nothing to tolerate.[20]

He faults the adaptation for lacking Gide's personal connection to the subject matter. In criticizing gay-oriented works, Bentley believes strongly that gay stories should be told from the gay perspective. Without saying so, he could have meant his perspective. He complains:

> The Goetzes' play seems to have been conceived to carry a message of tolerance; if it does not spring from an understanding of the original *Immoralist*, it springs from sympathy for the married homosexual who wrote it. The play is a portrait of Gide seen through the spectacles of a generous humanitarianism.[21]

In the closet still as a gay man but posing as a liberal political activist, Bentley is defending the gay cause, defining the gay aesthetic, and identifying authors and critics as gay.

Bentley also discussed many issues concerning homosexuality in his critical monograph *What Is Theatre?* (1956). In this text, he challenges playwrights to tackle the subject with full force. In spite of, or perhaps because of, his own closeted stance, Bentley is critical of playwrights who deal with the topic of homosexuality in too tentative a manner and force their characters back into the closet by the end of the play. These remarks confused some critics who felt he was condemning the subject matter as inappropriate for the theater. In *What Is Theatre?* he responds to these charges:

> I was praised recently for having intimated that there was too much homosexuality in current plays, but what I meant to imply was that there was not enough. Having gone so far, our playwrights will have to go further; having inflicted the subject on us, they will have to say

something about it and not snatch it back out of our hands in the last scene with a speech or two about the wickedness of false accusations. *Third Person* by Andrew Rosenthal comes as a partial answer to my prayer.[22]

Bentley gives a glowing review of *Third Person* and concludes:

> Though going much further in honesty than other Broadway treatments of the homosexual theme, it does not go the whole way, and, in fact, through lack of candor about the primitive sexual needs of human beings, ends up—quite unintentionally, I imagine—as a defense of platonic friendship against sex. Such a notion is an evasion of the issue: homosexuality is validated on condition that it isn't sexual![23]

He also praises actor Bradford Dillman for not evoking stereotypes in his portrayal of the gay character, Kip. These arguments, uttered during the 1950s, prefigure the arguments of the Gay and Lesbian Association against Defamation some thirty years later.

Also in this volume, Bentley evaluates Tennessee Williams's *Cat on a Hot Tin Roof*. Bentley acknowledges that the play is one of Williams's first to present homosexuality as a theme. However, Bentley wants more. He criticizes Williams for backing off the gay cause:

> His [Brick's] father, however, explains that this [Brick's drinking] is an evasion: the real reason is that he is running away from his homosexuality. At this point, the author abruptly changes the subject (to the father's mortal illness) and never really gets back to it.[24]

Still later in his essay, Bentley makes a surprisingly insightful assessment of bisexuality and accuses Williams of ignoring this possibility.

> In the circumstances we can hardly be surprised that he [Brick's friend Skipper] proves impotent; yet he reaches the startlingly excessive conclusion that he is homosexual and kills himself. Surely the author can't be assuming that a man is either a hundred per cent heterosexual or a hundred percent homosexual?

Finally, Bentley asks the following loaded—considering his marriage of the time—question in regards to the credibility of the characters: "If a girl has a hunch that her husband is homosexual, does she simply clamor for him to sleep with her?"[25] In this, Bentley speaks from experience. With such insights, he cracks open his closet door.

As his own developing desires came closer to the surface, Bentley showed greater willingness to let down his primary professional facade.

As a critic, he could assume the pose of a figure more powerful than the vulnerable playwright. His posing allowed him to work within the status quo, within the political and social system. In doing so he was able to attain higher status, respect, and position. However, beneath these posings, one could find Bentley the artist, Bentley, the oppressed individual, angry, lashing out against an intolerant system. In his criticism, and increasingly as his repressed voice began to be heard in his plays, he championed underdog characters and disenfranchised groups and criticized the social order for being rigid and oppressive.

Bentley's emergence from the closet as a playwright was tentative. He was not capable, until *Lord Alfred's Lover,* of revealing enough of his personal life to be highly successful as a creative writer. His early works, few and far between, trade heavily on classical myth, which serves to preserve his straight facade as a critic and thinker who is merely dabbling in adaptation and not attempting to be a "full fledged" playwright. However, the workings of subaltern desire are nonetheless discernible in a technique we can identify as *queening,* a term coined by David Van Leer signifying the importation of rhetoric or motifs common to the queer community into heterosexual plots.[26] The choice of adapting Greek material itself, of course, is highly suggestive. This historical period was already associated in modern times with pagan rituals and homoerotic images and practices. Bentley adapted classical myths to depict a world that more closely resembled the contemporary 1950s, a world of sexual and political oppression, corruption, and the clash between spiritual and social mores. While he studiously avoided direct representation of homoeroticism, he treated themes of forbidden love and honor in the face of oppression that expressed transgressive passion even as they argued for containing it.

His earliest play, *Orpheus in the Underworld* (1956), focuses on an unsanctioned love and its consequences. In this play, Orpheus declares his passion for Eurydice in spite of the god Hymen's warnings. Once he declares his love, as Bentley himself had discovered when his inappropriate passion for the elusive Fred became apparent to school authorities, his fate is sealed. This play can be seen as a tribute to the honor and courage it takes to declare a forbidden love, or a defense for those who do not; a defense of the closet. Had Orpheus not declared his love, the gods would not have looked at him and Eurydice unfavorably. Had he respected the gods and controlled his passion in the underworld, he would have won her back. The lessons are clear. Self-control and self-restraint must prevail, the same as with the rules of the closet.

Bentley published two more Greek adaptations as companion pieces in 1967: *A Time to Live*, a twist on the Antigone story, and *A Time to Die*, an adaptation of the story of King Peleus. Like his *Orpheus*, *A Time to Die* depicts forbidden love and the fate of a political outcast. Antigone must die for her principles. Her truth is her inspiration. In contrast to the heroine of Sophocles, Bentley's Antigone does not stand up to Creon, but rather for him. She is ambivalent about her brother's condition. She is cajoled by Haimon and Tiresias to bury Polynices to restore the balance of power between Thebes and Argos. However, it is Creon, torn between his love for Polynices and his duty as king, who convinces her to bury Polynices, and she does so on Creon's behalf. Antigone is the only character in this play who is not in a closet. Creon is a humanitarian and family man posing as a tyrant. Tiresias is a political man posing as a philosopher. Haimon is a back stabber posing as a dutiful son. However, Antigone's act allows each of the three characters to protect his closet and she, alone, pays the consequences. Her honesty, her love for her family, her courage cost her her life. Antigone champions the truth, for which, she asserts, we must be willing to fight: "We have to keep some part of ourselves, and that the center, secure, inviolate, even at the cost of deadly battle with the dragon wherever we may find him, even coiled round a corpse."[27] In this play, those who maintain the closet survive but suffer a loss of dignity. The war continues without any of the three men standing up for his beliefs. They appear to be manipulative and conniving.

In the second play, *A Time to Live*, the honorable character, rather than being forced to die, is forced to continue his life as a leader. This is the story of King Peleus at the end of the Trojan War. His grandson Pyrrhus, along with Andromache, a Trojan, had sired a bastard son, Mollossus. His jealous wife Hermione and her lover Menelaus plot to kill Pyrrhus and his young child. Meanwhile, Peleus wishes to cede the throne to Pyrrhus, who agrees to ascend if Peleus will declare his bastard child a rightful heir. Upon the murder of Pyrrhus, Peleus decides to struggle against Menelaus, legitimize Mollossus and Andromache, and retain the throne in spite of his old age. Again, Bentley "queens" by emphasizing queer themes in a heterosexual context. A story of longing for social legitimization, his adaptation captures the stigmatization and demonization felt by gay men and lesbians before Stonewall. Significantly, Bentley's mythical outsiders, in spite of local prejudice, find sanctuary at the temple. While scorned by the political and social order, they are protected by the spiritual order. And when Peleus, representing honor and justice, finally validates them, he does so in the name of religion and family as well as throne: "Let our mourning be tempered with rejoicing! It is a token wherein I now take this child-son of Greek Pyrrhus, Trojan and Andromache—and on my sole authority declare him LEGITIMATE."[28] Prejudice, then, according to Bentley, need not necessarily be a function of church or state, but rather, of misguided individuals and societal mores.

In the years that followed, between Stonewall and *Lord Alfred's Lover,* Bentley dropped his poses one by one. His plays became more self-expressive and his political activism more candidly tied to his own gay life.

The Red White and Black (1970) was a transitional play, written immediately after and celebrating the message of Stonewall. With music by Brad Burg, it was a "stage show for a rock group of 4 musicians and about 10 singing actors. Its form was not that of a drama, but of a narrative poem."[29] Published in *Liberation* magazine in May 1970, it was reminiscent of the projects of the Living Theatre. The production contained highly political dialogues and songs condemning the Vietnam War, sexism, racism, and homophobia. He titled three successive songs in the piece "Be Gay but Be Careful," which told of the problems in picking up "straight" men; "The Male Bitch," which glorified male drag; and "Goodbye Christopher," which described a straight person's perspective on Stonewall. In a companion piece entitled *Vigilante,* Bentley wrote of homophobia and gay bashing:

And to appease your passions vivisectional,
Your tastes and sadistic and your raging hate,
The Lord your God has made the homosexual
for you to libel, beat up, and castrate.[30]

However, at the time of this play, Bentley, just as he did in his critical work years earlier, was still posing as a liberal heterosexual. He did not acknowledge his own homosexuality, and his attacks on capitalism and the U.S. government wrapped up his gay activism in a cloak of other issues. While he was writing from the closet, his work on behalf of "gay liberation" nonetheless came quickly on the heels of the Stonewall Riots, and was not echoed in much of the liberal theater and antiwar drama of the time. He also went further than he had before in depicting closeted gay individuals. Amid dialogue peppered with quotations by Walt Whitman, Oscar Wilde, and others, in a clever commentary on the "closet" itself, he attacked hypocritical anti-Communist henchman Roy Cohn. In particular, he compared Cohn to conservative and homophobic Cardinal Spellman. He never, however, directly exposed Cohn's homosexuality, strangely respecting Cohn's own closet, even though many in the gay underground of the time knew about Cohn's proclivities. Finally, he used many references that became the primary subject of his next play.

Are You Now or Have You Ever Been: The Investigations of Show-Business by The Un-American Activities Committee (1972) used actual characters and testimony from the hearings in a fictionalized format. This play was Bentley's strongest defense of the closet. While characters struggle to remain silent about their behavior and affiliations and to champion their right to privacy, a huge governmental conspiracy threatens them. They are asked not only to expose private information about themselves, but about others as well. In his preface, Bentley quotes William O. Douglas:

> The struggle is always between the individual and his sacred right to express himself on the one hand, and on the other hand the power structure that seeks conformity, suppression, and obedience. At some desperate moment in history, a great effort is made once more for the renewal of human dignity.[31]

Telling the tale of the end of privacy from the point of view of the closet was highly charged emotionally for Bentley. His characters were closet Communists, along with their friends and colleagues. Many of these people were linked similarly to the gay underground with which Bentley was undoubtedly linked. He knew these people, and they knew him. From Gertrude Stein and her coterie of artists and free thinkers to Jack Kerouac, Allen Ginsberg, and the beat generation, this underground group of artists, political leftists, and gays and lesbians had existed in some form or another throughout the twentieth century. The McCarthy hearings sought to destroy this way of life. This conservative backlash and its fallout had fueled tensions leading to Stonewall and to Bentley's personal coming out.

While Bentley's play champions privacy and an extension of the closet, it also advocates honesty and self-preservation. In the play Lillian Hellman explains it succinctly in her letter to the committee as she prepares to refuse to incriminate anyone other than herself:

> I was raised in an old-fashioned American tradition and there were certain homely things that were taught to me: to try to tell the truth, not to bear false witness, not to harm my neighbor, to be loyal to my country. . . . It is my belief that you expect me to violate the good American tradition from which they spring [by testifying against her friends].[32]

This speech becomes an emotional high point of the play. Hellman stands for loyalty and privacy. Bentley, in his closet, did, too. However, he also presents the argument for unabashed truth as it was articulated on the stand by actor Paul Robeson:

> I stand here struggling for the rights of my people to be full citizens of this country. And they are not. . . . You want to shut up every Negro who has the courage to fight for the rights of his people, for the rights of workers, and I have been on many a picket line for steelworkers too. And *that* is why I am here today"[33]

The Robeson quote seems to indicate an end to silence and double lives. Bentley, in true liberal fashion, begins to equate the struggles of the African American population with those of the gay community.

Interestingly, Bentley uses Elia Kazan as one of his characters. He remains steadfastly in support of the man and his work, though not his act of betrayal.

> Gadge Kazan, whom I knew fairly well at one time, is a great deal better than just likable. He abounds in good qualities. That makes any act of his that may not be good all the more important and significant.[34]

In the volume with *Are You Now* were two other historical plays with a decidedly socialist bent: *The Recantation of Galileo Galilei* and *From the Memoirs of Pontius Pilate*. According to Bentley, critics have offered a gay reading of *The Recantation of Galileo Galilei,* asserting that the relationship between Galileo and Castillo, the young priest, was more romantic than professional. Although Bentley denied any intention of implying a sexual relationship,[35] there is evidence in the text to support the interpretation of a closeted playwright writing a closeted character in a closeted manner. The only characters who exhibit trust and loyalty in their relationship, Galileo and Castillo are drawn as mentor/protégé in the Socratic tradition. In the opening discussion of Castillo, the following covert, but erotically charged, exchange occurs:

> *Sarpi.* This is one student.
> *Sagredo.* And one that likes you.
> *Galileo.* All right. Was this one student, drawn from the large class
>   of young people that likes me, ready for the news?
> *Sarpi.* He certainly was.
> *Sagredo.* I enjoyed every moment of it: *I'd* like to have him as a
>   student.[36]

In addition, dynamics of the closet can be read in Galileo's recantation, or lie, to save his life. Bentley quotes John Berger in his preface: "Today the hero is ideally the man who resists without being killed. Cunning, as the mental faculty which is the equivalent of endurance, has become, not the better part of valor, but certainly an essential one."[37] He then quoted Rabbi Eybeschutz in Feuchtwanger's *Jud Suss:* "It is easy to be a martyr. It is much more difficult to appear in a shady light to the sake of an idea."[38] The story involves Galileo's struggle with the Christian community over his assertion that the earth is not the center of the universe. In his insincere recantation of this belief, he becomes a scientist posing as a religious zealot. He realizes that the world is not ready for his teachings. The lie offers a closet from which he can go on with his studies.

Bentley continued to make the same claims regarding his own queer identity. In describing his outrage at Yale's dean of freshmen, he explained: "[I should have] gone straight to the Dean . . . and said [I] liked Fred and it was none of his damn business. But it was 1940, so I went to the bathroom, felt I was going to vomit, and actually had diarrhea."[39] He continued in defense of his closet: "My training, after all, was in history—You have to understand the period. And me as a man of my period. . . . [T]he Dean of Frosh was actually raising my consciousness while dutifully enabling Fred to stay virginal, or at least straight." Bentley, like his Galileo, was forced to mask his true nature to accommodate the unenlightened masses of his time.

From the Memoirs of Pontius Pilate depicts the story of the life and death of Yeshu (Jesus). In this version, however, Yeshu is a human being unhappily posing as a messiah at society's behest. He confides in Judas:

> Consider. The word Messiah has been in my ears since childhood. Whispered by every passing breeze. Mouthed by every would-be soothsayer. Palestine is a land of dreams but, oh Judas, I have cause to wish fewer of the dreams were about me. Not thirty and already folklore! Those fairy tales about my mother, my birth, my childhood and youth![40]

The play depicts Yeshu's spiritual journey to discover why he is a prisoner of this image. How others perceived him provides the fuel for his inevitable murder. At the end of the play, Yeshu is given the same choice offered to Galileo, recant or be killed. Before he can make the choice, however, he collapses and is carried off to what will be his death. The answers he searches for do not come during his lifetime. But Judas has hinted at the mystery's resolution, telling him: "If someday you conquer, you are the Messiah. The imperative is to fight on till someday you conquer."[41] Rather than unquestioningly assuming and hiding behind his socially determined pose, Yeshu persists in searching for his own identity. All of the other characters—Pilate, Annas, Caiaphas, Judas, and Herod—become what the world expects from them. They wear their masks. Only Yeshu, who aims for a deeper truth in selfhood, will survive beyond his life span.

Bentley published *Expletive Deleted,* a drama about the White House tapes, in 1974. This is yet another play about government corruption and the wages of deceit. Nixon undergoes the consummate "outing." While other plays have defended the closet, this one seems to proclaim truth at all costs. Nixon's public image is completely at odds with his behavior. He lives in fear of exposure by a sensational media. In the end, with the truth told, and a terrible price paid, he is able to resume a somewhat normal life. The play marks Bentley's increasing frustration with his own dishonesty as it depicts the country's distrust and discouragement over the government's lies.

The Kleist Variations (1978) consists of three plays that use the philosophy of Heinrich von Kleist to investigate the themes of death, suicide, and sexual roles. These plays, though drawing on the work of an author known to have desired other men, contain little or no reference to the sexuality of either Kleist or Bentley. However, the published version of *The Kleist Variations* contains an interview by the Voice of America, wherein Bentley defends his championing gay liberation. Though he does not specifically disclose his own identity, he leads the interviewer, and thus the reader, to wonder.[42]

Fuller disclosure comes in *Lord Alfred's Lover* (1981), which analyzes the complex relationship of Oscar Wilde and Lord Alfred Douglas. Bentley remarks that while most playwrights saw this as a story about Wilde's imprisonment, he sees it as a coming-out story, embracing both his own and Wilde's experiences. He claimed the title was a joke, an irony. Bentley's Oscar Wilde was not Lord Alfred's lover because he did not understand himself as a sodomite until the very end of his life. In this play, his first to deal with same-sex desire as a central theme, Bentley describes the nature of his own double life, his own closeted existence, through the historical characters.

Like Wilde, Bentley attempted marriage and fathered two sons. In middle age, at the height of his literary success, the pressures of leading a double life finally led to his coming-out process. He later defended his choice to get married:

It's not that you went into a marriage knowing for certain you are
gay and deceiving your wife. You went into a marriage, typically,
not being certain and thinking that because you like or love a
woman, you will very likely end up totally straight. And you had
every reason to be straight in those days. No wonder that people
misunderstood you. You hadn't understood yourself, and you gave
out mixed signals.[43]

Rather than the prison sentence Wilde's revelations precipitated, Bentley's coming out, coincident with the post-Stonewall gay liberation
movement, brought greater personal freedom.

His next gay-themed play, *Round 2* (1991), proved a more torturous
process for Bentley. No longer relying on borrowed or historical subjects,
he invented his characters' voices based solely on his memory and experience.[44] In addition, *Round 2* marked Bentley's professional and personal acknowledgment of his homosexuality. It was also the first of Bentley's plays to be produced in his native England. Based on the pattern of
Arthur Schnitzler's *La Ronde,* it is a round-robin of ten sexual liaisons
where one partner of one affair meets a new person for the next
encounter. Many critics believed that the play was not appropriate for
the post-AIDS period. In fact, the Glines, the gay producing organization,
rejected the work when it was first submitted in 1986. During the publicity blitz for the opening of this show, Bentley spoke publicly with the
Advocate. In this article, he responded to critics who claimed that *Round
2* promoted a negative "gay image":

I wanted to write about the give-and-take of fairly typical, ordinary
gay people in how they conduct their love life and to be perfectly
natural and simple about it. The dialogue is based on things I have
observed and remembered. I did not have any ax to grind or try to
set up any positive images. I don't want [the situation to be one in
which] when you say "gay" everybody shouts "hurrah."[45]

Mindful of the era, however, Bentley did not repeat the pleas for "hedonism" that he called for in *Lord Alfred's Lover.* In fact, to appease these
critics, particularly those from the gay press, he later added a subtitle:
New York in the '70's, thereby distancing his play from the AIDS and the
sex-phobic gay community of the early 1990s.

In the fall of 1991, Bentley followed up his *Advocate* interview with
one in the *Tulane Drama Review.* Here and in other interviews he discussed many of his views about gay life, gay theater, and the need to portray nonflamboyant, nonglamourous gay characters.

There's a straight public for flaming queens and for pretty boys, especially if the latter are dying of AIDS. What the public won't take is that someone on 92nd street, not particularly good looking and not all that youthful, is not straight and not dying.[46]

This resistance, he claimed, kept his play *La Ronde* from being successful. "I have ten characters in the play, and only one is a transvestite. The other nine are ordinary people, not in the sense of being contemptible or mediocre, but in the sense that they would not be immediately recognizable as gay or straight."[47]

In addition, Bentley dismissed the idea of serving as a gay "role model": "It's an overdone idea—we don't have to be surrounded by them." He further condemned the idea of outing to advance the gay cause. He stated: "Is Malcolm Forbes a role model simply because he is famous and rich? If a person hasn't come out on his own, he is ipso facto not a role model."

Further, Bentley decried the "campy" gay stereotype and the notion that "sexuality" is the cornerstone of the gay character: "It's very difficult now to show a gay character for whom being gay is not the whole of his character. You'd never portray a heterosexual for whom heterosexuality is the only trait he has."[48]

Most recently, Bentley has angered gay activists and theater practitioners by siding with Catholic University's censoring Tony Kushner's *Angels in America.*

My own position, public and private, is of course closer to Kushner's than John Paul's but that doesn't mean I deny Catholics their right to keep off their premises material which they deem inflammatory if not actually damnable. To not-choose a play is not to censor it. A Catholic College is not an ACLU Office.[49]

Bentley was amused by the many angry responses to his letter subsequently published in *American Theatre.*[50]

Finally, Bentley has championed the cause of older gays and lesbians. He stated in an *Advocate* article promoting *Round 2:*

I think the general assumption is that gay men disappear at age 30 or so. Even the word gay probably communicates a youthful image. The straight world has worked out a few things that we haven't yet. . . . There is no such thing as a distinguished faggot.[51]

Over three decades, Bentley, as playwright, activist, and gay man, has come out. The codes with which he was compelled to write his early

plays and criticism have largely disappeared. But he achieved critical
fame while writing from the closet. Speaking broadly in his *TDR* interview in 1991, he acknowledged the workings of a "homosexual component" in lives and theater before it was labeled:

> But of course there was a homosexual component in theatre long
> before there were plays about it, long before the term "homosexual-
> ity." In the past there could be homosexual activity, but it didn't
> make the active person a "homosexual." And the change in lan-
> guage makes the past very hard to get at. If a naive person says
> "where are the homosexuals in the past?" They are nowhere
> because the word is nowhere. But if you look for the activity you'll
> find it. Similarly if you look for a gay component in theatre, you
> may find it.[52]

"Looking for it" in Bentley's career reveals that his queer desire,
while submerged as well as exposed, has fueled his theatrical passions
and shaped his writing and, in turn, the public perceptions and artistic
aesthetics he has influenced.

NOTES

1. Michael Bertin, ed., *The Play and Its Critic: Essays for Eric Bentley*
(New York: University Press of America, 1986), 9.
2. Eric Bentley, interview by the author, New York, April 15, 1997.
3. Eric Bentley, *The Kleist Variations: Three Plays by Eric Bentley* (Baton
Rouge: Oracle Press, 1982), 70.
4. Bentley, interview.
5. Eric Bentley, *The Playwright as Thinker* (New York: World Publishing,
1955), 94.
6. Ibid., 97.
7. Ibid., 106.
8. Ibid., 182.
9. Ibid., 227.
10. Eric Bentley, *The Dramatic Event* (London: Dennis Dobson, 1954), 108.
11. Ibid., 109.
12. Ibid., 93.
13. Ibid.
14. Ibid., 108.
15. Ibid., 146.
16. Ibid., 103.
17. Eric Bentley, *The Cult of the Superman: A Study of the Idea of Heroism*

in Carlyle and Nietzsche, with Notes on Other Hero-Worshippers of Modern Times (Gloucester, Mass.: Peter Smith, 1969), 199.

18. Ibid., 198.

19. Ibid., 208–9.

20. Eric Bentley, *The Dramatic Event* (London: Dennis Dobson, 1954), 207.

21. Ibid., 199.

22. Eric Bentley, *What Is Theatre: A Query in Chronicle Form* (London: Dennis Dobson, 1957), 105.

23. Ibid.

24. Ibid., 59.

25. Ibid., 60.

26. David Van Leer, *The Queening of America* (New York: Routledge, 1995), 19.

27. Eric Bentley, *A Time to Die* and *A Time to Live* (New York: Grove Press, 1969), 51.

28. Ibid., 91.

29. Eric Bentley and Brad Burg "The Red, White, and Black," *Liberation,* May 1970, 4.

30. Ibid., 57.

31. Eric Bentley, *Rallying Cries: Three Plays by Eric Bentley* (Washington, D.C.: New Republic, 1977), x.

32. Ibid., 57.

33. Ibid., 71.

34. Ibid., 7.

35. Bentley, interview.

36. Bentley, *Rallying Cries,* 93.

37. Ibid., 85.

38. Ibid.

39. Bentley, *The Kleist Variations,* 68.

40. Bentley, *Rallying Cries,* 183.

41. Ibid., 194.

42. Bentley, *The Kleist Variations,* 67.

43. Gerard Raymond, "A Sage's Advice: Eric Bentley Muses on the Real Life Drama of Love and Sex," *Advocate,* April 9, 1991, 75.

44. Bentley, interview.

45. Raymond, "A Sage's Advice," 75.

46. John Luis DiGaetani, "The Thinker as Playwright: An Interview with Eric Bentley," *Drama Review* 35 (fall 1991): 90.

47. Ibid., 90.

48. Raymond, "A Sage's Advice," 75.

49. DiGaetani, "The Thinker as Playwright," 91.

50. Bentley, interview.

51. DiGaetani, "The Thinker as Playwright," 92.

52. Ibid., 90.

Designers and Dancers

The Electric Fairy

The Woman behind the Apparition of Loie Fuller

Bud Coleman

When she died, Loie Fuller (1862–1928) was mourned by the Parisian press: "a magician is dead," and "a butterfly has folded its wings."[1] "The famous creator of the serpentine . . . [has] closed her eyes to that light of which she had demanded so much."[2] Arguably one of the most famous performers in the world during the first quarter of the twentieth century, the years since Loie's death have shrouded this legendary woman in obscurity. The legacy of this American performer and designer has been problematized by the breadth of her multitalented artistry and her sexuality. Like the ephemeral light surrounding her on stage, her numerous accomplishments have vanished, leaving little documentation of her significance as actor, singer, dancer, choreographer, playwright, producer, costume designer, lighting designer, inventor, film director, museum founder, war relief organizer, and woman with homoerotic desires. Using her aged mother and later her dancing school as the "reason" she had no time for a heterosexual marriage, Loie was able to live without the prop of a man by her side; the last twenty-three years of her life she shared with her lover, manager, and artistic collaborator, Gabrielle Bloch.[3]

One of the few performers to enjoy sustained popularity with the public, critics, and fellow artists throughout her entire career, Loie Fuller at first glance appears a most unlikely candidate for this distinction. It is probable that no other performer in the history of dance has ever been able to transcend a portly frame and lack of dance training in the manner that Loie conquered the world. In a flattering article written for the *San Francisco Chronicle* in 1896, the reporter explained to readers that Loie was "not a sylph" but rather a woman "built like a column—round and firm and compact."[4] In 1900, Arsène Alexandre marveled at this "plump little, gay, bustling lady, drolly and naively careless in her dress" who could transform into "the marvelous dream-creature you see dancing madly in a vision swirling among her dappled veils which change ten thousand times a minute."[5] Wearing costumes of her own design made of hundreds of yards of gossamer-thin silk, Loie performed in a riot of color provided by multihued electric lamps, which she also designed. Incorporating innovative spatial arrangement, with her imaginative light and costume designs, Loie transformed herself into kinetic sculpture. She masked her corporeal presence with swirling fabric set ablaze in effervescent light: motion itself. As a woman who loved women, Loie had little interest in presenting a female dancer who was framed in a male heterosexual gaze. She fashioned not a stage persona—female dancer as object—but rather embraced the notion that she could present the essence of movement without the visible presence of the human body.

Several chroniclers of Loie's career agree with Clare de Morinni that her choreography did not survive her because she "had little personality of her own." Instead, "her essential talent was for stage decoration."[6] It is perhaps more productive to view Loie's choreography as spatial design rather than dance in that she was not concerned with steps, posture, gesture, and movement as vehicles with which to present her body to the public. Loie more than once articulated this idea, noting that " 'Light' and 'Color' thrown on great masses of silk, was my real representation and not dancing at all." Her performance utilized "rhythmical movement," which she "called dance for want of a more appropriate title."[7] Loie endowed fabric and light with the power, exuberance, and grace thought to belong exclusively to the dancing body.

The abstract nature of her work inspired radically different interpretations of her dances, positioning her work as the zeitgeist of different eras and artistic movements. *L'Art Nouveau,* with its whirling patterns of sinuous, curling lines, which celebrated women, plants, and flowers, saw in Loie's dances its art animated. Stéphane Mallarmé, the most important literary figure of the era, recognized her explorations into the emotional quality of color and proclaimed Loie to be the personification of Symbolist ideals by virtue of the metamorphic images in her dances.[8] Modern art enthusiast and critic Roger Marx saw in Loie's dances the spirit of the early Greeks: "the antique soul seems to be reincarnated."[9] The famous Parisian sculptor Roche (Fernand Massignon) stated unequivocally in 1903 that

> The luminous and naive Loïe Fuller dance is a product of American nature. The light effects are those of the unique atmosphere of the

Colorado canyons and only Florida butterflies in their flight, can compare with her graceful movements and the chaste and diaphanous floating of her draperies.[10]

Given the fact that Loie created every aspect of her performance with the exception of the music, Jules Claretie saw in her work the "theatre of the future . . . a feministic theatre. . . . if, as in Gladstone's phrase, the nineteenth century was the working-man's century, the twentieth will be the women's century."[11] Similarly, while some saw in Loie's fabric shapes that suggested flowers, fire, the wind, waves, et cetera, others could see in these undulating forms vulvar imagery, thus creating a highly charged erotic performance atmosphere. In a radical departure from typical critiques of dancers, observers of Loie's work were not moved to discuss her personality and/or her body on stage, but rather the physical manifestations of movement that they witnessed. The visions of this moving scenography of fluttering silk were, in a sense, neutral, allowing for multiple interpretations: art nouveau, Symbolist, Greek, American, feminist, erotic, and so on.

As Gilson MacCormack points out in Loie's obituary for *Dancing Times,* the story of Loie's "rise to fame is as dramatic as the most hardened reader of romantic fiction could wish for."[12] Unfortunately, a fair amount of the written work concerning Loie Fuller is exactly that, fiction—a situation she encouraged. As a producer, she rapidly learned the importance of publicity, so when there was no new dance, lawsuit, or illness to report, she would confide to a journalist some autobiographical tidbit that often contradicted her previous utterances. Loie offers her biographer no less than eight possible birth dates and countless renderings of other important events in her life. As subject and creator of her own career and the mythology surrounding it, Loie guaranteed that her historical record would be as open to interpretation as her theatrical presentations.

In addition to plethora of "facts" concerning Loie's life and career, contemporary critics have an additional hurdle in assessing her work because no one has successfully re-created her costumes, lighting, or choreography, and much about her personality and behavior is uncongenial to those who hold that she is significant as a performer, choreographer, and designer. While Loie lived in a lesbian relationship with another woman and actively promoted the work of other female performers, like other "first generation" New Women, she did not write about or discuss her sexuality, as did Natalie Barney, Renée Viviene, and

Radclyffe Hall. Loie also rejected the moniker of artist, often remarking to the press, "I suppose I am the only person who is known as a dancer but who has a personal preference for Science."[13] For years Loie maintained a laboratory employing six men who conducted experiments with light, color, and fabric. The celebrated astronomer Camille Flammarion arranged for Loie to become a member of the French Astronomical Society in recognition of her investigations into the physical properties of light. Loie's seemingly contradictory persona—innovative dancer/popular vaudeville performer, artist/scientist, chaste abstainer/lesbian, American/Parisienne—can only be understood if all facets of her life and career are examined.

The Creation of an Apparition

Born Mary Louise Fuller in Fullersburg, Illinois, a small town sixteen miles from Chicago, her family moved to the Windy City after Loie's birth (January 15, 1862). Loie made her theatrical debut at the age of four as Little Reginald in a Chicago stock company production of *Was She Right?* (as an adult she often performed boys' roles). Stints as a temperance lecturer and Shakespearean "reader" preceded her professional acting debut in 1877—at the age of fifteen—in a touring pantomime spectacle, *Aladdin.* In 1878 she made her New York debut in Dion Boucicault's *The Shaughraun,* moving on to various stock companies, vaudeville, and burlesque, producing a play she had written *(Larks),* and touring with Buffalo Bill. After a year as a member of London's Gaiety Theatre Company, Loie returned to New York to resume her sputtering acting career. In her autobiography, *Fifteen Years of a Dancer's Life* (1913), Loie describes her role in *Quack, M.D.,* where she had to perform a scene in which her character was hypnotized. Since actors had to provide their own costumes, Loie elected to wear a silk skirt an acquaintance had sent her from India.

> My robe was so long that I was continually stepping upon it, and mechanically I held it up with both hands and raised my arms aloft, all the while that I continued to flit around the stage like a winged spirit. There was a sudden exclamation from the house: "It's a butterfly! . . . It's an orchid!"[14]

Loie's imagination was far more persuasive than her memory—she told several different, highly dramatic stories of how she acquired her first silk skirt.

Loie's experiments with her skirt were variations on popular main-
stays of the vaudeville circuit. Performers of the nautch dance, commonly
attributed to India, Arabia, or Turkey, wore a full skirt made of translu-
cent fabric. More erotic than exotic, the silhouette of the body was visible beneath the sheer material as the dancer swayed her hips. The typical
skirt dancer emphasized the sinuous undulation of her arms and wore a
midcalf-length skirt to better showcase the technical virtuosity of her
feet. By radically increasing the size of the skirt, Loie took the emphasis
off the body, thus significantly changing the focus of these two popular
dances. As a thirty-year-old actress who was a little over five feet tall with
a tendency toward plumpness, she replaced the exotic, sensual appeal of
the nautch and skirt dances with patterns and shapes created by her
swirling silk garment. Loie, the costume designer, greatly assisted Loie,
the performer, by mitigating her physical imperfections.

Eager to capitalize on her triumph in *Quack, M.D.*, Loie met resistance from theatrical managers who knew her as an actress and singer,
not as a dancer. In the extravaganza *Uncle Celestin* (1891) Loie was at
last able to present her dance in a Broadway theater the way she had conceived it, in a darkened auditorium and illuminated by colored electric
lights following her own lighting design. Critics praised Loie, whose performance was "not a skirt dance, although she dances and waves a skirt.
It is unique, ethereal, delicious. . . . [T]he audience . . . insist upon seeing
her pretty piquant face before they can believe that the lovely apparition
is really a woman."[15] The manager of *Uncle Celestin* was grateful for the
publicity Loie generated while the show was on the road, but in New
York at the Casino Theatre Loie's name was absent from lithographs
advertising the show. When the manager refused to give Loie proper
billing and a promised raise, she quit the show at the end of its first week
and was replaced by another "serpentine" dancer, Minnie Renwood.

The balance of 1892 in New York saw nothing but repetitions of the
Uncle Celestin experience for Loie. Though singled out for praise by the
critics, theater managers refused to give her more money, better billing,
or artistic control. Nevertheless, Loie continued to promote herself with
awe-inspiring diligence, at one point scheduling performances in three
different theaters—two in Manhattan and one in Brooklyn—on the same
evening. Since she appeared between the acts of a comedy or musical, she
timed the evening so she could travel from theater to theater.

Loie realized that there was no interest in her native land in serious
dance; "The notion of going to Paris possessed me. . . . I wanted to go to
a city where, as I had been told, educated people would like my dancing

and would accord it a place in the realm of art."[16] Loie and her mother traveled to Europe, first performing in Berlin, Hamburg, and Cologne before they reached Paris, where she applied to the manager of the Paris Opéra, since he "ought to be receptive of innovations in dancing."[17] M. Gailhard offered her four performances a month since there were already "serpentine" dancers performing in Paris. Not only was this contract offer not acceptable to Loie, she was shocked to learn that one of the dancers was an American acquaintance, Mabelle Stuart. Loie convinced the management of the Folies-Bergère to dismiss her imitator. During the next eight days, while Loie prepared her own program, she danced in the great music hall under her own imitator's name. Loie made her formal Parisian debut November 5, 1892, with a forty-five minute program consisting of four solo dances: "Serpentine" (see fig. 17), "Violet," "Butterfly," and one later called "La danse blanche." One reviewer declared that Loie's performance was a "success without precedence in this theatre."[18] Opened in 1869, the Folies-Bergère had built its reputation with variety entertainment—acrobats, dancing girls, jugglers, wrestlers, animal acts, et cetera. While the nudes arrived later, the can-can did its part to excite male patrons. Loie not only was lauded by writers and artists, but as "La Belle Americaine" she was embraced by patrons who had shunned Montmartre's music halls for their bawdy entertainment. Loie single-handedly made the Folies-Bergère respectable by initiating matinee performances for women and children. Taking the city by storm, Loie's initial engagement ran over three hundred performances. She was also grateful that appreciative Parisians christened her "La Loïe," since *loie* means "goose."

Loie may have heard about the Parisian demimonde when she was in New York or performing in London, a place where she might escape the Victorian repression of a hetero-patriarchal world. While the fashionable salon world of the 1890s that Proust later immortalized, with its aged duchesses, wigged and rouged homosexual men, and homosexual women in tuxedos, did exist, there is no evidence Loie joined this world even after her spectacular engagement at the Folies-Bergère. While the South Bank set may have attended Loie's performances, they did not invite her to their salons. Whatever cachet Loie's fame and sexual predilection might have had, she was not rich, well read, or articulate. Indeed, even after living in Paris for thirty-six years she still could not speak the language fluently. Loie Fuller may have made the Folies-Bergère respectable, but this did not make her a great artist; she was the star of Montmarte, not the Paris Opéra. Just as she invented her own

FIG. 17. Loie Fuller in her original costume for the
Serpentine Dance, around 1891.

(Courtesy, Billy Rose Theatre Collection, New York Public Library for the Performing Arts.)

artistic medium, Loie created her own homosocial world, even though by the turn of the century there were Parisian salons that catered to European lesbians.[19]

Loie's choice not to express her sexuality openly in her choreography or design work was not a weakness, but rather a shrewd business decision. Painfully aware of the fate of Oscar Wilde and the 1918 "Cult of

Clitoris" scandal that broke out in London concerning dancer Maud
Allan,[20] Loie went out of her way to make sure that no hint of scandal
would compromise her public life or career. Even in libertine Paris, when
the marquise de Belbeuf and Colette performed a scene of lesbian love in
a pantomime skit at the Moulin Rouge in 1907, they were very nearly
arrested. At the age of sixty-five Loie tried to block the publication of
Isadora Duncan's autobiography because, as she told her lawyers, the
chapter that insinuated that Loie was a homosexual was "scurrilous and
false."[21] Loie had nothing against Isadora personally. Indeed, she
launched the young dancer's European career in 1901 and attended one of
her final concerts in 1926, even going so far as to get Isadora's autograph
on a program. But what Loie considered her private life was not for public consumption.

As a designer—of sets, lights, costumes, and movement—Loie was
unusual in that she put herself on stage. However, just as she edited her
public persona by omitting her sexuality, similarly she abstracted her performative physical presence. While some in the audience saw in her work
the sinuous "feminine" shapes of art nouveau, others reveled in the
power of the New Woman who technologized her body in order to
become pure energy: movement and light. Loie's matinees at the Folies-
Bergère—and indeed most of her performances for the rest of her
career—were attended primarily by women and children. These performances were considered by the press and advertised by promoters as
being "respectable," insinuating that there was nothing sexual in her performances. What most male critics undoubtedly missed was an ample
bosom, wasp waist, and a well-turned ankle, and therefore they saw
nothing sensual in a heterosexual context in Loie's programs. Women in
the audience, especially those with homoerotic desires, however, saw in
Loie's fluttering silk an abstracted display of feminine sexuality: fluid and
enveloping.

Loie's costumes not only obliterated her dancing body, but more
importantly provided a large surface to catch the ever-changing beams of
light she designed. Many of her early costumes (in the 1890s) were deco-
rated to provide a literal reference to the subject of each dance. The costume for the "Butterfly Dance" (1893) was emblazoned with the images
of seven large monarchs; Salomé's costume for her "Flower Dance"
(1895) was festooned with garlands of fabric roses; for "Dance of the Serpents" (1896) the skirt was painted to show numerous sinewy vipers flick-
ing their tongues at the dancer's waist. As Loie increased the complexity
of her lighting designs, her later costumes utilized natural silk without

ornamentation or dye, allowing the ever-changing light to "decorate" the garments. In 1894 Loie patented a costume design that incorporated wands (aluminum or bamboo) sewn into the silk that permitted "the folds of the garment to assume variegated and fanciful waves of great beauty and grace."[22] For "In Lys de Nile" (1895), Loie devised a costume containing five hundred yards of gossamer-thin silk; manipulating the fabric, she could send swells of cloth twenty feet up into the air.

The novelty of Loie's dance creations, and the popular success they enjoyed, spawned a host of imitators in America and abroad. In 1892 Loie unsuccessfully sued Minnie Renwood, her *Uncle Celestin* replacement, for infringement of her copyright; the New York Circuit Court denied protection because her dance did not fall within the meaning of a "dramatic composition" as defined in the Copyright Act. Two months into her initial run at the Folies-Bergère, three women in Paris and one in London were imitating her dances. To protect herself, Loie began to file patents, not for her choreography, but for many of the technical devices that formed a crucial part of her performance. Unfortunately, these safeguards did not stem the flow of imitators who were to vex Loie throughout her career. The most successful of the impersonators, Ida Pinckney—from Forest City, Iowa—often used Loie's name, or claimed to be Ida Fuller, Loie's sister-in-law.

In order to heighten the effect of her complicated lighting designs on her swirling silk, Loie darkened the auditorium and eliminated the use of footlights—practices by no means common in the 1890s. As she increased her repertoire of dances, she began to experiment with different spatial arrangements, starting with her own "black box": black chenille fabric formed the wings, borders, and backdrop, and black carpet covered the stage floor. For "Fire Dance," her most famous dance, Loie patented a stage setting (1893) that necessitated replacing a section of the stage floor with a plate of glass, which was then illuminated from underneath. Dancing to Wagner's "Ride of the Valkyries," Loie appeared to glow from within as the light played on her silk fabric. As the orchestra began to play, a dim, purple flame appeared to glow in the center of the stage. Animating the bottom of her skirt as the burning ember grew into a fire, Loie slowly began to raise the pole extensions in her costume. Matching the frenzy of the score, the silk, now red, yellow, orange, and magenta, moved faster and faster, leaping high into the air. Roche sighed, "Never will more splendid flames illuminate the triumph of an artist."[23] Jean Lorrain reported that Loie stood "in blazing embers, and did not burn," but exuded light.[24]

A variation on the glass floor for "Fire Dance" was Loie's use of a mirrored pedestal that made the dancer appear to float. The mirrored pedestal reflected the black draperies, thus elevating the dancer and concealing the structure used for this purpose. The pedestal was constructed with a glass surface so that light could illuminate the dancer from underneath. In 1895, she patented the "Mirror Room," a stage set of mirrors that formed a small octagonal room. This setting seemingly multiplied the number of dancers on stage and embellished the choreography since the reflected figures optically moved from one mirrored surface to another. While these patents protected various mechanical devices, the most important of Loie's technical secrets were safeguarded only by the confidence of her electricians; for many years her brother Burt was her chief electrician. To accomplish some of her spectacular lighting effects, Loie painted plates of glass with various pigments in abstract designs. She created further variations by altering the texture of the glass slide itself, and by projecting a light beam through two slides while slowly removing one of the plates. Critic Roger Marx was moved to praise "the opulent fairyland of light" that Loie created, basking in the "excess of beauty which results from a marvelous illumination and the intoxication to the eye that is given by the undulating nuances of the play of colors."[25]

Incandescent electric lights had been used in the theater for scarcely ten years when Loie made her debut at the Folies-Bergère in 1892. She was one of the first to recognize the potential of this new medium and to successfully exploit its possibilities; Adolphe Appia would not publish his first work on lighting for another three years. Loie understood the simplest principle of light, that to be perceived, it must have a surface on which to make contact. Instead of projecting light on a flat screen hung at the back of the stage, Loie transformed herself into a constantly changing, three-dimensional canvas. By enlarging the kinesphere of the dancer with pole extensions, and enhancing the fantastic shapes created by the silk fabric with her sophisticated lighting designs, Loie Fuller filled the stage with movement on a unprecedented scale. She had her electricians physically move light instruments about, as well as use revolving discs in front of the lamps to change colored slides. Her "Fire Dance" required fourteen electricians, and another necessitated thirty-six men, each assigned to his own lighting instrument. Fearful of imitators, Loie never wrote out a complete light plot or a master cue sheet. Instead, each electrician was cued during the performance by Loie's gestures, heel taps, and other signals arranged during rehearsal.

As her choreography, set design, lighting design, and fabric construction became more sophisticated, so did Loie's choice of music. First dancing to popular tunes, she now danced to Beethoven, Chopin, Delibes, Gluck, Mendelssohn, Purcell, Schubert, Schumann, and Stravinsky. Massenet gave Loie unrestricted performing rights to his music without royalty, and Gabriel Pierné conducted for her. Her sensitivity to music and her flair for the dramatic in many ways made up for her lack of formal dance training. Loie was not interested in choreographing a dance whereby the steps mirrored the rhythm and tempo of the music: "I try to follow the musical waves in the movements of the body and the colors. . . . Music is the joy of the ears; I would wish to make it the delight of the eyes, to render it pictorial, to make it visible."[26] For Loie, light and color were equal partners with the medium of choreography. By creating a visual analogue for music, Fuller liked to say that she could see music; Claude Debussy remarked upon witnessing Fuller dance to his *Nocturnes, Nuages, Fêtes, and Sirènes* that he had heard his music for the first time.[27]

To usher in the new century, the Exposition Universelle of 1900 was held in Paris to celebrate technological advances and French colonial expansion. Loie Fuller was the only American performer on the boulevard of cabaret theaters built for the fair. It is nothing short of remarkable that this plump, thirty-eight-year-old performer had become not only the most famous dancer in Europe, but also the undisputed queen of the exhibition.[28] While the Paris World Exhibition of 1889 viewed the Eiffel Tower as a symbol of the spectacular ascent of man, the 1900 exhibition located the source of this achievement in two structures at the base of the Eiffel Tower: the Palace of Women and the Pavilion of the Decorative Arts.[29] Roger Marx, inspector-general of French provincial museums, no longer embraced the wrought-iron architecture of the 1889 fair as the apex of modernity; rather he praised the feminine, interior world of craft arts. For Marx, the "soaring grace" of the exposed wrought-iron construction of the Eiffel Tower was replaced by the "soaring grace" of the dancer Loie Fuller.[30] But Loie was not the archetype of woman, she was a woman who controlled electric light. The *Hachette Guide to the Exhibition* explained

> The Palace of Electricity contains the living, active soul of the Exhibition. . . . Without electricity the Exhibition is merely an inert mass devoid of the slightest breath of life. . . . The magic fluid pours forth: . . . The soul of the Palace brings Light and Life.[31]

The abstract nature of Loie's dance allowed the art nouveau movement to see in her work their botanical and entomological flowing forms, but at the same time her use of this new "magic fluid" meant that Loie had created a truly new dance for a new century. Loie combined the three main attractions of the exhibition—Palace of Women, Pavillion of Decorative Arts, and Palace of Electricity—by presenting the New Woman framed by the shapes of art nouveau and brought to "life" by electricity.

The 1900 exposition celebrated two main themes, modern scientific advancement and colonial expansion. Pavilions representing France's nineteen colonies employed one simple marketing strategy: display of female sexuality to suggest the attainable, voluptuous charms of France's colonial holdings. As producer, Loie sought to capitalize on the European vogue for anything "oriental" by performing at the Paris exposition on a double bill with a Japanese troupe, featuring the actress Sada Yacco. Sir Henry Irving saw the company in Boston and wrote them letters of introduction; the press dubbed "Mme. Yacco, Japan's Ellen Terry" for her restrained acting style.[32] The stunningly beautiful Yacco, while undeniably perceived as exotic, was at the same time not presented erotically. As a dancer and producer, Loie managed to gesture toward exploitation of colonialist women, yet at the same time distancing herself from it. Rhonda K. Garelick notes that while Loie's "veil dances owed much to the Oriental 'belly dance' (prominently featured at the World's Fair), they actually involved no 'belly' at all." Loie's dances did not tantalize, for "they did not *un*veil any parts of her body."[33] The program presented at the Théâtre Loïe Fuller combined the antique Orient and the modern West without the commodification of the women who performed inside.

The years between her Parisian debut in 1892 and the exhibition of 1900 can be seen as the apex of Loie's career; in 1896 Loie returned to New York, no longer a struggling actress but the highest-paid performer in vaudeville, commanding a price double that of Lillian Russell. Loie was guaranteed one thousand dollars a night at Koster and Bial's Music Hall in New York City. On a bill with ten variety acts (comedians, jugglers, acrobats, etc.) Loie's thirty-minute set was so popular she stayed for four weeks at Koster and Bial's, performing six nights a week to full houses. Loie repeated this success in Boston. Historians later proclaimed that the 1895–96 season at the Boston Theatre had "doubtless never been equaled in a single season at any other playhouse in the world," because its roster of stars included Joseph Jefferson III, Nat C. Goodwin, Maurice Barrymore, Eleanora Duse, Helena Modjeska, Marie Dressler, John Philip Sousa and his band, the Boston Symphony Orchestra, Ignace Paderewski, and Loie Fuller.[34]

Loie was embraced by the general public, intellectuals, and artists, her popularity measured not only by strong box office but by the Loie

Fuller posters, scarves, jewelry, handkerchiefs, skirts, and lamps that flooded the shops. The core of her solo repertoire was created in this period, as her design aesthetic matured. Needless to say, not all of her experiments were successful.

Realizing the inherent limitations of restricting her repertoire to solo dances, Loie tried productions on a larger scale. With music by Gabriel Pierné and a libretto by Armand Sylvestre, the first of these extravaganzas was the pantomime *Salomé* (1895). Surrounded by a large cast and an elaborate set, Loie no longer appeared ethereal or mysterious. Critic Jean Lorrain saw only an "unhappy acrobat [who] is neither mime nor dancer; heavy, ungraceful, sweating and with make-up running at the end of ten minutes of little exercises . . . she manoeuvers her veils and her mass of materials like a laundress misusing her paddle."[35] With the premiere of the Oscar Wilde/Richard Strauss opera *Salomé* (1907), Loie staged a second pantomime, *Tragédie de Salomé* (1907), with a libretto by Robert d'Humière and music by Florent Schmitt. While the technical effects were universally acclaimed, Loie's performance as a mime was again deemed to be unsatisfactory.

For her first Salomé production, Loie conceived of the character not as the cold-blooded temptress of legend, but as a young girl in whom the "miracle of faith" had made "a mystical Salomé, chaste almost."[36] Loie had taken the most popular subject of the skirt and nautch dances, Salomé's Dance of the Seven Veils, and subverted its heterosexual construct. When she mounted a second version in 1907, the new libretto featured a Salomé consistent with other turn-of-the-century renderings— evil, seductive, voluptuous; Loie hetero-eroticized her second Salomé in order to align the character to popular taste. Loie's two Salomé productions were critical failures because her abstract dance form was unsuited to the presentation of a narrative story, and Loie was unsuccessful presenting a female stage character that inspired heterosexual eroticism.

The Woman behind the Veils

While fantasy clouds part of Loie's history, a vacuum exists concerning many details of her personal life. As with most of her personal alliances, the exact character of her first documented relationship is in question. When Loie was in her late twenties, she met Col. William Hays, the nephew of Rutherford B. Hayes. After a tour of the West Indies, which was partially produced by Hays, Loie owed him ninety-two hundred dollars. In May 1889, the two signed an unusual contract: "I William B. Hays, in the presence of God, do take Loie Fuller for my lawful wife."[37] When Loie sued Hays in 1892 for bigamy, it was revealed in court that there had never been a church ceremony and they had never lived together.

Before Loie brought her husband to court, Hayes had been spreading rumors around New York that Loie was a "monster of immorality."[38] During the trial, however, he issued the following statement to ward off a suit for slander: "I, William B. Hayes, of my own free will and accord, do hereby publish and declare that I firmly believe that Loie Fuller is free from all taint of immorality or misconduct of any kind."[39]

Regardless of how she lived her personal life in New York, once Loie established her dancing career in Paris, she was known by the European cultural world to be a lesbian.[40] She now surrounded herself with a homosocial world that she was able to maintain for the rest of her life: she employed women as secretaries, maids, chefs, and masseuses; established an all-female dance school; and ran an all-female dance company.

Fifteen years Loie's junior, Isadora Duncan had arrived in Paris with the same goal as her predecessor—to dance. When Isadora saw Loie perform in the 1900 exposition, she was impressed with this "luminous vision." "No imitator of Loie Fuller has ever been able even to hint at her genius! . . . She was one of the first original inspirations of light and changing colour. I returned to the hotel dazzled and carried away by this marvelous artist."[41]

When Loie saw Isadora dance to a Chopin prelude, she declared it to be "the most beautiful thing in the world," and subsequently invited Isadora to join a tour of Germany she had already booked for Sada Yacco.[42] Although Isadora was taken aback by the sight of Loie surrounded by a "dozen or so beautiful girls" who were "alternately stroking her hands and kissing her," she accepted the terms of the tour.[43] Isadora, embracing the ideal of New Woman and the equality of women in human relations, was no doubt attracted by the idea of this woman-centered world that Loie created and sustained, but Isadora soon found herself in situations she did not understand or could not control. In Leipzig, Isadora relates she was kissed "passionately" by a red-haired girl in the Fuller entourage called Nursey, "because she was always ready to soothe and nurse any one who had a headache."[44] "In spite of my admiration for the art of Loie Fuller," Isadora began to ask herself what she "was doing in this troupe of beautiful but demented ladies."[45] Nursey was assigned to be Isadora's roommate in Vienna: "About four o'clock in the morning Nursey arose and, lighting a candle, advanced towards my bed proclaiming, 'God has told me to choke you!' "[46] Isadora was able to escape even though Nursey "was hot upon my footsteps."[47]

While Isadora Duncan was writing her autobiography, *My Life*, she was involved in an intimate relationship with the notorious Mercedes de Acosta, whom Robert A. Schanke discusses in another chapter in this volume.[48] Although Isadora does not mention this relationship in her memoirs, she does note "that the highest love is a purely spiritual flame which is not necessarily dependent on sex," which included heterosexual and homosexual relationships.[49] Although not mentioned by name in *My Life*, Isadora was clearly describing Loie's lover Gabrielle Bloch[50] when she wrote about the "strange figure dressed in black tailor-made" who was in "the midst of these nereids, nymphs, [and] iridescent apparitions. . . . I was at once attracted by this personality but felt that her enthusiasm for Loie Fuller possessed her entire emotional force, and she had nothing for me."[51]

Regardless of whether Isadora took leave of Loie in Vienna because she "was frightened to death by my surroundings"—as she wrote in her autobiography—or because her romantic overtures to Gabrielle were rebuffed, it is clear that Isadora's career directly benefited from Loie's brief sponsorship. The Hungarian impresario Alexander Gross was so taken by the young American at one of Loie's arranged performances that he signed Isadora to thirty performances at Budapest's prestigious Urania Theater, which proved to be the triumphant beginning of her career in Europe.

Reflecting on her unqualified success at the Folies-Bergère, Loie would explain, "I was born in America but made in Paris."[52] Her 1892 debut at the Folies-Bergère not only launched her career, but "From that day on I had adventure after adventure."[53] Certainly one of the most important adventures in Loie's life was her relationship with Gabrielle Bloch. Gabrielle saw Loie perform in her first season at the Folies-Bergère; the fourteen-year-old Gab was so taken by Loie that she penned this tribute to the woman who wore "celestial robes": "Soul of the flowers, soul of the sky, soul of the flame, Loie Fuller has given them to us. Words and phrases avail nothing. She has created the soul of the dance, for until Loie Fuller came the dance was without soul! . . . The inanimate becomes animate."[54]

Beginning in 1905, Loie lived with Gabrielle in what was commonly known as a lesbian relationship.[55] This partnership attracted attention since Gab was sixteen years younger than Loie and always dressed in male clothing. Amid recollections of Sarah Bernhardt, Alexandre Dumas, Queen Marie of Romania, and Auguste Rodin, Loie devotes an entire chapter of her 1913 autobiography to her longtime companion and manager.

> For eight years Gab and I have lived together on terms of the greatest intimacy, like two sisters. . . . her voice is of velvet, her skin and locks are of velvet, her eyes are of velvet and her name ought to be *Velours*. If one could compare her to a living creature a boa constrictor would be most appropriate, for her movements are like those of a snake. There is nothing sinuous, nothing rampant about them, but the *ensemble* of her motions suggests the suppleness of the young adder.[56]

When Gab took up residence with Loie in 1905, she shared not only her private life, but was very visible publicly as Loie's business partner. Loie was involved in many different projects: producing herself and her dance company; producing artists like Hanako and Sada Yacco; orchestrating war relief work for France, Belgium, and Romania; promoting visual artists like Rodin; designing lights; directing films; and so on. While Gab operated primarily as Loie's assistant, on other projects Gab was independent of Loie. During World War I, the ambulance train running between France and Belgium was under the supervision of Gabrielle Bloch, and she was given screen credit for several screenplays she wrote for Loie.

When Loie died in 1928, she and Gab had lived together for twenty-three years. An indication of the public knowledge of their relationship can be gleaned from this condolence note written by Marie Curie:

> Dear beloved Gab,
>   I have just learned from the papers the sad news . . . I thought Loïe was getting better and can scarcely believe this sudden blow, so awful for all those who loved Loïe. . . . I embrace you very tenderly and very firmly, dear Gab, and think of you and of our Loïe.[57]

Loie would boast to reporters that she "was born to be a mother and to spend most of my days in the kitchen, but some strange perversity of fate led me to the motherhood of dancing."[58] Establishing a school of dance the same year her beloved mother passed away, Loie moved from daughter to "mother" without the complications of having children of her own. No doubt the formation of the school and a permanent company in 1908 were also motivated by Loie's advancing age; now in her midforties, Loie could no longer physically sustain an evening of solo dance. While Loie had been staging large company pieces since 1895, she had been the only "skirt dancer" surrounded by actors. With the formation of the school, Loie altered her dance-mime formula to choreograph for her dancers, her "instruments of light."[59] Loie's previous group works contained male and female characters, whereas with the formation of her school, she choreographed almost exclusively for girls and young women. (Over the thirty years of the company's existence, at least two boys danced with the troupe, yet the majority of the time it was an all-female group.) Abandoning the heavy sets and literal stories of her previous pantomimes, Loie transformed her young dancers into abstractions, going to the point of giving them new names: Peach, Buttercup, Smiles, Chocolate, Pinky, and so on. At the school, Loie encouraged her students to move naturally, to discover their own individuality, but on stage her pupils were to remain anonymous. In addition to foregrounding the group over the individual, Loie also choreographed many dances where the performers danced as much to each other as to the audience. This homosocial world possessed a homoerotic tension that was very different from the image of Loie performing solo. While Loie subverted the male gaze in her solo work by obliterating her body with yards of silk, her group works for young women delineated a woman-only world: the presence of a man was neither wished for nor necessary.

Critic Georges Pinoch saw the troupe in 1912 and remarked, "It seems to me that the little students of Loie Fuller are less attentive about being precise than the little girls instructed in dance by her illustrious emulator [Isadora Duncan]. On the other hand, they have a lighter grace, and with their wild little movements they create a whimsy that is more lithe and well-balanced."[60] Loie did not teach her charges specific dance steps, but rather principles of movement, as she explained.

> The difference between natural dancing and that promulgated by Isadora Duncan is that she teaches and dances the old Greek classic motions. It is something definite—something of form. Natural dancing is the conversation of the senses and the soul. Something in a bar of music suggests something to our mind, and accordingly our bodies shape themselves and move in sympathy with that idea.[61]

Upon Loie's death in 1928, Gab kept the school and the company going, ceasing operations only with the German occupation of France in 1940.

No less significant than Loie's relationship with Gab was her friendships with Queen Marie of Romania and Alma Spreckels, two relationships that fostered events of historical importance. Strikingly beautiful, Marie was the daughter of Alfred, duke of Edinburgh, and Grand Duchess Maria of Russia, making her the granddaughter of both Queen Victoria of England and Czar Alexander II of Russia. While still crown princess, Marie had seen Loie Fuller dance at the Roumanian National Theatre in 1902. Impressed with the performance, Marie invited Loie to perform at the palace. At the end of her engagement in Bucharest, Loie had not received a wire for funds that she needed to travel to her next engagement, in Rome. With an entourage of twelve and several thousand pounds of equipment to ship, Loie was in dire straits. Never one to shrink from an association with the powerful and mighty, Loie appealed to her new acquaintance, Marie, and the crown princess loaned Loie the funds to travel to Rome. Thereupon commenced a friendship and correspondence that was to last for the rest of their lives.

While Loie occasionally asked her society and royal acquaintances for assistance, Loie's nature was not to take advantage of these relationships. In the case of Marie, Loie rejoiced in the "artist's soul I met in the wilderness and saw in the sunshine of truth."[62] Loie not only devoted a considerable amount of energy in assisting Queen Marie, personally and politically, she also solicited the aid of others in the Romanian cause. Moved by the desperate situation in Romania, Loie came to Jassy and volunteered as a Red Cross nurse during World War I. For her war relief work, Loie received military decorations from Romania, France, and Belgium.

Grateful for Loie's charity work, their friendship was also a great sense of personal comfort to Marie: "I feel that you long to stretch your protecting arms over me, defending me against vices in ways I cannot grasp with my royal mind! God bless you Loie dear. Your Marie."[63] While a spirit of warmth pervades most of Marie's correspondence to Loie, several of the extant letters warn "Loïe Dear" that while the queen's love might be unconditional, the realities of her life placed limitations on their relationship.

> I do not wish you to be nervous when you write to me, all our friendship was based upon our great trust in each other. I must be disappointing sometimes, as you feel immense possibilities in me, but you can only fix half my attention in spite of the great work of love you are doing for me, in spite of my being the central thought of your existence. I have a separate life, am held by a thousand things we have never even had the time to tell each other.[64]

A product of the Victorian age, Queen Marie (1875–1938) clung to the romanticism of the nineteenth century in spite of the twentieth-century calamities she was forced to contend with. But in Loie, Marie not only found another idealist, but also a friend who supported her artistic efforts as a writer and painter. Marie gave Loie exclusive rights to make stage and/or screen productions of her short stories. One of Marie's fairy tales, "The Lily of Life," Loie not only made into a dance, but she later made into a film (1920).

While the Panama-Pacific International Exposition of 1915 marked Loie's successful return to the United States as an international star, it was also an event that brought Loie into contact with two wealthy American philanthropists. Alma de Bretteville Spreckels (1882–1962), the wife of sugar baron Adolph Spreckels, devoted herself to the cultural future of San Francisco by establishing the California Palace of the Legion of Honor and the Maritime Museum. Loie convinced her wealthy friend that Rodin's work deserved a place in San Francisco; the Legion of Honor's collection includes eighty-five works by Rodin donated by Mrs. Spreckels.

Railway and road construction magnate Samuel Hill (1857–1931) had circled the globe seven times and fought in both the Russian and German armies. As one of his many projects, Hill purchased seven thousand acres in the Columbia River valley along the Washington-Oregon state line with the intent of establishing a Quaker agricultural community. Undaunted by Maryhill's failure to attract settlers, Hill began work on a fortresslike home, its reinforced concrete walls soaring fifty feet into the air. Running out of enthusiasm and money, Hill abandoned work on the mansion, so Loie convinced him to turn it into a museum for French art. On July 24, 1917, Sam wrote to Loie, "After the eloquent pleading of today, I have decided to dedicate my new chateau at Maryhill, Washington, to a museum for the public good, and for the betterment of French art in the far Northwest of America. Your hopes and ideals shall be fulfilled, my dear little artist woman."[65] Hill, whose eccentric idealism surpassed even Loie's, later refined his ideas for the Maryhill Museum of Fine Arts, dedicating it to world peace, his daughter Mary, and the queen of Romania.

Bolstered by entreaties from Sam and Alma, Loie secured Queen Marie's promise to make her first visit to the United States in order to attend the museum's dedication on November 3, 1926. After a reception with President Calvin Coolidge, the queen boarded a special ten-car train

that transported her across the country. When the train halted in Maryhill, Washington, it was one hundred miles from the nearest city. On
board the train were two million dollars worth of paintings, statuary,
and memorabilia from the queen, intended for a museum that had neither windows nor a roof. Speaking before two thousand assembled
guests, Marie hid her disappointment and confusion and focused on
Hill's idealism, rather than on the architectural skeleton behind her. One
reporter was moved to write that the queen's address was "one of the
most dramatic and magnificent things this chronicler has ever witnessed,
and it is doubtful if any American public official could have the wit and
courage to seize a disaster as she did and turn it into a triumph."[66]

What influence Loie had over politicians and the wealthy patrons
who agreed to organize Queen Marie's United States tour quickly
eroded; the committee that she had assembled to promote the queen's
visit dismissed her. Despite her position on the museum's board of
trustees, Loie did not attend the Maryhill dedication ceremony for fear of
further embarrassing Marie. Whether forced by the committee or motivated by her wounded pride, Loie composed a press release that
explained, "I have nothing whatever to do with the visit and mission of
Her Majesty the Queen of Roumania except to manifest a lifelong devotion to one whom I consider the noblest woman in the world and any
statement to the contrary is false and unfounded."[67] Marie, aware of the
discord among her American organizers, though unable to keep Loie in
her entourage, nevertheless honored the dancer during the 1926 Maryhill
dedication.

> Some have wondered at the friendship of a queen for a woman
> whom some would call lowly. That woman is Loie Fuller. Her name
> has often been slighted. That woman stood by me when my back
> was to the wall. That woman gave me her life in my hour of need.
> She went all over America getting aid for my people. This has almost
> been forgotten by the rest of you, but I could no longer be silent. In
> this democracy, there should be no gap between the high and the
> lowly. As woman to woman, I wish there would be no doubt in any
> heart that that woman gave me hope.[68]

Queen Marie not only honored Loie publicly at Maryhill, she also sent
Loie a fifteen-page letter upon her return to Romania, acknowledging her
inability to prevent Loie being dismissed by the planning committee. In
this heartfelt epistle, the queen begs Loie not to let others destroy their
friendship.

The world is trying to tear us asunder, trying to make us misunderstand each other, to make us doubt each other, to make our interest clash. . . . [T]here is one grief I have not been able to put from me and that is the noncomprehension of our friendship by the world at large.

It has tried to ridicule it, to belittle it, to tear it up by the roots, to make me see absurdity in it—but all in vain, I am your friend still. . . . I suppose that there is a simplicity, a depth in our love and understanding, that the world, ever looking for complications, cannot comprehend. . . . They seek motives. Why this friendship? What can be my motive? and especially what can be yours?

There is a simple explanation, it can be given in one word: Love—But nobody believes that explanation, it is too simple, so they would rather stand by their scoffing! . . . Carry on, faithful Loie, grit your teeth, do not weaken, do not give way, your spirit is stronger than your tired body, your Love is greater than the hate which is trying to destroy you. . . . Your Marie.[69]

Sam Hill died five years after the museum's dedication and thus never saw Maryhill completed. It would remain unfinished for fourteen years, but Alma Spreckels took up the challenge, opening it to the public in 1940. Although *Time* magazine called it "the loneliest museum in the world,"[70] Maryhill houses an outstanding collection of works by Rodin (courtesy of Loie's negotiations with the artist), the Queen Marie Gallery featuring jewelry, furniture, and Russian icons donated by the queen, and the only permanent museum gallery in the world devoted to Loie Fuller, containing sculpture, drawings, posters and photographs celebrating the *Feé Lumineuse*.

Sam Hill's biographer, John Tuhy, raises the possibility of a love affair between Sam and Loie. Responding to one of her ideas concerning Maryhill, Sam wrote in 1923, "Your idea grows on me, as does my love for you." A month later, Sam reassured Loie that he had "finished" with love interest Alice Barton, hoping for an invitation to Paris.[71] While this correspondence in no way confirms or negates a romantic attachment, an interesting letter from Sam's son to a cousin in 1947 reveals no love lost between the Hill family and Loie Fuller.

I happen to remember that in my father's estate there were some drawings by Rodin, that were pronounced by experts as having no market value. They might have even been spurious, as they were sold to my father by the late Loie Fuller, who was a first-class chiseler, as well as being several other things of even more doubtful value.[72]

Having spent over twenty years of her life championing the work of artists such as Rodin, Théodore Rivière, Pierre Roche, Sada Yacco, Hanako, and even Queen Marie's short stories, Loie flirted with a permanent legacy of her own. In 1927 Loie began a flood of letters to Sam Hill soliciting his participation in founding a Loie Fuller Museum in Paris. Conceived as a Paris satellite of the Maryhill Museum, Sam was attracted to the idea but did not have the resources to undertake the venture. During the 1950s, Alma Spreckels tried to generate support to build a Museum of the Dance in San Francisco as a memorial to Loie Fuller, but twenty years had passed since the dancer's death, and Alma could find little endorsement for this project.

A Legacy of Light

Following the war, Loie organized many tours for her pupils, but her own professional appearances became less and less frequent. During the 1920s, Loie created a series of shadow dances for her students. Front and rear projections manipulated the dimensions of the stage and collaborated with her dancers in creating "optical conjurings." Loie's troupe had a great success in London in 1923 with *Ombres Gigantesques;* utilizing mammoth projections, an enormous hand appears to pluck at the dancers, while a giant foot descends to crush them later. The company returned to London in 1927 with the *Shadow Ballet,* a dance influenced by Loie's film experiments. At the age of sixty-five, this was to be Loie's last public performance. Loie died January 1, 1928, of complications brought on by pneumonia and breast cancer, and was buried in her beloved Paris. The location of her burial was in accordance with her wishes: "I like New York, but Paris has been kinder to me."[73]

All over Europe and America Loie Fuller was imitated, but never successfully, largely because of the care she took to keep secret the technical and artistic designs of her electric lighting. She choreographed over 135 dances, but they were (and are) impossible to re-create because there exists no record of the movement, the exact construction of the costumes, or light plots. In this day of computer-assisted special effects, Fuller's inventions may seem simplistic. But for late-nineteenth-century audiences, the opportunity to view stage lighting as something more than mere illumination was a "revelation of the peculiarly beautiful effects gained by a triple union of music, light, and the grace of wind-blown fabric," according to a reviewer for San Francisco's *Argonaut.*[74] Though Loie left behind no body of revivable choreography nor a codified dance technique, her legacy is nevertheless prodigious.

In the 1890s she darkened the auditorium, stripped the stage of scenery and footlights, and created decor using the movement of fabric and light. With her masses of silk and optical devices, Loie focused on movement, not on the dancer. Since Loie's dance was intended to be neither erotic nor sensual, her desexualized dances subverted the heterosexual gaze. By removing the visual presence of her body from the dance, she could more completely embrace the abstract, and therefore become whatever fantasy the audience wanted to project on to her.

Early in her career as a dancer, Loie was praised for signing "the death warrant of the high kick and the throbbing wobbles" of the skirt and nautch dances. In 1893, the *New York Herald* announced that Loie had created "a new dance," making other dance forms appear "stupid, commonplace, and old fashioned."[75] Despite acclaim while she was alive, most subsequent dance historians give only Isadora Duncan and Ruth St. Denis credit for originating the genre of modern dance. St. Denis sought to expand this view to include a

> maternal triumvirate . . . of contemporary dance pioneers. Isadora, Loie and myself. Although Loie was older than either Isadora or I, we were basically contemporaries and although we went our own ways and did individual things, we presided over the birth of a new era in the art of dance.[76]

Among the pioneers of modern dance, it should be remembered that Loie antedated them in the use of classic music for dance accompaniment, in her theory of "natural" movement to express emotion, in disposing of the corset as part of a dance costume, and in her training of young dancers.[77] Loie Fuller was also the first to devise an evening in the theater that consisted only of solo dance, without the addition of dialogue, songs, or commentary.[78] Fifty years after she had seen Loie dance at the 1900 exposition, Ruth St. Denis wrote,

> It was a revelation to me of what could be done with lights and veils—huge, incredibly-moving silk clouds—and the play of lights upon them. I have never forgotten her marvelous "Fire Dance" and, above all, "The Lily"—that almost-intangible shape rising in unearthly splendor from a base so that the whole effect was one of some magical lotus flower manifested out of thin air before our astonished eyes.[79]

Motivated by what she considered to be a cultural oversight, St. Denis created a dance to honor "La Loïe." "I have long felt that our acknowledgment, and therefore our gratitude, should belatedly go to one who brought a great gift to Europe and America—and one who, certainly has not received full credit for her labors in the Lord's vineyard of Beauty."[80] *The Ballet of Light,* presented with the Los Angeles Philharmonic Orchestra in the Hollywood Bowl, on August 3, 1954, was a "tribute to a great artist whose contribution toward lighting has yet to be acknowledged."[81]

Another artist influenced by the work of Loie Fuller was the painter and stage designer Pavel Tchelitchew. His memories of her performances inspired his designs for several Balanchine ballets, notably *Errante* (1993), with its dreamlike silk costumes and phantasmagorical lighting.

While Loie's performative work can be read as the theatrical manifestation of the New Woman, offstage she did not speak about women's suffrage. In contrast to the power of her on stage abstraction, the offstage Loie was not mysterious or ethereal; rather she was a short, dowdy woman with spectacles framing her big blue eyes. As one reporter commented in 1909, "One couldn't find anything affected about Miss Fuller with a microscope."[82] Loie Fuller lived the life of a liberated woman, but it was not a cause she championed for other women. Her arena was not the lectern, but the stage. Rhonda Garelick reminds us that on stage Loie transformed herself into a commanding apparition of light and movement and was "recognized as a lesbian by the worlds of art, music and literature," but was at the same time "viewed as a kind of sexless and spritely maiden aunt from America."[83] Loie's life was a study in contradictions: an American who lived in France for over thirty-five years and never learned to speak the language fluently; a portly woman with no formal dance training who fashioned herself into the most famous dancer in the world; a performer who not only paved the way for the modern dance movement, but who also had significant impact on light, set, and costume design; a theater artist who did not showcase the human body on stage, but rather the "charm of color and light."[84] For Mauclair the presence of these contradictory elements was liberating, since "Loie Fuller tears us away from the conflicts of ordinary life, and leads us to the purifying landscapes of dreams."[85] In his *Historie de la Danse* (1904), Ménil marvels at the suggestive poetry of Loie that transported her audiences on "the starry and luminous path of hashishien dreams."[86]

Loie knew that her dreams would not be realized in her lifetime. She told Andre Riguad in 1923, "I must be content to trace the path; but I am certain of being followed and someday one will realize the theatre of light, of which I have dreamed."[87] Prophetically, Queen Marie wrote Loie in 1927, "It may not be in this world that you will enjoy recognition." But she consoled her friend that "one day, when your long struggle will be over, you will enter a light more marvelous than all the wonderful lights that you, light's great master, lit for us poor mortals, here, on this suffering earth."[88]

NOTES

1. Quoted in John E. Tuhy, *Sam Hill—the Prince of Castle Nowhere* (Portland, Ore.: Timber Press, 1983), 224.

2. Quoted in Richard Nelson Current and Marcia Ewing Current, *Loie Fuller: Goddess of Light* (Boston: Northeastern University Press, 1997), 335.

3. Rhonda K. Garelick, "Electric Salome: Loie Fuller at the Exposition Universelle of 1900," in *Imperialism and Theatre*, ed. J. Ellen Gainor (New York: Routledge, 1995), 98.

4. "La Loie Fuller, Queen of Dancers," *San Francisco Chronicle*, November 13, 1896, n.p.

5. Arsène Alexandre, "Le théâtre de La Loie Fuller," *Le Théâtre*, August 11, 1900, 24.

6. Clare de Morinni, "Loie Fuller: The Fairy of Light," *Dance Index*, March 1942, 46.

7. Quoted in Current and Current, *Loie Fuller*, 339.

8. Sally R. Sommer, "Loie Fuller's Art of Music and Light," *Dance Chronicle* 4, no. 4 (1981): 394.

9. Quoted in Margaret Haile Harris, "Loïe Fuller: The Myth, the Woman, and the Artist," *Arts in Virginia*, fall 1979, 27.

10. Quoted in Harris, "Myth," 27.

11. Quoted in Loie Fuller, *Fifteen Years of a Dancer's Life* (Boston: Small, Maynard, 1913), 282.

12. Gilson MacCormack, "Loie Fuller," *Dancing Times*, February 1928, 686.

13. Quoted in de Morinni, "Loie Fuller," 47.

14. Fuller, *Fifteen Years*, 31.

15. Quoted in Sally R. Sommer, "Loïe Fuller," *Drama Review* 19, no. 1 (1975): 57.

16. Fuller, *Fifteen Years*, 46.

17. Ibid., 51.

18. Quoted in Margaret Haile Harris, *Loïe Fuller: Magician of Light* (Richmond: Virginia Museum, 1979), 18.

19. Shari Benstock, *Women of the Left Bank: Paris, 1900–1940* (Austin: University of Texas Press, 1986), 48.

20. Current and Current, *Loie Fuller*, 329.

21. Quoted in ibid.

22. Harris, *Magician*, 18.

23. Quoted in Harris, "Myth," 24.

24. Quoted in Frank Kermode, "Loïe Fuller and the Dance before Diaghilev," *Theatre Arts*, September 1962, 16.

25. Quoted in Harris, *Magician,* 20.

26. Quoted in Sommer, "Art," 390.

27. Sommer, "Art," 398.

28. Garelick, "Electric Salome," 85.

29. Debora L. Silverman, *Art Nouveau in Fin-de-Siècle France* (Berkeley and Los Angeles: University of California Press, 1989), 7.

30. Ibid.

31. Quoted in ibid., 299.

32. Quoted in Shelley C. Berg, "Sada Yacco: The American Tour, 1899–1900," *Dance Chronicle,* 16, no. 2 (1993): 168.

33. Garelick, "Electric Salome," 86.

34. Eugene Tompkins and Quincy Kilby, *The History of the Boston Theatre, 1854–1901* (Boston: Houghton Mifflin, 1908), 442.

35. Quoted in Harris, *Magician,* 20.

36. Quoted in ibid.

37. Quoted in Morinni, "Loie Fuller," 41.

38. Quoted in Current and Current, *Loie Fuller,* 36.

39. Current and Current, *Loie Fuller,* 39.

40. Garelick, "Electric Salome," 98.

41. Quoted in Isadora Duncan, *My Life* (New York: Liveright, 1927), 95.

42. Fuller, *Fifteen Years,* 228.

43. Duncan, *My Life,* 94.

44. Ibid., 97.

45. Ibid.

46. Ibid., 98.

47. Ibid.

48. Ann Daly, *Done into Dance: Isadora Duncan in America* (Bloomington: Indiana University Press, 1995), 170, 249.

49. Duncan, *My Life,* 285.

50. Bernice Scharlack, *Big Alma: San Francisco's Alma Spreckels* (San Francisco: Scottwall Associates, 1995), 53.

51. Duncan, *My Life,* 96.

52. Quoted in Patricia Failing, "Loïe Fuller, Art Nouveau Muse," *Antiques World,* September 1979, 50.

53. Fuller, *Fifteen Years,* 58.

54. Quoted in ibid., 264–65.

55. Current and Current, *Loie Fuller,* 120.

56. Fuller, *Fifteen Years,* 250–51.

57. Marie Curie, letter to Gabrielle Bloch, undated but c. 1928, Maryhill Museum of Art archives.

58. " 'La Loie,' Flitting about Her Hotel Room, Describes Her Art," *Musical America,* September 11, 1909, 3.

59. Quoted in Morinni, "Loie Fuller," 51.

60. Quoted in Sommer, "Art," 396.

61. "Flitting about Her Hotel Room," 3.

62. Quoted in Hannah Pakula, *The Last Romantic: A Biography of Queen Marie of Roumania* (New York: Simon and Schuster, 1984), 340.

63. Queen Marie, letter to Loie Fuller, May 30, 1921, Maryhill Museum of Art archives.

64. Queen Marie letter to Loie Fuller, March 23, 1921, Maryhill Museum of Art archives.

65. Sam Hill, letter to Loie Fuller, July 24, 1917, Maryhill Museum of Art archives.

66. Quoted in Pakula, *The Last Romantic,* 353.

67. Quoted in ibid., 345.

68. Quoted in Tuhy, *Sam Hill,* 244.

69. Queen Marie, letter to Loie Fuller, March 15, 1927, Maryhill Museum of Art archives.

70. Quoted in Earl Clark, "Sam Hill's Castle in the Columbia," *American West* (April 1988): 40.

71. Tuhy, *Sam Hill,* 224.

72. James N. B. Hill, letter to D. B. Hill, February 5, 1947, Maryhill Museum of Art archives.

73. "Evolution of Dance," *New York Herald,* August 27, 1893, n.p.

74. "La Loie," review of La Loie Fuller and Her Famous Artists, *Argonaut,* June 5, 1915, 370.

75. "Evolution of Dance," n.p.

76. Quoted in Walter Terry, "The Legacy of Isadora Duncan and Ruth St. Denis," *Dance Perspectives,* Winter 1960, 31.

77. Morinni, "Loie Fuller," 51.

78. Daly, *Done into Dance,* 62.

79. Ruth St. Denis, program for *The Ballet of Light,* August 3, 1954, Hollywood Bowl, New York City Public Library at Lincoln Center, Dance Collection.

80. St. Denis, program, n.p.

81. St. Denis, program, n.p.

82. "Flitting About Her Hotel Room," 3.

83. Garelick, "Electric Salome," 98.

84. Quoted in Current and Current, *Loie Fuller,* 339.

85. Quoted in Garelick, "Electric Salome," 90.

86. Quoted in Harris, *Magician,* 22.

87. Quoted in Sommer, "Loïe Fuller," 67.

88. Queen Marie, letter from to Loie Fuller, March 15, 1927, Maryhill Museum of Art archives.

"Not as Other Boys"

Robert Edmond Jones
and Designs of Desire

Jane T. Peterson

In the 1910s and 1920s, Robert Edmond Jones (1887–1954) led the vanguard of scenic artists who were adapting the European design principles of Adolphe Appia, Edward Gordon Craig, and Max Reinhardt to the American theater. The "New Stagecraft," as the American incarnation of these principles came to be known, transformed design from a slavish reliance on literal reproduction into a suggestive evocation of a drama's essence. With its emphasis on simplification and mood, Jones's designs strove for a "poetic, total theatre"[1] rather than an iconography rooted in imitation.

During the first two decades of his career, Jones's theories and designs had a far-reaching impact on commercial and experimental theater alike, including a number of historically significant "firsts" in American theater. His improvised setting for *The Glittering Gate* in 1914 launched the Washington Square Players; he set the stage for two one-act plays in Hutchins Hapgood's house that were the initial productions of the Provincetown Players in the summer of 1915; his designs for Harley Granville-Barker's 1915 production of *The Man Who Married a Dumb Wife* are acknowledged as the first incarnation of the New Stagecraft on the Broadway stage; his designs for Vaslav Nijinsky's 1916 *Til Eulenspiegel* marked the first time that an American had designed for the famed Russian Ballet; and his 1917 direction of Ridgely Torrences's *Three Plays for the Negro Theatre*, the first time that black actors had performed on Broadway in dramatic roles, has been acclaimed as "the most important single event in the entire history of the Negro in American theatre."[2] He designed for venues as diverse as the Neighborhood Playhouse and the Theatre Guild, the American Laboratory Theatre and the Metropolitan Opera. Extensive collaboration with producer-director Arthur Hopkins, in addition to working with a variety of other commercial producers like

Jed Harris and Brock Pemberton, infused the principles of the New Stage-craft into the commercial Broadway theater. As colleague and mentor, his association with other numerous designers (most notably Donald Oenslager, Jo Mielziner, and Mordecai Gorelik) helped assure that his ideas were assimilated by future generations of American scenic designers.

Despite Jones's significance as one of the influential forces shaping the style of modern American theater practice, his life and work have yet to be fully explored and documented. Apart from a smattering of schol-arly articles and unpublished dissertations, there are no comprehensive analyses of his designs; no biography has been written to date, and most details of Jones's personal life remain hidden from public scrutiny. To complicate matters, his papers at Harvard University appear, to this writer, to have been sanitized of virtually all personal references, and the manuscript Jones had been working on just before his death was report-edly burned by his sisters.[3]

The paucity of personal information arouses one's curiosity, if not suspicions. What is *not* disclosed and *why?* To find answers to such ques-tions, the researcher is required to explore the gaps among the facts that are known about the subject's life. One must identify patterns that emerge from the accretion of these gaps and explore the subtext within the silences. One also becomes adept at interpreting innuendo as well as cautiously embracing rumor and gossip, which can contribute to an oral history.[4]

My long-held suspicion that the gaps in the story of Bobby Jones's life were, at least in part, a function of his very closeted homosexuality was affirmed by a particularly authoritative oral transmission of histori-cal information. A well-known senior theater scholar who wishes to remain anonymous provided confirmation of Jones's homosexuality to Kim Marra, one of the coeditors of this volume. During our source's graduate studies in the late 1940s, he was friends with an older gay man, who, prior to pursuing an advanced degree, had been one of Jones's assis-tants for many years and had gleaned direct knowledge of Jones's per-sonal life. This former assistant arranged for Jones to visit the school, and it was in the context of this visit that the former assistant revealed Jones's homosexuality to our source. While one utilizes knowledge gained through the theatrical grapevine with a healthy degree of trepidation, it is this kind of information upon which gay and lesbian history must often rely. When combined with the known facts of Jones's life and work, this friend-of-a-friend variety of oral history is an indispensable tool in the project of more fully recovering Jones's contributions to theater history.

If, as the evidence suggests, much of Jones's personal life was intentionally concealed by his family, one must look at what was surreptitiously revealed about the artist in and through his work. In light of Jones's stature as a scenographer and theorist whose work has affected generations of American designers, it is incumbent on us to begin to decode the dynamics that animate this work.

It is the purpose of this article to read (or more accurately, to reread) the text of Jones's early career and creative work to help reveal the private person behind the public persona. An overview of Jones's early life, the years prior to his sojourn in Zurich to enter psychoanalysis with Jung, provides the context for an investigation of the period encompassing his most significant design work. Four productions (*Macbeth, The Hairy Ape, Desire under the Elms,* and *The Great God Brown*) are then examined in closer detail to reveal the dynamics of desire to which Jones gives visual expression.

Primarily as a designer and occasionally as a director, Robert Edmond Jones continually employed the tools of his trade to explore his own subaltern desires that were frequently concealed behind a veneer of heterosexual respectability. Both his art and his life reveal a tension between Jones's puritanical New England upbringing and his transgressive sexual desires that found expression in pre- and postwar New York and its theater. This article examines how Jones's subverted desires served as both a source of conflict and of inspiration, shaping his artistic production into a coded palette of homoerotic desire. While time and space constraints do not allow a complete analysis of his work or life, this study suggests ways that future investigations can employ Jones's subaltern sexuality as a lens through which to read both his life and work.

As Jones scholar Dana Sue McDermott astutely observes in her detailed examination of the artist's preprofessional life, the conflicted dynamic between Jones's practical, puritanical New England background and his (impractical) passion for the theater was a powerful, formative force.[5] Born in Milton, New Hampshire, he was the son of Fred Jones, a farmer who preferred cultivating his mind to cultivating the soil, and Emma Cowell Jones, an accomplished pianist who gave music lessons to children in the area.[6] Another significant influence on the young Bobby Jones was his grandmother, Emma's mother and a former teacher of Latin, English, and drawing, who lived in the Jones household.

The young Bobby Jones clearly inherited the familial aptitude for literature and the arts. He read voraciously, played the violin, and by the age of nine was resolved to be an artist, owing in large part to the materials and tutelage provided by his grandmother.

While these artistic talents and literary aptitudes would eventually serve him well in his chosen vocation, they set him apart from other boys his age. Bobby's life of the mind was in sharp contrast to the more physical activity preferred by his peers. "When schoolwork and chores were done and his two brothers raced to the river to fish or went off to join a game of baseball at which they both excelled, Robert was allowed, if he chose to, to practice, or sit and draw, or to disappear into the barn cupola to read or dream his interminable dreams."[7]

Despite the idyllic description of Jones's rural childhood conjured up in Mary Furber's biographical essay, the reality for Jones was something "large and terrible, an almost Lincolnesque life."[8] Images of his grandmother's "Jehovah-like wrath" pervaded a home filled with "its secret, interior drama—the drama of strong, devoted, violent, cross-grained characters."[9] The discomfort the young artist felt amid these powerful familial forces was only compounded by his alienation from his peers as the young Jones "heard it murmured . . . that he was not as other boys."[10]

Jones found an environment more amenable to his needs and desires when he entered Harvard University on scholarship in 1906. Its urbane atmosphere must have come as a great relief to the aesthetic New Hampshire boy. He played violin in the university orchestra, designed posters and costumes for Harvard theatricals, and devoured the theater and dance performances in the Boston area before graduating in 1910.

While the family initially encouraged Jones's artistic interests, his desire to pursue art as a career ultimately put him into conflict with his family's expectations for a "practical" career choice along the lines of his brothers: Charles was an insurance agent in Yonkers, and Philip chose the ministry (eventually becoming pastor of a major Presbyterian church in Manhattan). A pragmatic solution appeared to be a career in portraiture, but two more years of halfhearted efforts as a graduate assistant in Harvard's Department of Fine Arts ended in failure.

After leaving Harvard in 1912, Jones moved to New York and was able to reconcile his own artistic needs with his family's expectations by pursuing a career in theatrical design. "Theatre was sheer pleasure to [Jones], something his puritanical inheritance refused to allow him to think of as a career. When he at last succeeded in combining design and painting with theatre, he was profoundly grateful."[11] On a professional level, at least, his internal struggle between subjective desires and objective authority was resolved.

Jones's professional talents first manifested themselves in a passion for fabrics and costumes. "He loved colors and materials and liked to handle them."[12] Not only did this passion for costume suit his new career, but it also provided an outlet for his flamboyant persona. Considered a "character,"[13] often a code word for homosexual, Jones was given to posing à la Oscar Wilde (fig. 18). He affected long hair and a long beard, and "[h]e posed a good deal—to himself as well as to others; he did not have any individuality of his own yet so he borrowed one."[14] Nor did he sustain any one pose for very long but used his chameleon-like propensity to adopt his identity to current circumstances. "The truth is that even intimate friends of this innovator scarcely know how he looks, for his looks, like his personality and his achievements in the theatre are constantly being formed and reformed out of the mutable substance of the times."[15]

Despite Jones's talent with fabric, his new career as a costume designer for theatrical producers Ray Comstock and Morris Gest was short lived. Jones quit in anger after Morris Gest reportedly walked on some of the designer's sketches that had been lying on the floor. The proud young artist ended up sleeping on park benches, where Harvard classmate John Reed found him.[16]

In early 1913, journalist and political activist John Reed (who would later document the 1917 Russian Revolution in *Ten Days That Shook the World*) was investigating the Paterson, New Jersey, silk strike for *The Masses*. He was also the lover of wealthy art patron and socialite Mabel Dodge. Through the largess of Reed and Dodge, Jones was given a place to live and the opportunity to design and stage his first New York production.

Mabel Dodge had instituted her famed salon at 23 Fifth Avenue in 1912 as a means of mitigating her boredom. Melding the bohemian and radical elements of Greenwich Village with the bluebloods of New York society, Dodge's gatherings included blacks and whites, "socialists and anarchists, Freudians and free-lovers, artists and activists."[17] Fluid boundaries and transgressive sexualities were tolerated, if not welcomed. Carl Van Vechten, an openly gay married man and Dodge's close friend, had encouraged the salon's creation. Jones found this atmosphere so much to his liking that he took up residence in one of Dodge's guest rooms.

To a young man conflicted by the psychic struggle between social expectations and personal desires, 23 Fifth Avenue must have been a haven. Located two blocks from Washington Square, Dodge's apartment was near the geographic hub of Greenwich Village. By 1913 the Village had become "the most famous bohemian community in the country."[18] Its reputation for "tolerating nonconformity (or 'eccentricity') . . . held

FIG. 18. Robert Edmond Jones at work. Although undated, the photo was most likely taken after 1926.

(Courtesy, Billy Rose Theatre Collection, New York Public Library for the Performing Arts.)

out the promise of making the Village a safe and even congenial place for homosexuals to live."[19] As noted by Susan Clark in her essay in this volume, Barnes also sought sanctuary and anonymity in the Village during this same period. As bohemians or homosexuals, both Jones and Barnes were free to be themselves in this new home.

Not all of Dodge's salon guests were bohemians or bluebloods, however. Radicals of all stripe were welcomed, and one notorious guest was "Big Bill" Haywood, leader of the International Workers of the World (IWW). His socialist politics inspired Dodge to mount a pageant depicting the plight of the striking silk workers in New Jersey. Madison Square Garden was rented and Jones was charged with designing the sets and staging the action. "'Our Bobby Jones,' as Reed began to call him, insisted on making it a Gordon Craig affair."[20]

Since Dodge and Reed intended to leave for Europe immediately after the pageant, they raised money in the name of the "Robert E. Jones Transportation and Development Company," which allowed Jones to accompany them. Van Vechten joined them in Paris, and "Carl was maliciously charmed with Bobby and tormented him—teasing him playfully, frightening him dreadfully—the New England ascetic."[21] When Jones's hopes to study with Edward Gordon Craig in Italy were not realized, he went instead to Germany, where he studied informally at Max Reinhardt's Deutsches Theatre in Berlin until forced to return with the outbreak of World War I. Although Jones was familiar with the theoretical writings of Craig, Appia, and Reinhardt prior to his European journey, it was during this trip that he became immersed in their practical application.

Returning to New York in 1914, Jones again took up lodging in Dodge's apartment, and their symbiotic relationship provides valuable insight into Jones's associations with women. Dodge, the world-weary socialite, admittedly used the young designer to assuage her ennui. "Bobby made me forget this [sense of futility] sometimes. He was so young-minded, so full of fantasy. . . . his vitality bubbled up in ecstasy and enthusiasm. I had little of this at the moment so I borrowed his. In this way we are all vampires sometimes. I really dipped into Bobby's pool of life and drank."[22] Jones, on the other hand, "attached himself to me and I became his mother."[23] This maternal bond was strengthened after Jones, who nearly died from a ruptured appendix, was saved, he believed, by Dodge's having willed him back to life. "He said I had created him, that I was his real mother."[24]

The security of Dodge's home and maternal protection allowed Jones the freedom to fully channel his transgressive passions into the theater. He was no longer constrained by the repressive atmosphere of his own family, which forced those passions into hiding. And their relationship was mutually satisfying; Dodge clearly fed off Jones's passions and vitality, helping her to endure her privileged, if emotionally unfulfilled, life. Despite the fact that Dodge was only eight years Jones's senior, their interdependent needs were clearly platonic and not sexual. As a matter of fact, Dodge noted that Jones had difficulty forming affectional relationships with other people; he "couldn't understand anyone's having any *personal* feelings about anything when there was so much to do in the theatre. He was always one or [*sic*] those for whom real life is unreal and only stage life true."[25]

Jones was intent on immersing himself in the "true life" of New York theater and quickly made a name for himself and for the theories of the

New Stagecraft. His critically acclaimed designs for the New York Stage Society's presentation of Harley Granville-Barker's production of *The Man Who Married a Dumb Wife* (1915) launched his professional career and heralded a new voice in the theater. One of the opportunities ensuing from this success was the commission to design Vaslav Nijinsky's 1916 production of the ballet *Til Eulenspiegel.* Jones referred to the collaboration as "an experience so novel and so startling that it altered the course of my entire life"[26] and designated a particularly "bitter moment" as the point at which "my belief in myself as an artist is born."[27]

Jay Scott Chipman's essay in this volume notes a similar transformative experience for lighting designer Jean Rosenthal. The sensual moving body of a dancer on stage not only aroused same-sex desires in both artists but also provided inspiration for their work. However, Rosenthal's artistic relationship with Martha Graham could be compared to a mutually beneficial affair of many years, while Jones's artistic association with Nijinsky was more like a tempestuous one-night stand. Despite the differences in duration, the impact of innovative, even transgressive, dancers on the two designers was truly transformational and lasting.

Working on the *Til Eulenspiegel* project must have appealed to Jones on several levels. The plot, taken from German folklore, follows the exploits of a roguish prankster who defied the customs and conventions of the common folk until he was arrested and hanged. Til's defiance of social authority reiterated Jones's own essential conflict: the struggle between transgressive behavior and repressive authority of social convention. Even Til's use of disguise (priest, professor, clown) was reminiscent of Jones's penchant for changing his personality as well as his fashion.

Of course, the opportunity to work closely with the famed danseur would have held the greatest appeal for Jones; the transgressive nature of both Nijinsky's art and his personal life must have been irresistible to the young designer. In a reminiscence consisting of a series of "flashbacks," Jones offers glimpses of their volatile time together: from the exhilaration of mutual creativity that carries them "far into the night" working at each other's elbow to being the brunt of the famous danseur's hatred and rage when the sets first are brought on stage. Even thirty years after the experience, the powerful, often conflicting emotions that Nijinsky evokes are palpable. Although it is ostensibly a record of artistic and cultural miscommunication, the subtext can be read as a narrative of lovers' short, turbulent relationship. However, without further evidence, one can only speculate on the exact nature of this clash of genius.

Another, more grounded and less fiery relationship also developed from the Granville-Barker production of 1915. Jones's designs for that production so impressed fledgling producer Arthur Hopkins that he hired the young artist for his Broadway production of *The Devil's Garden* later that year. This began a collaboration between the two men that spanned three decades and numbered forty-seven productions.

Philosophically, Jones and Hopkins were cut from the same cloth. Both had traveled in Europe in 1913 and had been deeply affected by the theories of Max Reinhardt and Gordon Craig. Stripping the stage of unnecessary clutter, each propounded the belief that design should serve only the needs and themes of the play, and each strove for artistic integrity, which they placed above commercial potential. The aesthetic principles and idealism that guided Hopkins's producing career were clearly compatible with Jones's vision of the theater, forming "a natural fusion"[28] between the two men.

Any relationship of such duration and depth should be read for its homoerotic connotations, which are unmistakably suggested in Hopkins's effusive description of their emotional bond. "The angels that watch over our destinies occasionally reveal a rare gift for casting. It is not only marriages that are made in Heaven."[29] Obviously, their bond went well beyond the boundaries of a business association and into the realm of emotional connection.

Both the personal and professional aspects of the Jones-Hopkins relationship merit closer scrutiny in future studies. Although Hopkins was married to actress Eva O'Brien, it must be determined if their relationship was more a social convenience than a physical commitment. It would also be productive to investigate if the homoeroticism, even latent homoeroticism, in the Jones-Hopkins relationship found expression in their professional work. For example, did their alliance with lesbian actress Alla Nazimova for two Ibsen plays in 1918 allow a forum for a queer aesthetic to be disseminated on the commercial stage?

While these and other insights into their relationship remain to be decoded, there is one clear advantage that Jones did reap from his alliance with Hopkins. Due in large measure to the commercial and critical success of their early collaborations, Jones was accorded full membership in the male-dominated world of the theater, which, as queer scholar George Chauncey reminds us, was a very gay world indeed. "The degree to which men participated in the gay world depended in part on their jobs. Some occupations allowed men to work with other gay men in a supportive atmosphere, even if they had to maintain a straight façade in dealing with customers and other outsiders. Men who worked in the . . .

theater industry, among other occupations, often found themselves in such a position."[30]

As rewarding as Jones's personal and professional associations with Hopkins may have been, by 1923 he felt the need for a distinct turn away from the commercial theater and toward the avant-garde. Teaming up with playwright Eugene O'Neill and critic-producer Kenneth Macgowan, the three formed the Experimental Theatre. Jones's friendship with Macgowan went back to their undergraduate years at Harvard (he had worked on Macgowan's production of *The Scarecrow*), and the two men had toured Europe together in 1921 to assess the state of theater in several countries. The result was *Continental Stagecraft* (1922) with text by Macgowan and illustrations by Jones. The artist's association with O'Neill was of a more recent vintage, however, stemming from their collaboration on Hopkins's productions of *Anna Christie* (1921) and *The Hairy Ape* (1922).

The Triumvirate, as the Experimental Theatre came to known, sought a theater whose focus was experiment in production. A phoenix that arose from the ashes of the original Provincetown Players, "It [was] to be a directors' theatre, as it had been a playwright's."[31] It was under these auspices that Jones was able to hone his skills as a director—first as a codirector with James Light and later as solo director. As "stage director in chief" Jones was able to assume considerable control over the selection, conception, and direction of the plays presented, especially the successful productions of O'Neill's *Desire under the Elms* and *The Great God Brown*.

This last production culminated the collaboration of the Triumvirate and denoted the beginning of a significant change in both the life and work of Jones. Before the play closed, he had left for Zurich to undergo psychoanalysis with famed analyst Carl Jung and was entertaining the possibility of abandoning the theater altogether. McDermott, who has written extensively of Jones's relationship to Jungian psychotherapy and theory, suggests that Jones was going through what Jung refers to as a midlife crisis, an intense period of questioning one's basic values and making major changes in one's way of living.[32] The periodization of Jones's life into pre- and post-Zurich, therefore, is a convenient demarcation for both his life and work.

Biographers have noted that Jones underwent a profound change at this time, but little speculation has been given to the nature of that change. While the details of his extended analysis with Jung may never be fully revealed, it is plausible to suggest that the psychic struggle between

Jones's inner, homoerotic desires and the outer, social prohibitions against any form of transgressive sexuality that dominated his upbringing had reached a crucial impasse.

Jones's personal life provokes intriguing questions, but it is his work that provides tantalizing insights into his homoerotic desires and psychosexual conflict. A look at four significant pre-Zurich productions—*Macbeth* (1921), *The Hairy Ape* (1922), *Desire under the Elms* (1924), and *The Great God Brown* (1926)—suggests ways homoerotic desire permeates Jones's work. Each production explores the intense psychic conflict between transgressive desires and the boundaries of social acceptability, the same conflict with which Jones was struggling.

The dynamic emerging from the collision of inner, subjective needs and outer, social expectations as played out in productions of the pre-Zurich period reveals a designer in the throes of creative and personal exploration. While Jones was pushing the envelope of aesthetic style and visual form, his own psychic struggle was being disclosed on stage. A similar struggle is evidenced in the work of Djuna Barnes, according to Susan Clark. Barnes's "theatre of 'restraint'" also explores the inner worlds of her characters through a verbal and visual modernist poetics not unlike Jones's New Stagecraft. Both artists utilized their theatrical skills to express the hidden truths of their lives.

All four of Jones's productions discussed here explore transgressive desires and the fatal consequences of acting on those desires. The productions also progress from abstract representation toward more realism, thereby bringing the struggle out of the scenographic closet, if you will. They also reflect a movement away from the constraints of commercial theater (objective demands) and toward a greater degree of creative control for the designer (subjective desires). *Macbeth* was designed for Arthur Hopkins as a commercial, Broadway production. Although *The Hairy Ape* was produced under the auspices of the more experimental Provincetown Players, Hopkins held the rights to the play, thereby creating a situation of shared production credit: Hopkins codirected with James Light and Jones codesigned with Cleon Throckmorton. The last two plays, however, were produced by the Jones-Macgowan-O'Neill triumvirate, an experimental situation in which Jones was able to exert considerable control as both designer and director.

The 1921 production of *Macbeth* was one in a series of plays that the Hopkins-Jones team created with the Barrymore dynasty. They had scored a critical triumph the previous year with their adaptation of Shakespeare's *Richard III,* starring John Barrymore, and they had every reason to believe that their success would be replicated with the Scottish play starring Lionel Barrymore. Unfortunately, however, the same critic who praised Jones's designs for *Richard III* as "incomparably the most beautiful Shakespearean investiture this country has known"[33] also forecast (not unlike *Macbeth's* weird sisters) that "we are all always absurdly haunted by the fear that Mr. Jones is about to overstep himself."[34] And overstep himself he did, as *Macbeth* became Jones's first critical failure.

Critic Alexander Woollcott's first impression of *Macbeth* was one of "shock" that the designer would, in Woollcott's estimation, focus attention on the design at the expense of the play.[35] His less-than-flattering review is valuable, however, for providing a vivid verbal description of Jones's design.

> [Jones] has set upon the stage certain cubistic properties which, not in themselves but in their present association, are quite horrible imaginings. An Inverness that looks like a fiercely extracted tooth, a Dunsinane that suggests waste-basket cuttings strewn through space, a path for the sleepwalker that threads its way through gewgaws which may strive to suggest the graveyard of her hopes but which actually suggests a forest of giant snowshoes battered by storm.[36]

Woollcott applauded Jones's aesthetic objective to move out of the two-dimensional world of theatrical realism into a three-dimensional, sculpted environment for actors, and he felt that Jones had accomplished this objective, at least in several memorable moments, in the designs for *Richard III*. What he objected to in *Macbeth* was Jones's "half-hearted, irresolute effort to do more—when, to be both mystical and exact, he tries to move out of three dimensions into four."[37] *Macbeth* did, indeed, try to do "more," but rather than moving in the direction of mysticism as suggested by Woollcott, one must read the production as an overt movement into psychological exploration.

The inner, psychic focus of the production was clearly articulated in a *New York Times* article Arthur Hopkins wrote prior to the production's opening. Seeking to liberate the Shakespearean drama from "its vessel of tradition" and to realize the universality as "a play of all times and all people," he and Jones chose a highly stylized and psychologically charged production concept. Claiming no concern for the

> conscious motives that have been ascribed to Macbeth and Lady Macbeth . . . we believe the real causes were deeper seated than conscious motive, and, furthermore, that the same causes exist today in

all people . . . that strong people can be picked up by forces they do not understand, are helpless to combat, and by which they are dashed to utter destruction.[38]

While these forces that lead to "utter destruction" appropriately are never specified, it is apparent that these inner forces—transgressive desires and needs—are in conflict with outer social constraints and morality.

It is interesting to note that, at the time of the production, both Hopkins and Jones were in psychoanalysis with Dr. Smith Ely Jelliffe, an eclectic therapist who employed dream interpretation among his analytical techniques.[39] The stylized, otherworldly quality that pervaded the production was undoubtedly influenced by these analytic experiences. The opportunity to explore the inexorable forces of desire and identity confronting the Scottish thane would have been compelling to both men at this point in their lives and careers.

Macbeth, introduced in absentia as a hero to be rewarded for his bravery and nobility, is seen as much more human and less heroic two scenes later. The witches' prophecy that he would be king is enough to whet his lust for power, thereby forcing Macbeth into an identity conflict. At the same time that he desires the throne, he fears the very thing he desires, as his wife so astutely observes: "art thou afeared / to be the same in thine own act and valor / as thou art in desire" (I.vii.39–41). To obtain the object of his desire, Macbeth must transgress the laws of nature and society by committing the crime of regicide. Desire comes with a high price, and it is Macbeth's internal struggle between wanting and fearing that propels the action of the play.

As a psychological portrait of fear and desire, Jones's production design reflected the Scotsman's interior landscape. In our post-Beckettian age, the theatrical depiction of abstract psychological terrain is familiar territory, but with the theater of the early 1920s only slowly emerging from the grip of literal presentation, the Jones-Hopkins depiction was baffling and disquieting to audiences. Unlike the design concept for *Richard III*, which, for all of its abstraction, was still grounded in a recognizable reality, *Macbeth* operated on a wholly symbolic level. For *Richard III* Jones had employed a variation of a unit set; during most scenes, a large, looming structure suggestive of the Tower of London provided the background. In *Macbeth*, however, the bonds of reality were severed and replaced with symbolic shapes more suggestive of mood and emotion than of a specific time or place. The acting area was described as "a glowing platform in space,"[40] a territory of intense light enveloped by a black void. The cones of light illuminating the stage offered sharp contrast to the surrounding darkness and allowed characters to walk in and out of the light, shadowy figures haunting the recesses of the space. Woollcott's "extracted tooth" was, in fact, a series of tilted, triangular shapes, suggestive of Renaissance arches piercing the darkness, simultaneously indicative of vaulting ambitions and skewed motivations.

Perhaps the most provocative scenic elements in the production were three huge silver masks suspended over the stage in both the witches' scene and the banquet scene. These forms were enlarged versions of the masks worn by the witches; with abstracted eyes and mouth through which light eerily glowed, they presided over the action on the stage. Suggestive of the omniscient fates who possessed men's souls, their resemblance to human skulls also accentuated the psychological dimension of Macbeth's struggle.

The struggle with identity in addition to the attraction/repulsion dynamic of desire articulated in the action of *Macbeth* were patterns with which Jones would have found great identification. However, the production of O'Neill's *The Hairy Ape* (1922) provided Jones an artistic environment within which to objectify his own struggle more openly.

Eugene O'Neill's *Hairy Ape* depicts the hypermasculine world of firemen or stokers on a steam-powered ocean liner. The opening scene, set in the bunk area, immediately establishes an all-male milieu of drunk and noisy seamen, many of whom are stripped to the waist. Functioning as both sleeping quarters and recreation area, O'Neill's first scene melds the public with the private into an image of homosocial intimacy.

Despite his middle-class background, the all-male domain of rough, raw, working-class laborers was attractive to Jones, who felt "a kinship of some sort . . . with miners, truck drivers, working people and the down-and-out."[41] This erotic attraction also motivated the popular phenomenon of "slumming" that gave middle-class men "a chance to cultivate and explore sexual fantasies by opening up to them a subordinate social world in which they felt fewer constraints on their behavior."[42] The opportunity to depict this all-male world of tough seamen onstage (slumming on a grand and graphic scale) would have been irresistible to Jones's middle-class homoerotic desires.

The sexual implications of this social milieu are reinforced by the stoker's other domain located within the bowels of the ship: a geographical concept referred to as the "stokehole." The term *stokehole*, referring to the space about the opening in a furnace or boiler, is taken from the

Dutch *stoken* meaning "to poke." While too obvious for further comment, the sexual connotations of this and many other nautical terms (*seaman, stoker*, etc.) must not be overlooked. Nor should one ignore the well-known fact that the homosocial world of sailors is a space of considerable homoerotic activity, both at sea and on land.

In the noisy underbelly of the ship, the massive engines that propel the ship are fed with coal; the mechanized, modern world is maintained only through the intense physical labor of these beasts of burden. Pervasive parallels between the men and apes reiterate the level of physical need and animal instinct at which these men operate. Drink and the camaraderie of fellow stokers provide life's pleasures; women or "goils," depersonalized by the men who refer to them simply as "skoits," are not needed or wanted in this masculine world. The companionship and sense of belonging engendered by this male milieu are sharply contrasted to women's essential unfaithfulness. "Dey don't wait for no one. Dey'd double-cross yeh for a nickel. Dey're all tarts, get me? Treat 'em rough, dat's me. To hell with 'em. Tarts, dat's what, de whole bunch of 'em."[43]

O'Neill's characters, with the exception of Yank, function as types rather than individuals and are distinguishable primarily through their ethnic accents. This deliberate avoidance of characterization creates an image of undifferentiated masculinity. Despite his simian similarity to other stokers, Yank is set apart from them by his powers—albeit limited—of reason. Yank's need to "tink" places him in a position of ambiguity that is manifested in feelings of displacement. Yank desires a "home," a place to belong. It is likely that Jones experienced a strong identification with Yank, who was "not as the other men."

Yank's sense of displacement is exacerbated by his encounter with Mildred Douglas, an emissary from the normative society, whose intrusion into Yank's world only intensifies his desire to belong. The Jones-Throckmorton designs for the ship's forecastle graphically depicted this collision between desire and an authority that threatens that desire. The space where Yank felt most at home became an expressionistic reflection of the stoker's inner self. As the conflict between his desire to belong and the social forces that threatened that desire intensified, a pattern of crisscrossing right-angled pipe cutouts became progressively distorted, the angles increasingly skewed.

The grotesque exaggeration of Mildred and her aunt as anemic and artificial further enhanced the production's expressionism: inertia replaced energy, and posturing displaced sincerity. This expressionistic technique culminated in scene 5, when Yank invades their Fifth Avenue world. Gaudy décor and masks were used to accentuate the artificiality of the uptown denizens. The stylization and use of masks placed the inner/outer conflict in bold relief: the outer, artificial self is frozen into an exaggerated facade, a dramatic and theatrical technique that Jones and O'Neill explored more fully in *The Great God Brown.*

O'Neill's class critique is also embedded in the play's binarism between the manufactured and natural worlds that operates most potently in the images of entrapment: the free and natural animal is set in opposition to the man-made world of steel ships and cages. Yank's ambiguity reflects a similar position between the natural and manufactured. Despite his claims of identification with the new world ("I'm steel and steam and smoke and de rest of it"),[44] he cannot escape his true animal-like self. He is trapped, belonging to *both* worlds and *neither* world at the same time. Yank's desire to fit in, to belong, ultimately takes him to the gorilla cage at the zoo. As a tragedy of desire, his identification with the ape can be read as capitulation to his most instinctual needs or transgressive physical desires. However, just as in *Macbeth,* succumbing to those desires has fatal consequences. The resolution of the psychic struggle between the inner and outer selves comes at an extremely high price.

Yank's psychic exploration mirrored Jones's own desire to belong within a comfortable homosocial world despite intrusive social pressures from family and social norms to thwart that sense of belonging. Jones operated in both worlds but was apparently not comfortable in either. O'Neill's expressionistic script, however, provided Jones the opportunity to objectify this psychic landscape on stage in a more overtly homosocial expression. As the second O'Neill play of his design career, it also afforded Jones greater familiarity with the emerging playwright's ideas and themes.

The affinity that designer and playwright shared for the psychosocial themes being explored in O'Neill's plays was motivation, at least in part, for the formation of the Triumvirate. In addition to the artistic freedom this new coalition provided Jones, it also allowed Jones and O'Neill to work in a close, collaborative environment. Apart from a thematic affinity, it is interesting to speculate on Jones's possible homosexual attraction to the handsome writer. Whatever the nature of this affinity, however, it proved mutually beneficial to both men, as evidenced by the triumph of *Desire under the Elms* (1924).

Produced in the Experimental Theatre's second season, *Desire under the Elms* was the fifth collaboration between designer and playwright. It was, however, the first O'Neill play that Jones single-handedly directed.

Steeped in the theories of Craig and Reinhardt, Jones propounded the concept of a production as a unified entity emerging from the vision of a single creative artist. Working principally as a designer, Jones was limited in his ability to achieve his objectives. Within the structure of the Triumvirate, however, Jones was able to merge the three functions of producer, director, and designer, providing him the venue within which to fulfill his vision.

Desire under the Elms was the perfect vehicle for Jones to exercise his creative vision. The tale of transgressive desire and lust was set amid the stony soil of a nineteenth-century New England farm, a background not unlike his own New Hampshire roots and one he shared with the playwright. A tragedy of Oedipal sin modeled on Euripides' *Hippolytus* and Racine's *Phaedra,* O'Neill's rendition of the ancient myths explored the nature of desire in many of its manifestations. Peter and Simeon Cabot lust for their freedom from the thankless toil on their father's farm. When Eben Cabot buys their share of the land, they waste no time in setting off for the West, the American symbol of limitless freedom. Eben's desire, on the other hand, is to possess the farm despite his father's claim to the same. Ephraim Cabot, flinty patriarch of the all-male family, desires soft companionship. When sleeping in the barn with the cows no longer satisfies that desire, he sets off in search of a mate. Each of the Cabots wears his desires on his sleeve; lust for land as well as lust for the services of Min, the neighborhood whore, are proudly proclaimed. This bold expression of their desires must have appealed to Jones, who knew no such freedom in his childhood home full of "secret, interior drama."

Abbie Putnam, the young woman Ephraim marries, also desires the farm, contesting Eben's claim and bringing a new level of subtlety into the expression of desire within the Cabot household. As the object of Abbie and Eben's desire shifts from the land to each other, they must try to hide that desire. Even the truth about the birth of their son must be hidden as they convince Ephraim that it is his offspring. The secreted, closeted nature of the young couple's transgressive love is fully revealed only after the child is murdered and they are led off to prison.

Despite similarities with the two previous plays (especially the severe punishment for the expression of transgressive desires), *Desire under the Elms* displays a distinct thematic progression: desire is overtly sexual in nature. In *Macbeth* the transgressive desire was objectified as lust for temporal power; in *The Hairy Ape* the desire for belonging, the need for a home, can easily be read as a desire for a homosocial world, but the sexual nature of that desire is still subverted by social norms. In *Desire under the Elms* social norms are flagrantly flouted as the illicit love is not just desired but acted upon.

Jones's production design for *Desire under the Elms* moved away from the more abstract and stylized concepts of the two earlier plays to be firmly grounded in the memories of his childhood. The wholly symbolic presentation of Macbeth's interior landscape and the expressionistic presentation of homosocial desire in *The Hairy Ape* are replaced with bold strokes of stark realism. The less abstract, but no less symbolic, design for *Desire under the Elms* was a continuation of the inner/outer dynamic explored in the earlier plays. Although based on O'Neill's suggestion and sketches for the play, the design "bears a strong resemblance,"[45] including its buff color, to Jones's family home in New Hampshire. He created a two-story New England farmhouse whose exterior walls could be removed to reveal the four rooms on the interior of the house: the more public kitchen and parlor downstairs; the private area of the sons' bedroom and Ephraim's bedroom upstairs. Through the removal and replacement of the wall units, the action (both physical and psychological) within the house could be disclosed. For example, as Eben's and Abbie's mutual distrust gives way to a powerful attraction, the design was able to help physicalize their internal struggle. In the second scene of act 2 the two bedrooms are simultaneously revealed and, try as they may to ignore it, the attention of each is focused on the other's bedroom. Their mounting desire ultimately transcends the wall, and, as they give into these powerful forces, the parlor, abandoned since the death of Eden's mother, becomes the site of their illicit love. The transgressive desire is no longer being acted out in the private sphere but is brought out into the public domain of the house.

Just as the title proclaims, *Desire under the Elms* explores the powerful reality of sexual desire; passions seething below the social facade prove too compelling to be ignored. As in the previous two plays, the transgressive nature of their desire results in dire retribution. However, Jones's design reflects a significant shift from an interior, more abstract psychological realm to the outer, more realistic social arena. Not only do the characters act on their desires, but it is evident in the party scene (act 3, scene 1) that everyone except Ephraim knows of their illicit love. Their transgressive desire has become public, and it is through public acknowledgment of this desire at the end of the play that the young pair arrives at a sense of self-acceptance and peace. Abbie's and Eben's experience of conflict between transgressive desire and social prohibition resonated with Jones's own personal struggle. As director and designer of *Desire under the Elms,* he was able to give a visually graphic and sensitive rendering of this dilemma.

Although O'Neill and Jones collaborated on other Triumvirate productions, some of which explored the dynamics of desire in its multitude of guises, it is *The Great God Brown* (1926) that merits the most attention. Less overtly sexual than *Desire under the Elms,* it is significant for what it reveals about Jones's internal conflict. The culmination of the Jones-O'Neill collaborations of this period, it was also Jones's last major design before his "crisis" period of 1926–27. Jones's creative exploration of the split between the inner and outer selves reached a climax with this production and helped precipitate the need for a thorough self-examination of the artist's personal and professional life.

The Great God Brown graphically delineates the struggle between the public and private selves of two men, William Brown and Dion Anthony, whose careers and lives are inextricably intertwined. Brown is a practical, hardworking young man whose architectural firm is successful, if uninspired; Dion is the impractical, poetic, and gifted artist. As the obverse of the other, each desires what the other has: Brown wants Margaret's (Dion's wife) love and Dion's talent; Dion wants Brown's ability to compromise one's ideals enough to survive in the real world. After Dion dies in Brown's house, the businessman assumes the artist's persona. Playing dual roles, Brown takes Dion's place in Margaret's life and continues to run his own business. As this duplicitous double life begins to take its toll, both Brown and his Dion persona begin to lose their grasp on reality. The Dion persona vows to kill Brown as a resolution to the mounting anxiety. When it is announced that Brown is dead, "Dion" is suspected of the crime. Before Brown-Dion is killed by the police, Cybel (the woman Brown has kept as a mistress) realizes that the two personas have merged into a single being and appropriately refers to him as Dion Brown.

Jones employed masks in order to effect the transformations within and among the characters. The actors' faces portrayed the characters' inner selves, while a mask held up in front of their face revealed the outer, public persona. Young Dion's mask was "a fixed forcing of his own face—dark, spiritual, poetical, passionately super-sensitive, helplessly unprotected in its childlike, religious faith in life—into the expression of a mocking, reckless, defiant gayly scoffing and sensual young Pan."[46] As Dion's artistic sensitivity collides with the harshness of reality, the childlike becomes cynical, and the sensual Pan is replaced with a sneering Mephistopheles.

Jones and O'Neill previously had explored the use of masks in *The*

Hairy Ape and *The Ancient Mariner*. However, this particular use of the mask was new theatrical territory for both artists. In the two earlier works, masks were employed to obliterate character depth: masks highlighted the cardboard two-dimensionality of character in *The Hairy Ape* or the unindividuated chorus in *The Ancient Mariner*. Masks in *The Great God Brown*, on the other hand, revealed the inner world of the character in a wholly tangible form. They physicalized the disparity between the inner and outer selves; the hiding and dissembling required to maintain the public persona is graphically and poignantly demonstrated. Kenneth Macgowan, author of *Masks and Demons* (1923), claimed in a program note that this play was "the first example of the use of the mask to dramatize changes and conflicts in character. The old Greeks employed the false face to denote merely emotion and physical suffering. O'Neill uses it 'to picture the conflict between the inner character and the distortions which outer life thrusts upon it.'"[47]

Undoubtedly this psychic conflict resonated with Jones. In his analysis of the original production, O'Neill scholar Ronald Wainscott observes that Jones "certainly demonstrated an unusual sensitivity to the material"[48] and "had a special sensitivity to the play."[49] If this "special sensitivity" was his own homoerotic struggle, then the coincidence of his "midlife crisis" with the run of this production bears examination. While Jones's arduous production schedule prior to Zurich may have contributed to his need to leave the theater and rekindle his creative energies, it does not explain why "only a chosen few people, among them Dr. Jelliffe, Eugene O'Neill and Arthur Hopkins, knew the reason for Jones being in Zurich."[50] It is reasonable to suggest that the psychic exploration that he had been undertaking in his designs and that culminated in *The Great God Brown* proved too emotionally threatening to the artist.

Jones undoubtedly identified with both Brown and Dion. Dion, named for the Greek god Dionysus, is imbued with the same wildness and danger associated with the god. In addition to Dionysus's identification with orgiastic revelry, the sexual ambiguity of this astonishingly beautiful but effeminate god of legend must have appealed to Jones's queer aesthetic, if not his self-image. Despite his scoffing at convention, Dion yearns for the ability to survive in the real world, however morally ambivalent that world might be. Brown, on the other hand, is firmly rooted in reality but desires to escape the bonds of pragmatism and to take flight on the wings of Dion's idealism. During the production, the taking off and putting on of masks objectified the characters' inner and outer selves. Queer historian George Chauncey notes that many "gay men, for instance, described negotiating their presence in an often hostile world as living a double life, or wearing a mask and taking it off."[51] Although these selves remain separate and distinct throughout most of the play, this convention begins to collapse toward the end as the two selves merge into each other. One can speculate that the melding of his two selves (the inner self of homosexual desire and the more conventional public persona) was too threatening to Jones. If the two worlds were collapsed into a single reality, one risked possible public exposure of the transgressive desires. Rather than risk a psychic emergence from the closet, Jones fled to Zurich, seeking the tools to reconcile the internal struggle.

One strategy by which to read this internal struggle can be taken from Jones himself. In a letter to Kenneth Macgowan written while undergoing analysis, he suggested that Jung's description of the extraverted intuitive type most aptly described his personality.[52] In Jung's typology of the personality, the extraverted type focuses primarily on the objective or outer world. "If a man thinks, feels, acts and actually lives in a way that is *directly* correlated with the objective conditions and their demands, he is extraverted. His life makes it perfectly clear that it is the object and not this subjective view that plays the determining role in consciousness."[53] When the objective or outside world takes precedence over the subjective in a person's consciousness, "his inner life is subordinated to external necessity, *though not without a struggle.* . . . The moral laws governing his actions coincide with the demands of society, that is, with the prevailing moral standpoint."[54]

Adjustment to the objective situation (normative standards and morality) is not made without its psychological price. "A purely objective orientation does violence to a multitude of subjective impulses, intentions, needs and desires and deprives them of the libido that is their natural right."[55] Jung's extravert is an individual whose actions are dictated by the morality and expectations of society at the expense of the person's true needs and desires. For an extraverted type such as Jones, the powerful social sanctions against same-sex desire would overwhelm and thwart transgressive libidinous desires, but not without considerable internal struggle between the subjective desires and the objective authority.

The intuitive component of Jones's personality helps illuminate the fact that the "reality" of the stage took precedence over the more mundane realities of life. According to Jung, the "intuitive is never to be found in the world of accepted reality-values, but he has a keen nose for anything new and in the making. . . . The intuitive's morality is governed neither by thinking or feeling; he has his own characteristic morality, which consists in loyalty to his vision."[56] While this aspect of his personality may have hampered Jones in his emotional and personal life, it was certainly an asset in his professional career, as his impressive list of "firsts" attests.

If, as this essay posits, Jones's personal struggle was a manifestation of the internal conflict between transgressive, homosexual desire and objective prohibition, a brief look at one of Jung's ideas on homosexuality will shed light on the ramifications analysis had on the post-Zurich Jones. Jung acknowledged the reality of homosexual attraction but believed it was misplaced psychic energy that needed to be redirected toward a more spiritual object. Convinced that Freud's sexual definition of the libido must be replaced with a concept of undifferentiated psychic energy,[57] Jung transformed Freud's physical, bodily orientation into a more psychical, almost spiritual, orientation where "sexual feelings are to be understood as really meaning our longing for inner wholeness and integration—as being about our embodied souls, not only our bodies."[58]

Jones returned to New York in 1927, and it is useful to examine how he integrated these Jungian concepts into his post-therapeutic life and work. It is evident that he made significant accommodations toward a more spiritual orientation of inner wholeness, and that the integration of the spiritual with the physical was reflected in his new work. For example, even though the aesthetic principles underlying Jones's early work always had a spiritual dimension, it was in this later period that he began to systematically articulate those ideas on the page in addition to the stage. In a series of lectures and articles, most notably *The Dramatic Imagination* (1941), Jones elaborated this spiritual longing in theatrical terms.

While Jones's focus on a spiritual component was advantageous to his theoretical writing, its benefit to his design work is questionable. Despite claims of renewed energy after his return from Zurich,[59] an appraisal of his career after 1927 reveals that he trod a safer path. His designs, while frequently inspired, lost much of their innovative edge. The majority of his commissions were for established, mainstream producers; virtually gone were the little-theater experiments. His most critically acclaimed productions of this period, such as *The Green Pastures* (1930), *Mourning Becomes Electra* (1931), and *The Ice Man Cometh* (1946), were significant more for their drama than their design. What had once been revolutionary had now become commonplace.

The designer's efforts to effect a spiritual orientation of inner wholeness were not solely relegated to his professional life. Significant changes were made in his personal life as well, as the renovation of his family home in New Hampshire attests. Here he created a physical space to which he could occasionally retreat and in which he ultimately died after a prolonged illness in 1954. This renewed involvement with family signals a shift away from (or at least an integration with) his previous New York–based identity. The moral openness of the city, a space where Jones could act out his homosexual needs and desires in relative anonymity, was being replaced with, at least in part, the moral puritanism of his childhood home and family.

Although evidence suggests that Jones did not completely abandon homoerotic affiliations, one must examine another significant accommodation Jones made toward a more conventional lifestyle: his marriage to Margaret Carrington in 1932. At the time of his marriage, Jones was forty-five and Carrington ten years his senior. The two had become coworkers and friends when Carrington was engaged by the Hopkins-Jones team in the early 1920s as vocal coach for John Barrymore's Shakespearean roles. The sister of Walter Huston, Carrington had been an opera singer of some note until a vocal accident ended her career. After her injury she developed and taught a rigorous vocal training technique whose devotees included Alfred Lunt, Orson Welles, Lillian Gish, and Walter Huston.[60] A previous marriage to William Carrington, wealthy businessman and art patron, allowed Margaret to "finally become the millionaire she always knew she would be."[61] Shortly after her marriage to Carrington, however, he was thrown from a horse and was confined to a wheelchair for the remainder of his life. His death in 1931 left her a financially comfortable widow.

Jones's marriage to the older Carrington bears striking similarity to his relationship with Mabel Dodge, and one can presume that the marriage was also platonic rather than sexual. Along with companionship, each benefited professionally from the relationship. Russell Lewis, Jones's personal assistant who lived with the couple in their Santa Barbara, California, villa, claimed that "the Jones-Carrington alliance was one of true affection and deep professional respect."[62] Lewis's assessment, however, raises as many questions as it answers. Certainly the term "alliance" smacks more of a business arrangement than a romantic involvement, while "affection" and "respect" are feelings more appropriate to a friendship than to a love relationship. And one must ask if there was a homoerotic component to Jones's relationship with his "personal assistant," frequently a coded phrase for a closeted relationship. Although the exact nature of these relationships has yet to be decoded, it is plausible that the social respectability of marriage, not to mention their mutual respect for each other as artists, prevailed over passion for the forty-five-year-old Jones.

Despite the personal and professional accommodations toward "inner wholeness" that mark Jones's post-Zurich period, the struggle between objective demands and subjective desires that pervaded his early life was not entirely expunged. Rather, it is transliterated into Jones's belief in the dual nature of human existence. In the essay entitled "Curious and Profitable," he asserts, "At the root of all our living . . . is a consciousness of our essential duality. . . . Life . . . is a never ending dialogue between the outer self and the inner self which together make up our dual nature."[63] It is this duality, this conflicted dynamic between the inner and outer selves, that played itself out in the designer's personal life as well as his designs.

One must read Jones's designs for the stage (his public persona) as an exploration of his personal struggle between homosexual desire and social expectations. This conflicted dynamic was most potent in Jones's pre-Zurich years, which comprised his queerest period. *The Great God Brown* became the culmination of a series of plays in which Jones probed his own psyche to explore the transgressive nature of desire and the conflict between the "inner character and the distortion which outer life thrusts upon it." With each successive production the inner self that desires was revealed in a more public, if not more realistic, way. For example, the Hopkins-Jones *Macbeth* explores the desire for power by probing the inner recesses of the principals' psyches. Although the characters act in a very public way, their motivations are best understood through their subconscious. An extremely abstract design scheme, therefore, was employed to bring the inner world of the Macbeths to the stage. While power is the object of desire in *Macbeth,* the desire for belonging that suffuses *The Hairy Ape* takes on a more overtly transgressive homoerotic guise. It is clearly the company of men that Yank desires. In Jones's designs the realistic world of the stokers melded with Yank's psychic struggle into an expressionistic vision of longing and desire. The stylized elements of the scenery were in counterpoint to the gritty realism of the stokers and created a visual amalgam of the inner and outer worlds of the play. The stylization of *The Hairy Ape* is abandoned for stark realism in the austere world of *Desire under the Elms.* The desire in the play is overtly sexual and, although the characters initially resist these forces, they ultimately capitulate to the illicit love. Jones's designs mirrored the more open, publicly proclaimed desire with a realistic style of production. *The Great God Brown* probes the merging of the inner and outer selves, although stylistically it reiterates the expressionism of the earlier *The Hairy Ape*. The convention of masks and actors' faces to represent the two selves was a stunningly graphic representation of the psychic struggle.

Beneath a veneer of heterosexual respectability depicted onstage lies Robert Edmond Jones's more secret self. It was observed that his scenery "stands out in memory . . . but always with something held back."[64] Only when we decode what was being held back will we truly understand the power and genius of Jones's scenographic talent. We must probe behind both his literal and metaphorical masks that gave expression to the duality of his nature, the conflict between his inner and outer selves.

NOTES

1. Eugene O'Neill, *"The Theatre We Worked For": The Letters of Eugene O'Neill to Kenneth Macgowan,* ed. Jackson R. Bryer (New Haven: Yale University Press, 1982), 69n.

2. James Weldon Johnson, *Black Manhattan* (1930; New York: Da Capo, 1973), 175.

3. Dana Sue McDermott, telephone conversation with author, May 8, 1998.

4. Lesley Ferris, "Kit and Guth: A Lavender Marriage on Broadway," in *Passing Performances: Queer Readings of Leading Players in American Theater History,* ed. Robert A. Schanke and Kim Marra (Ann Arbor: University of Michigan Press, 1998), 200.

5. Dana Sue McDermott, "The Apprenticeship of Robert Edmond Jones," *Theatre Survey,* November 1988, 193–212.

6. For additional information on Jones's early youth see Mary Hall Furber, "The Scene: New Hampshire, U.S.A.," in *The Theatre of Robert Edmond Jones,* ed. Ralph Pendleton (Middletown, Conn.: Wesleyan University Press, 1958), 7–13.

7. Furber, "The Scene," 11.

8. Elizabeth S. Sergeant, "Robert Edmond Jones: Protean Artist," *Fire under the Andes* (Port Washington, N.Y.: Kennikat Press, 1927), 39.

9. Ibid., 39–40.

10. Ibid., 41.

11. Furber, "The Scene," 13.

12. Mabel Dodge Luhan, *Movers and Shakers* (New York: Harcourt, Brace, 1936), 315.

13. Sergeant, "Robert Edmond Jones," 39.

14. Luhan, *Movers and Shakers,* 315.

15. Sergeant, "Robert Edmond Jones," 37.

16. Kenneth Macgowan, "Robert Edmond Jones," *Theatre Arts Monthly* 9 (1925): 723.

17. George Chauncey, *Gay New York: Gender, Urban Culture, and the Making of the Gay Male World, 1890–1940* (New York: Basic Books, 1994), 232.

18. George Chauncey, "Long-Haired Men and Short-Haired Women: Building a Gay World in the Heart of Bohemia," in *Greenwich Village: Culture and Counterculture,* ed. Rick Beard and Leslie Cohen Berlowitz (New Brunswick, N.J.: Museum of the City of New York, 1993), 152.

19. Ibid., 153.

20. Luhan, *Movers and Shakers,* 204.

21. Ibid., 217.

22. Ibid., 315.

23. Ibid.

24. Ibid., 318.

25. Ibid., 219.

26. Robert Edmond Jones, "Nijinsky and *Til Eulenspiegel*," *Nijinsky: An Illustrated Monograph,* ed. Paul Magriel (New York: Henry Holt, 1946), 45.

27. Ibid., 59.

28. Arthur Hopkins, *Reference Point* (New York: Samuel French, 1948), 96.

29. Ibid., 95.

30. Chauncey, *Gay New York,* 274.

31. O'Neill, *Letters to Macgowan,* 48.

32. Dana Sue McDermott, "Creativity in the Theatre: Robert Edmond Jones and C. G. Jung," *Theatre Journal* 36, no. 2 (1984): 216.

33. Alexander Woollcott, "Second Thoughts on First Nights," *New York Times,* February 27, 1921, sec. 6, p. 1.

34. Alexander Woollcott, "The Play," *New York Times,* March 8, 1920, 7.

35. While it is fairly well known that Alexander Woollcott was a gay man, it is not surprising that his reviews of Jones's work did not address the homoerotic symbolism in the designs considering that it was 1921.

36. Woollcott, "Second Thoughts," 1.

37. Ibid.

38. Arthur Hopkins, "The Approaching 'Macbeth,'" *New York Times,* February 6, 1921, sec. 6, p. 1.

39. Dana Sue McDermott, "The Void in *Macbeth*: A Symbolic Design," *Themes in Drama 4: Drama and Symbolism,* ed. James Redmond (Cambridge: Cambridge University Press, 1971), 120.

40. Woollcott, "Second Thoughts," 1.

41. Mordecai Gorelik, "Life with Bobby," *Theatre Arts* 39 (April 1955): 94.

42. Chauncey, *Gay New York,* 36.

43. Eugene O'Neill, *The Hairy Ape,* in *The Plays of Eugene O'Neill,* (New York: Modern Library, 1982), 1:211.

44. Ibid., 209.

45. McDermott, "Apprenticeship," 193.

46. Eugene O'Neill, *The Great God Brown* (New York: Horace Liveright, 1926), 14.

47. Kenneth Macgowan, program note *The Great God Brown,* clipping file, Museum of the City of New York.

48. Ronald H. Wainscott, *Staging O'Neill: The Experimental Years, 1920–1934* (New Haven: Yale University Press, 1988), 189.

49. Ibid., 199.

50. McDermott, "Creativity in the Theatre," 214.

51. Chauncey, *Gay New York,* 6.

52. McDermott, "The Void in *Macbeth,*" 118. While Jung's typology of the personality was a three-part construct (extravert/introvert; intuitive/sensation; feeling/thinking), Jones identifies himself with only two of the three categories.

53. C.G. Jung, *Psychological Types* (Princeton: Princeton University Press, 1971), 333–34.

54. Ibid., 334; emphasis added.

55. Ibid., 338.

56. Ibid., 368.

57. Christine Downing, *Myths and Mysteries of Same-Sex Love* (New York: Continuum, 1989), 108.

58. Ibid., 110.

59. McDermott, "Creativity in the Theatre," 215.

60. Lawrence Grobel, *The Hustons* (New York: Charles Scribner's Sons, 1989), 97.

61. Ibid., 96.

62. Paul Robert Waldo, "Production Concepts Exemplified in Selected Presentations Directed by Robert Edmond Jones," Ph.D. diss., University of Oregon, 1970, 377.

63. Robert Edmond Jones, *Towards a New Theatre,* ed. Delbert Unruh (New York: Limelight Editions, 1992), 77, 78.

64. Sergeant, "Robert Edmond Jones," 44.

A Lifetime in Light

Jean Rosenthal's Careers, Collaborations, and Commitments to Women

Jay Scott Chipman

Jean Rosenthal's remarkable career as a stage lighting specialist began at Yale, where, starting in 1930, she studied lighting design with Stanley McCandless, long recognized as one of the early experts in American stage lighting. After graduation, at age twenty-one, Rosenthal was fortunate to find work with the Federal Theatre Project in New York City, where she soon became acquainted with numerous young artists, including John Houseman, lighting expert Abe Feder, and director Orson Welles. These contacts led to a contract for the Broadway run and national tour of Leslie Howard's *Hamlet* in 1936; as electrical technical director, Rosenthal seized the opportunity to demonstrate some of her own ideas about lighting at a time when the field was still dominated by males.

When Welles and Houseman formed the Mercury Theatre in 1937 after the controversy surrounding their defiant staging of Marc Blitzstein's *The Cradle Will Rock,* Rosenthal accepted the job of technical director and lighting manager (see fig. 19). She supervised the electricians and challenged herself to achieve the complex scenic and illumination demands requested by Welles with few instruments and an almost nonexistent budget. To do so she developed a systematic method for recording instrument placement and cue settings, a system that Simon Callow asserts "enabled the Mercury to be more ambitious in terms of light than any other theater."[1]

Rosenthal chose not to relocate when Welles and Houseman took the Mercury to Hollywood in 1938 and, instead, supported herself by taking a faculty position at the Neighborhood Playhouse School of the Theatre. In 1940 she cofounded Theatre Production Service (TPS), a successful mail-order house for dispersing technical theater information and

Fɪɢ. 19. Jean Rosenthal, age twenty-six, on stage at the Mercury Theatre in 1937.

(Courtesy, Billy Rose Theatre Collection, New York Public Library for the Performing Arts.)

equipment. Rosenthal also became increasingly in demand as a lighting designer and gradually accumulated an impressive list of production credits, including, between 1941 and 1969, lighting for forty-five plays and thirty-one musicals on Broadway, seventy-three ballets at the New York City Ballet, thirty-four ballets at the American Ballet Theatre, fifty-three dances for Martha Graham, five seasons with the American Shakespeare Festival, two seasons at the New York City Opera, a season at the Metropolitan Opera, and numerous consultations for educational, civic, and commercial construction projects. Not only did she help promote lighting design to the status of a profession, but she set the standard for professionalism and excellence within the field.

Though quickly sketched here, Rosenthal's achievements leave little doubt that, as friend and biographer Lael Tucker Wertenbaker has insisted, she be considered an "historic figure in her field, recognized for her particular creative genius."[2] It is dismaying, therefore, as Mary Callahan Boone has recently pointed out, that "Rosenthal's specific contributions to lighting design in mainstream theatre have themselves remained largely invisible."[3] Boone takes a step toward remedying the situation in her article and, as well, offers a feasible explanation for its occurrence. "Rosenthal's quiet demeanor, her politeness, her highly tactful mode of collaboration with other artists, and her willingness to background her own contributions became her trademarks," Boone notes.[4] These trademarks effectively coincided both with gender expectations of women during the historical moments in which Rosenthal was working, and the "subordinately collaborative role demanded of the theatrical lighting designer."[5] One way Rosenthal's career may be viewed, Boone rightly stresses, is as "an attempt to work within the established cultural, professional, and artistic hierarchies, which all demanded she and her art be subordinate, if not invisible."[6] While valued for being unobtrusive during her lifetime, that same unobtrusiveness has contributed to Rosenthal, her methods, and her artistry being undervalued in theater history studies.

This essay aims to consider Rosenthal's achievements within a context of both theater history and, since same-sex collaboration and lesbian erotics were instrumental in her artistic development, within the history of sexual diversity. First, I situate Rosenthal's career and professional relationships with women within a context of lesbian social history. I acknowledge the difficulty of determining Rosenthal's sexual orientation and suggest reasons why this difficulty occurs. To recover her as a figure in lesbian and gay theater history, I then advocate that she be viewed as a "woman-committed woman" and examine three of her most significant professional and personal same-sex relationships with women, two of which may be viewed in contemporary terms as domestic partnerships. I conclude with an analysis of Rosenthal's long-term artistic collaboration with dancer Martha Graham, including a homoerotic reading of Rosenthal's lighting so that I may illuminate the dynamics of sexuality in production design.

My intention is that these sections have both a cumulative and fragmenting effect that can elicit this historical agent's elusive subjectivity. The analysis exploits the tensions that arise from knowledge rendered incomplete by the passage of time and lack of "hard" evidence about intimate sexual behavior and the complex workings of desire.

Cultivating a "Careful Impersonality"

In the quantity of printed material by or about Jean Rosenthal there is no evidence to suggest that she self-identified as a lesbian, nor is it likely that she would have confided such information to acquaintances given the high value she placed on her privacy. Wertenbaker attests to this trait in the preface to *The Magic of Light,* citing Rosenthal's "warmth, which reserved to itself a deep personal privacy and never invaded yours," as among the factors that made her such a cherished friend.[7] Given lesbian social history in the twentieth century and Rosenthal's personal circumstances, the lack of such evidence isn't surprising.

Of crucial significance, however, is that Jean Rosenthal lived during a time, 1912–69, when some women did, privately and/or publicly, self-identify as lesbians. Many, particularly those living in urban areas, even considered themselves part of a lesbian culture. From a historical perspective the formation and existence of an identity or culture specifically and publicly named lesbian is of value because, among other things, it contributes to a fuller understanding of sexuality and gender in twentieth-century American society and informs the complexities of women's relationships.[8] It is important for this study in particular because, as Rosenthal lived almost all of her life in New York City and worked in the performing arts, it would have been virtually impossible for her not to be aware of the existence of lesbian and gay individuals and cultures. Simply put, whether or not she *self-identified,* she would have had sufficient knowledge about homosexuality *to identify it as a phenomenon.*

The odds for this are further increased when one considers that Rosenthal's father was a physician and her mother a psychologist. Her parents were Romanian immigrants who believed in providing their three children with the most progressive education possible (a belief that governed their choice of the Ethical Culture School in the Bronx, William Fincke's Manumit School in Pawling, New York, and the Friends' Seminary in Manhattan). It is highly likely, therefore, that Rosenthal and her brothers were acquainted with at least some of the discourse of turn-of-the-century and early-twentieth-century sexologists, including that often disparagingly associated with homosexuality. In addition, with the family's appreciation of the arts and life in Manhattan in the late 1920s, it is very possible they encountered the cosmopolitan sexual liberalism and taboo-breaking Bohemianism (including experiments with lesbianism) prevalent during those years (notably in Greenwich Village).

Despite whatever knowledge of same-sex relations Rosenthal may have accumulated from her liberal environment and education (including her year and a half at the Neighborhood Playhouse School of the Theatre and three years at Yale), America's social and sexual climate had changed when it came time for Rosenthal to enter the nation's work force during the depression. As Lillian Faderman has astutely pointed out, not only did women have considerable difficulties supporting themselves in a nation that needed fewer workers, but they also had "to brave the increasing hostility toward independent females" that intensified as a result of widespread economic hardship.[9] Rosenthal's jobs and the responsibilities delegated to her brought her face-to-face with these potentially daunting circumstances.

From the age of twenty-one, when she managed technical operations for the Federal Theater Project's Municipal Wagon Theatre in New York City, and with the responsibilities subsequently delegated to her during employment on Leslie Howard's *Hamlet,* at Unit 891, and at the Mercury Theatre, Rosenthal often found herself supervising male coworkers. Noting that the technical fields of the theater historically had remained "a closed male world," Rosenthal tells of relying on courtesy "to overcome rude prejudice" and of cultivating "a careful impersonality, which disregarded sex," in order to create an atmosphere of collaboration with men who may have resented her presence. Demonstrating her expertise and her appreciation for the expertise of others was her primary strategy for negotiating this difficulty. That it was successful is evidenced by her comment, "I did know my stuff, and I knew the technicians knew theirs. I honored, truly, their knowledge and their prerogatives. And gradually they came around—from stagehands to directors—to honor mine."[10] This comment about proving one's worth to gain success in a male-dominated profession echoes the sentiments expressed decades earlier by playwright and director Rachel Crothers, as documented elsewhere in this volume.

As Rosenthal's livelihood was dependent upon acquiring cooperation in the face of such obstacles, undoubtedly she would have seen little advantage to any action that would have given her coworkers ammunition to reject her leadership. This would certainly have included any admission or appearance of same-sex attraction, the discourse of which, as Faderman notes, continued to be dominated by "medical opinions regarding the abnormality of love between women."[11]

During World War II there was, by necessity, a shift in attitude toward accepting women in the workplace, a recognition of female independence, and, to some degree, a validation of love relationships between women both in the service and in civilian life. But these changes proved short-lived. At the end of the war, society took a conservative turn that had a strong impact in all these areas (and would continue to have an impact well through the 1960s). As Americans trying to attain some degree of "normalcy" struggled to reintegrate male veterans into the labor force and the domestic sphere, women were overtly and subliminally encouraged to relinquish their jobs and independence. Those who refused to do so often were treated with hostility and suspicion. Rosenthal resisted the pressure to conform and managed to survive. What's more, due to recognition of her expertise in the area of technical theater production, she was even asked to help train returning veterans. Because of the strength of her professional contacts, her likability, and her reputation for quality work, Rosenthal's career not only survived this social crisis but flourished and expanded through the 1950s and 1960s.

The two-and-a-half-decade span following the war, with regards to lesbian culture, was grim. With the increasing acceptance of psychoanalysis as a means of mediating and policing mental health, the dominant image manufactured for women who loved women was one of sickness to be cured on the analyst's couch. As a result, notes Faderman, not only lesbians but women in general sought to avoid appearances of same-sex affectional preferences, fearing being discredited as mentally unhealthy "before any other aspect of [their] personality or behavior could be considered."[12] An additional blow was dealt by McCarthyism in the 1950s with pronouncements associating homosexuality with communism that prompted a climate of paranoia and intimidation. If women, as Faderman states, wanted to "maintain the advantages of middle-class American life . . . and the careers to which it led," they did well to conceal any aspect of their life that could be construed as abnormal, including alternative sexuality.[13]

Rosenthal, who as an unmarried woman and an independent businesswoman would already be suspect, had much to lose in a culture all too ready to damn without evidence. In the political climate of the 1940s, 1950s, and 1960s, Rosenthal would have had considerable incentive to deny lesbian self-identification.

It is significant that Rosenthal remains mostly silent about *any* romantic involvements. While one may speculate that this occurs because of the concern for personal privacy mentioned by Wertenbaker, or because of a desire to protect her career, or out of a sense of propriety, the exact reason or reasons are unclear. Only once, in fact, does she breach her silence. In *The Magic of Light* she refers to Willy Nolan, a technician with whom, among other projects, she collaborated on the reconstruction of a theater for the Marquis de Cuevas Ballet in 1944. Before going on to describe her admiration for his knowledge of stage machinery she remarks, "I think we had fallen in love, a little, when I was 'that girl at the Mercury.'"[14] Characteristically, she offers no details of the nature of their "love" nor the length of its duration. Whether the comment can be read as an indicator of bisexuality or as a smokescreen to conceal her commitment to women is not evident.

Commitments to Women

In negotiating the lack of material evidence about Rosenthal's sexuality and the problematics of labeling behaviors and practices ahistorically, Leila J. Rupp's eloquently articulated concept of the woman-committed woman is helpful, especially regarding women's same-sex relationships in pre-Stonewall America. While acknowledging that there were women during this period who came to identify their feelings and experiences as "lesbian," Rupp posits the simultaneous existence of a broader category of women whom she designates "women-committed women." She describes women-committed women as those "who would not identify as lesbians, but whose primary commitment in emotional and practical terms, was to other women."[15] To illustrate her concept, Rupp documents two types of relationships she would classify as "women-committed" with examples of participants in the postsuffragist women's rights movement: (1) women who lived in long-term or lifelong domestic relationships with other women, and (2) women who became infatuated with a charismatic woman leader. Rupp's analyses facilitate enlargement of the range of what can be considered same-sex relationships between women, especially when contemporary definitions, particularly evidence of sexual activity, cannot be ascertained. Her method allows for analysis of the many differences and similarities among women-committed women.[16]

In addition to these two useful categories of relationships, Rupp's model is flexible enough also to encompass behaviors and practices occurring within long-term business and artistic collaborations. In cultural climates where even casual acquaintances between women might be considered suspect and, therefore, cause for oppression, business and artistic partnerships offer possible sources for commitments among women while sustaining an acceptable appearance within a context of necessary professional contact. Given the hostile climate for independent women in the late 1940s, 1950s, and 1960s, it is feasible to classify several of Jean Rosenthal's personal and professional associations as women-committed relationships.

In *The Magic of Light* Rosenthal states her belief that in the commercial theater "you make contacts, not friendships." While these contacts, based on "a kind of instantaneous response to the people with whom you work," may be "thrilling and rewarding" and "perfectly lovely relationship[s]" for the length of their endurance, Rosenthal writes, when the association is over, "you return to your home base and they return to theirs." As a result, she concludes, "I have been pretty much of a loner through all these associations."[17]

It is evident, however, that Rosenthal cultivated several relationships that moved beyond the point of professional contact to a level that was also personal. Most of these relationships were with women; three such liaisons proved particularly significant. To the casual observer, perhaps the professional aspect may have been the only one in view; it justified the existence of the relationship and shielded the more personal emotional attachment from unwelcome scrutiny.

Rosenthal's coworkers at Theatre Production Service (notably an all-female enterprise during its first years), provided her with a "much needed sense of organized professional community" that she felt was missing elsewhere in her work. Central among these coworkers was Nananne Porcher, hired by Rosenthal during the war, who later became her "invaluable stage manager for ballet and opera."[18] Porcher shared Rosenthal's work ethic and was an able collaborator who advocated Rosenthal's aesthetic ideals. "When it comes to doing my lighting my way," Rosenthal writes in *The Magic of Light*, "Nan is fierce and implacably determined to carry out my original intentions."[19] Historian Anne MacKay, who was employed by Rosenthal at Theatre Production Service from 1950 to 1952, affirms Porcher's expertise and dedication to Rosenthal's artistic vision. "Nan knew everything about Jean's lighting; she was the stage manager, gave all the cues, [and] saw all the light plots. [She] understood what Jean was doing and why."[20] Rosenthal mentored Porcher and, in the late 1950s while production director at Dallas Civic Opera, provided her with practical opportunities to learn lighting design. These interactions indicate that a high level of commitment between the two women existed on the professional level.

MacKay provides insight into the working environment at TPS in the early 1950s, stating that Rosenthal was attempting to establish her career as a lighting designer while "desperately trying to make the business work so that she would have a backup income"[21] (see fig. 20). Notably, MacKay writes, "there were no men around except the professionals they worked with."[22] She also clearly remembers the absence among the women of "all the social time heterosexual women spend with men," a silence that contributed to "all their energy and artistic attention [being] focused on the job."[23] While the work received primary emphasis, consistent with Faderman's analysis, a space for same-sex professional interaction was cultivated at TPS.

In a profile story on Rosenthal published in The *New Yorker* in February 1956, Winthrop Sargeant mentions that Rosenthal was sharing an apartment with Porcher in midtown Manhattan. Identifying Porcher as "one of [Rosenthal's] colleagues" and the production manager of the New York City Ballet, Sargeant describes her as "a formidably efficient woman" and, in one of the few glimpses into Rosenthal's home life, comments that Rosenthal "leaves most of the cooking to Miss Porcher."[24] Sargeant also informs readers that Rosenthal's friends were practically all theater people and that "her contact with them is for the most part professional."[25] J. K. Curry's essay about Rachel Crothers in this volume documents a parallel instance of journalistic curiosity about the practicality of shared living arrangements as possible means of explaining to readers a career woman's lack of a heterosexual relationship.

Given Rosenthal's at least decade-long professional association with Porcher and the shared living arrangement, it would be fair to assume that Porcher by 1956 had moved beyond the point of a professional contact to that of a more personal companion. The nature of their commitment had shifted and the intimacy of their friendship and shared understandings facilitated Porcher's ability and determination to carry out Rosenthal's intentions. As evidenced in the article, however, the work relationship is still intact and receives primary emphasis in the public press. The living arrangement is presented matter-of-factly and with no indication of how long the two had shared the apartment. Not surprisingly, given the magazine and the period, there is no discussion of same-sex affection.

As Rupp has advised, in the 1950s women, especially those who enjoyed the status of working professionally, "might live together without raising an eyebrow."[26] This would appear to be the case here. Details of Rosenthal's and Porcher's private life as domestic partners remain unknown. MacKay, however, confirms that at work "Nan and Jean were very comfortable with each other" and observes that they had a "terrific

FIG. 20. Jean Rosenthal in her office about 1962.

(Courtesy, Billy Rose Theatre Collection, New York Public Library for the Performing Arts.)

working relationship, efficient and lots of humor."[27] It was MacKay's impression that "Jean was Nan's life" and that "Nan's devotion and experience made life easy for Jean."[28] It is interesting to note, therefore, that for all the anecdotes Rosenthal includes about Porcher in *The Magic of Light,* she does not mention living with her. The comment Rosenthal *does* make, that "sometimes I have lived alone and sometimes shared my apartment," elides the fact that she shared her apartment with another woman.[29]

Neither does Rosenthal mention Marion (Mickey) Kinsella. It is Wertenbaker who, in the preface to *The Magic of Light,* introduces Kin-

sella as a figure in Rosenthal's life, identifying her as "Jean's on-the-job
lighting assistant who was an artist and sculptor the rest of her time." (A
program from the musical *Saratoga,* which premiered in New York on
December 7, 1959, lists Kinsella as "Production Assistant to Miss Rosenthal," indicating that their professional relationship dated at least from
that time.)[30] Wertenbaker also states that Rosenthal "shared a lovely
house" with Kinsella on Martha's Vineyard, Rosenthal's favorite retreat
from the stresses of work and the city, and the place where Rosenthal,
recovering from cancer surgery in 1968, spent much of her time.[31]
Although there is no indication of the length of time they resided together
nor any details of the relationship between the two women, Wertenbaker
supplies just enough information to indicate that at some point the relationship expanded to a level of personal as well as professional commitment. Like the earlier relationship between Rosenthal and Porcher, the
one between Rosenthal and Kinsella evolved into a domestic partnership.

Kinsella is credited with designing the stage decor for Rosenthal's
final lighting project before her death, Graham's *Archaic Hours,* a prestigious assignment that would have given her the opportunity to work in
close collaboration with the ailing Rosenthal. Furthermore, upon Rosenthal's death on May 1, 1969, Houseman identifies Kinsella as the person
who called him with the news.[32] Together with the information about living arrangements, this evidence suggests that Kinsella was committed to
providing care for Rosenthal during her recovery from surgery and during the last year of her life. The shared devotions between the two women
motivated Kinsella to serve Rosenthal as an artistic assistant and as a
caregiving personal companion.

Though sketchy, these few details indicate perhaps most significantly
that Rosenthal cultivated a second decade-long relationship with a
woman, and that the friendship involved the practical circumstances of
sharing a home in conjunction with continued professional association
that benefited the careers of both. Once again there is no conclusive evidence of a sexual relationship between the two women, but the evidence
of mutual commitment is sufficient to warrant consideration in the terms
Rupp outlines. Furthermore, since Rosenthal professionally mentored
both Porcher and Kinsella and secured employment opportunities for
them, more evidence surfaces of a woman-centered assistance network.
The same-sex relationships of Elisabeth Marbury and Elsie De Wolfe,
Rachel Crothers and Mary Kirkpatrick, and the collaboration of Cheryl
Crawford, Margaret Webster, and Eva Le Gallienne in the American
Repertory Theatre venture are other pertinent examples.[33]

The third relationship that deserves examination involves Lael Tucker Wertenbaker. This relationship differs from the first two in that Wertenbaker never resided with Rosenthal as a domestic partner, nor did she ever work in the area of lighting or technical theater. Wertenbaker, a novelist and freelance writer, states that she met Rosenthal in 1958. Though she does not divulge the circumstances of that meeting, Wertenbaker does mention discussing with Rosenthal early in their acquaintance the possibility of collaborating on a book about Rosenthal's career and the art of lighting design. She also claims to have spent "a lot of odd time with Jean" and comments about watching her work in the theater. "This was time well spent," she writes, though Rosenthal's professional work precluded making headway on the writing project.[34] The project, which eventually came to be known as *The Magic of Light,* evolved into a long-term collaboration, one that Wertenbaker persisted in completing.

For Rosenthal's part, she promised Wertenbaker that she would design lighting for her autobiographical family novel *Death of a Man* should it ever be dramatized, no matter how many other commitments she had. Rosenthal kept this promise in 1962 when Garson Kanin adapted the novel as *A Gift of Time.* Additionally, when commissioned in 1964 to design and produce a sound and light production for the restoration of Boscobel, a historic house on the Hudson River near Garrison, New York, Rosenthal insisted that Wertenbaker collaborate with her by writing the script. This appreciation of Wertenbaker's writing is also evident in Rosenthal's cooperation with the writing of *The Magic of Light* and entrusting her woman friend to design and edit it.

This relationship reverses the pattern noted above. Rosenthal and Wertenbaker's acquaintance developed into a friendship that came to include professional artistic collaboration. This collaboration, in a historically significant way, documented the artistic skills of both women (as well as Kinsella's) and advanced the careers and historical appreciation of both. Notably, I believe, Rosenthal identifies Wertenbaker as "my friend," one of the few people she designates with that term.[35] Given the cultural climate, the two women's intimacy could be rationalized as having the writing project as a basis.

Each of Rosenthal's relationships described here is based on a high level of mutual commitment between the women involved. That all three relationships became intimate and were sustained over at least a decade is especially significant in a profession where, as Rosenthal herself noted, associations frequently are terminated or interrupted following the completion of a single project. These factors, and the fact that Rosenthal's relationships with her male professional collaborators for the most part did not shift to a more personal level, would support the thesis that Rosenthal was a woman-committed woman.

Knowledge of the relationships with Porcher, Kinsella, and Wertenbakers help to construct a more complete historical portrait of Rosenthal. As an independent woman artist and businessperson, she established and maintained intimate friendships and domestic partnerships with other women in a climate often hostile to both women's intimacy and independence from men. These close same-sex affiliations are a part of her history, of theater history, and of the history of woman-committed relationships in theater.

Fascination, Devotion, Collaboration

In *Martha Graham: Portrait of the Lady as an Artist,* photographer Martha Swope chronicles a portion of Graham's modern dance repertoire from the late 1950s and early 1960s, capturing glimpses of Graham's artistic vision and personal charisma as a performer in a series of stark black-and-white photographic images.[36] Swope's photography also documents the artistry of Jean Rosenthal, whose stage lighting designs for Graham not only provide illumination for the performances (and for the photographs) but also, through dramatic use of light and shadow, heighten the mood and atmosphere of the compositions. Particularly haunting in this collaborative context, and particularly memorable, are those photographs where the face or the body of Graham herself receives primary focus due to Rosenthal's lighting, especially those Swope takes from a rear or side angle. In many of these shots sources of illumination are revealed, glowing brightly above and beyond the performer from the darkened auditorium or wings. These photographs visually symbolize the tangible bond between these two highly respected women artists and the aesthetic achievement resulting from their same-sex collaboration.

Rosenthal's lengthy association with Martha Graham differs from the three presented above in several key ways. Not only was it considerably longer in duration, spanning four full decades, and confined primarily to professional work, but it involved a level of infatuation on Rosenthal's part that is different from her involvements with the other women. Because Graham often performed in their artistic collaborations, the relationship spilled from backstage to onstage, expressing its dynamics in more material and complex ways.

In *The Magic of Light* Rosenthal credits Martha Graham as having
had "the most lasting and dominant influence on my life and way of
thinking."[37] This influence began in 1929 when seventeen-year-old Jean
Rosenthal enrolled at the Neighborhood Playhouse School of the Theatre, where Graham was on the faculty teaching dance.[38] While Rosenthal's aversion to performing limited her receptivity to Playhouse training, she acknowledges that "we students learned a great deal because our
instruction came from such stimulating people."[39]

One of the most stimulating people for Rosenthal was Graham,
whose personality and purpose, she admits, "fascinated her." In addition
to discovering a shared interest in Greek mythology, Rosenthal, writing
years later, recalls Graham's "intense sensuality and her equally intense
spirituality" that "were spent to exhaustion in her dancing." She envied
Graham's "stark beauty of saint-and-sinner combined in one woman"
and understood why Louis Horst, Graham's lover and the Playhouse's
teacher of dance composition, was captivated by her.[40] Describing Graham as "a woman of imagination, of total purpose toward what she
wanted to achieve," it is not unlikely that the teenage Rosenthal was, as
is suggested by Saul Goodman, "carried away by the sheer personal magnetism, creative drive, and inventiveness of one of the greatest artists of
our time."[41] Rosenthal's comments suggest not only a fascination with
Graham's persona and an appreciation for her artistic skills but also, in
her identification with Graham's lover, an element of homoerotic desire.

Martha C. Vicinus's examination of female teacher-student relationships is helpful at this juncture. Vicinus theorizes that it was commonplace for female students to develop an idealized love for an older, publicly successful woman during periods when women were pioneering new
public roles and professional occupations.[42] Expressed for the most part
in nonsexual behavior, the pleasure of such love was fulfilled instead,
Vicinus suggests, by channeling one's powerful emotions into a higher
cause such as religion, education, or the general betterment of others.
Self-control was exerted (and valorized) and the student's love expressed
through symbolic acts.[43] For the teacher's part, as she was in a position
to help with the careers of her protégées, many women urged their students "to seize the new opportunities opening up for women and to enter
new occupations."[44]

Although Vicinus's research is confined to examinations of all-girl
English boarding schools at the turn of the century, the adult Rosenthal's
remembrance of her teenage fascination with Graham falls within the
pattern. In 1929 Graham was establishing her reputation in dance by

inventing a new vocabulary of expressive movement. Her artistic standards for herself and her students were absolute and merciless, requiring an enormous degree of self-sacrifice and dedication to the work. When a stairway accident put an end to Rosenthal's dancing, she became Graham's technical assistant, a position that allowed Rosenthal to work in close proximity to Graham, to watch Graham dance, and to channel her infatuation into artistic creation. She was able to symbolically express her commitment to Graham by becoming a backstage collaborator in Graham's achievements. Whether it could be called an idealized love or not, Rosenthal's actions and comments indicate a strong devotion to Graham.

This loyalty and devotion continued for four decades as Rosenthal became Graham's treasured lighting designer and, once TPS was established, supplier of all technical necessities. "I went to [Martha] when she wanted me," writes Rosenthal in *The Magic of Light.* "To do one or two new works for Martha a year was a part of my life and a renewal of my own interior spirit."[45] This comment, and an observation by LeRoy Leatherman that the adult Rosenthal's demeanor toward Graham was "still that of a student, humble, soft-spoken, in the presence of an adored master," are not only evidence of how immensely Rosenthal valued her relationship with Graham, but are also indicators of Rosenthal's intense personal and professional loyalty and emotional investment in another woman.[46]

It is not clear how actively Graham encouraged Rosenthal to pursue her career goals in a newly developing field dominated by males. In her autobiography, however, Graham gives herself credit as stimulus. "Soon, it was clear to both of us that [dancing] was not [Jean's] path," Graham writes in *Blood Memory,* "I suggested lighting and for years she would work with me and experiment."[47] Rosenthal cites her association with Graham as "really the first [I] had in terms of lighting design."[48] She also acknowledges Graham's influence in a 1961 *New York Times* article, complimenting Graham and other "present day choreographers who have created original concepts in the dance field." In doing so, she asserts, they have "in the process utilized, and thereby encouraged, creative efforts in related fields."[49]

Graham's reciprocation of Rosenthal's loyalty and professional commitment cannot really be questioned given her steadfast maintenance of their long professional collaboration. A reciprocated emotional investment is more difficult to assess, though Leatherman's descriptive insider's view that "a subtle change takes place in Martha with Jean on the premises" seems to point toward an affirmation. Coupled with his remark that "Jean's presence seems to banish uncertainty" due to her "deeply reassuring knowledge of the intricacies and technicalities of stage production," the comment indicates that Graham treasured the deep bond of trust and artistry cultivated through years of friendly collaboration that, in practical and emotional terms, can be identified as woman-committed.[50]

In *Blood Memory* Graham calls attention to Rosenthal's "most extraordinary gesture" of designing lights and providing production services for her production of *Archaic Hours*. Although weakened by recurrence of cancer, Graham writes that "Jean got permission to come out of the hospital in an ambulance. She sat on a stretcher with me in the aisle of the City Center Theatre and supervised the last work she would ever light."[51] Rosenthal died ten days after *Archaic Hours* had its premiere, making one of her comments in *The Magic of Light* prophetic. "Martha's was the first work I did," she writes, "and I hope it will be the last."[52] That she was able to complete the project is testimony to Rosenthal's sheer will power, to her professional dedication, and to the power of her devotion to Graham.

Lighting/Touching

Wertenbaker recalls a captivating image of Rosenthal "when the lights had been focused and colored to her satisfaction, standing in the light, happily dabbling her fingers in it, as if it were a tangible substance, and nodding."[53] This impression of the designer in what is seemingly physical contact with light helps to explicate Rosenthal's own comment: "Light is quite tactile to me. It has shape and dimension. It has an edge. It has quality and it is an entity."[54]

Being in the light, for Rosenthal, was a sensory experience. As Wertenbaker's recollected image illustrates, not only did Rosenthal feel she was able to touch the light, but also, reciprocally, she was able to sense it touching her. In accordance, light (whether natural or artificial) was for her an interactive, sensible substance that "affects everything [it] falls upon."[55] This affective quality, for Rosenthal, made it a powerful, expressive scenic tool for the performing arts, one that a skillful designer could use to accentuate the emotional content of a scene, to enhance an individual's performance, and to "tie together disjointed moments so that they accumulate into a lasting and significant impression."[56] "Short of music itself," she insisted, "no medium at the artist's command may be as lyrical as light."[57] This lyrical quality was also recognized by early dance and lighting pioneer Loie Fuller, who, as Bud Coleman notes in this volume, bathed her silk-draped body with moving colored light to create sensuous floral, fiery, and serpentine shapes for her turn-of-the-century dance performances.

The theoretical underpinnings of Rosenthal's ideas can be linked to Swiss theater artist Adolphe Appia, whose early-twentieth-century treatises on scenography include some of the first aesthetic discussions of stage lighting. Rosenthal's comments suggest her familiarity with Appia's writings, whether from her Yale studies or because of her continued interest in theater history and stylistic innovation. Appia provided a foundation upon which future artists could build, including a particularly resonant argument for a transmission of desire through stage lighting.

By using light, Appia asserted, "anything is possible in the theater, for it suggests unmistakably, and *suggestion* is the only basis on which the art of the stage can expand without encountering any obstacles."[58] This was especially true, he believed, when facing the challenge of suggesting psychological states and symbolic values (for example, the complexities of desire). Attempts to evoke them through realistic means, Appia felt, would always be inadequate. Lighting, however, could complement and enhance other means of representation and, like music, communicate "that which belongs to the 'inner essence' of all vision."[59] Both light and music, he believed, were artistic media capable of extraordinary subtlety, each possessing the capacity to express or suggest emotional nuance.

Appia's technique for capitalizing upon light's expressive powers involve a layering process. After installing equipment to provide a stratum of relatively immobile diffuse light for general visibility, instruments then are added as an overlay of that general illumination in order to create "active" light.[60] More mobile and flexible, this light is subtly manipulated for dramatic effect, conveying "emphasis and counterpoint as a visible correlative to the flow of the music-drama itself." Used in combination, the two layers of light "create, sustain, and modulate mood and atmosphere."[61]

By carefully coordinating the intensity, color, texture, and duration of these light layers, Rosenthal knew that she as a designer could "release [light] emotionally" and therefore "touch" both spectator and performer.[62] She recognized, in other words, the agency of the designer and acknowledged that not only the lights but also the designer who patterns them have an impact on "how [spectators *and* performers] see what [they] see, how [they] feel about it, and how [they] hear what [they] are hearing."[63]

In performances, Rosenthal, as the lighting designer, occupied a complex subjective position. Her lighting, the material product of hours of conferences, rehearsal viewing, plotting, and cuing, was her artistic contribution to the collaborative process, a technical expertise for which she received professional credit. Practically, her designs provided general illumination and sensory stimulation for both performer and spectator. Rosenthal's lighting also, however, carefully enhanced the emotional content of the text, communicating subtle symbolic messages to the spectator and enveloping the performer within a tactile substance corresponding to the environment of the textual fiction.

The designs represent, as well, Rosenthal's personal response to the performers and the material being performed. Though always sensitive to the demands and wishes of her collaborators, her desires, sensibilities, preferences, and stylistic decisions charged the final "look" and "feel" of the performance. Her lighting designs, therefore, not only enhanced the emotional nuances of the performance text, but transmitted her personal feelings in a tangible series of tactile light patterns. Her lighting must be viewed as a technological extension of her self-identity as an artist and as a woman, affording her an expanded capacity for sensual experience. Perhaps Rosenthal, watching her lighting designs materialize in rehearsal or performance, or in her imagination, perceived herself "touching" everything in the performance space.

The notion of lighting as touching, of light as a material expression of desire, is particularly useful when considering Jean Rosenthal's collaborations with performers. Rosenthal stated that it was a pleasure for her to work with stars who made active use of lighting as part of their performances, who took "full advantage of whatever skill I bring to making his or her performance work."[64] Though both male and female performers capitalized upon her skills, it is significant that Rosenthal almost exclusively refers to women performers in *The Magic of Light*. One may speculate that part of Rosenthal's pleasure in working with women who understood how her lighting could contribute to the effectiveness of their performances involved two additional unacknowledged factors. She desired, first of all, to touch them, and light provided the means to do so. Second, they desired to be touched with light, specifically Rosenthal's light. Light, in a very real sense, became a source of symbolic, sensual, and consensual same-sex communication.

As designing for the dance was Rosenthal's "most constant love," her greatest pleasure derived from lighting/touching Martha Graham.[65] This is not surprising given their personal and professional history. Graham actively responded to the sensory stimulus Rosenthal's lighting provided. "I am absorbed," she confesses in Blood Memory, "in the magic of light and movement."[66] Her almost exclusive use of Rosenthal as her lighting designer attests that Graham was absorbed in the magic of Rosenthal's lighting, a fact Rosenthal deeply appreciated. "When [Martha] sees a light come up and hit a certain spot on the stage," Rosenthal told an interviewer, "she plays with it, avoiding it, working around it for the confused, soul-searching movements of the dance and landing up right in the light for an affirmative ending. She uses lights as they should be used."[67] Rosenthal's descriptive comment hints of flirtation, courtship, and union between dancer and light. It can be read as a symbol of Rosenthal's desire to touch her with light and of Graham's desire to be touched by light.

Rosenthal's design method, involving frequent attendance at rehearsals, accentuates and elaborates upon this dynamic of desire. Only after repeated viewings of Graham's preparatory work would Rosenthal create her light plot, a practice that led to her statement that "the lighting came from Martha, from the interior of Martha." "The changes were keyed to the physical impulse, the human body," she writes in The Magic of Light, "not to the music or form. There had to be a kinetic connection, an interior reaction."[68] Rosenthal's remarkable claim implies that during rehearsals she scrutinized Graham's body for the visual clues that would allow her "to get on Graham's wave length," to attain an intimate knowledge of Graham's body, movements, and interior impulses in order that she might create a successful fusion of light and movement.

What Rosenthal repeatedly viewed in rehearsal and performance has been described by Agnes DeMille as "the most sensual [dance] technique ever evolved."[69] As Graham's signature style of contraction and release centered in the dancers' diaphragm and pelvis, the repetitions and variations of pelvic thrust infused Graham's performances with images that often were perceived as explicitly sexual. Graham shrugged off criticism, publicly championing "a certain beauty about sex that can only be expressed through eroticism." "I know my dances and techniques are considered deeply sexual," she comments in Blood Memory, "but I pride myself in placing on stage what most people hide in their deepest thoughts."[70]

Rosenthal watched Graham rehearse, seeking evidence of the kinetic

connections of Graham's physical impulses to guide her lighting decisions. She viewed a dance vocabulary composed of erotic images and sensual rhythms danced by a "lusty and highly sexed woman" who "lived in
passion."[71] Though in sharp contrast to her own modesty and carefully
guarded privacy, Rosenthal's "organic" designs were complicit in
enhancing Graham's eroticism and celebration of sexuality. The lighting
contributed not only to aesthetic pleasure of performers and spectators,
but also to their erotic pleasure. This applied to Rosenthal herself. When
Rosenthal "touched" Graham with light, she was sharing in an erotic
exchange. When she viewed Graham performing in her lights she could
imagine herself enfolding Graham in a series of sensuous embraces or
caresses.

The merging of light and movement in Graham's performances created a "totality," an "instinctual realization of a mind and spirit" that
Rosenthal confided was "hair-raisingly beautiful" for all concerned.[72]
This is an important acknowledgment of sensory stimulation received
from the dynamics of performance. Though not specifically erotic, it indicates the emotional power of Graham's sensual performances and Rosenthal's involvement and investment in them.

Rosenthal's technique of merging of movement and light, and her
desire to touch with light combined with a performer's desire to be
touched by light, was not limited to Graham. In lighting Mary Martin's
"ineffable grace and vitality," for example, Rosenthal's strategy involved
plots "full of motion" to match Martin's physical vivacity. "You treat
her like quicksilver," she writes, "light glancing from her shining surface" (a comment that directly acknowledges Rosenthal's light "touching" Martin's body).[73] Martin considered Rosenthal an artist who "used
lights instead of oils," marveling at Rosenthal's skill in finding the perfect
blend of color and texture to "project 'me' best."[74]

When lighting Lynn Fontanne, Rosenthal concentrated on
Fontanne's "ability to be absolutely and beautifully still." Describing her
lighting sessions with Fontanne as "meticulous affairs," Rosenthal notes
with pleasure the actress's concern with the details of lighting. "Lynn
went through every one of her lines," Rosenthal writes, and "in each
position the lights were focused" to her satisfaction. She also comments,
with a familiar hint of fascination and infatuation already seen in her discussion of Graham, on Fontanne's "magical voice" and "physical
beauty," which could create "humor, radiance, sexuality, intelligence—
and the desire on the part of every woman in the audience (including,
presumably, Rosenthal herself) to be Lynn Fontanne."[75]

Rosenthal's specific mention of Mary Martin and Lynn Fontanne is significant since both were reputed to be lesbian or bisexual.[76] For Rosenthal to express her pleasure in lighting/touching them suggests more explicit lesbian erotics, especially if she was aware (through the grapevine or other contacts) of their inclinations. Margaret Leighton and gay icons Maria Callas, Angela Lansbury, and Bette Davis are also mentioned by Rosenthal as favorite stars with whom she worked, each having a savvy for using lighting to her best advantage. For each, Rosenthal's desires included a wish to help them fulfill their obligation to "remain beautiful," a task she viewed as a "special problem" for any lighting designer and one that could be accomplished by "touching" the performers with light.[77]

The primary focus of this essay has been to recover lighting designer Jean Rosenthal as a figure in lesbian, bisexual, and gay theater history. To do so I employed a layering strategy, each section of the essay building upon and reverberating back through those that preceded it. In this way Rosenthal emerges as a complex historical figure, and the images of her are continually being adjusted and reenvisioned in light of new information.

A review of Rosenthal's career reveals a wealth of significant achievements as a designer, businesswoman, and consultant. She collaborated with some of the most influential artists working in the performing arts during the mid–twentieth century, many of whom requested her services due to her impeccable reputation for quality results. The quantity and scope of Rosenthal's work are impressive. It is even more impressive when one considers her success in a male-dominated field when women were actively discouraged from working professionally. That she was able to flourish is a tribute to her persistence, stamina, and ability to adapt.

Twentieth-century lesbian social history reveals circumstances that would have discouraged Rosenthal from self-identifying as a lesbian. Although there were women who did identify themselves as lesbians, there is no evidence to suggest Rosenthal was one of them. She did, however, form strong personal and professional relationships with women that can be analyzed as woman-committed attachments. Her professional relationships and same-sex partnerships with Nananne Porcher and Marion Kinsella and her long-term association with Lael Tucker Wertenbaker can be viewed as convincing evidence that Rosenthal's primary commitment in emotional and practical terms was to other women.

Rosenthal's lengthy collaboration with Martha Graham provides further evidence to bolster this claim. Her youthful infatuation with the sensual, innovative, hardworking dancer was channeled into a lifelong adoration and professional commitment. Given these circumstances, there is a basis for a homoerotic interpretation of Rosenthal's lighting designs for Graham and other glamourous women performers as artistic, material expressions of her devotions and desires. Her designs for women performers can be viewed as affectionate same-sex encounters in which she "touches" the performers with light, as conscious or unconscious channels for the emotional release of desires that, due to cultural constraints, might have no other outlet.

A complete portrait of Rosenthal does not emerge. But if we adapt one of Graham's well-known sayings, a resonant description of Rosenthal's artistry comes into focus. "Desire is a lovely thing," Graham writes, "and that is where dance comes from, from desire." Like dance, Rosenthal's lighting, too, was "a kind of fever chart, a graph of the heart" shaped by desire.[78] Rosenthal danced with light, embracing her performing partners with sensuous, desirous luminosity.

NOTES

1. Simon Callow, *Orson Welles: The Road to Xanadu* (London: Jonathan Cape, 1995), 330.

2. Lael Wertenbaker, preface to *The Magic of Light*, by Jean Rosenthal and Lael Wertenbaker (Boston: Little, Brown, 1972), vii.

3. Mary Callahan Boone, "Jean Rosenthal's Light: Making Visible the Magician," *Theatre Topics* 7, no. 1 (1997): 82.

4. Ibid., 78.

5. Ibid., 79.

6. Ibid., 82.

7. Wertenbaker, preface, v.

8. Here I'm indebted to the work of Leila J. Rupp, who makes these points in association with her study of women involved in the postsuffrage women's movement. Leila J. Rupp, "'Imagine My Surprise': Women's Relationships in Mid–Twentieth Century America," in *Hidden from History: Reclaiming the Gay and Lesbian Past*, ed. Martin Bauml Duberman, Martha Vicinus, and George Chauncey Jr. (New York: Penguin, 1989), 408.

9. Lillian Faderman, *Odd Girls and Twilight Lovers: A History of Lesbian Life in Twentieth-Century America* (New York: Columbia University Press, 1991), 93.

10. Rosenthal and Wertenbaker, *The Magic of Light*, 35.

11. Faderman, *Odd Girls*, 93.

12. Ibid., 138.

13. Ibid., 145.

14. Rosenthal and Wertenbaker, *The Magic of Light*, 36.

15. Rupp, "Imagine My Surprise," 408.

16. Ibid., 409.

17. Rosenthal and Wertenbaker, *The Magic of Light*, 29.

18. Ibid., 24. After Rosenthal's death Nananne Porcher would become president of Jean Rosenthal Associates.

19. Ibid., 126.

20. Author's e-mail correspondence with Anne MacKay on Thursday, October 29, 1998. MacKay is the author of *Wolf Girls at Vassar: Lesbian and Gay Experiences, 1930–1990* (New York: St. Martin's Press, 1993)

21. Anne MacKay, e-mail to the author, October 28, 1998.

22. Anne MacKay, e-mail to the author, October 30, 1998.

23. Anne MacKay, e-mail to the author, November 3, 1998.

24. Winthrop Sargeant, "Profiles: Please, Darling, Bring Three to Seven," *New Yorker*, February 4, 1956, 58.

25. Ibid., 57.

26. Rupp, "Imagine My Surprise," 407.

27. Anne MacKay, e-mail to the author, October 30, 1998.

28. Anne MacKay, e-mail to the author, October 25, 1998.

29. Rosenthal and Wertenbaker, *The Magic of Light*, 39.

30. Wertenbaker, preface, v. Kinsella also provided illustrations for *The Magic of Light*. She is listed in a 1984 brochure in the Jean Rosenthal Associates clipping file at the Billy Rose Theatre Collection, New York Public Library at Lincoln Center, as a space consultant. Significantly, Anne MacKay, e-mail to the author, October 25, 1998, noted that Kinsella shared a residence with lighting designer Tharon Musser in the early 1950s. Kinsella's residing with Rosenthal was, therefore, Kinsella's second same-sex shared living arrangement and her second with a prominent lighting designer.

31. Wertenbaker, preface, viii. Following Rosenthal's death, Kinsella shared the house on Martha's Vineyard with Porcher. A recent Internet search found the two women still jointly listed at the Martha's Vineyard residence.

32. John Houseman, *Final Dress* (New York: Simon and Schuster, 1983), 386.

33. Please see Kim Marra's essay on Marbury and De Wolfe and Jay Plum's essay on Crawford in *Passing Performances: Queer Readings of Leading Players in American Theater History*, ed. Robert A. Schanke and Kim Marra (Ann Arbor: University of Michigan Press, 1998).

34. Wertenbaker, preface, v.

35. Rosenthal and Wertenbaker, *The Magic of Light*, 68.

36. LeRoy Leatherman, *Martha Graham: Portrait of the Lady as an Artist* (New York: Alfred Knopf, 1966).

37. Rosenthal and Wertenbaker, *The Magic of Light*, 13.

38. With no particular career goals and due to her unconventional early education Rosenthal was refused admission to the colleges to which she had applied. Rosenthal remarks that her parents sent her to the Neighborhood School of the Playhouse, despite her having no predilection for dancing or acting, "simply to broaden my horizons." Ibid., 13.

39. Ibid., 14.

40. Ibid.

41. Ibid., 13; Saul Goodman, "Meet Jean Rosenthal," *Dance Magazine* 36 (February 1962): 19. Agnes DeMille includes a quote from Dorothy Bird, another Graham dance student at the time Rosenthal was studying dance, who provides an enlightening glimpse at the feelings Graham engendered in her teenage pupils. "Everyone was hypnotized, absolutely magnetized by Martha. It was like a mass falling in love, but much, much more. It was more than a crush. She opened our eyes to the arts. I was on fire." Agnes DeMille, *Martha: The Life and Work of Martha Graham* (New York: Random House, 1991), 130.

42. Martha Vicinus, "Distance and Desire: English Boarding School Friendships, 1870–1920," in Duberman, Vicinus, and Chauncey, *Hidden from History,* 213.

43. Ibid., 216–17.

44. Ibid., 221.

45. Rosenthal and Wertenbaker, *The Magic of Light,* 131.

46. Leatherman, *Martha Graham,* 126.

47. Martha Graham, *Blood Memory* (New York: Doubleday, 1991), 99.

48. Rosenthal and Wertenbaker, *The Magic of Light,* 13. Ernestine Stodelle usefully notes that in the thirties no one had ever heard of a lighting designer for dance. Instead, choreographers were responsible for their own lighting and supervised as the stagehands set up and positioned the equipment. Stodelle also comments that it was Louis Horst who first suggested that Graham utilize Rosenthal in the capacity of lighting designer. Ernestine Stodelle, *Deep Song: The Dance Story of Martha Graham* (New York: Schirmer Books, 1984), 83.

49. Jean Rosenthal, "The Art and Language of Stage Lighting," *Theatre Arts,* August 1961, 6.

50. Leatherman, *Martha Graham,* 126.

51. Graham, *Blood Memory,* 99. Wertenbaker's account has Rosenthal in a wheelchair (preface, viii–ix).

52. Rosenthal and Wertenbaker, *The Magic of Light,* 131.

53. Wertenbaker, preface, vi.

54. Rosenthal and Wertenbaker, *The Magic of Light,* 39.

55. Ibid., 3.

56. Ibid., 63.

57. Ibid., 89.

58. Adolphe Appia, "Comments on the Staging of *The Ring of the Nibelungs,*" in *Adolphe Appia: Essays, Scenarios, and Designs,* trans. Walther R. Volbach, wd. Richard C. Beacham (Ann Arbor: University of Michigan Press, 1989), 93.

59. Adolphe Appia, *Music and the Art of Theatre,* in *Adolphe Appia: Texts on Theatre,* ed. Richard C. Beacham (London: Routledge, 1993), 51.

60. Appia, *Art of Theatre,* 52.

61. Richard C. Beacham, *Adolphe Appia: Theatre Artist* (Cambridge: Cambridge University Press, 1987), 27.

62. Rosenthal and Wertenbaker, *The Magic of Light,* 72.

63. Ibid., 3.

64. Ibid., 34, 71.

65. Ibid., 77.

66. Graham, *Blood Memory,* 8.

67. Ellen Violett, "Name in Lights," *Theatre Arts,* December 1950, 27.

68. Rosenthal and Wertenbaker, *The Magic of Light,* 129.

69. DeMille, *Martha,* 237.

70. Graham, *Blood Memory,* 211.

71. DeMille, *Martha,* 201.

72. Rosenthal and Wertenbaker, *The Magic of Light,* 131.

73. Ibid., 33.

74. Ibid.

75. Ibid.

76. For discussion of Martin, see Stacy Wolf, "The Queer Pleasures of Mary Martin and Broadway: *The Sound of Music* as a Lesbian Musical," *Modern Drama* 39, no. 1(1996): 51–63, and "Mary Martin: Washin' That Man Right Outta Her Hair," in Schanke and Marra, *Passing Performances,* 283–302. For a discussion of Fontanne, see Jared Brown, *The Fabulous Lunts: A Biography of Alfred Lunt and Lynn Fontanne* (New York: Atheneum, 1986); and Sam Abel, "Staging Heterosexuality: Alfred Lunt and Lynne Fontanne's Design for Living," in Schanke and Marra, *Passing Performances,* 175–96.

77. Rosenthal and Wertenbaker, *The Magic of Light,* 33.

78. Graham, *Blood Memory,* 6.

Notes on the Contributors

Kim Marra is Associate Professor of Theatre Arts and American Studies at the University of Iowa. With Robert A. Schanke, she coedited *Passing Performances: Queer Readings of Leading Players in American Theater History*. Her articles and reviews primarily on gender and sexuality in late-nineteenth- and early-twentieth-century United States theater history appear in *Theatre Survey, Theatre Journal, TDR, Journal of Dramatic Theory and Criticism, Theatre Research International, Theatre Annual, ATQ: Journal of Nineteenth-Century American Literature and Culture, New England Theatre Journal, Journal of American History, August Wilson: A Casebook, Staging Difference: Cultural Pluralism in American Theater and Drama,* and *Performing America: Cultural Nationalism in American Theater.* She has served on the editorial boards of *Theatre Survey* and *Theatre History Studies,* as Book Review Editor for *Theatre Survey,* and, for two terms, as a member of the Executive Committee of the American Society for Theatre Research.

Robert A. Schanke is Professor of Theatre at Central College, Iowa, where he has served as Chair of the faculty research and development committee. His articles on theater history appear in *Theatre Survey, Theatre Topics, Southern Theatre,* and *Central States Speech Journal.* He has contributed to numerous reference books and anthologies, including *Women in American Theatre, Cambridge Guide to American Theatre,* and *Shakespeare around the Globe.* He is author of *Ibsen in America: A Century of Change* (Scarecrow), *Eva Le Gallienne: A Bio-Bibliography* (Greenwood), and *Shattered Applause: The Lives of Eva Le Gallienne* (Southern Illinois). With Kim Marra, he coedited *Passing Performances: Queer Readings of Leading Players in American Theater History* (University of Michigan Press). He is editor of the journal *Theatre History Studies* and the Theatre in the Americas Series for Southern Illinois University Press. As Vice President for Membership and Marketing of the Association of Theatre in Higher Education, he currently sits on the Governing Council. He is completing a full-length biography of Mercedes de Acosta under contract with Southern Illinois University Press.

Jay Scott Chipman is Assistant Professor of Communication and Theatre at Nebraska Wesleyan University with a Ph.D. in theater history and performance studies from the University of Pittsburgh. He has made numerous conference presentations and has published in *Theatre Studies* and *The Gay and Lesbian Literary Heritage* (Henry Holt).

Susan F. Clark is currently completing a full-length study of *Uncle Tom's Cabin* in popular entertainment entitled *Sold Down the River*. The book will be the first to examine Stowe's work as it has been used by multiple mediums to reframe and reflect racial politics in America over the past one hundred and fifty years. Dr. Clark has taught at Smith College, Emerson College, the University of Southern Maine, and has recently been honored by a full year fellowship from the National Endowment for the Humanities. Other publications appear in *New Theatre Quarterly*, *The Journal of Popular Culture* and *The Drama Review*.

Bud Coleman is Associate Professor of Theatre at the University of Colorado at Boulder, where he is Director of the Certificate Program in Lesbian, Gay, Bisexual, and Transgender Studies. A former dancer with Les Ballets Trockadero de Monte Carlo, Fort Worth Ballet, Ballet Austin, and Kinesis, his publications have appeared in the *Austin American-Statesman*, *New York Native*, *Theatre History Studies*, *Theatre InSight*, and the *Gay & Lesbian Almanac* (St. James Press). He has served as the Chair of the Lesbian and Gay Focus Group of the Association for Theatre in Higher Education.

J. K. Curry is Assistant Professor of Theatre at Wake Forest University. Her publications have appeared in the *Journal of American Drama and Theatre*, *Theatre Journal*, *Northwest Drama Review*, and *American National Biography*. Her research interests include women and theatre and the nineteenth and early twentieth century American stage. She is the author of *Nineteenth-Century American Women Theatre Managers* (Greenwood) and the forthcoming *John Guare: A Research and Production Sourcebook* (Greenwood).

Mark Fearnow is Associate Professor of Theatre at Hanover College. He is the author of *Clare Booth Luce: A Research and Production Sourcebook* (Greenwood) and *The American Stage And The Great Depression: a Cultural History of The Grotesque* (Cambridge). He is a contributor to *The Cambridge Guide to American Theatre* and authored a chapter on

American playwrights and their theatres for the *Cambridge History of American Theatre*, Volume II. He has served as Book Review Editor for *Theatre Survey*.

Billy J. Harbin is Professor Emeritus in the Department of Theater, Louisiana State University, Baton Rouge. He coedited *Inside the Royal Court Theatre, 1956–1981: Artists Talk* (Louisiana State University Press) and has published articles in major professional journals, including *Theatre Journal, Theatre Survey, Theatre Notebook, Theatre History Studies,* and the *William and Mary Quarterly*.

Lisa Merrill is Professor of performance studies and rhetoric at Hofstra University and holds an appointment as Visiting Professor at Northwestern University for 2002. Her critically acclaimed biography, *When Romeo Was a Woman: Charlotte Cushman and Her Circle of Female Spectators* (University of Michigan Press), was awarded the Joe A. Callaway Prize for the Best Book on Drama and Theatre. She has published articles on gender, sexuality, and theatrical performance in *Women and Performance; Caryl Churchill: A Casebook* (Garland), *Encyclopedia of Lesbian Histories* (Garland). She is currently coeditor of Book Reviews for *Text and Performance Quarterly*.

Daniel-Raymond Nadon is Associate Professor at Kent State University Trumbull Campus. He has published a variety of reviews and articles in journals such as *Theatre History Studies, On Stage Studies, Journal of Dramatic Theory and Criticism, Comparative Drama,* and *Modern Drama*. He received one of the first Fulbright grants to Quebec, where he studied the works of gay Quebecois playwright Michel Tremblay.

Jane T. Peterson is Associate Professor of Theatre at Montclair State University in New Jersey. She specializes in theater history of the 1910s and 1920s, women in theater and contemporary playwrights of diversity. She is the co-author of *Women Playwrights of Diversity* (Greenwood) and has articles published in *Theatre History, Notable Women in Theatre,* the forthcoming *Art, Glitter and Glitz: Theatre in the 1920s, American National Biography,* and others.

Jeffrey Smart has an M.F.A. in playwriting from Indiana University and a Ph.D. in theater history and criticism from the University of Missouri, Columbia. He has taught at the University of Minnesota, Duluth, North-east Missouri State University (now Truman State University) and the University of South Florida at Sarasota.

Albert Wertheim is Professor of English and Theatre and Drama at Indiana University. He is the author of *The Dramatic Art of Athol Fugard: From South Africa to the World* (Indiana University Press) and has published widely on modern British and American, Restoration and Renaissance drama. He has served on the executive board of the MLA Drama Division and editorial boards of *American Drama, Theatre Survey,* and *South African Theatre Journal.* He is the past treasurer of the American Society for Theatre Research and past president of the Eugene O'Neill Society.

James Wilson is Assistant Professor of English at La Guardia Community College. He is currently working on a book about gay and lesbian theater and performance in the Harlem Renaissance entitled *"Bulldykes, Pansies, and Chocolate Babies": Performance, Race, and Sexuality in the Harlem Renaissance.*

Index